Greif zu und kauf mich!

Displays als Erfolgsmotor für Marken und Handel

Move people to buy more

Displays build brands in-store

STI Group (Hrsg.)

Deutscher Fachverlag

Impressum

Projektleitung:	Claudia Rivinius, STI Group, Lauterbach
Artdirektion und Titel:	Ingo Götze, Frankfurt am Main
Gestaltung:	Gerhard Berger, berger design, Darmstadt
Produktion:	Hans-Jürgen Wulf, DFV, Frankfurt am Main
Projektmanagement:	Caroline Schauwienold, DFV, Frankfurt am Main
Redaktion:	Martina Leinhos, Lörzweiler
Übersetzungen:	Fiona Bartholomew, Frankfurt am Main
Herausgeber:	STI Group
Druck:	abcdruck GmbH, Heidelberg
Buchbinderische Verarbeitung:	Josef Spinner Großbuchbinderei GmbH, Ottersweier

Verlagsgruppe Deutscher Fachverlag
Mainzer Landstraße 251
D-60326 Frankfurt am Main

www.dfv-fachbuch.de

ISBN: 978-3-86641-216-3

©2010 by
Deutscher Fachverlag GmbH, Frankfurt am Main, Germany

Die Wiedergabe von Warenbezeichnungen, Handelsnamen oder sonstigen Kennzeichen in diesem Buch berechtigt nicht zu der Annahme, dass diese von jedermann frei benutzt werden dürfen. Vielmehr kann es sich auch dann um eingetragene Warenzeichen oder sonstige gesetzlich geschützte Kennzeichen handeln, wenn sie nicht eigens als solche markiert sind.

Imprint

Project management:	*Claudia Rivinius, STI Group, Lauterbach*
Art direction and cover:	*Ingo Götze, Frankfurt am Main*
Design/Layout:	*Gerhard Berger, berger design, Darmstadt*
Production:	*Hans-Jürgen Wulf, DFV, Frankfurt am Main*
Project management:	*Caroline Schauwienold, DFV, Frankfurt am Main*
Copy editor:	*Martina Leinhos, Lörzweiler*
Translations:	*Fiona Bartholomew, Frankfurt am Main*
Editor:	*STI Group*
Printed by:	*abcdruck GmbH, Heidelberg*
Bookbinder:	*Josef Spinner Großbuchbinderei GmbH, Ottersweier*

Mix
Produktgruppe aus vorbildlich bewirtschafteten Wäldern, kontrollierten Herkünften und Recyclingholz oder -fasern
www.fsc.org Zert.-Nr. GFA-COC-001159
© 1996 Forest Stewardship Council

The use of descriptions of goods, trade names or other hallmarks in this book is for identification only and does not justify the assumption that they can be used publicly. In fact, these marks are or may be registered marks or other legally protected marks of their respective owners.

Inhaltsverzeichnis / Table of Contents

Editorial 8
Ein Medium der Extra-Klasse: Das Display
Frank Ohle

Grußwort 10
Florian Langenscheidt

Editorial 8
The display: a medium in its own class
Frank Ohle

Opening remarks 10
Florian Langenscheidt

I. Die Ursprünge des Displays – Von der Antike bis zur Selbstbedienung 11
Sophie Wittl, Christoph Häberle

I. The Origins of the Display – From Antiquity to Self-Service 11
Sophie Wittl, Christoph Häberle

II. Die Entwicklung des POS-Marketings 26
Bernd Hallier

II. The Development of POS Marketing 26
Bernd Hallier

III. „Draußen zuhause":
Markenführung – Am Point of Sale
Acht POS-Biografien besonders prominenter Marken 36
Hans-Georg Böcher
    GILLETTE – Triumph einer neuen Idee 40
    MILKA – Die „zarteste Versuchung, seit es Schokolade gibt" 54
    NESCAFÉ – Löslicher Kaffee seit 1938 66
    NESQUIK – Der Kakao mit dem lustigen Hasen 76
    NIVEA – Die schneeweiße Creme in der blauen Dose 84
    PHILIPS – Eine der ersten Design-Marken der Welt 98
    REXONA – Die weltweit größte Deo-Marke 110
    RICOLA – Vom Nischenprodukt zum Weltmarktführer 122

III. "At home outdoors":
Brand Management – At the Point of Sale
Eight exemplary POS biographies of well-known brands 36
Hans-Georg Böcher
    GILLETTE – the triumph of a new idea 40
    MILKA – the "creamiest chocolate temptation ever" 54
    NESCAFÉ – instant coffee since 1938 66
    NESQUIK – the cocoa with the funny bunny 76
    NIVEA – the snow-white cream in the blue jar 84
    PHILIPS – one of the world's first design brands 98
    REXONA – the world's number one deodorant brand 110
    RICOLA – from niche product to global market leader 122

INHALTSVERZEICHNIS | TABLE OF CONTENTS

IV. **Shopper Insights: Was Kunden bewegt** 132
  1 Point of Purchase-Marketing im Einzelhandel – Weniger Shopper Confusion, mehr Shopper Convenience 134
  Hendrik Schröder
  2 Der neue „Wettbewerb um Preis und Qualität" – Wie Käufer in Europa ihre Kaufentscheidungen verändern 148
  Louise Spillard
  3 Lösungen für Kunden im Handel 156
  Jon Kramer

IV. *Shopper Insights: How Customers tick*............ 132
  1 Point of purchase marketing at retail – Less shopper confusion, more shopper convenience 134
  Hendrik Schröder
  2 The 'contest for value' - how shoppers in Europe are making their buying decisions 148
  Louise Spillard
  3 Solving for shoppers 156
  Jon Kramer

V. **Was Verkaufsförderung bewegt: Die Effizienz von POS-Maßnahmen** 164
  1 Von Shopper Insights zu betriebswirtschaftlichen Erfolgskennziffern 166
  Susanne Czech-Winkelmann
  2 Der Wirkungsgrad von Marketingaktionen im Handel Marktuntersuchungen in niederländischen Supermärkten nach der Vision Tracking-Methode ... 178
  Bram Nauta

V. *Driving sales promotion: the effectiveness of POS activity 164*
  1 From shopper insights to economic success indicators 166
  Susanne Czech-Winkelmann
  2 The effectiveness of marketing at retail Vision tracking market research in Dutch supermarkets 178
  Bram Nauta

VI. **Das Display der Zukunft: POS 2.0 – Display 2.0** 186
  1 Die Rolle des Displays im Supermarkt der Zukunft 188
  Günter Bauer
  2 The Future of Retail 198
  Raphael Stix
  3 360°-Marketing: Displays als Erfolgsfaktor von Marken und Handel 204
  Tom Giessler

VI. *The Display of the future: POS 2.0 – display 2.0... 186*
  1 The display in the supermarket of the future 188
  Günter Bauer
  2 The future of retail .... 198.
  Raphael Stix
  3 360 degree marketing: the display as a success factor for brands and retailers 204
  Tom Giessler

VII. Der POS der Zukunft – Die Zukunft des POS-Marketings 218	*VII. The POS of the future – the future of POS marketing* *218*
1 Zurück in die Zukunft: „Greif zu und kauf mich!" – Die Umwerbung des hybriden Verbrauchers .... 220 Michael Schellenberger	*1 Back to the future: "Move people to buy more!" – How to reach the hybrid consumer ....220* *Michael Schellenberger*
2 Die Zukunft des POS-Marketings .... 224 Michael Gerling, Marlene Lohmann	*2 The future of POS marketing....................224* *Michael Gerling, Marlene Lohmann*
3 Werbeformen für die Märkte von morgen..... 234 Claudia Endl	*3 Advertising for the stores of the future ....234* *Claudia Endl*
VIII. Integrierte Kommunikation: Vom Solisten zum Orchester................ 246 Frank-Michael Schmidt, Henk Knaupe	*VIII. Integrated communication: From soloist to orchestra* .... *246* *Frank-Michael Schmidt, Henk Knaupe*
IX. Die Zukunft des Displays .... 256 Christoph Häberle	*IX. The future of the display.............................. 256* *Christoph Häberle*
X. Abbildungs-, Quellen- und Literaturnachweise 264	*X. Reference* *264*
XI. Die Autoren 288	*XI. The Authors* *288*

EDITORIAL

FRANK OHLE

Ein Medium der Extra-Klasse: Das Display

FRANK OHLE

The display: a medium in its own class

Was bewegt Menschen dazu, ein bestimmtes Produkt zu kaufen? Die Antwort auf diese Frage beschäftigt Marktforscher, Psychologen, den Handel und die Markenartikelhersteller seit vielen Jahrzehnten. Sie ist dabei so komplex wie vielschichtig und täglich kommen neue wissenschaftliche und praxisbezogene Erkenntnisse über den Käufer – den so genannten Shopper – hinzu.

Einig sind sich die Experten, dass für die Kaufentscheidung neben dem Produktversprechen die Produktpräsentation im Handel – am POS (Point of Sale) – eine entscheidende Rolle spielt. Was die Bretter für den Schauspieler, das ist der Handel für die Marke: eine Bühne.

Am POS findet ein beständiger Wandel statt. Im Mittelpunkt des Interesses steht heute jedoch weniger das Produkt, sondern vielmehr der Shopper und seine Suche nach auf ihn zugeschnittenen Angeboten. Bei der Erschließung neuer Märkte ist es daher entscheidend, mit der Art der Warenpräsentation den „First Moment of Truth" – den ersten Eindruck – für die eigene Marke zu gewinnen.

Vom Point of Sale zum Point of Communication

Dabei schließt das Thema Verkaufsförderung die Verpackung mit ein, denn diese unterstützt den Produkt- und Markenauftritt und macht das damit verbundene Produktversprechen erlebbar – gemäß der Erkenntnis: Gut verpackt ist halb verkauft.

Die Entwicklung der Verkaufsförderung ist eng mit der Entwicklung des Handels verzahnt. Seit dem Siegeszug der Selbstbedienung haben sich Displays als „Markenmacher" etabliert. Anfang der 60er Jahre wurden in Deutschland erstmals Displays aus Wellpappe in Serie gefertigt. Die Idee der temporären Zweitplatzierung hatte der Unternehmer Wilhelm Stabernack, der das Fundament zur heutigen STI Group schuf, in den USA entdeckt und nach Deutschland transferiert. Er wurde somit zum Vater der ersten Displayfertigung in Europa.

Heute hat diese Form der POS-Kommunikation einen festen Platz im Marketing-Mix und auch im Budget der Planer, die alleine in Europa jährlich mehrere hundert Millionen Euro in Displays investieren. Die

What moves people to buy a product? This question has been occupying the minds of market researchers, psychologists, retailers and suppliers of branded goods for several decades. The answer to this question is as complex as it is multi-faceted, and every day we gain new scientific and practice-oriented insights about the buyer, the shopper.

Experts will agree that the product's promise and its presentation at the POS (point of sale) play an equally important role in whether or not the customer decides to buy a product. The store is for brands what the boards are for actors: a stage.

The POS is subject to continuous change. At the POS, not the product, but the shopper is at the centre of attention, the shopper in his search for products and solutions that are tailored to his particular needs. This should be borne in mind when entering new markets, because it is essential for retailers to win at the "First Moment of Truth" and impress the customer with an intriguing presentation of their products.

From the Point of Sale to the Point of Communication

Sales promotion includes the issue of packaging because, as an important part of the product's or brand's presentation, it makes the product's promise come to life – according to the maxim: well packed is half sold.

The development of sales promotion is closely linked to the development of retail. Ever since the introduction of self-service, displays have become "brand builders". In Germany, the first corrugated cardboard displays went into mass production in the early 1960s. Wilhelm Stabernack, who laid the foundations of what is today known as the STI Group, can be credited with bringing the concept of a temporary secondary product presentation to Europe, having seen it in action during a trip to the US. He was to become the father of the first display production in Europe.

Today, this POS marketing tool is an integral part of the marketing mix and also of the budgets of planners who invest hundreds of millions of euros in displays every year in Europe alone. The STI Group has grown with the market and has inspired the market by continuously deve-

Entwicklung kreativer Displayideen immer wieder neue Impulse gegeben, so dass sie heute als führender europäischer Displayanbieter regionale Auftritte für lokale Marken ebenso realisiert wie multinationale Kampagnen für Global Brands.

Displays sind und bleiben der Erfolgsmotor für Marken und Märkte, eingebunden in 360°-Kommunikationskampagnen, multimedial animiert oder immer öfter auch international standardisiert.

Das vorliegende Buch spannt einen Bogen über 50 Jahre Markengeschichte am Point of Sale. Internationale Experten aus Wissenschaft, Markenartikelindustrie, Handel und der Kommunikationswirtschaft beleuchten die POS-Kommunikation von gestern, heute und morgen.

Als Herausgeber ist es der STI Group wichtig, die vielfältigen Aspekte zu beleuchten, welche die Warenpräsentation am POS beeinflussen – und zwar sowohl auf nationaler als auch auf internationaler Ebene. Daher gilt der Dank an dieser Stelle den Autorinnen und Autoren – allesamt Experten und anerkannte Persönlichkeiten auf ihrem Gebiet – die sich für dieses Thema begeisterten. Sie haben in ihren Archiven recherchiert, aktuelle Marktdaten analysiert, wissenschaftlich geforscht und für den Blick in die Zukunft ihre gesamte Expertise einfließen lassen.

Das Ergebnis halten Sie jetzt in Ihren Händen: das erste Buch zum Thema Display, dessen Titel die zentrale Aufgabe dieses Marketing-Mediums zum Ausdruck bringt: „Greif zu und kauf mich!": Displays steigern den Abverkauf der beworbenen Produkte im Handel und beschleunigen den Griff des Shoppers.

Prof. Dr. Frank Ohle
Vorsitzender der Geschäftsführung der STI Group

leader among display suppliers in Europe, a partner for local brands and their regional presentations as much as for the multinational campaigns of global brands.

The displays is, and will remain, a central success driver for brands and stores alike, whether they are integrated into 360 degree marketing campaigns, equipped with digital signage or, as is increasingly the case, standardized for international use.

This book covers 50 years of brand history at the POS. Leading international scientists, manufacturers of branded goods, retailers and communications experts elaborate on how POS communication worked in the past, where it stands today, and what it may look like in the future.

As the editor, STI Group is committed to highlighting all of the large number of aspects that have an effect on product presentation at the POS, nationally as well as internationally. I would like to thank all the authors, all of them experts and respected figures in their fields, for their dedicated enthusiasm. They dived into their archives, analysed latest figures, conducted scientific research and injected all of their expertise into a vision of the future.

You are now holding the result of these efforts in your hands: the first book ever written on and for the display. Its title reflects the display's central function as a marketing medium: "Move people to buy more!" Displays increase the sales of promoted products at retail and encourage the shopper to buy.

Prof. Dr. Frank Ohle
Chief Executive Officer of STI Group

„Man sieht sie fast überall – beim Schaufensterbummel, beim Einkaufen im Supermarkt, in der Wartehalle des Flughafens oder in Banken. Die Rede ist vom Display in zwei- oder dreidimensionaler Form, als Bodenaufsteller oder Deckenhänger, als Probierstand oder Thekenaufsteller, als Schüttgondel oder Stanzfigur, bestückt mit Ware oder Prospekten, oder einfach als Schauobjekt. Nur gut ein Jahrzehnt hat es gebraucht, um das Display als innovatives Werbemedium im Handel zu etablieren."

Dipl.-Kfm. Wilhelm Stabernack 1975

„They can be seen almost everywhere – in shop windows, in the supermarket, in airport waiting areas or in banks. What we are talking about is the display, two or three-dimensional displays, floor stands or danglers, demonstration stands or counter displays, free-standing dump-bins or stands, product displays or leaflet holders, or displays that are simply meant to draw the customer's attention. It took less than roughly a century to establish the display as an innovative advertising medium at retail".

Wilhelm Stabernack, Master's degree in Business Administration, 1975

GRUSSWORT | OPENING REMARKS

FLORIAN LANGENSCHEIDT

Liebe Leser,

FLORIAN LANGENSCHEIDT

Dear readers

Marken sind wie Macheten. Sie schlagen Schneisen durch den Dschungel des Warenangebotes. Sie sind wie Mantras, die Türen öffnen zu inneren Räumen großer Erinnerungstiefe und Assoziationsintensität. Wenn Religion und Ideologie als sinnstiftende Systeme nicht mehr greifen, sind es manches Mal die Marken, die Identität verleihen und Sinn geben. Sie schenken Orientierung und Halt, sind Leitplanken auf den Autobahnen des Konsumentenlebens. Sie transportieren Werte und machen diese erfahrbar, sie ermöglichen Gruppenzusammengehörigkeit und Individualität zugleich. Der Ausweis als Sinnbild für die eigene Identität steckt in der Regel tief innen in der Brieftasche – die Marke hingegen wird stolz und selbstbewusst durch den Raum der Öffentlichkeit getragen, weil sie ohne übertriebene Bescheidenheit von sich sagen kann: „Hier bin ich. Das bist Du. Vergiss alles andere."

All das wäre schon mehr als spannend genug für zahlreiche große Bücher. Designexperten könnten über Logos und Wort-Bild-Marken, Farben und Typografie, Packaging und Ästhetik nachdenken. Ökonomen könnten trefflich darüber streiten, wie sich der Brand Value – bei großen Markenartiklern milliardenschwer – am besten so präzise berechnen lässt, dass er auf der Aktivseite der Bilanz aufscheinen kann. Psychologen könnten ein Kategoriengerüst aus den Balken Relevanz, Aktualität, Identität, Authentizität, Tradition und Einmaligkeit errichten, um den Mythos Marke verstehbar zu machen. Manager könnten darüber berichten, wie weit sich eine Marke ausdehnen lässt und wie sie mit dem Verhältnis zwischen Corporate Brand und Sub Brand umgehen. Marketingfachleute könnten erklären, warum gute Markenführung große Preisprämien ermöglicht und so die hohe Preissensitivität schnäppchenverliebter Konsumenten drückt.

Das Thema Marke wird Wirtschaftsjournalisten und Publizisten immer neu und mit immer neuer Relevanz und Aktualität beschäftigen. Das vorliegende Buch stellt das Display als entscheidendes Instrument der Markenkommunikation in seinen Mittelpunkt. Es spannt einen weiten Bogen von der Geschichte und Entwicklung des Displays bis hin zu aktuellen und zukunftsweisenden Betrachtungen und greift somit erstmals dieses für den Markenerfolg bedeutende Thema in umfassender Weise auf. Es ist vor allem die Unmittelbarkeit, die dieses Medium so spannend und bedeutend macht. Denn unmittelbar vor der Kaufentscheidung bietet das Display häufig die letzte Möglichkeit, eine Marke spannend und oft erstaunlich kreativ zu inszenieren. Deshalb verstehe ich dieses Buch als wichtigen Beitrag zur Markenkultur und wünsche ihm eine breite und interessierte Leserschaft.

Dr. Florian Langenscheidt
Verleger Deutsche Standards Editionen und Gesellschafter der Langenscheidt-Verlagsgruppe
München, Frühjahr 2010

Brands are like machetes. They blast their way through the jungle of goods on offer.
They are like mantras opening doors to inner spaces of deep memories and intense associations. Where religion and ideologies fail as meaningful systems brands at times offer identity and meaning. They give orientation and support. They are crash barriers on the motorway of consumption. They convey value and make value tangible. They make group affiliation and individuality possible at the same time. Often brands are more important than the identification in people's wallets because they allow them to move in the public sphere proclaiming without excessive modesty: "Here I am. That's you. Forget about the rest".

All that would be exciting enough for several thick books. Design pundits could reflect on logos and composite marks, colours and typography, packaging and aesthetics. Economists could argue splendidly about how to calculate brand value – worth billions in the case of large brands – precisely enough to make it appear on the asset side of the balance sheet. Psychologists could develop a categorical framework from the pillars relevance, currency, identity, authenticity, tradition and uniqueness to help comprehend the myth of the brand. Managers could tell us how far a brand can be stretched and how they handle the relation between corporate brand and sub-brand. Marketing experts could explain why good brand management can allow brands to charge higher prices and thus lower the high price sensitivity of bargain-loving consumers.

The phenomenon brand and its changing relevance will continue to occupy the minds of economic journalists and publicists in ever new ways. This book, covering a wide range of aspects of the display like its development and history, is a perfect case in point. Especially since, according to my knowledge, it is the first publication to cover a subject of importance for brand success in such a comprehensive and historical way. For it is its visual immediacy that makes the display such an exciting and important medium. In the seconds preceding the buying decision the display is often the last possibility to present a brand in an exciting and often astonishingly creative way.
That is why I believe the present book to be an important contribution to brand culture. I am sure it will find a wide and interested circle of readers.

Dr Florian Langenscheidt
Publisher of Deutsche Standards Editionen and partner of the Langenscheidt publishing group
Munich in spring 2010

I. DIE URSPRÜNGE DES DISPLAYS – VON DER ANTIKE BIS ZUR SELBSTBEDIENUNG | THE ORIGINS OF THE DISPLAY – FROM ANTIQUTITY TO SELF-SERVICE

Wandbild aus Grab I der Pyramide von Sakkara
Mural from tomb 1 of the Saqqara pyramid

DIE URSPRÜNGE DES DISPLAYS – VON DER ANTIKE BIS ZUR SELBSTBEDIENUNG
THE ORIGINS OF THE DISPLAY – FROM ANTIQUITY TO SELF-SERVICE

Sophie Wittl, Christoph Häberle

Die Ursprünge des Displays – Von der Antike bis zur Selbstbedienung

Die Übersetzung des Begriffes „to display" aus dem Englischen bedeutet „zur Schau stellen, abbilden, anzeigen, darstellen, ausstellen, offenbaren". Die zentrale Aufgabe eines „Displays" ist damit definiert, nämlich als „stummer Verkäufer" Ware repräsentativ anzubieten, um deren Verkauf zu fördern.
So handelt es sich bei einem Display um ein Verkaufsförderungsinstrument, das direkt am Point of Sale (POS) eingesetzt wird, um den Absatz von Produkten zu steigern. Dieses wird an exponierter Stelle außerhalb des Regals platziert, so dass die gezeigten Artikel prominent hervorgehoben werden, um sich von Wettbewerberprodukten zu differenzieren.

Neben den drei Hauptfunktionen Aufmerksamkeit zu erzeugen, repräsentativ zu differenzieren und den Verkauf zu fördern, übernimmt das Display zunehmend weitere Aufgaben. Selbstverständlich sind dies die Logistik- und Schutzfunktionen, die gewährleisten, dass Produkte sicher im Laden ankommen, die Raumfunktion – ein Display bietet im Laden zusätzliche Stellfläche für Produkte – und die Vermittlungsfunktion, die Produkte, Produktgruppen oder Marken dem Kunden wirksam kommuniziert.

Anhand ausgewählter historischer Epochen wird die Entwicklungsgeschichte des modernen „Displays" und dessen elementare Funktionen dargestellt, um die sich zukünftig wandelnden Anforderungen erkennen zu lernen.

Ohne Wettbewerb keine Verkaufsförderung – Wirtschaftsleben in Ägypten

Die Sesshaftwerdung des Menschen sowie Ackerbau und Viehzucht waren Voraussetzung wie Ursprung für die Entstehung des „ersten großen zentralen Staates der Menschheitsgeschichte"[1]: Ägypten. Die Wirtschaft basierte auf einer Überschussproduktion der Landwirtschaft, durch die ein arbeitsteiliges System mit neuen Berufen entstand.[2] Bauern und Handwerker arbeiteten im Auftrag des Staates und hatten eine vom Königshof („Pharao") gesetzlich festgelegte Arbeitsleistung zu erbringen. Die ägyptische Wirtschaft

Sophie Wittl, Christoph Häberle

The Origins of the Display – From Antiquity to Self-Service

The English verb "to display" means "to present, to show, to provide on a screen, to express, to exhibit, to manifest". This leads us to the main definition of the "display" as a "silent salesman" offering products in a representative way to promote sales. Hence a display is a sales-promoting tool used directly at the point of sale (POS) to increase the sale of goods. The display is positioned in a prominent place outside the store shelf, presenting the products in a way that catches the attention and distinguishes them from competing products.

Apart from its three key purposes of drawing attention, distinguishing in a representative way and promoting sales, the display performs a large number of new functions. Naturally, these are logistic and protective functions that make sure the products arrive safely at the stores, the function of increasing the space for products in the store and the mediation function of making the customer familiar with a product, product group or brand.

In the following the historical development of the modern "display" and its fundamental functions during select historical periods will be presented in order to learn to identify changing requirements in the future.

No sales promotion without competition – business life in Egypt

The end of nomadic life and the change to a permanent settlement together with agriculture and farming were the conditions and the origins of the "first major central state in human history"[1]: Egypt. Economy was based on excess agricultural production that led to a system based on division of labour and new professions.[2] Farmers and craftsmen were under state control and forced by law to work for the king ("Pharaoh") for a determined period of time every day. Egypt's economy was based on planned economy.[3] Trade was rudimentary and dominated by barter trade because the state provided the population with all the food and other supplies it needed for every-day life. Small local markets emerged for the exchange of excess products as wall paintings show. No money was used in Egypt in 400 BC.

Abbildung 1: Geflügelverkauf, dargestellt auf einem Sarkophag aus Ostia
Figure 1: The sale of poultry as shown on a sarcophagus from Ostia

Abbildung 2: Straßenszene in Pompeji
Figure 2: Street scene in Pompeii

basierte auf der Planwirtschaft.³ Der Handel war rudimentär entwickelt und funktionierte als Tauschhandel, da die Bevölkerung vom Staat mit allem Lebensnotwendigen versorgt wurde. Kleine lokale Märkte zum Tausch von Überschüssen entstanden, wie Wandmalereien zeigen. Geldgeschäfte gab es bis etwa 400 v. Chr. keine. Seit 4000 v. Chr. dienten Körbe, große Blätter oder Schalen als Verpackung ausschließlich zur Lagerung, zum Transport und zum Schutz der Waren – also reinen Logistikfunktionen. Verkaufsförderung wurde nicht gezielt beabsichtigt, da weder die Vielfalt noch der Wettbewerb von Gütern dies erforderte.

Since 4000 BC baskets, large leaves and bowls were used exclusively to store, transport and protect goods, all being entirely logistic functions. Sales promotion was not intended due to the lack of product variety and competing products.

Präsentation schafft Begehrlichkeit – Römisches Reich

Bereits im Römischen Reich bestand großes gesellschaftliches Interesse am florierenden Einzelhandel. Neben einfachen lokalen Märkten und Messen, auf denen Bauern ihre Erzeugnisse verkauften, existierten in den Städten Läden und sogar einige von Kaufleuten oder Handwerkern betriebene „Einkaufszentren". Speziell durch den Wohlstand der Bürger Roms entstand ein Markt für Luxusgüter, die Stadt wurde mehr und mehr zum Konsumzentrum.⁴ Großzügig gaben zunehmend zu Wohlstand gekommene römische Bürger ihre Sesterzen aus, der Einkaufsbummel - das genussvolle Konsumieren - gehörte bereits zur römischen Freizeitbeschäftigung.⁵ Die Warenpräsentation im wachsenden Warenangebot gewann an Bedeutung. Die meisten Geschäfte lagen im Erdgeschoss mehrstöckiger Mietshäuser mit Ladentheken direkt zur Straße. Der Kunde konnte bedient werden, ohne das Geschäft betreten zu müssen.

Abbildung 1 zeigt den Ladenverkauf von Geflügel, welches weithin sichtbar an einer galgenähnlichen Konstruktion hängt oder in Schalen ansprechend präsentiert ist. Die Ladentheke zur Straße bewirkte, dass potenzielle Kunden unmittelbar am Verkäufer vor-

Presentation creates desire – the Roman Empire

In the Roman Empire there was great interest in society in the flourishing retail market. Apart from the simple local markets and trade fairs where farmers sold their produce there were stores in the cities and even some "shopping centres" run by salesmen or craftsmen. A market for luxury goods emerged for the wealthy citizens of Rome, the city gained more and more importance as a centre of consumption.⁴ The increasing number of Romans that had achieved wealth freely spent their sesterces and savoured consumption and regular shopping sprees in their free time.⁵ The presentation of the growing range of goods gained importance. Most stores were located on the ground floor of multi-storey houses and had counters directly facing the street. The customer could be served without entering the store. Figure 1 shows a store selling poultry hanging clearly visible on a gallows-like construction or nicely presented in bowls. From his street-facing counter the seller could call out immediately to potential customers who walked directly past the store.⁵ Goods were placed on the counter at eye-level with the customer, they were clearly visible in their open bowls and needed no advertising. The counter area with its shop window character had a mediation function.

Figure 2 shows a store with a sign engraved into the right side of its

I. DIE URSPRÜNGE DES DISPLAYS – VON DER ANTIKE BIS ZUR SELBSTBEDIENUNG | THE ORIGINS OF THE DISPLAY – FROM ANTIQUTIY TO SELF-SERVICE

beigingen und direkt angesprochen werden konnten.[5]

Die Ware wurde auf der Verkaufstheke in Augenhöhe der Kunden ausgestellt, sie war durch die offenen Schalen gut sichtbar und warb für sich selbst. Die Auslage hatte den Charakter eines Schaufensters, also vermittelnde Funktion.

Abbildung 2 zeigt einen Laden, auf dessen rechter Seite ein in Stein gemeißeltes Ladenschild Werbezwecken diente. Üblich in Rom war auch, Körbe und Krüge außerhalb des Ladens auf der Straße zu positionieren. Zusätzliche Gestelle und Auslagetische neben dem Eingang erweiterten die Ladentheke. Diese Verkaufsförderungsinstrumente waren häufig so groß und sperrig, dass sie den erwünschten Besucherstrom in den engen Gassen massiv beeinträchtigten.[5]

Den Handeltreibenden kam die ausladende Bauweise entgegen, denn auf diese Weise waren Passanten gezwungen, an den Auslagen langsam vorbeizugehen. Zwangsläufig fiel der Blick auf das in Augenhöhe befindliche Warenangebot. Das „en passant" entstandene Interesse entschied, ob sich der Weg ins Ladeninnere lohnte. Die Inhaber der Läden reagierten dabei unmittelbar auf das Freizeitverhalten der wohlhabenden Römer. Diese wurden nicht nur als Bedarfskäufer, sondern auch als Genusskäufer begriffen, die sich gerne beim Einkaufsbummel[5] vergnügten und informierten. Die dargebotene Ware war das perfekte Medium, um Kundeninteresse zu wecken.

Dem Display kommt hier die zentrale Funktion der Vermittlung zu. Ware musste produktadäquat angeboten werden und der Kunde musste mit der Ware konfrontiert werden. Darüber hinaus erweiterten römische „Displays" zusätzlich zur begrenzten Verkaufstheke die Lager- und Präsentationsfläche der kleinen voll gestellten Läden und übernahmen Raumfunktionen.

Pietät versus Konsum – Die verdeckte Warenpräsentation im Mittelalter

Mit dem Untergang des weströmischen Reiches erlangte die Kirche im Zuge der Christianisierung zunehmend an Macht. Im Laufe des Mittelalters (etwa 5. bis 14. Jahrhundert) vollzog sich der Übergang von grundherrschaftlicher Naturalwirtschaft zur Geldwirtschaft. Damit verlagerte sich die Wirtschaftsmacht in die Städte, weg vom

stone wall that had an advertising purpose. It was also common use in Rome to position baskets and jugs on the street in front of the store. Additional racks and tables enlarged the store counter. These sales promoting structures were often so big and bulky that they made it extremely difficult for the flow of customers the shopkeeper targeted to pass through the narrow lanes.[5] Traders welcomed the sprawling constructions because they forced passers-by to walk slowly past their offerings. Inevitably the potential customer would see the products that had been displayed at eye-level. The interest that might have incidentally been raised while passing by would decide on whether or not the store was entered. Shopkeepers reacted directly to how wealthy Romans behaved in their free time. They shopped not only out of necessity but also for pleasure and liked to enjoy and inform themselves during their shopping spree.[5] The goods offered were the perfect medium to raise the customer's interest.

Thus the display performs a mediation function. The customer had to be presented and confronted with the product in the right way. In addition Roman "displays" also had the function of enlarging the limited counter, storage and presentation space of the stores that were usually crammed with goods.

Piety versus consumption – hidden product presentation in the Middle Ages

With the decline of the Roman Empire in the west and Christianisation the power of the church increased. In the course of the Middle Ages (around 5th to 14th century) the economy gradually moved from being one dominated by landowners and barter trade to a monetary economy. Economic power shifted away from the countryside and an agrarian economy to the cities. Increasing foreign trade weakened rural production and led to the rise of feudalism. Guilds ruled over social and economic matters in medieval cities. The monetary economy gained increasing importance and led to early forms of capitalism. Merchants and hucksters achieved financial independence and increased their power and influence. The end of the late Middle Ages saw the rise of the bourgeoisie. While the church's omnipresent authority deeply disapproved of any consumption-oriented attitude in

Abbildung 3: Laden für Lebensmittel und Haushaltswaren, um 1390
Figure 3: Food and houseware store, around 1390

Abbildung 4: Fliegender Händler mit Bauchladen, um 1480
Figure 4: Hawker with vending tray, around 1480

Land und von der Agrarwirtschaft. Wachsender Fernhandel führte zu einer Entwertung der ländlichen Produktion sowie feudalen Machtverhältnissen. Das mittelalterliche Zunftwesen bestimmte die sozialen und wirtschaftlichen Vorgänge in den Städten. Die Geldwirtschaft gewann zunehmend an Bedeutung und führte zu frühen Formen des Kapitalismus. Kaufleute und Krämer erlangten finanzielle Unabhängigkeit und zunehmend Macht und Einfluss. Gegen Ende des Spätmittelalters begann die Zeit des aufsteigenden Bürgertums. Während zu Beginn des Mittelalters der omnipräsente Machtanspruch der Kirche konsumorientierte Grundhaltungen der Menschen zutiefst missbilligte, entstand durch zunehmenden Fernhandel ein vielschichtiges Warenangebot des täglichen Bedarfs: luxuriöse Textilien, Gewürze aus fernen Ländern, Obst und Südfrüchte bis hin zu Zitronen.[6]

Die Einzelhändler des Mittelalters – die Krämer – waren in Zünften organisiert und hatten ihre Läden nach festen Regeln zu führen, die auch die Warenpräsentation reglementierten: „Im Hintergrund standen die Regale mit den Schnittwaren. Borten, Gürtel und ähnliche Waren wurden in Kisten aufbewahrt, die Gewürze in Gewürzkästen. [...] Es durfte jedoch nicht zuviel Ware gezeigt, der Käufer sollte nicht zum Kauf gereizt oder gar einem anderen Zeitgenossen abgelockt werden. So durften auf dem Ladentisch selbst nur Reis, Hirse, Backpflaumen, Lorbeer, Mandeln und Johannisbrot in offenen Säcken stehen, die kostbaren Gewürze mußten [!] im Kasten verschlossen sein. Ebenso mußten [!] Schnittwaren sofort nach dem Ausschneiden wieder in die Regale zurückgelegt und damit dem Blickfeld entfernt werden. [...] So wollte es die Erfurter Krämerzunft um 1500 haben."[7]

Abbildung 3 zeigt einen Gemischtwarenladen, auf dessen Verkaufstheke geschlossene Körbe und runde Kisten präsentiert sind. Nur ein Sack Reis ist offen, der Verkäufer wiegt daraus gerade

the early Middle Ages, now increasing foreign trade created a varied offer of everyday goods: luxury textiles, spices from distant countries, fruit including tropical fruits such as lemons.[6]

Medieval retailers, the hucksters, were organised in guilds and had to run their stores according to strict regulations that also regarded the presentation of goods: "In the background there were shelves with draperies, trimmings, belts and similar products were kept in boxes, spices in spice boxes. [...] Shopkeepers were instructed not to display too many goods, urge the customer to buy or even poach the customers of other shopkeepers. Only rice, millet, dried prunes, laurel, almonds and carob bean were allowed on the counter, the precious spices had to be [!] locked away in boxes. Fabrics and textiles had to be [!] returned to the shelves immediately after cutting so that the customer could no longer see them. [...] that is the way the Erfurt Guild wanted it in 1500."[7]

Figure 3 shows a general store with closed baskets and round boxes on its counter. Only a sack of rice is open, the shopkeeper is weighing some rice from the sack for a customer. In the back there are shelves with small clay and glass vessels and bound bales of fabrics or other goods. Candles in different sizes were hanging from the ceiling. Fresh goods like fruit and vegetables were sold at the market.[8] Conform with the demands of theologians and guild regulations goods were presented indirectly and hidden in vessels. The strict medieval regulations clearly reflect the authorities' belief that openly presented goods had a beckoning and seducing effect on people and that the visual effect of the goods contributes "to overcoming the distance that separates seller and buyer".[9]

Apart from the respected hucksters there were other retailers who were not organised in guilds. Figure 4 shows a hawker with his vending tray touring the town. Merchant and salesman in one he sells

I. DIE URSPRÜNGE DES DISPLAYS – VON DER ANTIKE BIS ZUR SELBSTBEDIENUNG | THE ORIGINS OF THE DISPLAY – FROM ANTIQUTITY TO SELF-SERVICE

etwas für die Kundin ab. Im Hintergrund befinden sich Regale mit kleinen Gefäßen aus Ton und Glas sowie verschnürte Ballen mit Ware. Von der Decke hängen Kerzen in verschiedenen Größen. Frische Waren wie Obst und Gemüse wurden auf dem Markt verkauft.[8] Um den Vorstellungen der Theologen und den Regeln der Zünfte zu entsprechen, präsentierten die Krämer ihre Waren indirekt und verdeckt in Gefäßen. Die strengen mittelalterlichen Vorschriften belegen deutlich die Erkenntnis der Obrigkeit, welch anziehende und verlockende Wirkung offen gezeigte Ware auf Menschen hat und dass die optische Wirkung der Ware „die trennende Distanz zwischen Käufer und Verkäufer" überwinden hilft.[9]

Neben den angesehenen Krämern gab es weitere, nicht in Zünften organisierte Kleinhändler. Abbildung 4 zeigt einen fliegenden Händler mit Bauchladen, der in der Stadt unterwegs war. Kaufmann und Verkäufer in einem präsentierte er seine Waren in Form eines Bauchladens aus einer flachen Kiste mit einem Tragriemen aus Leder.[9] Mit seiner Warenpräsentation und seinem Rufen lockte der Händler potenzielle Kundschaft an (die wohl früheste Form des 1:1-Marketings). Der Bauchladen entspricht einem mobilen Display, er dient zugleich als „Schaufenster und mobile Ladentheke".

Differenzierung standardisierter Massenprodukte – Die Industrialisierung

Mit zunehmender Industrialisierung in der zweiten Hälfte des 18. Jahrhunderts änderte sich die Bedeutung des Displays erneut. Absolutismus und Grundherrschaft waren überwunden, der Zunftzwang lockerte sich. Die Voraussetzungen für die freie Ausbreitung des Handels, der Kapitalbildung und der technischen Erneuerung waren gegeben. Die Industrialisierung bewirkte einen massiven gesellschaftlichen Wandel von individuell handwerklicher zu standardisiert industrieller Tätigkeit. Auf allen Ebenen der volkswirtschaftlichen Produktion hielten industrielle Produktionsmethoden, Arbeitsteilung, Automatisierung, Standardisierung zur Produktions- und Effizienzsteigerung Einzug. Eine mehrheitlich bäuerliche Gesellschaft durchlief einen raschen Wandel zu einer industriellen

his goods from a flat case with a leather carrying strap.[9] By presenting his goods and shouting he attracts potential customers (probably the earliest form of one-to-one marketing). The vending tray corresponds to the mobile display, it is "shop window and store counter" in one.

The differentiation of standardised mass products – the industrialisation

The display's meaning was changed once more by the growing industrialisation in the second half of the 18th century. Absolutism and feudalism were things of the past, the guilds were loosening their grip. The conditions were given for free retail growth, capital formation and technical progress. Industrialisation brought about a massive social transformation resulting in the shift from individual craftsmanship to standardised industrial production. Industrial methods of production, division of labour, automation and standardisation entered all levels of national production to boost production and efficiency. The largely rural society was rapidly replaced by an industrial society. Around 1850 approximately two-thirds of the population was self-sufficient. In the course of the industrialisation society changed rapidly to become largely dependent on external supply.[10] The emerging class of skilled workers no longer worked on the fields but for the monetary economy. They had to buy their groceries in stores. That led to strong retail expansion. Numerous stores opened (general stores and corner shops) that catered for people's daily needs. Small retailers mainly used their store furniture to present their goods. The key piece of furniture in the corner shop was the counter, which separated the customer from the salesperson and the mostly loose and unpackaged goods that were stored in shelves and drawers behind the counter. The shopkeeper or the salesperson recommended products the customers may want to buy and personally guaranteed their quality.

The end of the 19th century saw the beginnings of numerous suppliers of branded goods like Maggi, Bahlsen, Nivea, Persil, Osram, Uhu, Coca Cola, Kellogg's and Heinz. This development was driven by industrialisation and the resulting mass production of standardised goods as well as the increasing distance between manufacturer and consumer.

Gesellschaft. Während um 1850 etwa zwei Drittel der Bevölkerung Selbstversorger waren, kehrte sich der Anteil im Laufe der Industrialisierung rasch um zur mehrheitlichen Fremdversorgung.[10] Die entstehende Klasse der Fabrikarbeiter bestellte keine Ackerflächen mehr, sondern arbeitete auf Basis der Geldwirtschaft. Sie waren darauf angewiesen, ihre Nahrungsmittel zu kaufen. Ab Mitte des 19. Jahrhunderts führte dies zu einem sprunghaften Anstieg des Einzelhandels. Zahlreiche Fach- und Einzelhandelsgeschäfte (Kolonial- oder Tante-Emma-Läden) zur Deckung des täglichen Bedarfs entstanden. Dem kleinen Einzelhändler stand zur Präsentation der Waren vor allem seine Ladeneinrichtung zur Verfügung. Das zentrale

Abbildung 5: Tante-Emma-Laden
Figure 5: Corner Shop

Einrichtungselement im Tante-Emma-Laden war die Theke, sie trennte die Kundschaft vom Verkäufer und von den meist losen, unverpackten Waren, die dahinter in Regalen und Schubladen aufbewahrt wurden. Der Krämer oder Verkäufer empfahl seiner Kundschaft entsprechende Produkte und garantierte mit seiner Empfehlung für deren Qualität.

Sowohl als Folge der Industrialisierung und der damit einhergehenden Massenproduktion standardisierter Produkte als auch aufgrund zunehmender Distanz zwischen Hersteller und Konsument entwickelten sich Ende des 19. Jahrhunderts zahlreiche Markenartikelhersteller. Es ist die Blütezeit des Markenartikels (wie z. B. Maggi, Bahlsen, Nivea, Persil, Osram, Uhu, Coca Cola, Kellogg's, Heinz). Die massenhafte Produktion von Gütern des täglichen Bedarfes bedeutete für das individuelle Produkt die Notwendigkeit einer starken Differenzierung. Das Markenprodukt und die Repräsentation der Marke auf Verpackungen oder Displays geriet zum elementaren Differenzierungsmerkmal, das synonym für die Qualität des Produktes stand. Es versprach Sicherheit und mit zunehmendem finanziellen Wohlstand der Käuferschaft wurde es rasch als soziales Statussymbol wahrgenommen.

Neben unzähligen kleinen Einzelhandelsgeschäften entwickelten sich nun auch erste Warenhäuser, deren prunkvolle Einrichtung und Fülle an Waren die Menschen staunen ließ. Um 1900 entstanden vor allem in Großstädten größere Kaufhäuser und Kaufhausketten (u. a. Karstadt 1881, Hertie – Hermann Tietz 1882). Die Warenhäuser stellten zunächst keine bedrohliche Konkurrenz für die kleinen Einzelhandelsgeschäfte dar, Ende der 1920er Jahre betrug der Anteil der Einzelhandelsgeschäfte noch etwa 75 %.[10] Im

It was the golden age of branded goods. In the days of mass production of every day goods each product needed to distinguish itself strongly from the others. Brands and their presentation on packs or displays stood out clearly from non-branded products and soon became synonymous with quality. Brands evoked a feeling of trust and were soon conceived as status symbols by a growing wealthy shopping public.

In a market dominated by countless small stores the first department stores opened their doors. Their splendid furnishings and vast product range amazed customers. Around 1900 larger department stores and department store chains such as Karstadt (1881) and Hertie – Hermann Tietz (1882) appeared mainly in large cities. Department stores were not yet a threatening competition for smaller stores, in the late 1920s small retail establishments still accounted for 75 % of the market.[10] Department stores displayed goods openly and gave "partial self-service", the early beginnings of self-service. The customer was served by the sales staff only on request and was free to walk around and have a look around.[11] Customers no longer needed advice from salespersons on branded products they knew well from commercials and advertisements. Advertising, consequent brand appearance as well as dedicated packaging and displays made sure that these products had long become ingrained in customers' minds as coveted product personalities with added value. When corner shops started to sell branded goods their sales staff also lost their advisory function. The customer now relied on the brand's visual presentation on packs and displays rather than on advice from sales staff.

Abbildung 6: Versandschachteln, die gleichzeitig als Thekendisplay dienten, links 1905, rechts 1933

Figure 6: Shipping boxes that could also be used as counter displays, left 1905, right 1933

Warenhaus wurden Produkte offen in Form der „Teilselbstbedienung" – den ersten Anfängen der Selbstbedienung – präsentiert. Der Kunde wurde nur auf Wunsch vom Personal beraten, ebenso konnte er sich frei bewegen und umschauen.[11] Die Beratung zu Markenartikeln durch den Verkäufer wurde unnötig, da diese sich durch ihr konsequentes Markenerscheinungsbild, ihre Verpackung, ihre Displays und wachsende Bekanntheit durch Werbung in der Öffentlichkeit längst als begehrenswerte Produktpersönlichkeiten in den Köpfen der Käufer festgesetzt hatten und Mehrwert generierten. Mit dem Einzug von Markenartikeln in Tante-Emma-Läden wurde auch hier die Beraterfunktion des Verkäufers überflüssig. Der Kunde verließ sich auf das visuell Präsentierte einer Marke – auf Verpackung und Display.

Die Markenartikelhersteller analysierten für ihre Verkaufsförderungs- und Werbemaßnahmen das Einkaufsverhalten der Menschen. Befanden diese sich im Laden, so war ihr Blick zwangsläufig auf die Theke gerichtet, dort erfolgte die Bedienung und auch beim Warten war man der Theke zugewandt. Verständlich daher, dass zunächst der Thekenaufsteller entwickelt wurde.

Die dargestellten Thekendisplays von Dr. Oetker (Abbildung 6) dienten einerseits als Transportverpackung, andererseits als markenrelevante Präsentationsfläche. Sie wurden direkt auf die Theke gestellt, der Deckel wurde hochgeklappt, so dass die Produkte gemeinsam, in einer der Marke entsprechend gestalteten Schachtel, präsentiert wurden und nicht zusammen mit Packungen anderer Wettbewerber ins Regal wanderten. Das Aufstellen auf der Theke gewährleistete das offene Zur-Schau-Stellen der Produkte, d. h., die Artikel gelangten nicht hinter die Theke und damit aus dem Blickfeld des Kunden.

Zur Unterstützung des Verkaufs boten Markenartikelhersteller Verkaufsmöbel an, speziell gestaltete und mit dem jeweiligen Signet versehene Schränke. Die Schränke (Abbildung 7) hatten einerseits die Aufgabe, die Produkte sicher aufzubewahren, andererseits diese sichtbar zu präsentieren und den Abverkauf durch die Sonderplatzierung zu steigern. Zudem boten sie zusätzliche Verkaufsfläche, die Produkte beanspruchten keinen Platz in Schubladen oder Regalen.

To improve their promotion and advertising efforts suppliers of branded goods analysed customers' buying behaviour. When in the store, customers' eyes were inevitably directed towards the counter, where sales staff were sure to help with advice. When waiting customers also tended to face the counter. It is therefore only logical that the counter display was the first display to be developed.

The featured counter displays from Dr Oekter (figure 6) were transport package and presentation platform in one. The display was placed directly on top of the counter and its lid opened to present the products all together in a brand-specific box instead of ending up in the shelves with competing products. The position on the counter guaranteed that the products were openly displayed and were not positioned out of the customer's sight behind the counter.

To support the sale of their products suppliers of branded goods provided retailers with furniture, specially designed cabinets featuring the company's logo. The cabinets (figure 7) served to provide safe storage while at the same time showcasing and promoting the sale of products in a prominent place. They also created new space, products no longer took up room in drawers and shelves.

Contrary to the confined space of corner shops branded goods suppliers had much more room in department stores. This allowed branded goods suppliers to think up particularly impressive constructions and forms of presenting their products in an eye-catching way as for example in the case of the house built entirely from Persil packs (figure 8).

The existence of the branded article is of fundamental importance for the development of the display. It was the brand that gave products on sale in the store an identity customers grew to. The display plays an important role in conveying brand and product messages and creating value, in particular for branded goods.

Abbildung 7: Verkaufsschränke „Dr. Oetker" für 300 bzw. 500 Päckchen, 1914
Figure 7: "Dr Oetker" display cabinets for 300 or 500 packs, 1914

Abbildung 8: Haus, aus Persilpackungen gebaut
Figure 8: House built of Persil packs

Im Gegensatz zu den beengten Verhältnissen im Tante-Emma-Laden stand den Markenartiklern im Warenhaus einiges mehr an Platz zur Verfügung. Daher konnten sich die Markenartikler besonders beeindruckende Formen und Aufbauten einfallen lassen, um ihr Produkt in Szene zu setzen, wie beispielsweise ein Haus ganz aus „Persil"-Packungen (Abbildung 8). Auffallend einprägsam wurde dabei speziell die Produktverpackung im Gedächtnis verankert.

Für die Entwicklung des Displays ist das Entstehen des Markenartikels von fundamentaler Bedeutung. Erst durch die Marke bekamen Produkte, die im Einkaufsladen verkauft wurden, für den Verbraucher ein Gesicht. Das Display übernimmt gerade im Bereich der Markenartikel eine wesentliche Funktion des Vermittelns von Marken- und Produktbotschaften und damit der Wertschöpfung.

Verkaufseffizienz durch Selbstbedienung

Zwei Weltkriege, Inflation und Wirtschaftskrisen behinderten in der Zeit bis 1945 die Entwicklung des Einzelhandels. In die durch kleine Tante-Emma-Läden geprägte Handelslandschaft in Deutschland platzten Ende der 40er Jahre aus Amerika kommend neue Formen des Handels. Die mit dem Tante-Emma-Prinzip verbundene persönliche Beziehung und Dienstleistungsbereitschaft zwischen lokalem Händler und Kunden wurde aufgelöst durch anonyme Handelsformate. Der Supermarkt, geprägt durch große Verkaufsflächen und wenig Personal, sowie umfangreichem Angebot an Lebens- und Genussmitteln, Drogerieartikeln und Gütern des täglichen Bedarfs expandierte. Der Trend zur Selbstbedienung sparte Personal, längst erledigten Markenartikel ihre Kommunikationspflicht unabhängig vom Verkaufspersonal. Herbert Eklöh, ein

Sales efficiency through self-service

During the period leading up to 1945 the development and growth of retail was hindered by two world wars, inflation and economic crises. In the late 1940s new retail concepts were imported to Germany from America and fundamentally changed the country's corner shop dominated retail landscape. The personal relationship between customer and local retailer and the related service mentality disappeared with the decline of the corner shop and was replaced by anonymous retail formats. Supermarkets with their typical large selling space and reduced sales staff, their vast offer of food and drink, luxury foods and beverages such as alcohol, coffee and tobacco, personal care products and every-day goods were expanding rapidly. The trend towards self-service reduced staff levels, as the brand no longer needed salespersons to communicate with the customer. A chemist called Herbert Eklöh opened the first German supermarket in Osnabrück in 1938. He had to close again because of the reluctance of customers towards the idea of self-service. The rise of the supermarket started with the opening of the first self-service store of retail cooperative "Produktion" in Hamburg in 1949. The number of self-service stores increased from 20 in 1950 to 1,379 in 1957. The EDEKA group introduced self-service in 1954, the non-food range was expanded in 1959. The success of the self-service concept led to other retail concepts such as department stores, specialist department stores, self-service department stores, discounters and large specialist stores. Self-service meant that the article itself had to do the presenting and explaining - one of the display's fundamental functions. The display removes the article from the shelf, thus separating it from similar products, and presents it in a place where it is noticed even from a distance. Self-service provided the display with its key function – the function of being a "silent salesman". In pre-self-service days the counter stood between the goods and the customer, barring immediate access to the product. The salesperson had a mediation and

DIE URSPRÜNGE DES DISPLAYS – VON DER ANTIKE BIS ZUR SELBSTBEDIENUNG | THE ORIGINS OF THE DISPLAY – FROM ANTIQUTIY TO SELF-SERVICE

Abbildung 9: Display „Persil" mit Roll-Palette, 1966/67
Figure 9: "Persil" roll pallet display, 1966/1967

Abbildung 10: Bodendisplay „Pretty Hair", 1969
Figure 10: "Pretty Hair" floor stand display, 1969

Abbildung 11: Bodendisplay „Perla", 1960er Jahre
Figure 11: "Perla" floor stand display, 1960s

gelernter Drogist, eröffnete 1938 den ersten deutschen Supermarkt in Osnabrück, der aufgrund geringer Akzeptanz des Selbstbedienungsprinzips seine Pforten zunächst schließen musste. Als 1949 in Hamburg der erste SB-Freiwahl-Laden der Konsumgenossenschaft „Produktion" eröffnete, begann der Siegeszug der Selbstbedienung. Von 20 Selbstbedienungsläden 1950 stieg die Zahl auf 1.379 im Jahr 1957 an. 1954 führte der EDEKA-Verbund das Selbstbedienungsprinzip ein, 1959 wurden verstärkt Non-Food-Produkte ins Sortiment genommen. Weitere Betriebsformen des Einzelhandels, wie Warenhäuser, Fachkaufhäuser, SB-Warenhäuser, Verbrauchermärkte, Discounter und Fachmärkte, folgten dem Erfolg des Selbstbedienungsprinzips. Durch die Selbstbedienung muss sich die Ware verstärkt selbst anbieten und erklären – eine elementare Aufgabe des Displays. Es nimmt die Ware aus dem Regal, d. h. aus dem Umfeld ähnlicher Produkte, heraus und macht schon von Weitem auf sie aufmerksam. Deshalb bekam das Display durch die Selbstbedienung seine wichtigste Funktion – nämlich als „stummer Verkäufer". Bisher trennte der Ladentisch die Produkte von den Kunden und versperrte so den direkten Zugriff auf die Ware. Die Bedienung war als Vermittlerin und Beraterin zwischen Käufer und Ware tätig.[12] Durch das Wegfallen der Bedienung und damit auch der Verkaufstheke wird einerseits die räumliche Distanz zwischen Ware und Käufer verringert. Andererseits wird die Ware anonym, da sie überregional verkauft wird und nicht mehr vom vertrauten Bauern, Bäcker oder Metzger aus dem Ort stammt.[12] Dem Display kommt durch die angemessene Präsentation der Waren die Aufgabe zu, die vermittelnde und damit verkaufende Funktion der Bedienung zu ersetzen. Gleichzeitig informiert es Kunden und bietet Orientierung im wachsenden Warenangebot, das eine fachliche Beratung zur damaligen Zeit immer notwendiger gemacht hätte.

Die Markenartikelhersteller erkannten das wirtschaftliche Potenzial rasch. Sie beschränkten sich nicht mehr nur auf den Einsatz von Thekendisplays, sondern wurden zu Hauptnutzern der neuen Bodendisplays aus Wellpappe, die in Deutschland in den 60er Jahren eingeführt wurden. In den USA gab es diese bereits, da das Selbst-

advisory role in the relationship between customer and product.[12] The disappearance of service and, consequently, also the sales counter narrowed the distance between the product and the customer. At the same time, the product, which was no longer sold by the farmer, baker or butcher next door, became anonymous.[12] By representing the goods in an adequate way the display replaced the salesperson in his mediation and sales roles. The display further offered information and orientation to a customer, who is confronted with an expanding product range, a fact that in former times would have required professional advice.

Branded goods suppliers were quick to recognise the economic potential. They soon moved on from the counter display to become the main users of corrugated cardboard floor stand displays that were first introduced in Germany in the 1960s. They were already being used in the US, where self-service had been established. As a result of self-service the customer was left to himself in the store. The advice known from the corner shop was replaced by packs and displays. They conveyed the product's quality and brand.

Similarly to the counter display, which at the beginning was nothing more than a simple shipping box that could also be used as a counter-top presentation, the first floor stand displays were also shipping boxes. The shipping boxes were stacked on top of each other and ripped open so that the products could be seen. Together with an eye-catching poster this construction proved to be a very inexpensive form of display. (figures 9 and 10).
Next to corrugated cardboard other materials were used for the construction of displays. In the case of Perla a washing basket was used for a bin. The writing "Please serve yourself!" on the socket of the Perla display was an obvious invitation to self-service. (figure 11) Similar signs suggesting self-service were put up in the store (figure 12) to make the customer familiar with the new way of shopping.
The 1960s saw the development of many creative and eye-catching types of displays. The Planschi display has a corrugated cardboard socket with an inflatable duck on top that was used as a bin for goods. The display was sure to attract customers' attention. Children in particular are likely to have been keen on having "Planschi fun" when they saw the duck. (figure 13)

bedienungsprinzip sich durchgesetzt hatte. Durch das eingeführte Selbstbedienungskonzept waren die Kunden im Laden auf sich gestellt. Die vertraute Beratung aus dem Tante-Emma-Laden ersetzten Verpackungen und Displays. Sie kommunizierten Qualitäten von Produkt und Marke.

Ähnlich der Entwicklung des Thekendisplays, das zunächst eine reine Versandschachtel war, die den Zusatznutzen der Thekenpräsentation aufwies, wurden auch für den Aufbau der ersten Bodenaufsteller Versandkartons verwendet. Die Versandkartons wurden übereinander gestapelt und aufgerissen, so dass die Produkte sichtbar waren. In Verbindung mit einem Plakat, das Fernwirkung erzeugte, war dies eine sehr preisgünstige Variante des Displays (Abbildungen 9 und 10). Neben Wellpappe wurden auch andere Konstruktionsmaterialien für Displays eingesetzt. Beispielsweise dient beim Perla-Display ein Wäschekorb als Warenschütte. Die Aufschrift „Bitte bedienen Sie sich selbst!" auf dem Sockel des Perla-Displays fordert den Kunden zur Selbstbedienung auf (Abbildung 11). Dieser Hinweis erfolgte auch durch die Beschilderung im Laden (Abbildung 12) und brachte somit den Kunden das neue Prinzip des Einkaufens näher.

In den 60er Jahren entstanden ebenso bereits sehr kreative und auffällige Displayformen. Das Planschi-Display besteht aus einem Sockel aus Wellpappe, worauf eine aufblasbare Ente montiert wurde, die zur Warenaufnahme diente. Das Display zog sicherlich die Blicke der Kunden auf sich. Vor allem Kinder wollten höchstwahrscheinlich aufgrund der Ente den „Plantschi-Spaß" haben (Abbildung 13).

Abbildung 12: Augsburg, erster Selbstbedienungsladen
Figure 12: The first self-service store in Augsburg

Verführung zum Konsum – 1980er und 1990er Jahre

Nachdem in den 1980er und 1990er Jahren mit wachsendem gesellschaftlichen Wohlstand das Streben nach Erhöhung des persönlichen Lebensstandards durch Konsum enorm anstieg, wurde die wirtschaftliche Zielsetzung darauf ausgerichtet, Einkaufen als gesellschaftliches Freizeiterlebnis zu positionieren. Die Verführung des Kunden zum Kauf stand im Mittelpunkt aller Verkaufsaktivitäten. Speziell in Shopping-Zentren und Malls entstanden erste Konzepte des „Erlebniskaufs". Begriffe wie „Impulskauf", „Quengelzone" und „Warendruck" wurden zu Bewertungskriterien erfolgreicher Verkaufsstrategien. Dauerhafte Einkaufswelten mit luxuriösen Erlebnisprofilen (Exotik, Fitness, Wellness etc.) in spezifischem Ambiente wurden inszeniert. Fassadenähnliche Motto-Dekorationen mit Animationsprogrammen, polysensuellen Geruchs-

The temptation to consume – the 1980s and 1990s

With the growing social wealth and the pursuet of raising standards of living which consumption triggered in the 1980s and 1990s came the redefinition of economic objectives - shopping was now to become a social leisure experience. Enticing the customer was now at the centre of all sales activities. New "shopping experience" concepts were rolled out especially in shopping centres and malls. Terms like "impulse purchase", "whining area" and "product pressure" came to define how successful sales strategies are. Permanent theme areas were set up in stores that offered lush exotic, fitness or well-being experiences in dedicated environments. Dedicated theme decorations were created which looked like store fronts and were accompanied by animation programmes, multi-sensory scent and sound experiences, entertaining games and interactive temporary and permanent displays became commonplace in stores.

Even though these shopping experience areas are perfect for temporary promotions, they are today carefully assessed regarding their long-term economic benefits. On the other hand permanent displays such as profitable brand shops and complex shop-in-shop systems were designed in particular for high-end brands in multi-brand stores including sophisticated flagship store fittings that respond to the highest standards of brand representation.

Abbildung 13: Bodendisplay „Plantschi", 1960er Jahre
Figure 13: "Plantschi" floor stand display, 1960s

und Klangerlebnissen, Unterhaltungsspielen sowie interaktiven Temporär- und Permanentdisplays entstanden. Für temporäre Aktionen perfekt, wird der langfristige wirtschaftliche Nutzen dieser Einkaufswelten mittlerweile sorgfältigst geprüft. Auf der anderen Seite entstanden besonders im Bereich der Premiummarken in Form von Permanentdisplays profitable Markenshops sowie komplexe Shop-in-Shop-Systeme für Multi Label-Stores bis hin zu aufwändigen Einrichtungen von Flagshipstores mit höchstem Anspruch an Aspekte der Markenrepräsentation.

Fazit

Die Ausführungen zur Entwicklung des Displays zeigen deutlich, dass die Funktionen des Displays immer in enger Abhängigkeit zu den gesellschaftlichen und ökonomischen Bedingungen einer bestimmten Zeitepoche stehen. In jedem Fall steht das Display immer an vorderster Front der Verkaufsförderung, es ist der Katalysator in der Kunde-Produkt-Beziehung:

- Es konfrontiert den Kunden mit der Ware und bietet diese produktadäquat an.
- Es verringert die Distanz zwischen Kunde und Ware.
- Es fokussiert die Aufmerksamkeit auf die Ware.
- Es schafft formale Differenzierung gegenüber Wettbewerberprodukten.
- Es verbessert die Orientierung in einem unübersichtlichen Warensortiment.
- Es kommuniziert dem Betrachter inhaltlich die Qualitäten eines Produktes, dessen Marke und evoziert Wertvorstellungen in unserem Bewusstsein.
- Es fordert vom Betrachter mentale Auseinandersetzung und verankert sich bleibend in der Erinnerung.

Vorauszusehen, welche neuartigen Anforderungen dem Display in Zukunft zukommen werden, ist sicherlich nicht einfach. Soziologen, Zukunfts- und Trendforscher sowie Marktforscher sind hier gefordert, Antworten auf die drängende Frage, welche gesellschaftlichen und ökonomischen Entwicklungen zukünftig unser Kaufverhalten beeinflussen, zu geben.

Conclusion

The observations made on the development of the display show clearly that the display's function is always closely linked to the social and economic conditions of a certain period in time. In all cases the display is key to sales promotion, it is the catalyst in the relationship between customer and product:

- *It confronts the customer with the product and presents the product in an adequate way.*
- *It narrows the distance between customer and product*
- *It focuses the attention on the product.*
- *It distinguishes the product from competing products.*
- *It improves orientation within a confusing product range.*
- *It conveys information to the customer about the product's quality, its brand and evokes judgements of value in the customer's consciousness.*
- *It mentally engages the customer and leaves a lasting impression.*

Obviously it is not easy to predict what new requirements the display will face in the future. Sociologists, futurologists, trend analysts and market researchers are called upon to find answers to the pressing question of what social and economic developments will influence people's buying behaviour in the future.

Sophie Wittl   Christoph Häberle

II. DIE ENTWICKLUNG DES POS-MARKETINGS | THE DEVELOPMENT OF POS MARKETING

Einzelhandel in den 50ern
Retail in the 1950s

DIE ENTWICKLUNG DES POS-MARKETINGS
THE DEVELOPMENT OF POS MARKETING

Bernd Hallier
Die Entwicklung des POS-Marketings

Die Evolution des POS-Marketings

Der Point of Sale ist ein Begriff, der in Deutschland erst in der Nachkriegszeit eingeführt wurde – er kann differenziert werden in POS und POS-Marketing. Der POS ist heute die gesamte Ladenfläche; POS-Marketing ist der absatzwirtschaftliche Prozess, der alternativ zur klassischen Werbung in den Medien vom Händler auf der Verkaufsfläche praktiziert oder geduldet wird. Die Entwicklung des POS-Marketings ist eng verknüpft mit der Geschichte des Handels und der Geschichte der Verpackung – beide Berührungspunkte sind miteinander verzahnt und bedingen einander:

- Der Handel hat sich Ende der 40er Jahre von der Bedienung zur Selbstbedienung umpositioniert, was viele neue Vertriebstypen hervorgebracht hat.
- Die Einführung der Selbstbedienung war nur möglich durch entsprechende Verpackungen und Behältnisse.

Diese Markt-Evolution wurde durch POS-Marketing unterstützt; zugleich durchlebte das POS-Marketing beständig Veränderungen.

Von der Bedienung zur Selbstbedienung

Der erste revolutionäre Schritt des Wandels im Handel war die Einführung der Selbstbedienung:

- Die Ware musste standardisiert vor-verpackt werden (also nicht mehr während des Verkaufsvorgangs).
- Präsentationsmöbel mussten für potentielle Käufer zugänglich sein.
- Die „Empfehlung" des Ladeninhabers wurde abgelöst durch die Verpackungsbeschriftung, -grafik und Regalpräsentation.
- Die Anonymisierung des Kunden eliminierte die Beratung durch den Ladeninhaber/Marktleiter im Kundendialog einerseits und ermöglichte anderseits dadurch die Ladenmultiplikation.

Aus dem „Tante Emma"-Bedienungsladen entstand zuerst das SB (Selbstbedienung)-Geschäft, später durch das ISB (Institut für

Bernd Hallier
The development of POS marketing

The evolution of POS marketing

In Germany, the term point of sale was introduced only in the post-war era. The term can be differentiated into POS and POS marketing. Today, the POS is defined as the entire store space. POS marketing is the marketing process that differs from conventional advertising in the media and is used or tolerated by the retailer on the sales floor. The development of POS marketing is closely linked to the history of retail and the history of packaging. Both aspects are closely connected to each other and are mutually dependent:

- *At the end of the 1940s, retailers moved from service to self-service which created many new forms of distribution.*
- *The shift to self-service was possible only through the introduction of packaging and containers.*

This market development was supported by POS marketing. At the same time POS itself was subject to constant change.

From service to self-service

The introduction of self-service marked the first revolutionary step towards change at retail:

- *Goods had to be pre-packed (they were no longer packed during the sale process).*
- *Presentation furniture had to be accessible to potential customers.*
- *"Recommendation" by the store owner was replaced by front of pack labelling and graphics as well as shelf presentation.*
- *Customers became anonymous, which made advice from the store owner or manager redundant in customer dialogue, but at the same time enabled store multiplication.*

The traditional corner shop was replaced first by the self-service store, which was later defined as a store with a space of up to 400 m². Larger stores were termed supermarkets. It may be of interest to note that the first 20 self-service stores were introduced between 1949 and 1950 across the whole of Germany. In 1952,

Kassenzone der 60er
Checkout area in the 1960s

Selbstbedienung), definiert als Läden mit Flächen bis zu 400 Quadratmetern; über jene Verkaufsflächen hinausgehende Geschäfte erhielten den Begriff „SuperMarkt". Interessant mag sein, dass die Einführung der ersten 20 Selbstbedienungsläden zwischen 1949 und 1950 flächendeckend über die ganze Bundesrepublik Deutschland erfolgte. 1952 bewegten sich die ersten 80 Betriebe zwischen 35 (!) und 330 Quadratmetern; sie gehörten zu 52 Prozent den Konsumgenossenschaften, zu 38 Prozent den Lebensmittelfachbetrieben, zu sieben Prozent dem selbstständigen Einzelhandel und zu drei Prozent den Warenhäusern. Erstmals führte 1958 das ISB eine Sortimentsbreitenerhebung durch. Im Schnitt hatten die SB-Geschäfte zu jenem Zeitpunkt circa 1.000 Artikel, davon 100 Nonfood (Wasch-, Putz- und Reinigungsmittel).

Von „Tante Emma" zum Massendistributeur

In der zweiten Entwicklungsstufe wurden in den 60er und 70er Jahren die atomistischen lokalen Händlerstrukturen durch regionale Filialsysteme ersetzt. Namen, wie Stüssgen/Köln, Latscha/Frankfurt, Kupsch/Würzburg, standen für regionale Marktführer mit einer Agglomeration von 50 und mehr Geschäften, die in einer Region konzentriert waren.

Das POS-Display ist Waren- und Werbeträger und füllt als Zweitplatzierung Versorgungslücken bei den expandierenden

the first 80 stores had spaces ranging between 35 (!) and 330m². Around 52% of the stores were owned by retail cooperatives, 35 % belonged to food companies, 7% to independent retailers and 3 % to department stores. The German Institute for Self-Service, Institut für Selbstbedienung (ISB), conducted a survey on assortments for the first time in 1958. It found that at the time, self-service stores offered an average of 1,000 products including 100 non-food products like cleaning products.

From corner shop to mass distribution

In a second development the atomized local retail market structure, consisting of small single-unit retailers, was replaced by a system of regional store chains in the 1960s and 1970s. Market leaders of the time include Stüssgen in Cologne, Latscha in Frankfurt and Kupsch in Würzburg. These companies had 50 stores or more in a particular region.

The POS display is a platform for goods and advertising. Used as a secondary placement it fills the gap in the supply of expanding retail partners. In the 1960s and 1970s, the secondary placement was also a tactical tool of "push marketing" used for the introduction of new branded goods, because it attracted the customer's attention. For the connected refunds, the secondary placement was also extremely popular with buyers of retail companies. The industry offers advertising sub-

II. DIE ENTWICKLUNG DES POS-MARKETINGS | THE DEVELOPMENT OF POS MARKETING

Der EAN-Code und Scanning ermöglichen die Produktbezeichnung auf dem Kassenzettel.
EAN and Scanning made it possible to print the product name on the receipt.

Handelspartnern. Für Neueinführungen von Markenartikeln ist die Zweitplatzierung in den 60er/70er Jahren zugleich ein taktisches Tool des „Push-Marketings", denn sie erregt die Aufmerksamkeit der Konsumenten. Gleichzeitig ist sie bei den Einkäufern des Handels aufgrund der Kostenerstattung – die Industrie zahlt für Displays einen Werbekostenzuschuss (WKZ) – äußerst gefragt. Teilweise kommt es zu Platzierungsüberschwemmungen im Handel und die Displays kämpfen um die besten Plätze.

Mit der zunehmenden Artikelanzahl und der steigenden Kaufkraft geht eine Vergrößerung der Läden einher, es entstehen neue Betriebsformen. Für die oberhalb der Supermärkte liegenden SB-Warenhäuser wird die Verkaufsfläche für 1966 mit 0,25 Mio. Quadratmetern angegeben – für 1976 mit 4,6 Mio. und 1986 mit 6,7 Mio. Der bundesdeutsche Einzelhandelsumsatz wuchs in dieser Zeit von 138,7 Mrd. DM über 315,9 Mrd. auf 531,3 Mrd.; d.h., die Flächenausdehnung übertraf die makroökonomische Umsatzentwicklung bei weitem! Der Grund der Flächenexpansion lag in dem diversifizierten/segmentierten Angebot: Aus einem Joghurt entwickelte sich Joghurt diverser Geschmacksrichtungen, mit unterschiedlichen Fettgehalten, in unterschiedlichen Konsum- und Gebindegrößen.

Die quantitative Expansion ging einher mit einer qualitativen Veränderung. Die Plattform dieser Modernisierung war die 1966 erstmals vom ISB und der Messe Düsseldorf durchgeführte EuroShop-Messe. Bestand das erste EuroShop-Logo aus dem stilisierten Bild eines Ladens und eines Schaufensters, so symbolisierte ein Jahrzehnt später das zweite (und heute noch gültige) EuroShop-Logo das Summenzeichen der Kassen und damit auch das Zusammentreffen von Angebot und Nachfrage! Ging es bei den EuroShop-Veranstaltungen der 60er Jahre um die Schaufenstergestaltung, den Ladenbau, die Kühlmöbel und Kassen, so rückten zu Beginn der 70er Jahre die Beleuchtung, die Schauwer-

sidies for displays, called Werbekostenzuschuss in German, or WKZ for short. This sometimes led to a flood of placements at retail, resulting in fierce competition among displays for the best in-store locations.

The increasing number of goods and rising spending power led to the expansion of store space and the emergence of new distribution forms. The total space of self-service department stores, which are bigger than supermarkets, was 250,000m² in 1966. That number increased to 4.6m in 1976 and to 6.7m in 1986. German retail sales rose from 138.7m in 1966 to 315.9m in 1976 and to 531.3m in 1986. This means that store space expansion was substantially stronger than macro-economic sales growth! Store space expansion was prompted by product diversification and segmentation. First there was only plain yoghurt, then came yoghurt with different flavours and differing fat content offered in various sizes.

Quantitative expansion was accompanied by qualitative change. EuroShop, the trade show staged by ISB and exhibition organiser Messe Düsseldorf for the first time in 1966, was the platform for that modernisation. The first EuroShop logo was a stylized image of a shop and shop window. A decade later, the EuroShop logo was changed to symbolise the sign formerly shown on the subtotal key of German cash registers, its two opposite arrows forming a star and thus highlighting the interaction of supply and demand. While the EuroShop events of the 1960s concentrated on shop window decoration, shop fitting, refrigeration equipment and cash registers, the focus shifted to lighting, visual advertising and sale promotion in the 1970s. Under the leadership of ISB, which is today the EHI Retail Institute, EuroShop has become the engine of technical innovation, inspiration and motivation for the industry.

A glance at history shows that in terms of macro-economic space expansion retailers were "driven" and "drivers" at the same time. The

bung und die Verkaufsförderung in den Fokus. Die EuroShop entwickelte sich unter der Leitung des ISB (heute EHI Retail Institute) zum Motor der technischen Innovation, der Inspiration und Motivation der Branche.

Der Blick in die Geschichte zeigt, dass der Handel auch bei der makroökonomischen Flächenexpansion nicht nur „Getriebener", sondern ebenfalls „Treiber" war. Das Schlagwort jener Zeit lautete „Diversifikation". Nahezu alle Filialbetriebe starteten mehr oder minder breitgefächert neben ihren Lebensmittelgeschäften zusätzlich mit Fachmarkt-Vertriebslinien. Ein Beispiel hierfür ist die Firma Allkauf.

Durch diese Diversifikation wurde bundesweit eine Veränderung der Markt- und Unternehmensstruktur in Bewegung gesetzt. Auch die bis dahin mehr branchenorientierte Marktkonzentration wurde in andere Marktsegmente übergreifend hineingetragen – teilweise kombiniert mit ersten Schritten einer Internationalisierung des Handels.

Vom Point of Sale zum Point of Purchase

Die Einführung des Scannings Mitte der 70iger Jahre brachte den Händlern in den 80-iger/90-iger Jahren die Datenübersicht über den wirklichen "Abverkauf" pro Laden und pro Marke sowie über die Warenbestände. Handel und Industrie kamen zu der gemeinsamen Erkenntnis, dass es weniger um „Push" – sondern vielmehr um „Pull" – Aktivitäten des Konsumenten (also des „Purchase") bei den Handelsaktionen gehen sollte. Der POS wurde zum POP definiert und beispielsweise durch Organisatoren wie POPAI (Point of Purchase Advertising International) strategisch bei den Mitgliedern aber auch propagandistisch auf

Allkauf-Diversifikation / Diversification at Allkauf

1968	Erstes SB-Warenhaus	First self-service department store
1976	Möbelhäuser	Furniture stores
1978	Fotofachgeschäfte	Photo shops
1981	Reiseveranstalter	Tour operators
1985	Optikfachgeschäfte	Optician shops

Quelle/Source: Retail Institute

catchword of the time was "diversification". Almost all store chains added a more or less large number of specialist distribution channels to their food stores. The company Allkauf is an example for this.

This diversification triggered a change in market and company structure, across the whole of Germany. Market concentration, formerly focused mainly on the individual industries, started to diversify into new markets, in part accompanied by tentative steps towards internationalisation.

From point of sale to point of purchase

Scanning was introduced in the mid-1970s and in the 1980s and 1990s provided retailers with data about real sales figures per store and brand as well as inventory levels. Both industry and retail came to the conclusion that retail promotions should focus on the "pull" activities of the consumer (meaning the "purchase") rather than the "push" activities. The POS was newly defined as the POP and

In den 80ern wurde die Kassenzone schrittweise ein technisches Cockpit.
In the 1980s the checkout area gradually turned into a technical cockpit.

II. DIE ENTWICKLUNG DES POS-MARKETINGS | THE DEVELOPMENT OF POS MARKETING

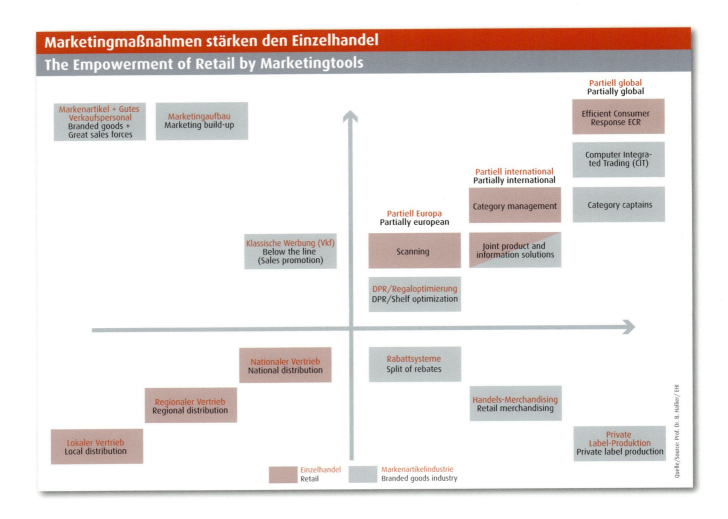

zahlreichen Verträgen oder in Publikationen dokumentiert. Auch die Namensgebung der 1974 gegründeten deutschen Vergabestelle der EAN-Nummer „Centrale für Coorganisation CCG" (heute GS1) spiegelt diesen Zeitgeist wider. Letztendlich laufen ebenfalls die gemeinsam von Handel und Industrie Mitte der 80er entwickelten Ansätze der „Direkten Produktrentabilität (DPR)" und auch die heutigen ECR-Bemühungen mit allen Aktivitäten entlang der Total Supply Chain in dieselbe Richtung: Der POP soll optimiert werden.

Die DPR-Ansätze waren eng gekoppelt an die „Anforderungen des Handels an Verpackungen"; damit griff der Handel erstmals in ein Kompetenzgebiet der Industrieseite ein – sowohl unter dem Aspekt der Ökonomie (Verpackungsvolumen) als auch der Ökologie (Mehrweg versus Einweg). Eine Erweiterung der ursprünglichen Produkt-Promotion liegt im so genannten „Category Management", denn erstmals geht es bei der Optimierung der „Kategorie" nicht mehr um die Produkte einer einzelnen Firma, sondern um die Sortimentszusammensetzung über alle Anbieter einer Warengruppe hinweg. Damit gewinnt der Handel die Hoheit über den Laden zurück, denn der Händler hat weniger Interesse an einer Marke als vielmehr an der Sortimentsgestaltung!

was strategically documented by organisers like the international assocation Point of Purchase Advertising International (POPAI) with its members, but also in several lectures and publications. "Centrale für Coorganisation CCG", the name the German provider of bar code numbers, today known as "GS1", chose for its foundation in 1974, reflects that zeitgeist. In the end, the "Direct Product Profit (DPP)" initiatives launched jointly by industry and retail in the 1980s as well as today's Efficient Consumer Response (ECR) efforts and all related supply chain activities have the same objective of optimising the POP.

DPP's approach was closely linked to "retail's packaging requirements". For the first time, retailers entered a field of competence previously reserved to the industry both in terms of economy (packaging volumes) and ecology (reusable against disposable). So-called "category management" represented the extension of original product promotion because the focus of product optimization was no longer on the products of an individual company, but on the assortments of all suppliers of a certain product category. In this way, retail regained authority over its stores because the retailer is interested in the assortment rather than in the brand.

Auf die Ausrichtung des Handels an den Bedürfnissen des Shoppers geht sicherlich das Shopping-Center als neue Betriebsform zurück. 100 Jahre nach der Einführung der Warenhäuser (um 1875) als „Alles-unter-einem-Dach-Konzept", die sich zum Anker des innenstädtischen Einkaufs entwickelten, wurde circa 1975 die Idee des sortimentsübergreifenden Einkaufs revitalisiert. Allerdings basierte das neue Konzept auf der Mobilität der Konsumenten und führte zu einer Verlagerung der Ladenflächen in die Stadtrandzonen. Betriebsorganisatorisch besteht des Weiteren der Unterschied darin, dass die Verkaufsfläche eines Warenhauses zentral gesteuert wird, während das Shopping-Center eine Agglomeration von Händlern in einer baulichen Einheit (laut EHI-Definition mit mindestens 10.000 Quadratmetern) beherbergt.

Vom Point of Purchase zum Point of Differentiation

Betrachtet man die mikroökonomischen Aktivitäten des POS-Marketings, so werden für Berechnungen von ECR-Modellen/POP-Offerten seitens der Industrie in der Regel soziodemografische Daten der Region für die Planung der Sortimente genutzt:

Surely, the shopping centre as a new form of distribution was a key driver for retail's orientation towards the needs of their customers. A decade after the introduction of department stores (roughly in 1875) as an "everything-under-one-roof" concept that became the anchor format of inner-city shopping areas, the idea of purchasing across all product categories was revived in 1975. The new concept, however, was based on the mobilisation of the customer and led to a shift of retail space to out-of-town areas. A further difference, in terms of operational organisation, is that the sales areas of department stores is controlled centrally, while shopping centres consist of an agglomeration of retailers in a property unit with a space as defined by EHI of at least 10,000m².

From the point of purchase to the point of differentiation

Considering the macro-economic activities of POS marketing in order to calculate ECR models/POP offers, the industry usually uses social demographic data of a certain region to plan product assortments. Inevitably, various average values lead to a standardised assortment at retail.

Modernes Einkaufszentrum: Europa Passage in Hamburg
A modern Shopping center: The Europa Passage in Hamburg

II. | DIE ENTWICKLUNG DES POS-MARKETINGS | THE DEVELOPMENT OF POS MARKETING

Moderne Zahlprozesse funktionieren wahlweise via Mobiltelefon oder Fingerabdruck.
Modern payment processes include payment by mobile phone or fingerprint.

Diverse Durchschnittswerte führen dabei zwangsläufig zur Vereinheitlichung der Sortimente der Händler.

Angesagt ist jedoch in oligopolistischen Märkten der Laden als „Point of Differentiation" (POD)! Hatten die Top-5-Händler 1980 zusammen nur einen Marktanteil von circa 26 Prozent, so liegt dieser in 2010 bei über 80 Prozent; d.h., die großen Player treffen in fast allen Regionen aufeinander. Die Handelsunternehmen müssen sich daher in ihrem eigenen Auftritt voneinander unterscheiden. Im Vordergrund der Handelsaktivitäten steht nicht mehr die Ubiquität des Markenartikels, sondern die Profilierung des eigenen Ladens als Marke - eventuell auch über Handelsmarken (Private Label-Produkte) als Unterscheidungskriterium. Erfolgreiche Händler in Großbritannien (Tesco, Sainsbury) haben mittlerweile in vielen Marktsegmenten über 50 Prozent des Markenartikelsortiments durch Private Label-Produkte ersetzt.

Berücksichtigt man, dass alleine in Deutschland jedes Jahr 30.000 neue Artikel auf den Markt gebracht werden, anderseits ein guter Supermarkt insgesamt nur 20.000 bis 25.000 Artikel führt, so wird das Konfliktpotenzial für Neueinführungen der Markenartikelindustrie deutlich.

Zur Vermeidung dieses Dilemmas sind verstärkte kundenspezifische Promotionen denkbar, die exklusiv von Industrie- und Handelsunternehmen gemeinsam durchgeführt werden. So gab es bereits in den 80er Jahren Ansätze der Martin Brinkmann AG,

In oligopolistic market structures, however, the store as a "point of differentiation" (POD) is an issue. In 1980, the five leading retailers together had a market share of around 26 %. That figure will rise to 80 % in 2010. This means that the same big players can be found in almost all regions. Retailers are thus forced to individualise their presentation to distinguish themselves from others. The focus is no longer on the omnipresence of the branded product, but on the store's distinction as a brand, possibly by using private label products as a distinguishing feature. Successful British retailers like Tesco and Sainsbury's have meanwhile replaced more than 50 % of their branded goods offer by private label products in many market sectors. Considering that 30,000 new products are launched on the market every year in Germany alone, but that a good supermarket has only 20,000 to 25,000 products on offer, it becomes clear that suppliers of branded goods face a potential conflict when introducing new products.

Manufacturers and retailers could jointly organise more exclusive customer oriented promotions to avoid this dilemma. As early as the 1980s, Martin Brinkmann AG launched exclusive promotional campaigns for various cigarette brands in select stores and store chains. The stores participating in the campaigns had an unique event-like atmosphere during the promotional period that differed greatly from the usual secondary placement in the till area. In Germany, a tournament of the card game of Skat that took place in the Lüneburg Heath region even made it into the headlines of the tabloid Bild!

für verschiedene Zigarettenmarken exklusive Promotionaktionen mit ausgewählten Märkten und Handelsketten durchzuführen. Die jeweils unter Vertrag genommenen Märkte hatten während der Promotionszeit einen einmaligen Event-Charakter, der sich von den üblichen Zweitplatzierungen an der Kassenzone deutlich abhob. Über ein in der Heide durchgeführtes Skatturnier wurde seinerzeit sogar in der Bild-Zeitung berichtet!

Point of Diffentiation Plus

Der „POD Plus" im Zeitabschnitt 2000 bis 2025 ist komplexer und mehrdimensional. Das erfolgreiche Zukunftsmodell des POD ist integraler Bestandteil einer umfassenden Corporate-Identity-Strategie des Handels: Standort, Ladenbau, Ladentechnologie, Sortimente und Preispolitik, wie sie jeweils modellhaft in den beiden ersten „Future Stores" der Metro getestet wurden/werden, müssen aufeinander abgestimmt sein. Auch Themen wie „Corporate Social Responsibility" spielen heute für den Erfolg von Handelsunternehmen eine wichtige Rolle.

Der POD kann unter Einbindung technologischer Innovationen verstärkt Sachthemen im Kundendialog kommunizieren. Geht man von der EHI-These aus, dass Handelsunternehmen circa ein Prozent ihres Umsatzes in EDV investieren, so ist dies z. B. beim US-Unternehmen Wal-Mart ein Jahresvolumen von circa 3 Mrd. Euro – also eine Größenordnung, die dem Jahresumsatz von bekannten Markenartikelunternehmen entspricht. Produkt- und Konsumentendaten werden unter der Voraussetzung der Zustimmung der Kunden gespeichert und miteinander auf den unterschiedlichen Ebenen verknüpft. Hierbei kann natürlich im Rahmen von Kundenclubs auch interaktiv kommuniziert werden. Abzuwarten bleibt, ob sich hieraus Communities bilden, die zu einer Verknüpfung des stationären Handels und des Internets führen – aber auch Kundenbewertungen eines Standortes oder die Nutzung des POS als Ort spontaner selektiver Kundengruppen sind denkbar: Der POD Plus erhält Event-Charakter – oder wandelt sich (überspitzt) in einen POC, den Point of Customer.

Point of Diffentiation Plus

The "POD Plus" of the period 2000 to 2025 is more complex and multidimensional. The successful POD model of the future is an integral part of an extensive corporate identity strategy for retail. Location, shop fitting, store technology, product assortments and pricing policies as tested in an exemplary way by Metro in its first two "Future Stores" must be well coordinated. Issues like corporate social responsibility also play an important role for retailers today.

In consumer dialogue, the POD and integrated technological innovations can help convey particular topics. Based on EHI's assumption that retail companies invest around 1% of sales in electronic data processing (EDP), in the case of US retail group Wal-Mart that amounts to around 3bn euros, which is more or less the annual turnover of a major branded goods group. Assuming the consent of customers, product and consumer data is stored and linked on various levels. Naturally, this allows interactive communication within customer clubs. It remains to be seen whether communities will form from this and contribute to linking stores to the Internet. It may also lead to customer ratings of locations or the use of the POS as a place for spontaneous selective costumer groups. The POD assumes an eventlike character or, put bluntly, turns into a POC, the point of customer.

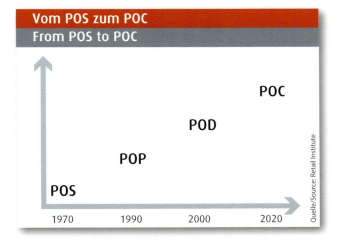

Vom POS zum POC / From POS to POC

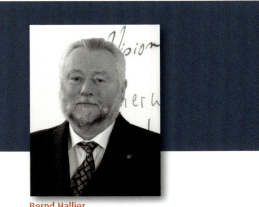

Bernd Hallier

III. | „DRAUSSEN ZUHAUSE" – MARKENFÜHRUNG – AM POINT OF SALE | "AT HOME OUTDOORS": BRAND MANAGEMENT – AT THE POINT OF SALE

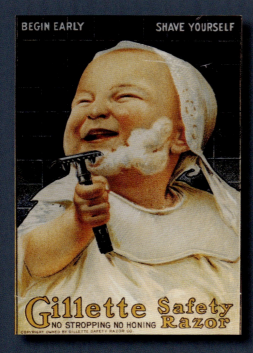

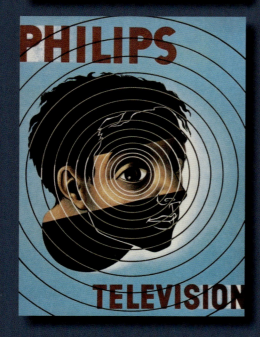

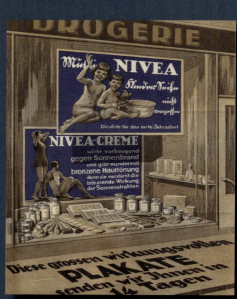

Hans-Georg Böcher

„DRAUSSEN ZUHAUSE":
MARKENFÜHRUNG – AM POINT OF SALE
ACHT POS-BIOGRAPHIEN BESONDERS PROMINENTER MARKEN

"AT HOME OUTDOORS":
BRAND MANAGEMENT – AT THE POINT OF SALE
EIGHT EXEMPLARY POS BIOGRAPHIES OF WELL KNOWN BRANDS

III. „DRAUSSEN ZUHAUSE": MARKENFÜHRUNG – AM POINT OF SALE | "AT HOME OUTDOORS": BRAND MANAGEMENT – AT THE POINT OF SALE

Marken leben von der Perpetuierung und selbstähnlichen Wiederholung ihrer Botschaft. Markenführung hat viel mit Produktions- und Vertriebskompetenz zu tun, noch mehr aber mit strategischer Kommunikation des Markeninhalts. Unbestritten ist der Ort des Kaufakts ein zentraler „Tatort", den Markenartikler traditionell in ihre Kommunikationsmaßnahmen einbinden. Anders jedoch als bei der Produktverpackung, wo der Markenartikler die Koordinaten seines Auftritts bis ins Detail selbst bestimmt, und anders auch als bei der klassischen Werbung, wo ihm durch Medien maßgeschneiderte Werberäume nach Wunsch angetragen werden, sind die Orte des Kaufakts nicht das wahre, angestammte „Zuhause" der Marken.

Denn im Handel regiert nun einmal der Händler. Und dessen Interessen sind mit denen des im Wettbewerb stehenden Markenherstellers keineswegs identisch. So ist der Ort des Kaufakts, im angelsächsisch geprägten Marketing-Jargon vertriebsorientiert als „Point of Sale" bezeichnet, eben ein durchaus umkämpfter „Punkt".

Auf ihn spitzt sich Vieles zu: Hier schneiden sich und hier berühren sich Hoheiten, Zuständigkeiten, Kompetenzen und Ambitionen. Es ist nur verständlich, dass die Fläche des Handels nicht per se die Fläche seiner Lieferanten sein kann. Und dennoch haben es einige ganz große Marken seit Jahrzehnten bereits verstanden, die fremden Flächen mit einem großen Auftritt (und durchaus zum beiderseitigen Nutzen) erfolgreich zu bespielen. Sie haben sich dort breit, aber auch unverzichtbar machen können. Für sie ist das umkämpfte, sturm-umtoste Terrain des Handels dennoch zu einem zweiten „Zuhause" geworden.

To be successful brand messages must prevail throughout communication, clearly and consistently. Brand management has a lot to do with competence in production and distribution, but even more with the strategic communication of brand content. Without doubt the point of sale is a central "scene of action" suppliers of branded goods traditionally integrate into their marketing activity. But, even though suppliers of branded goods are involved in the design of the product's packaging and personally plan the product's presentation in detail, and despite the fact that above-the-line advertising is tailored to their particular needs by means of media, the POS is not where brands come from and where they feel truly "at home".

That is because retail is ruled by the retailer. And the retailer's interests are not at all identical to those of the competing supplier of branded goods. So the point in the store where the purchase is made, in English called the "point of sale" to emphasise the distribution side to it, is without doubt a rather competitive "point".

Many important aspects converge at the POS, where authority, responsibilities, competence and ambitions meet and interact. The retailer's space understandably cannot per se be the supplier's space. Still, for decades now, some very big brands have known how to use retail space that are not their own for highly effective and successful presentations that definitely benefit both sides.

These brands have managed to gain ground at the POS and make themselves indispensable there. What has always been a fought-over and dark territory, has now become a second "home" for these brands. It is meanwhile completely natural for them to feel "at home outdoors" – to use the slogan of outdoor

Diese Marken sind heute mit aller Selbstverständlichkeit „draußen zuhause" – um einen Claim des Outdoor-Spezialisten Jack Wolfskin zu benutzen. Verholfen hat ihnen hierzu allerdings keine Wetterkleidung, sondern eine Erfindung, die sich fast unbeachtet aus dem Vertrieb in den Handel „geschlichen" hat: das Display.

Aus den bedruckten Lieferkartons von einst, die sich später in „stumme Verkäufer" verwandelten, sind längst komplexe Gebäude geworden, Regalsysteme, Marken-Architekturen. Und diese steigern – teils als Shop-in-Shop-Systeme integriert – mittlerweile auch die Attraktivität der Handelsflächen, die sie bereichern. Über den zurückgelegten Weg, aber auch die Perspektiven jener Entwicklung, die das Display erst möglich machte, möchte dieser Beitrag anhand von acht ausgewählten Markenbeispielen berichten.

specialist Jack Wolfskin. It was not outdoor gear, however, that helped achieve this, but an invention that "sneaked" into the world of retail almost unnoticed: the display.

The printed delivery boxes of the past that later turned into "silent salespersons" have long developed into complex constructions, shelving systems and brand architectures. These displays, in part integrated into shop-in-shop systems, today increase the attractiveness of the stores that use them as additional promotional tools. The present article has chosen the stories of eight select brands to describe the display's development while taking a look at the developments that were possible only because of the display itself.

Hans-Georg Böcher

GILLETTE – the triumph of a new idea

In the US, people who make a fortune from nothing are appreciated as "self-made men or women". Rarely, very rarely, is this achieved twice in a lifetime. The American King Camp Gillette (1855 – 1932) was one of the few who managed to repeat the feat of rising from the ashes. After a big fire in Chicago, Gillette's material existence lay literally in ruins in 1871. Like his father and brothers, he was a successful inventor who had now lost everything he had to the flames. For 20 years, he eked out a living as a travelling salesman, his thoughts always fixed on making that one invention that would provide him with a second breakthrough.

Legend has it that his employer, the inventor William Painter (1838 – 1906), gave him the advice to follow his own example and create something people could use once and then throw away. Painter, who had made many inventions, became rich with the creation of the crown cork in 1892. Soon after Painter founded "Crown Holdings Inc" in 1893, the crown cork became the global standard beverage closure. What if his employee Gillette succeeded in doing the same for a different product?

The 40-year old is said to have been looking into the mirror when he had the brilliant idea to invent a double-edged, disposable razor blade. If he succeeded in inventing a shaving device that was safe (safety razor) men would not have to go to the barber shop for a shave anymore. And once in possession of such a shaving device, he believed, only the blades had to be exchanged. The disposable razor blade would be exactly the right catchpenny product to make its inventor rich. Gillete's vision was to produce his own standard product.

The tough path to success

Six years passed before the inventor Gillette found the right partner in 1901. The manufacture of thin steel blades with a sharp edge on both sides was a novelty and no easy task. Gillette trusted an originator like William Nickerson to live up to the challenge of producing such a blade. "The Gillette Company" was founded in 1901 and produced the first blades in 1903. In the first year, the company sold a total of 168 blades. The following year, 90,000 razors and 123,000 blades were sold. But anyone who believes that breakthrough came easy is mistaken. Many giveaways, promotions and low prices were needed

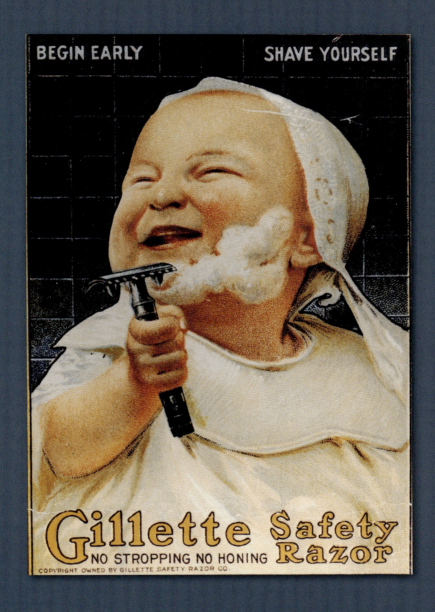

Früh krümmt sich… Echte Männer können mit dem Rasieren gar nicht jung genug anfangen. Anzeige aus der Frühzeit der Marke.
Practice makes perfect. For real men, it is never too early to start shaving. Advertisement in the brand's early years.

III. „DRAUSSEN ZUHAUSE": MARKENFÜHRUNG – AM POINT OF SALE | "AT HOME OUTDOORS": BRAND MANAGEMENT – AT THE POINT OF SALE

Der „Safety Razor" diente von Beginn der Etablierung eines Systems, das auf den Vertrieb der Klingen zielte. Diese trugen das Bildnis des Unternehmers um die Welt.
Right from the beginning, the „safety razor" aimed to establish a system for the distribution of the blades. The blades carried the image of the businessman all over the world.

In Deutschland nahm das Produkt in einem solchen Etui seinen Anfang. Eine beigefügte Bedienungsanleitung illustrierte mit Grafiken umständlich, wie die Selbstrasur stattzufinden habe (um 1908).
In Germany, the product started in a case like the one shown above. The enclosed instructions awkwardly explained in pictures how to shave (around 1908).

So wurde 1901 „The Gillette Company" gegründet, die 1903 ihre Produktion aufnahm. Im ersten Jahr sollen 168 Klingen verkauft worden sein, im zweiten Jahr bereits 90.000 Rasierer und 123.000 Klingen. Wer nun denkt, der Durchbruch sei von allein gekommen, der täuscht sich. Hinter den beeindruckend klingenden Zahlen standen viele Werbegeschenke, Promotion-Aktionen und Sonderpreise. Gillette war klar, dass sein Wettbewerber der Barbier war. Um die Selbstrasur zu etablieren, galt es, die Klingenpreise von Beginn an niedrig zu halten. Also gab Gillette notgedrungen seine neuartigen Klingen sogar unter Einstandspreis ab. Er wusste, dass erst die steigenden Produktionszahlen den Stückpreis senken würden. Also warb Gillette um neue Kunden, an die er seine Rasierapparate sogar verschenkte. Spätestens ab etwa 1910 hatte er sein Produkt etabliert. Gillette beherrschte nun den amerikanischen Markt. Im Jahre 1915 verkaufte Gillette, der inzwischen auch in Europa Fabriken unterhielt, weltweit mehr als 70 Millionen Klingen in alle Herren Länder.

Der „große Moment" kam für Gillette dann im Jahre 1917, als im Zuge des Kriegseintritts der Vereinigten Staaten in den

to achieve these impressive figures. Gillette knew exactly that his competitor was the barber. To make men shave themselves instead of going to the barber, he had to come up with blades that were cheap right from the beginning. Gillette conceded to sell his new blades below cost price. He was aware that he could keep unit prices low only by increasing production. So Gillette tried to win new customers by giving away his shaving devices for free. Around 1910, he had managed to establish his product and dominate the US market. By 1915, Gillette had also set up factories in Europe, and blade sales exceeded 70 million units worldwide.

Gillette's "great moment" came in 1917, when the US entered World War I, and the government ordered 36 million blades for their troops in Europe. To make sure their vital gas masks fitted properly, soldiers needed to be clean-shaven. This million-dollar deal turned Gillette into the world's leading producer and also into a fervent US patriot. Gillette also realised that the use of his blades during the war had a very important consequence. Returning from the war, an entire generation of men would now know how to shave properly, without the help of a barber.

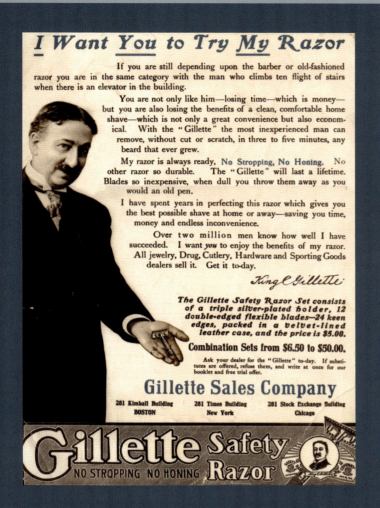

King Camp Gillette war nicht nur ein Erfinder, sondern auch ein Pionier des Marketing. Er wusste sich selbst als sein eigener „Testimonial" exzellent in Szene zu setzen.
King Camp Gillette was not only an inventor, but also a pioneer in marketing. He knew how to effectively promote himself as his own "brand ambassador".

Gillette, der auch als Autor sozialutopischer Bücher auf sich aufmerksam machte, war durch das Konterfei auf jeder Klinge eines der bekanntesten Gesichter der Welt. Er starb (als Folge des Börsencrashs) als armer Mann.
The face of Gillette, who also gained attention as an author of social-utopian books, was on every single blade. His face was one of the best-known faces around the world. He died poor (owing to the stock market crash).

Ersten Weltkrieg die US-Regierung bei Gillette zur Versorgung ihrer in Europa kämpfenden Truppen eine Bestellung von 36 Millionen Klingen in Auftrag gab. Die Soldaten sollten durch Selbstrasur dazu beitragen, dass die überlebenswichtigen Gasmasken eng an der Gesichtshaut anlagen. Ein Millionen-Deal, mit dem Gillette nicht nur zum weltweit führenden Großhersteller aufsteigen konnte, sondern mit dem er sich nun auch betont patriotisch in den USA zu positionieren wusste. Zugleich hatte der Kriegseinsatz seiner Klingen, das war ihm klar, eine ganz wesentliche Folge. Zurückgekehrt aus dem Krieg würde sich eine ganze Generation von Männern fortan kundig selbst zu rasieren wissen.

Der „1 Dollar-Look"

Gillette war weniger ein Techniker als ein Marketing-Genie. Einer seiner klügsten Schachzüge war ein ungewöhnliches, radikales Verpackungskonzept. Das zur Einführungszeit ja noch sehr erklärungsbedürftige Produkt des „Safety Razor" ließ Gillette in einer Kartonage verpacken, deren Äußeres dadurch eine Vertrauen erweckende Ausstrahlung gewann, dass es aussah wie staatliche Geldnoten. Das Verpackungsdesign kopierte einfach die Ausstat-

The one-dollar look

Gillette was more of a marketing genius than a technician. One of his cleverest moves was an unusual, radical packaging concept. During the introductory period, there was a great deal of explaining to do about the new product, so Gillette had his "safety razors" packed in confidence-inspiring cardboard packs that resembled banknotes. The notes on the packs looked like one dollar notes, but instead of the image of America's founder George Washington, the notes featured the "treasurer" (as he called himself) King Camp Gillette on their front. In a way, the unconventional design of the "safety razor" pack and its "state supporting" appearance (there was also an "official"-looking seal, a likewise official-looking reference to the US Patent Office and a right to return certified and signed by Gillette) created the impression that one dollar notes could be bought at the chemists. Indeed, in the initial stages of the safety razor, each blade was wrapped individually, the floral ornaments of its paper wrapper evoking the image of banknotes.

Considering that for decades every single one of the billions of blade wrappers that were sold around the world featured Gillette's image, we can assume that his face was possibly the best-known face around the world in those pre-television days.

III. „DRAUSSEN ZUHAUSE": MARKENFÜHRUNG – AM POINT OF SALE | "AT HOME OUTDOORS": BRAND MANAGEMENT – AT THE POINT OF SALE

Zur Einführung seines „Safety Razor" setzte Gillette Packungen ein, die den Charakter von Geldnoten imitierten. Sich selbst gab er auf der fiktiven „Banknote" als „treasurer" ein amtlich-seriöses Auftreten (Karton, um 1908).
For the launch of the "safety razor" onto the market, Gillette used packs that resembled banknotes. The notes featured the image of Gillette as "Treasurer", lending him an official and respectable appearance (Cardboard, around 1908).

Die „Blue Blade"-Klinge, eingeführt um 1930, war über Jahrzehnte hinweg der „Klassiker" des Hauses. Werbung in China, um 1985.
The "Blue Blade" was introduced around 1930 and was the brand's "classic" for decades. Advertisement in China, around 1985.

Aus der „Blue Blade" wurde „Fusion": Mit dieser Retro-Grafik gratulierte sich die Marke selbst zum 100. Geburtstag, Deutschland 2001.
"Blue Blade" was later renamed "Fusion". In this retro-style advertisement, the brand congratulated itself for its 100 birthday, Germany 2001.

tungsmerkmale der „1 Dollar-Note". An die Stelle des Staatsgründers George Washington trat hier jedoch der „Treasurer" (wie er sich bezeichnete) King Camp Gillette in Erscheinung. Das eigenwillige Packungsdesign des „Safety Razor" erweckte mit seinem „staatstragenden" Auftritt (zu dem unter anderem auch ein „amtlich" wirkendes Siegelzeichen, die offiziell erscheinende Bezugnahme auf das amerikanische Bundespatent sowie ein von Gillette mit Unterschrift beurkundetes Rückgaberecht beitrugen) gewissermaßen den Eindruck, man könne im Drugstore eine Dollarnote erwerben. Tatsächlich war auch jede einzelne Rasierklinge der Anfangszeit in ein papierenes Klingenbriefchen verpackt, dessen florale Ornamentik an Geldnoten erinnerte.

Wenn man bedenkt, dass über Jahrzehnte hinweg jedes seiner in Milliardenstückzahlen rund um den Globus vertriebenen Klingenbriefchen das Konterfei Gillettes zierte, dann wird klar, dass sein Gesicht in jener Ära vor der Erfindung des Fernsehens das möglicherweise am weitesten verbreitete des ganzen Erdballs gewesen ist.

The brand's appearance

The early internationalisation of the "Gillette" brand could be the reason why the brand had no visually coherent identity. The countless product varieties and presentations were held together by the image of the brand's founder. With the stock market crash and the following inflation, paper money lost much of its reputation. It was, at last, the end for the Gillette wrappers and its "pro-state" image. One of the most successful pack designs of all was that of the classic "BLUE Gillette BLADE", which came onto the market around 1930. This product would establish the colour blue as the colour that would later become firmly associated with the brand. In post-war Germany, the name "BLUE Gillette BLADE" was translated into "BLAUE Gillette KLINGE – EXTRA", thus strengthening the colour blue as the characteristic colour of the men's product line.

Gillette at the POS

Since its launch, the "Gillette" brand had been a pioneer of sales-oriented marketing and was extremely imaginative in its advertising. So it is no surprise that Gillette recognised its presentation at the POS as

In Deutschland folgte auf die „Blaue Klinge" die „Blaue Klinge Extra". Frühe Blisterpackung, Deutschland um 1960. Die Farbe Blau gab der Marke Halt.
In Germany, the successor to the "Blue Blade" was the "Blue Blade Extra". Early blister pack, Germany around 1960. The colour blue supported the brand in building an identity.

Das Sortiment wurde spätestens ab 1970 recht unübersichtlich. Eine klare Leitfarbe gab es nicht. Sortimentsübersicht um 1980.
In 1970, the product range started to be rather confusing. There was no dominating colour that could be identified with the brand. An overview of Gillette products, around 1980.

Erscheinungsbild der Marke

Die früh eingetretene Internationalität der Marke „Gillette" verhinderte womöglich das Herausbilden einer geschlossenen visuellen Markenidentität. Zusammengehalten wurden die unzähligen Angebotsformen und Markenauftritte vor allem durch das Bildnis des Firmengründers. Spätestens mit dem Börsenkrach und der nachfolgenden Inflation hatte das Papiergeld sein Ansehen verloren. Für die Gillette-Klingenbriefchen und deren „staatliche" Aura ging damit endgültig eine Ära zu Ende. Unter den verschiedenen Packungsdesigns sei auf das erfolgreiche Produkt des Klassikers „BLUE Gillette BLADE" hingewiesen, die seit etwa 1930 geläufig war. Mit dieser Sorte begann sich die blaue Farbe bei Gillette zu verankern. In Deutschland war in der Nachkriegszeit um 1960 aus der „BLUE Gillette BLADE" die „BLAUE Gillette KLINGE – EXTRA" geworden, die ihrerseits den Leitcharakter der Farbe Blau für die Herrenserie fortschrieb.

Gillette am POS

Die Marke „Gillette" war seit Beginn ihres Bestehens ein Pionier des absatzorientierten Marketings und ungeheuer ideenreich in

a challenge that required active involvement. In 1917, when Gillette received the million-dollar order from the US army, the company distributed advertising handbooks to retailers instructing them how to create a patriotic presentation for the brand in their shop windows, the so-called Patriotic Window Display, as part of the brand's "Gillette Service Week Campaign". At the centre of the window display was an outsize (Gillette) "US Service Set", surrounded by images of parading marine and infantry soldiers. The "Khaki Set" was created for the infantry troops, the "navy" naturally preferred the "US Service Set", which was identical but for the portrait of a sailor.

Even then, the branded goods supplier was actively involved in the presentation of its brand at retail. And the brand stayed true to this philosophy. Gillette tailored advertising methods to the needs of the individual markets around the world. Of course, the introduction of self-service strongly influenced Gillette's advertising. In 1977, a floor stand display was created for Gillette that was considered a tried construction at the time and allowed easy stocking. It consisted of only two parts: the pedestal and a poster that had a tray attached to it. The compact, space-saving display was ideal for small articles.

III. „DRAUSSEN ZUHAUSE": MARKENFÜHRUNG – AM POINT OF SALE | "AT HOME OUTDOORS": BRAND MANAGEMENT – AT THE POINT OF SALE

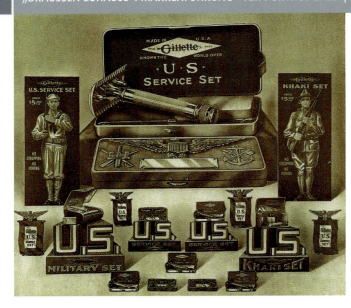

Patriotismus war gut für den Abverkauf. Gillette Service Week Campaign, USA 1917.
Patriotism helped boost sales. Gillette Service Week Campaign, US 1917.

Zweiteiliger Bodenaufsteller, Deutschland 1977
Two-piece floor stand display, Germany 1977

der Werbung gewesen. Wen wundert es da, dass der Auftritt am Point of Sale von Anfang an als Herausforderung begriffen und gestaltet wurde? Schon 1917, als Gillette den Millionenauftrag für die Streitkräfte erhielt, wurden den Handelspartnern Werbeschriften mit Anleitungen an die Hand gegeben, wie im Zusammenhang der „Gillette Service Week Campaign" ein patriotischer Auftritt der Marke im Schaufenster des Handels auszusehen habe („Patriotic Window Display"). Im Mittelpunkt stand hier, von Darstellungen paradierender Soldaten der Waffengattungen „Marine" und „Heer" flankiert, ein übergroßes (Gillette-)„U. S. Service Set". Streitkräfte des Heeres konnten das „Khaki Set" erwerben, solche der „Navy" dagegen bevorzugten sicherlich das baugleiche „U. S. Service Set", beworben mit der Darstellung eines Matrosen.

Schon damals gestaltete der Markenartikler aktiv die Inszenierung seines Auftritts im Handel. Dieser Philosophie blieb die Marke treu. In unterschiedlichen Märkten des Erdballs kamen die passenden Werbemittel zum Einsatz. Natürlich gab auch hier die Einführung der Selbstbedienung starke Impulse. Im Jahre 1977 wurde für Gillette ein Bodenaufsteller herausgebracht, der damals bereits als eine bewährte und leicht zu konfektionierende Konstruktion gelten konnte. Er bestand aus nur zwei Teilen: dem Sockel und dem Plakat mit anhängender Bodenplatte. Sein geringer Raumbedarf machte dieses Display besonders geeignet für Kleinartikel.

Eines der attraktivsten Waren tragenden Displays in der Geschichte dieser Werbegattung wurde 1996 von Gillette herausgebracht. Ziel war eine attraktive, Aufmerksamkeit weckende Zweitplatzierung für das Produkt „Gillette Sensor Excel". Die ungewöhnliche Antwort bestand in einem (im markentypischen Blauton

One of the most attractive displays ever was designed by Gillette in 1966. The objective was to create an attractive secondary placement for the product "Gillette Sensor Excel" that would grab the customer's attention. Gillette's rather unusual solution was an almost life-size Formula One racing car painted in the brand's typical blue. As the car would have taken up too much space on the sales floor if it had stood on its wheels, Gillette did not hesitate to turn it into a vertical position, so that the car stood upright in the store.

A shelf system was built into the car's interior, which consisted of two trays for shaving cream and aftershaves and two levels of euro hooks for blister packs. In this way, hanging blister packs with "Gillette" razor blades and standing metal dispensers with "Gillette" shaving cream could be presented together in the best possible way.

In 2000, an attractive black shelf display was designed to promote products from the men's care line "Arctic Ice". Products could be displayed on the pedestal as well as the two levels of trays. There were euro hooks above the trays for blister packs. 2002 saw the introduction of an innovative, almost daring display that presented men's and women's razors together for the first time. In order to retain the distinctive character of the products and their different target groups, a vertical line at the front divided the coated three-tier display into two parts, identified each by its own colour. Products for both men and women could so be presented for sale together on a small floor space (1/2 Chep pallet).

For the 2002 World Cup, Gillette developed a floor stand display with a chep pallet base. One side of its hexagonal bin featured the world cup trophy being held up by a player of the winning team. Its header

Regaldisplay in Form eines Formel-1-Rennwagens, Deutschland 1996
Formula One racing car shelf display, Germany 1996

„Arctic Ice", schwarzes Regaldisplay, 2000
Black "Arctic Ice" shelf display, 2000

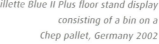

Gillette Blue II Plus, Bodendisplay als Schütte auf Chep-Palette, Deutschland 2002
Gillette Blue II Plus floor stand display consisting of a bin on a Chep pallet, Germany 2002

lackierten) Rennwagen der Formel Eins – in annähernder Originalgröße. Da das Fahrzeug auf dem Boden zuviel Handelsfläche belegt hätte, wurde es kurzerhand in die Vertikale gedreht. Es stand also aufrecht im Markt.

Das Fahrzeuginnere wurde nun mit einem Regalkorpus versehen, der außer zwei Tray-Ebenen, auf denen Rasierschaum und Aftershave dekoriert waren, an Eurohaken auch hängende Blisterpackungen auf zwei Ebenen aufnehmen konnte. So konnten die „Gillette"-Klingen im (hängenden) Blister-Pack mit den (stehenden) Metallspendern des „Gillette"-Rasierschaums optimal zusammen platziert werden.

Im Jahre 2000 wurde dann ein attraktives schwarzes Regaldisplay entwickelt, das Pflegeprodukte der Herren-Serie „Arctic Ice" bewarb. Hier ließ sich der Sockel ebenso dekorieren wie zwei Tray-Ebenen, über denen dann Eurohaken für Blister montiert waren. Innovativ, ja fast gewagt, war der Einsatz eines kombinierten Displays im Jahre 2002, das erstmals Rasierapparate der Herren- und der Damenlinie gemeinsam positionieren konnte. Um die Markenwelten der auf unterschiedliche Zielgruppen gerichteten Produkte getrennt zu halten, waren die auf drei Ebenen angeordneten Schütten ebenso wie der ummantelte Körper des Displays durch eine vorn an der Frontseite vertikal verlaufende Trennlinie in zwei Farbwelten aufgeteilt. So konnten auf geringer Standfläche (1/2-Chep-Palette) Erzeugnisse beider Anwendergruppen von Gillette gemeinsam abgesetzt werden.

Zur Fußball-Weltmeisterschaft 2002 wurde ein ebenfalls auf Chep-Palette fixiertes Bodendisplay herausgebracht. Die sechseckige Schütte zeigte auf einer Flankenseite das Motiv des empor-

card promised the buyers of "Gillette Blue II Plus", as part of the promotion, 40 % more product for the same price.

In the same year, petrol blue floor stand displays promoted the "Gillette Mach3" brand. A real "space and advertising miracle" was created with a blue "Gillette Sensor 3" floor stand display in 2003. Its back card featured a huge out-size, three-dimensional wet razor dummy together with 14 euro hooks. Razors in blister packs could be displayed on four levels, and small trays could be attached to the wall. By displaying the huge "three-dimensional dummy" in large detail, Gillette made the customer familiar with the exact way the particular razor model looked. Gillette managed to perform that difficult balancing act between advertising and sales in a very impressive way.

A display with a completely different design was created for the women's line "Gillette Venus Divine" in 2004. It had an elliptical, tiered plastic pedestal and a drawer inside its base. The display's back and sides were curved and the undulated structure on the right looked like shaving cream was pouring down its side. The products were hung up on euro hooks on the inside.

Another display targeting women was one designed for "Gillette Satin" in 2005. It was a pink and orange double sided shelf display. The products from the "Gillette Venus Vibrance" line were displayed on euro hooks on four levels.

In the same year, a eye-catching deep black shelf display was developed for the male customer under the name "M3 Power". The conspicuous bulges in the concave sides and the arched base of the display attracted a lot of attention. In terms of logistics, how did the introductory campaign succeed in delivering the product to

III. „DRAUSSEN ZUHAUSE": MARKENFÜHRUNG – AM POINT OF SALE | "AT HOME OUTDOORS": BRAND MANAGEMENT – AT THE POINT OF SALE

Kombiniertes Display für Herren- und Damen-Shaver, Deutschland 2002
Display for both men's and women's razors, Germany 2002

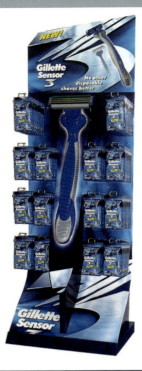

Gillette Sensor, blaues Bodendisplay mit großem 3D-Dummy des Rasierers, 2003
Blue Gillette Sensor floor stand display with large three-dimensional razor dummy, 2003

gereckten Weltpokals. Ein Aufsteckschild versprach den Käufern von „Gillette Blue II Plus" eine 40%ige Zugabe – bei gleichem Preis – aus Anlass der Handelsaktion.

Im gleichen Jahr 2002 wurde die Marke „Gillette Mach3" mit petrolfarbenen Bodendisplays unterstützt. Ein wahres „Raum- und Werbewunder" war ein blaues Bodendisplay für „Gillette Sensor 3", welches 2003 das Kunststück fertigbrachte, auf der Rückwand zugleich den Platz für eine lebensgroße XXL-Darstellung des Nassrasierers zu finden, der als dreidimensionaler Dummy aus Karton gefertigt war, und dabei gleichzeitig noch 14 Eurohaken aufzunehmen. Hier konnten, verteilt auf vier Ebenen, die Rasierer in Blisterpackungen abgesetzt und sogar kleine Trays eingeklinkt werden. Zugleich aber wurde die genaue Optik des Modells im „Großbild" eines riesigen „3D-Dummys" optisch vertraut gemacht. Ein schwieriger Spagat zwischen Werbung und Vertrieb, der hier besonders eindrucksvoll gelungen ist.

Eine ganz andere Gestaltwelt hatte dann 2004 ein Display für die Frauen-Serie „Gillette Venus Divine". Auf einem elliptischen, gestuften Kunststoff-Sockel, der als Tiefziehteil gefertigt war, baute sich ein organisch gebauter, geschwungener Mantel-Korpus auf. Die wellenförmige Struktur an der rechten Seite erinnerte an herabfließenden Rasierschaum. Im Inneren des Mantels fanden die Produkte an Eurohaken Aufnahme.

Ebenfalls an weibliche Kundschaft richtete sich später der in einer leuchtend-intensiven Farbwelt von Pink und Orange gehaltene Auftritt eines Regal-Doppeldisplays, das 2005 für „Gillette Satin"

almost all stores in Germany, Austria and Switzerland within ten days and sold half a million razors in only seven weeks?

The introductory campaign for the "Gillette Fusion" brand, which won the "Lebensmittel Zeitung Sales Cup" award in 2007, shows us how to achieve that. Right from the beginning, Procter & Gamble opted for POS marketing in addition to above-the-line advertising, knowing that the POS offered opportunity for secondary placements and attention-grabbing decorations. Within a very short time, eleven different displays were developed, which responded to the needs of the individual countries and presented the new brand in 15 countries in the best possible way.

This resulted in a large number of different requirements and display components, ranging from "euro hooks", eco-friendly bars and so-called "rolly dollies" to wooden pallets. A dedicated "giant pallet" was designed for British supermarket chain "Asda", and a special type of display was also designed for the Scandinavian market. Gillette's creative team faced a particular challenge when designing displays for countries that, for safety reasons, required so-called "safety cases" for razor blade packs, which made the design of the overall display structure extremely difficult. The display had to be designed in a way that allowed the stocking of various kinds of products according to whether the retail partner wanted to sell blades, razors or care products.

Four weeks after the first briefing, the first design drafts were drawn up in the company's headquarters in Geneva. Five months later, the first products were launched in Germany, Austria, Switzerland

Gillette Venus Divine, Thekendisplay, 2004
Gillette Venus Divine counter display, 2004

M3 Power, schwarzes Regaldisplay, 2005
Black M3 Power shelf display, 2005

Gillette Satin, Regal-Doppeldisplay, 2005
Twin Gillette Satin shelf display, 2005

aufgelegt wurde. Die Erzeugnisse der Serie „Gillette Venus Vibrance" konnten hier an Eurohaken auf vier Ebenen angebracht werden.

Für die männliche Kundschaft dagegen wurde 2005 unter dem Motto „M3 Power" ein auffälliges Regaldisplay in tiefschwarzer Farbstellung entwickelt. Dessen Korpus war durch die auffallenden Wölbungen an den konkav gestalteten Seitenwangen und dem gewölbten Bodensockel von hohem Aufmerksamkeitswert.

Wie kann man eine Einführungskampagne logistisch so gestalten, dass nach zehn Verkaufstagen nahezu alle Läden in Deutschland, Österreich und der Schweiz mit Ware versorgt und dass nach sieben Wochen bereits eine halbe Million Rasierapparate verkauft sind?

Die 2007 mit dem „Sales Cup" der „Lebensmittel Zeitung" prämiierte Kampagne für die Einführung der Marke „Gillette Fusion" zeigt, wie das möglich war. Von Beginn an wurde von Procter & Gamble neben klassischer Werbung auf den Point of Sale gesetzt, wo Zweitplatzierungsdisplays und aufmerksamkeitsstarkes Deko-Material zur Verfügung standen. Innerhalb kürzester Zeit wurden elf unterschiedliche Displaytypen entwickelt, die länderspezifisch konfiguriert waren und die neue Marke in 15 Ländern optimal präsentieren konnten.

Hieraus ergab sich eine große Vielzahl unterschiedlicher Anforderungen und Bestückungsvarianten – von „Eurohaken" über „Ökoleisten" bis hin zu „Rolly-Dollies" und Holzpaletten. Für die britische Supermarktkette „Asda" wurde beispielsweise eine eigene

and the UK. The launch in the other countries followed four months later. And, Gillette also "fuelled" the promotion of the "Fusion" razors at retail with a "firework" of events. As part of the promotion, around 35,000 men were shaved on the sales floor. Gillette's sales and marketing staff participated personally in the promotion on its starting day.

The figures were impressive: after only ten days, distribution had reached 96 %, and thanks to the "Fusion" range market growth was 50 % in the first month. In 2008, Gilette designed a combinable display called "duo display". It was used in particular in northern and eastern Europe, where retailers required small amounts of products and displays that took up little floor space.

The Gillette brands "Fusion Power Stealth" for men and "Venus Breeze" no longer had to share the same floor stand display. Now, each brand had its own brand "construction", which respected its individual colours and took up very little space. The "Fusion Power" structure stuck to the brand's typical black and orange contrast. The "Venus Breeze" display was held in the brand's colours light blue (on the outside) and violet (on the inside). The brands' products could be displayed on both sides of the narrow shelf display.

In 2009, a new asymmetric type of shelf display was designed for the brand "Gillette Gamer". It had trays on four levels with dedicated inserts for the Gillette packs. Its header card pointed to a 25 % discount given as part of a voucher campaign. The promotion was supported by football star Thierry Henry, whose image was featured on the side of the display.

„Giant Pallet" entwickelt, und auch für Skandinavien wurde ein eigener Displaytyp kreiert. Eine besondere Herausforderung für die Kreativen der Displayentwicklung war der Umstand, dass einige Länder aus Sicherheitsgründen für Klingenpackungen so genannte „Safe-Cases" einsetzten, was enorme Anforderungen an den Gesamtaufbau der Displays stellte. Darüber hinaus sollte die Bestückung sehr variabel gehalten werden können, so dass Klingen, Rasierer und Pflegeprodukte individuell nach den Wünschen der jeweiligen Handelspartner zusammengestellt werden konnten.

Von der Vorstellung der ersten Displayentwürfe im Headquarter des Konzerns in Genf – vier Wochen nach dem ersten Briefinggespräch – bis zur Auslieferung für den ersten Launch in Deutschland, Österreich und Schweiz sowie Großbritannien dauerte es fünf Monate. Die übrigen Länder folgten vier Monate zeitversetzt. Und auch auf der Fläche „brannte" das Promotion-Feuerwerk für den „Fusion"-Rasierer. Ungefähr 35.000 Männer wurden live rasiert. Dabei trat das Personal des Markenartiklers (aus Marketing und Vertrieb) zum Startschuss bewusst selbst als Promotor vor Ort auf.

Das Ergebnis in Zahlen war beeindruckend: Bereits nach zehn Verkaufstagen betrug die gewichtete Distribution 96 Prozent, und das Marktwachstum lag im ersten Monat dank „Fusion" bei 50 Prozent. Im Jahre 2008 wurde dann ein kombinierbares Display als „Duo-Display" herausgebracht. Dieser Displaytypus kommt vor allem in Nord- und Osteuropa zum Einsatz, wo geringere Warenmengen und auch geringere Stellflächen gewünscht werden.

Die Gillette-Marken „Fusion Power Stealth" auf der maskulinen und „Venus Breeze" auf der weiblichen Seite mussten sich hier nun nicht mehr ein gemeinsames Bodendisplay teilen. Vielmehr stand ihnen nun auf sehr schmaler Grundfläche ein der jeweiligen Marke und ihrer individuellen Farbwelt angepasstes, eigenes Marken-„Gebäude" zur Verfügung. So wie „Fusion Power" dem etablierten Kontrast von Schwarz und Orange treu blieb,

Waist-high floor stand displays were added for the 2009 "Fusion Gamer" campaign. They looked largely like regular displays, but the usual bins had been replaced by more complex ones that had a system of compartments with inserts specially designed for the individual packs, allowing easy organisation. The header card promoted the product by featuring the same images that were used in the TV commercials that accompanied the campaign in 2009. The TV spots featured the "avatars" of sports stars Thierry Henry, Roger Federer and Tiger Woods. At the POS, the stars (called "Gillette champions" in brand speak), shown in profile, were confronted with their own avatars. The header card read: "Now try it yourself!"

What started in 1914 as a brand-oriented shop window decoration suggested by King Camp Gillette, today is one of the most important and expressive features of Gillette's brand communication. The brand has long stopped approaching its customers only in TV commercials. For this former brand pioneer, attractive and multidimensional sales marketing of the highest quality is today a matter of course, and a tool used to shape the market.

Gillette Fusion, Thekendisplay, 2007
Gillette Fusion counter display 2007

Gillette Fusion, Bodendisplay, 2007
Gillette Fusion floor stand display, 2007

Gillette Fusion, Displayeinsatz mit integriertem Vorschubsystem, 2007
Gillette Fusion display tray with integrated feed system, 2007

Gillette Fusion, Regaldisplay, 2007
Gillette Fusion shelf display, 2007

Doppeldisplay (Kombination für Herren- und Damen-Shaver), Skandinavien 2008
Twin display for both men's and women's razors, Scandinavia 2008

konnte auch „Venus Breeze" mit den Farben Hellblau (außen) und Violett (innen) seine eigene Farbigkeit entfalten. Beiden Marken standen hierfür die Außen- und Innenseiten des schlanken Regaldisplays zur Verfügung.

2009 wurde für die Marke „Gillette Gamer" ein neuartiger Typus eines asymmetrisch aufgebauten Regaldisplays entwickelt, das Trays auf vier Ebenen bereithielt, die mit entsprechenden Einsätzen zum Einstecken der Packungen ausgestattet waren. Das oben aufgesteckte Markenschild wies auf einen 25%igen Preisnachlass im Rahmen einer Couponing-Aktion hin. Seitlich war als Werbepartner ein Porträt des französischen Fußballstars Thierry Henry integriert.

Für die „Fusion Gamer"-Kampagne 2009 kamen auch hüfthohe Bodendisplays zum Einsatz, die zunächst an die geläufigen Schütten erinnerten. An die Stelle der Warenschütte traten jedoch auch hier komplexe, Ordnung stiftende Steck-Systeme mit individuell auf die Packungsgestaltung zugeschnittenen Einsätzen. Das werbliche Markenschild wurde in Abstimmung auf die TV-Werbung gestaltet, die 2009 die Promotion-Aktion flankierte. Dort traten animierte „Avatare" der Sportstars Thierry Henry, Roger Federer und Tiger Woods in Erscheinung. Am Point of Sale wurden nun die im Profil gezeigten Stars (in der Markensprache als „Gillette-Champions" bezeichnet) mit dem (Ab-)Bild der ihnen gleichenden Avatare konfrontiert. Darunter war die Aufforderung zu lesen: „Probieren Sie nun selbst!"

Was um 1914 mit den Vorschlägen eines King Camp Gillette zur markenkonformen Schaufensterdekoration begann, ist heute zu einer der wesentlichsten und ausdrucksstärksten Sprachformen der Marke „Gillette" geworden. Längst begegnet diese ihrer Kundschaft nicht mehr nur noch im Werbefernsehen. Attraktives und mehrdimensionales Sales Marketing auf Top-Niveau ist für diesen Markenpionier von einst heute zur marktprägenden Selbstverständlichkeit geworden.

„*Gillette bietet weltweit innovative Produkte für ein optimales Rasurergebnis. Diesen Premiumanspruch wollen wir auch am Point of Sale transportieren. Wir arbeiten daher ständig daran, hochwertige und innovative Lösungen anzubieten, die auf die Bedürfnisse der Handelspartner abgestimmt sind, um durch aufmerksamkeitsstarke Platzierung am POS Mehrwert zu generieren.*"

Franz-Olaf Kallerhoff, General Manager, Customer Business Development, Procter & Gamble Germany/Austria/Switzerland

Franz-Olaf Kallerhoff

"*Gillette offers around the world innovative products for an ultimate shaving experience. And we want to take that high-end claim to the point of sale as well. We are working constantly on offering premium and innovative solutions that are tailored to the needs of retailers and guarantee a presentation at the POS that attracts attention and generates surplus value*".

Franz-Olaf Kallerhoff, General Manager, Customer Business Development, Procter & Gamble for Germany, Austria and Switzerland

Gillette Fusion, attraktives Shape-Display (mit Sylvie van der Vaart), Deutschland 2010

Attractively shaped Gillette Fusion display (with Sylvie van der Vaart), Germany 2010

Gillette Fusion, Regaldisplay, 2010

Gillette Fusion, shelf display, 2010

Gillette Fusion, Bodendisplay, 2010

Gillette Fusion, floor stand display, 2010

Gillette Venus Embrace, Bodendisplay, 2010

Gillette Venus Embrace floor stand display, 2010

Gillete Venus Embrace Regalhänger, 2010

Gillette Venus Embrace clip strip for shelves, 2010

Gillette Venus Embrace Regaldisplay mit vier Präsentationsebenen und Schaupräsentation eines Rasierers, Deutschland 2010

Gillette Venus Embrace shelf display with four levels and product demonstration of the Gillette razor, Germany 2010

MILKA – Die „zarteste Versuchung, seit es Schokolade gibt"

Wenige Marken haben sich mit einer starken Leitfarbe so nachhaltig ihre Präsenz im Handel und im Bewusstsein der Verbraucher erkämpfen können wie die Marke „Milka". Sie färbte nicht nur das Packungskleid ihrer Produkte lila, sondern gab gleich auch den Kühen auf den Almen eine neue Fellfarbe – zumindest in der Vorstellungswelt vieler Kinder. Doch davon später.

Ihren Ausgangspunkt nahm diese „typisch schweizerische" Marke in Neuchâtel. Hier hatte 1825 der soeben frisch von einer Amerika-Reise zurückgekehrte Philippe Suchard (1797–1884) im „Feuille d'Avis de Neuchâtel" die Gründung seiner Confiserie bekannt gegeben, in der neben den üblichen Desserts auch feine haus- und damit handgemachte Schokolade erhältlich sei. Ein Schlüsselerlebnis soll den kleinen Philippe 1807 im Kindesalter mit dem neuartigen Produkt der Speiseschokolade in Verbindung gebracht haben: Als zehnjähriger Bub hatte er auf ärztliche Verordnung den Auftrag, etwas Schokolade zur Stärkung seiner kranken Mutter zu besorgen. Ihn soll der damals gewaltige Preis von sechs Franken das Pfund ebenso beeindruckt haben wie die tatsächlich eingetretene Genesung der Mama. Suchard war sich später der Tatsache bewusst, dass die Zukunft des neuen Produkts nicht in der Luxuskategorie liegen konnte. Er setzte alles daran, die angesprochenen Zielgruppen zu verbreitern und „zu sehr billigem Preis eine gute Ware herzustellen".

Ein Deutscher als Vater der Milka

Als Carl Russ, ein 21-jähriger Kaufmann, im März 1860 beim Durchblättern der Tageszeitung eine Stellenanzeige des Hauses Suchard entdeckte, ahnte er wohl nicht, dass er dort später einmal eine im wahrsten Sinne des Wortes „führende" Stellung einnehmen würde. Und der erste Kontakt mit dem Gründer des Unternehmens, Philippe Suchard, verlief keineswegs erfolgreich, denn der junge Mann wurde abgelehnt. Ein Zufall wollte es, dass die Liebe ins Spiel kam, denn offenbar hatte der junge Russ das Gefallen der Tochter Suchards gefunden. Die junge Eugenie Suchard drang wohl so lange in ihren Vater, bis dieser trotz seiner Vorbehalte die Personalie an seinen Sohn abgab. Carl Russ konnte dann schon im April 1860 seine neue Stelle antreten. Und Eugenie wurde später seine Frau.

MILKA – the "creamiest chocolate temptation ever"

Only few brands have managed to secure such a lasting presence at retail, and stick thoroughly in the minds of customers for its typical colour as "Milka". The company not only wrapped its products in purple, but also gave the cows on the mountain pastures a new skin colour, at least that's what many children believed. But more about that later.

The story of this "typical Swiss" brand started in Neuchâtel. Upon returning from a journey to America, Philippe Suchard (1797–1884) founded a confectionery here in 1825 and announced it in the "Feuille d'Avis de Neuchâtel" newspaper. Apart from the usual desserts, the new company sold chocolate that was handmade in the confectionery. A personal experience in his childhood in 1807 is said to have had a crucial effect on his relationship with the new eating chocolate. At the age of ten, the doctor sent little Philippe to buy some chocolate to help his mother regain strength. The high price of six Swiss francs at the time impressed him just as much as the fact that his mother's health actually improved. Suchard later decided that chocolate should not be a luxury product. He did his very best to broaden the group of people the new product targeted, and "produce a good product that cost very little".

The German father of Milka

When the 21-year old merchant Carl Russ, flicking through the daily paper in 1860, came across a vacancy posted by the company Suchard, he could not have imagined that he would later literally assume a "leading" position in that company. And the first meeting with company founder Philippe Suchard was anything but successful, because the young man was refused. As coincidence would have it, love played its part. Apparently the young man had fallen for Suchard's daughter. Young Eugenie Suchard insisted with her father until be agreed to leave the decision to his own son. Carl Russ started to work for Suchard in April 1860. He and Eugenie were later married.

The 40 years the company was led by Russ can be considered its most fruitful years. By the time he retired in 1924, he had introduced many reforms and had turned the family-run company into a public company. He proved to be an early pioneer of modern brand communication, and without doubt successfully developed and built the company's

Dass Kühe ein lila Fell haben können, ist allgemein bekannt. Und zwar seit der legendären Werbekampagne von Young & Rubicam aus dem Jahre 1972.
Purple cows exist. Everybody knows that since the famous Young & Rubicam campaign in 1972.

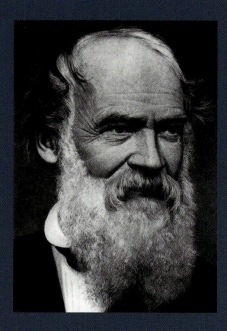

Der Unternehmensgründer Philippe Suchard (1797–1884), ein echter Schweizer, war von der stärkenden Kraft der Schokolade fasziniert.
Founder Philippe Suchard (1797–1884), a true Swiss, was fascinated by the strengthening effect chocolate has on the body.

Der Schwiegersohn des Firmengründers war ein Deutscher: Carl Russ (1838–1925). Er war der Erfinder der „Milka".
The company founder's son-in-law was German: Carl Russ (1838–1925). He invented Milka.

Die vierzigjährige Ära der Unternehmensführung unter Carl Russ, die erst 1924 endete, war wohl die fruchtbarste des Unternehmens. Russ hatte viele Neuerungen eingeführt, das Familienunternehmen in eine Aktiengesellschaft umgewandelt, hatte sich als früher Pionier der neuartigen Markenkommunikation erwiesen, und er hatte die ohne Frage wichtigste Marke seines Unternehmens entwickelt und erfolgreich aufgebaut: „Milka", abgeleitet von den Anfangsbuchstaben von „Milch" und „Kakao".

Milka – Eine Schokolade schreibt Werbegeschichte

Seit ihrer Einführung 1901 hatte die neue „Milka" alle Ausstattungsmerkmale des modernen Markenartikels: ein Produkt-Markenlogo, eine Herstellermarke („Suchard"), eine signifikante Leitfarbe und eine differenzierende Packung in den Regalen des Handels.

Und Milka tat viel dafür, um durch neue Werbetechniken und -methoden die Marke nachhaltig in den Köpfen der Verbraucher zu verankern. In der Anfangszeit des Markenwesens etablierte sich ausgerechnet das größenmäßig doch recht überschaubare Familienunternehmen Suchard als einer der führenden Pioniere der Markenwerbung in Europa. Unterschiedlichste Plakatmotive wurden

most important brand: "Milka", derived from the initial letters of the German words "Milch" (milk) and "Kakao" (cocoa).

Milka – a chocolate makes advertising history

Since its introduction in 1901, the new "Milka" had all the aspects of a modern branded article: a brand logo, a manufacturer's brand, a powerful colour and a packaging that stood out on store shelves.

Milka worked hard to leave a permanent impression on consumers by using new advertising techniques and methods. In the early days of brand business, it was, of all companies, the relatively small family-run company Suchard which established itself as one of the leading pioneers in brand advertising in Europe. The company developed greatly differing posters and experimented with sponsoring methods (for instance, Russ supported the young American Joseph Bruckner in his plan to be the first

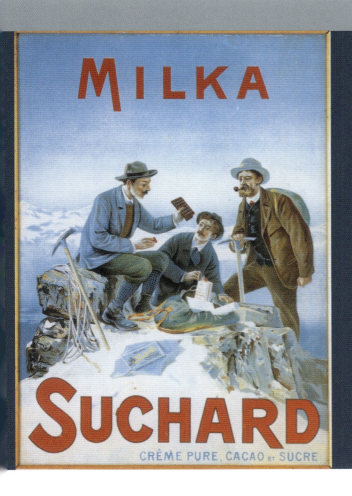

Milka war ein Werbepionier. Plakat um 1905.
Milka was a pioneer in advertising. Poster, around 1905.

Der „Milka-Bernhardiner" ist längst Reklamegeschichte. Er interpretiert einen Mythos und „apportiert" der Marke die „Herkunftsenergie" der Schweiz. Plakat um 1910.
Milka's St Bernhard has already gone down in advertising history. The dog represents a myth and "fetches" the "original energy" of Switzerland for the brand. Poster, around 1910.

aufgelegt; die Firma Suchard experimentierte mit Methoden des Sponsorings (Russ unterstützte beispielsweise das Vorhaben des jungen Amerikaners Joseph Bruckner, den Atlantik als erster in einem Heißluftballon zu überfliegen); und für das anspruchsvolle Verpackungsdesign in der lila Farbe mussten die neuesten Farb- und Drucktechniken der damaligen Zeit herhalten.

Viele der Plakat- und Werbemotive sind längst in die Geschichte dieser Gattung eingegangen. Beispielsweise das großformatige Lithoplakat, das drei Bergsteiger bei der Ersteigung eines eisigen Gipfels in den Hochalpen zeigt (um 1905). Unvergessen ist noch heute die Werbefigur eines Bernhardiners, den Milka um 1900 als erstes Maskottchen für diese Marke einsetzte. Anders als eigentlich bei den legendären Rettungstieren der Schweizer Bergrettung üblich, trägt der Milka-Bernhardiner gleichwohl kein Fässchen mit wärmendem Cognac an seinem ledernen Halsband, sondern – viel wichtiger – eine gut sichtbare Tafel „Milka"-Schokolade. Dieses

to cross the Atlantic in a hot air balloon). Suchard used the latest colour and printing technology of the time for its sophisticated packaging design in the colour purple. Many of Suchard's posters and adverts have gone down in advertising history. One example is the large lithographic poster showing three mountaineers on their way up to the peak of an icy mountain in the high Alps (around 1905). Another unforgettable character that appeared in Suchard's advertising was the St Bernard Dog, who became the company's first mascot in 1900. Unlike the usual barrel with warming cognac the famous rescue dogs wore for the Swiss Mountain Rescue, Milka's St Bernard wore a, much more important, bar of chocolate on his leather collar, for everyone to see. From 1905 on, thousands of St Bernards promoted the chocolate bar on various posters, enamel signs, promotional ashtrays, money trays and tins in several European countries.

The St Bernard also conveyed a clear brand statement: Milka is an authentic, essentially Swiss chocolate. As truly Swiss as the famous St Bernard.

Auf der Schokolade (hier Packungen von 1901, 1909, 1922, 1960 und 1988) wandelte sich nicht nur die Darstellungsweise der Kuh. Genial war der zart schmelzende Schriftzug des Markennamens, eingeführt 1909.

Not only the image of the cow changed on the chocolate over time (bars from 1901, 1909, 1922, 1960 and 1988). The new smooth logo that appeared on Milka bars in 1909, with letters that seemed to be melting, was a work of genius.

III. „DRAUSSEN ZUHAUSE": MARKENFÜHRUNG – AM POINT OF SALE | "AT HOME OUTDOORS": BRAND MANAGEMENT – AT THE POINT OF SALE

Genuss, wie ihn nur die „lila Kuh" verkörpert: Anzeige von 1981

No figure better embodies relish than the "purple cow": advertisement from 1981

Motiv warb seit etwa 1905 auf diversen Plakaten, Hinterglas-Schildern, Reklame-Aschenbechern, Zahltellern und Motiv-Blechdosen in unterschiedlichen Ländern Europas vieltausendfach für die neue „Milka"-Schokolade.

Zugleich transportierte es eine klare Aussage über die Marke: Milka ist eine echte, Ur-Schweizer Schokolade. So „schwyzerisch" eben wie der berühmte Bernhardiner.

Die lila Kuh

Noch heute wirbt die Marke bevorzugt in den Alpen, etwa, wenn sie eine riesige aufblasbare Milka-Kuh unübersehbar bei führenden Sportereignissen der Ski-Szene platziert. Überhaupt die „lila Kuh": Sie wurde längst zum eigentlichen Maskottchen dieser Marke. Die Idee, der auf den Packungen seit jeher zu findenden „Milchspenderin" der wertvollen Alpenmilch „ans Fell" zu gehen, hatte 1972 die Werbeagentur Young & Rubicam. In ihrer unnachahmlichen Kampagne griff die Agentur zu einem Schachzug, der die Welt des Surrealen sichtbar machte. Aus der Kuh auf der lila Packung wurde die lila Kuh. Sie ist heute gewissermaßen das „innere Bild" dieser Marke. Wie selbstverständlich liegt sie wiederkäuend auf den Almen der Hochalpen, steht lebensgroß, mit einer echten, großen Kuhglocke am Hals, in der Süßwarenabteilung des Handels und begrüßt die Kinder.

Selbst auf der Verpackung der Produkte ist das lila Tier zu finden. Und auch hier hat die Kuh sich durchgesetzt. Immerhin hat sie es

The purple cow

Milka, still today, prefers advertising in the Alps, for instance by positioning a huge inflatable Milka cow in a clearly visible spot during leading skiing events. Actually, the "purple cow" has long become the brand's real mascot. It was the idea of advertising agency Young & Rubicam in 1972 to "turn the coat" of the then omnipresent "giver" of precious alpine milk. In a matchless campaign, the agency made a clever move that made the surreal world become real. The cow on the purple pack turned into a purple cow. Today, the cow is so to say the brand's "inner image". As naturally as she lies on the mountain pasture, ruminating, she also stands in the sweets department of the store, full size with a real, large cow bell around her neck, saying hello to the children. The purple beast is also on the packaging of the products. The cow has prevailed over the farmer at her side, who had to give up and quit the field in the 1980s. What is the farmer against his cow in the minds of children? Now, untended by the farmer and without a guardian, the cow makes a new, confident appearance. Since 1988, the cow's skin on the Milka packs has the typical pattern that makes the white "Milka" logo on it easy to read.

Milka as a pioneer of sales marketing

It is not surprising that a brand that has made advertising history like no other has staged truly important and unusual advertising campaigns also at retail. We have already mentioned the life-size Milka cow used as an eye-catcher in various promotions.

Palettendisplay (1970er Jahre) zu einer markentypischen Promotion-Aktion, wie sie später Geschichte schreiben sollte. Denn 1995, als bei einem ähnlichen Malwettbewerb allein 40.000 Bauernhof-Motive zum Ausmalen an Kindergärten versendet wurden, malte jedes dritte Kind die Kuh mit einem lila Fell! Dies löste erregte Debatten über den Wirklichkeitsverlust und die Macht der Werbung aus.

Pallet display (1970s) for a typical Milka promotion that would later make history. In 1995, when 40,000 farmhouse colouring book images were sent out to children as part of a painting competition, one in three children painted a purple cow. An intense debate was sparked over the loss of reality and the power of advertising.

Ende der 1980er Jahre geschafft, dass der an ihrer Seite befindliche Bergbauer geschlagen das Feld räumen musste. Was ist – in der Phantasie der Kinder – eben schon ein Bauer im Vergleich zu seiner Kuh? Seit ihrem ersten Erscheinen ohne die „hütende" Aufsichtsperson hat sich die Kuh selbstbewusst ein neues Erscheinungsbild zugelegt. Denn seit 1988 wird sie auf allen Milka-Packungen mit jener typischen Fellmusterung gezeigt, in der das weiße Markenlogo „Milka" gut lesbar aufscheint.

Milka als Pionier des Sales Marketings

Bei einer Marke, die wie kaum eine andere Werbegeschichte geschrieben hat, verwundert es nicht, dass auch im Handelsbereich wirklich bedeutende, ungewöhnliche Werbeaktionen durchgeführt wurden. Auf die lebensgroße Milka-Kuh als Eyecatcher diverser Promotion-Aktionen wurde ja bereits hingewiesen.

Den inhaltlichen Bezug zur Welt der Alpen thematisierte Milka beispielsweise in den 1970er Jahren mit einem breit angelegten Malwettbewerb, der Kinder aufforderte, ein Bild der Alpen zu malen und an Milka zu schicken. Auf der Handelsfläche nahm die Aktion ihren Ausgang mit einem Palettendisplay, das in seinem Sockel einen großen Stauraum für Abverkaufsware integrierte und so einen Logistikvorteil bieten konnte. Über dem Sockel konnte der Abverkauf in einem Tray erfolgen. Ein aufgestecktes Plakat aus offsetbedruckter Wellpappe forderte die Kinder zum

In the 1970s, Milka organised a big painting contest that focused on the brand's ties with the alpine world. The children taking part in the contest were asked to paint a picture of the Alps and send it to Milka. In the store, the contest centred around a pallet display with a large integrated storage space in its pedestal, thus offering a logistical advantage. The products were sold off a tray on the pedestal. A corrugated cardboard poster, which was attached to the display, invited the children to take part in the contest, promising 1,000 German marks for the "ten prettiest paintings of the Alps".

In the late 1970s, the logistical advantages of pallet displays were applied to a variant that did not have the classic pedestal-and-tray structure. Instead, the display had eight trays, which were stacked on top of each other and could be removed one after the other after all products on the upper tray were sold. A header card pointed out that "every bar of Milka chocolate now offers things worth knowing about the Alps".

A particularly nice and charming display was designed in 1996. Milka introduced a walk-in Milka mountain hut somewhat reminiscent of the witch's house in Brothers Grimm's Hansel and Gretel fairy tale, which was built of bread and covered with cakes. The entire hut, which was specially designed for the launch of the miniture "Milkinis", was covered in colourful images. Not only the roof and the door and shutters, which could be actually opened and closed, were purple. There was also the familiar "purple cow" standing in front of the hut. An old friend was lying at her feat. Milka's helpful St Bernard was

Alpenhütte als „Knusperhäuschen" mit „Milka-Bernhardiner" und lila Kuh: eine erlebnisstarke Platzierung – und ein traumhafter Spielort für Kinder. Bodendisplay 1996.

"Gingerbread" mountain hut with the "Milka St Bernhard" and the purple cow: an exciting display – and a wonderful playground for children. Floor stand display 1996.

Mitmachen auf und lobte 1.000 DM aus für die „zehn schönsten selbstgemalten Alpenbilder".

In den späten 1970er Jahren wurden die Logistikvorteile des Palettendisplays dann in einer Variante ausgereizt, die auf den klassischen Sockelaufbau verzichtete. An dessen Stelle traten acht übereinander gestapelte Trays, die nach erfolgtem Abverkauf einfach nach und nach entfernt werden konnten. Ein Aufsteckplakat warb hier „Wissenswertes über Alpen" befinde sich „jetzt auf jeder MILKA-Tafel".

Ein besonders liebenswertes, charmantes Display wurde 1996 aufgelegt. Milka brachte, etwas erinnernd an die „Knusper-Häuschen" aus dem Kindermärchen „Hänsel und Gretel" der Gebrüder Grimm, eine begehbare „Milka-Alpenhütte" heraus. Die ganze Oberfläche dieser zum Launch der kleinen „Milkinis" aufgelegten Hütte war mit farbigen Motiven bedeckt. Nicht nur die aufklappbare Eingangstüre, das Dach und die beweglichen Fensterläden waren lila, sondern vor dem Haus stand auch die damals bereits vertraute „lila Kuh". Vor ihr hat sich auf dem Boden ein alter Bekannter niedergelassen. Hier begegnen wir noch einmal dem hilfsbereiten Milka-Bernhardiner. Die Hütte war natürlich für Kinder begehbar und dürfte ganz sicher nach dem Ende des Promotion-Zeitraums ein zweites Leben in zahlreichen Kinderzimmern gefunden haben. Besser kann man Markenheimat nicht inszenieren.

Natürlich war 1999 auch der 25-jährigen Geburtstag der Milka-Kuh ein Thema, das man in Promotion-Aktionen feiern konnte. Platzsparende Sekundendisplays konnten – auf einem schmalen Sockel aufgebaut – entweder Milka-Produkte abverkaufen (Ungarn) oder – besonders lustig mit der geschleckten Fell-Musterung – eigens aufgelegte CD's mit „heißen Hits auf kuhlen Scheiben" zum Abverkauf bringen.

Eine attraktive sechseckige Schütte wurde 2002 für Milka-Sub-Marken wie „Tender nuts", „LEO" oder „Wafelini" aufgelegt.

back. Of course, children could go into the hut, which is sure to have found a second home in many children's rooms after it was no longer needed for promotion at retail. There is no better way to orchestrate a brand's origin.

Naturally, the celebration of the Milka cow's 25th birthday in 1999 prompted various dedicated promotional events. In Hungary, for example, Milka products were sold on space-saving quick assembly displays with narrow pedestals. Another, particularly amusing display, was one that had the typical spotted pattern of the cow's coat, and offered a specially released CD with the latest hits under the motto "Heiße Hits auf kuhlen Scheiben". The slogan is a play with words on "Kuh", the German word for cow, and the similarly pronounced English word "cool".

In 2002, an attractive hexagonal bin was designed for Milka sub-brands like "Tender nuts", "LEO" or "Wafelini". Considering that Milka wanted to have large amounts of goods in the stores during the high seasons like Easter or Christmas, the function of displays gradually became increasingly logistical over the years. In the 1990s, eye-catching superstructures were created for displays that followed different themes. At Easter 2003, for instance, a paragliding purple Easter bunny appeared to be flying through a structure that looked like an Easter egg. At the side of the display, regardless of the bunny mascot, naturally, there had to be the famous "purple cow". The same year, Milka opted for a "scary" presentation for Halloween. A display in the form of a half cylinder was used, which, looking through it, showed a stage-like structure with a purple spooky castle.

Again in the same year, Milka promoted the products from the "From the heart" collection, which featured the "I love Milka" claim. Special Chep pallets were designed for the promotion. The sloping surface of their trays, one stacked on top of the other, allowed the products to slide into place. In 2004, the same design was used for a large floor stand display, which filled the entire surface of the pallet.

For the Milka "Choco & Rice", which was launched in Germany in 2008, Milka developed a shelf display, which proved to be a true "space miracle". With trays on five levels, it offered the highest possible sales

Heiße Hits auf „kuhlen" Scheiben bewarben den 25. Geburtstag der lila Kuh, Bodendisplay 1999

A display offered cds with latest hits for the purple cow's 25th anniversary, floor stand display 1999

Sekundendisplay zum 25-jährigen Geburtstag der Milka-Kuh, 1999

Quick assembly display introduced for the Milka cow's 25th anniversary, 1999

Sechseckige Schütte, Bodendisplay 2002

Hexagonal dump-bin 2002

III. „DRAUSSEN ZUHAUSE": MARKENFÜHRUNG – AM POINT OF SALE | "AT HOME OUTDOORS": BRAND MANAGEMENT – AT THE POINT OF SALE

Palettendekoration mit Hase als Paraglider, Ostern 2003
Paragliding bunny for pallet displays, Easter 2003

Da speziell zur Hochsaison wie Ostern oder Weihnachten große Warenmengen im Handel platziert werden sollten, übernahmen die Displays im Laufe der Jahre eine zunehmende Logistikfunktion. Für die emotionale Aufladung und den Transport des Markenbildes sorgten seit den 90er Jahren Palettenüberbauten, die thematisch ansprechend und auffällig gestaltet waren.

Für die Ostersaison 2003 fliegt beispielsweise ein lila Osterhase als lustiger Paraglider in einem Aufbau, der an ein Osterei erinnert. Seitlich angebracht und trotz des Hasen-Maskottchens unverzichtbar: die beliebte „lila Kuh". Eine „schaurige" Inszenierung dagegen wählte Milka im selben Jahr für die Unterstützung der Halloween-Produkte. Eine großformatige Dekoration in Form einer halben Trommel gibt den Einblick auf ein bühnenartiges Sichtfenster frei. Im Inneren der Bühne erscheint ein lila Gruselschloss.

Im gleichen Jahr 2003 bewarb Milka am Point of Sale auch die Produkte der „Von Herzen"-Kollektion, in der Milka mit dem Claim „I love MILKA" auftrat. Zur Unterstützung der Promotion brachte man „Chep"-Palettendisplays heraus, die als schräge Stapelschütten so gearbeitet waren, dass die Produkte nachrutschen konnten. Dieses Prinzip wurde auch für einen großen Bodenaufsteller 2004 verwendet, der eine volle Palettengrundfläche einnahm.

Für die in Deutschland 2008 neu eingeführte Milka „Choco & Rice wurde ein Regaldisplay entwickelt, das als kleines „Raumwunder" Trays auf fünf Ebenen integrieren und so ein Höchstmaß an Umsatz auf geringem Platz herbeiführen konnte. Das aufsteckbare Markenschild wies auf den Einführungscharakter der Aktion hin.

Technisch bemerkenswert war ein 2007 für den tschechischen Markt entwickeltes Bodendisplay, das vier Stapelschütten mit einem Aufsteckplakat kombinierte. Für die gewichtige Befüllung mit Schokolade musste eine Stabilisierung durch zusätzliche Stege in den Schütten erfolgen.

Palettendekoration „Halloween", Herbst 2003
"Halloween" spooky castle for pallet displays, autumn 2003

„Choco & Rice", Regaldisplay 2003
"Choco & Rice", shelf display 2003

„Von Herzen", Chep-Palettendisplay, 2006
"From the heart", Chep pallet display, 2006

Bodendisplay, Tschechien 2007
Floor stand display, Czech Republic 2007

Schachtdisplay mit Innendruck auf Palettenbreite, 2004
Pallet-size tier display with inside printing, 2004

Palettendekoration mit Milka-Kuh als Plüschtier, Muttertag 2009
Milka cow plush toy for pallet displays, Mother's Day 2009

63

III. „DRAUSSEN ZUHAUSE": MARKENFÜHRUNG – AM POINT OF SALE | "AT HOME OUTDOORS": BRAND MANAGEMENT – AT THE POINT OF SALE

Mega-Platzierung mit Alpenhüttendekoration, 2008
Huge display construction with mountain hut, 2008

Mit der begehbaren Alpenhütte im Originalformat hat Milka einen „Kommunikations-Klassiker" etabliert, der immer wieder aktualisiert und neu definiert werden kann. Für einige deutsche Großmärkte wurde 2008 beispielsweise zu diesem Thema eine regelrechte „Mega-Platzierung" umgesetzt, die logistische Ladungsträger mit einem stimmungsvollen Großplakat in eine Erlebnisdekoration verwandelte.

Zum Muttertag 2009 wurde dann zur Dekoration eines Palettenaufbaus ein attraktiver Aufsteller entwickelt: Eine auf einem runden Fußstück montierte Stange trägt eine kleine Alpenkulisse, in die eine als Plüschtier gearbeitete „lila Kuh" eingesetzt ist. Diese präsentiert sich charmant auf einer Blumenwiese vor dem Panorama der Berge. Ein Störer lobt die Qualität „Garantiert aus 100 % Alpenmilch".

Markenarchitektur – Auch für den permanenten Auftritt

Längst hat sich aus der lila Einwickel-Packung der Tafelschokolade von 1901 ein umfassendes Regalkonzept in dieser Leitfarbe entwickelt, das den Standort der Marke in den Märkten schon auf weite Distanzen visuell anzeigt. Bei der optischen Wirkung dieser Regale, die ein wesentlicher Schlüssel für die Kundenansprache ist, überlässt das Milka-Management nichts dem Zufall. Damit hat die dreidimensionale „Markenarchitektur" nicht nur die Zweitplatzierung erreicht, sondern prägt auch den eigentlichen, angestammten Auftritt der Marke auf der Handelsfläche. Für den Auftritt von Milka in Osteuropa beispielsweise wurde hierfür 2006

volume on a very small space. The attached header card called attention to the introduction of a new Milka product. Due to the heavy weight of the chocolate load, the inside of the bins had to be stabilised with additional bars. Milka developed a technically outstanding floor stand display for the Czech market in 2007 that had four stackable bins and a header card. Due to heavy weight of chocolate load, the inside of the bins had to be stabilised with additional bars.

The walk-in mountain hut Milka created at original size was a "communication classic", which could be permanently updated and redefined. In 2008, "mega displays" were used in some large stores that, equipped with a large atmospheric header card, turned a mere logistical load carrier into a true display experience.

In 2009, Milka developed an attractive display stand for Mother's Day. A small alpine scenery including a "purple cow" plush toy was attached to a bar that was fixed to a round base. The cow was charmingly placed on a flower meadow against an alpine backdrop. An eye-catcher promised a "100 % alpine milk guarantee".

Brand architecture – for a permanent presentation too

What started with the chocolate bar's purple wrapping in 1901, has led to the development of entire shelving concepts in the same colour that make sure the brand is spotted even from a distance. Milka's management leaves nothing to chance in creating the visual effect of these shelves, which is an essential key to customer approach. Three-dimensional brand architecture has thus been applied not only to secondary

Umfassende Regaldekoration für den Auftritt in Osteuropa, 2006. Auf drei Metern Regalbreite entfesselt die Marke hier auch in der Erstplatzierung ein Feuerwerk an Werbe-Ideen.
Large display construction designed for Eastern Europe, 2006. On a three-metre shelf, the brand produces a firework of advertising ideas, also at its traditional in-store department.

eine umfassende Regaldekoration entwickelt, die zeigt, wie es gehen kann. Auf drei Metern Regalbreite entfesselt die Marke hier auch in der Erstplatzierung ein Feuerwerk an stimmungsvollen Werbeideen. Zum Einsatz kamen hier am Regal erstmals klassische Verkaufsförderungselemente wie dreidimensionale große Kuhglocken in „Alpen-Optik", die als (einsteckbarer) Blickfang an einem langen lila Band vor den Regalen hingen. Und über den Regalen thronend, schufen, als oberer Abschluss, aufmerksamkeitsstarke Aufsteckplakate mit „Mood Pictures" die richtige „alpine" Stimmung für den harmonischen Gesamtauftritt der Marke.

placements, but also to the brand's regular place in the store's chocolate department. In 2006, an universal display, which was developed for the promotion of Milka products in eastern Europe, showed how it works. On a three-metre shelf, the brand managed to produce a firework of atmospheric advertising ideas, also at its traditional in-store department. For the first time, Milka used traditional promotional elements like large three-dimensional cow bells with an "alpine look", which hung from the shelves on long purple ribbons, thus drawing the customer's attention to the product. Attention-grabbing header cards with "mood pictures", which were attached to the top of the shelves, created the right "alpine" mood for an overall harmonious brand presentation.

"Verbraucher wollen heute nicht nur über die Medien an der Aura einer Marke teilhaben. Sie wollen die Markenwelt auch live erleben. Deshalb treffen wir uns mit unseren Konsumenten auch am Point of Sale. In Ergänzung zu unseren Fernseh-Spots inszenieren wir die Milka Welt – die Alpen, mit ihrer einzigartigen Natur und die vielfältigen Genuss-Erlebnisse - alles zum Anfassen. Milka ist eine Marke mit einem sehr hohen emotionalen Charakter, deshalb ist der direkte Kontakt mit unseren Konsumenten so wichtig – auch um immer wieder die Bindung zwischen Milka und Konsument als Erlebnis zu gestalten."

Hubert Weber, Vorsitzender der Geschäftsführung Kraft Foods Deutschland, Österreich und Schweiz

Hubert Weber

"Consumers today want to have part of a brand's aura not only in the media. They want to live the brand experience. That is why we meet our consumers at the point of sale. In addition to our TV commercials, we offer an entire Milka world – the Alps with their unique nature and the various ways of enjoying Milka products – and everything can be felt and touched. Milka is a brand that builds a strong emotional connection with its consumers, that is why direct contact is so important – we continuously turn the bond between Milka and the consumer into a true experience."

Hubert Weber, Managing Director of Kraft Foods Germany, Austria and Switzerland

NESCAFÉ – instant coffee since 1938

Some brands seem to have been here forever, almost as if they had existed in people's lives ever since mankind came into this world and had made those lives richer and easier by giving them the brand's particular products. Nescafé is one of those brands. First of all, instant coffee is a modern convenience product. The „birth of the brand", however, took place longer ago than some may image. Its roots go back to 1938, but the brand's idea had nothing to do with the goods typical of later times of emergencies, like the war.

In the Switzerland of 1938, troubles of the sort were still far away when the company Nestlé launched its instant coffee on 1 April. Prior to the launch, Nestlé sent out samples to several customers that met with positive, or even euphoric, reactions that supported the brand's introduction.

The brand's historical background

More or less since the middle of the 19th century, the emerging food industry developed early methods to turn perishable commodities into long-lasting products, which allowed longer storing and transportation times and were easier to prepare. The industry made very early attempts at producing a long-lasting "coffee preserve", but all attempts to create instant coffee failed. The industry managed to make the preparation of coffee easier, but the nature of the roasted coffee bean made it impossible to make coffee soluble.

Under the lead of Max Morgenthaler, extensive research was undertaken in Nestlé's laboratories to get closer to the goal of producing soluble coffee. The name "Nescafé" can be found in the test reports as early as 1932. As aroma preservation remained highly problematic, Morgenthaler's team was ordered to stop research on the black coffee powder. The team was only allowed to continue research on how to improve sweetened condensed milky coffee. Another task was to produce a tasty instant milky coffee. Morgenthaler worked on both tasks until 1935. As the solubility of the milky coffee left something to be desired, and the fixed mixing ration between coffee and milk did not appeal to consumer habits, it never made it onto the market. In the late summer of

Der „Aufstieg" der Marke nahm mit der „Patentdose" und der – für damalige Verhältnisse sehr convenience-orientierten – Portionspackung für eine Tasse ihren Anfang. Plakat, Schweiz 1949.
The brand's "rise" started with the "patented tin" and the – for the time very convenience oriented – one cup sachet. Poster, Switzerland 1949.

III. „DRAUSSEN ZUHAUSE": MARKENFÜHRUNG – AM POINT OF SALE | "AT HOME OUTDOORS": BRAND MANAGEMENT – AT THE POINT OF SALE

Der filterlose, lösliche Kaffee war neu. Seine Zubereitung musste damals noch umständlich erklärt werden. Bedienungsanleitung, um 1950.
The filterless instant coffee was a novelty. Explaining its preparation was still rather awkward at the time. Instructions, around 1950.

erlaubt. Ein weiterer Auftrag sah vor, einen geschmacklich guten Milchkaffee in Pulverform herzustellen. An beiden Aufgaben arbeitete Morgenthaler bis 1935. Da die Löslichkeit des Milchkaffees zu wünschen übrig ließ und das festgelegte Mischungsverhältnis der Anteile von Milch und Kaffee den Verbrauchergewohnheiten nicht zusagte, kam er nie in den Handel. So galten dann im Spätsommer 1935 die Kaffeeversuche sämtlich als offiziell beendet.

Morgenthaler indessen ließ die Sache keine Ruhe. Im Frühjahr 1936 hatte er auf eigene Faust ein fast geruchloses Pulver entwickelt, welches die konservierten Kaffee-Aromen erst beim Aufgießen mit warmem Wasser preisgab. Eine Sensation. Der technische Direktor soll sich zwar „erstaunt" gezeigt haben, dass Morgenthaler seine Kaffee-Forschungen noch immer verfolgte, wollte aber das Produkt gern degustieren. Beeindruckt von der Qualität des Kaffees lud er dann den Verwaltungsratspräsidenten der Nestlé zur Degustation ein. Der restliche Weg sollte von hier ausgehend den „Nescafé" als Weltmarke rund um den Globus führen. Innerhalb weniger Jahre eroberte der neue „Nescafé", verpackt in eine Blechdose mit patentiertem Deckel, die man deshalb als „Patentdose" bezeichnete, die Märkte in Großbritannien und Amerika.

1935, all coffee experiments were considered as officially terminated. But Morgenthal could find no peace. On his own account, he had developed an almost odourless powder, which freed the preserved coffee aroma only after warm water was added. A sensation. The technical director is said to have been very surprised that Morgenthal was still pursuing his coffee research, but was willing to taste the product. He was so impressed by the coffee's quality that he invited Nestlé's administrative board president to a coffee tasting. That paved the way to starting Nescafé's world dom-ination as a global brand. It took only a few years for the new Nescafé to conquer the US and UK markets, in a tin with a patented lid that was therefore called the "patented tin".

Marketing and packaging

Initially, Nescafé encountered obstacles in the market. The product was new and unknown. In Germany, many consumers got to know instant coffee through the CARE packages only after 1946. By then, it had already been successfully introduced into the US and England and had become familiar with many consumers there. It was the same for Nescafé, which was also introduced in the US and UK before it came to Germany in 1950.

Markenauftritt in der „Patentdose", um 1945
Brand presence in the "patented tin", around 1945

Marketing und Verpackung

Zunächst aber waren Marktwiderstände zu überwinden. Schließlich war das Produkt neu und ungewohnt. In Deutschland hatten viele Konsumenten erstmals über das CARE-Paket (ab 1946) den löslichen Kaffee kennengelernt, der in England und den USA damals bereits erfolgreich eingeführt und vielen Konsumenten vertraut war. Auch „Nescafé" ging den Weg in dieser Reihenfolge. Nach dem ermutigenden Start im angelsächsischen Raum wurde 1950 die Marke in Deutschland eingeführt.

Sie war hier ebenfalls in der Patentdose mit Papier-Rundumetikett verpackt. Kategorietypisch war der kaffeebraune Fond des Markenbilds, der das neuartige Produkt vertraut erscheinen lassen sollte. Daneben wurde in roter Farbe als Variante eine koffeinfreie Sorte aufgelegt: Deren Verpackungsdesign sprengte mit dem leuchtenden Rot ihres Labels selbstbewusst die Sehgewohnheiten des Kategorie-Umfelds. Was anders ist, bleibt haften: Heute noch ist Rot die Erkennungsfarbe der Marke, was mittlerweile in der Kommunikation durch eine rote Tasse visualisiert wird (Sorte „Nescafé Classic"), die beispielsweise als Onpack-Promotion mit

In Germany, Nescafé was also introduced in the familiar patented tin with a paper wrap around label. The colour of the product's brand image was the usual coffee brown to give the new product a familiar touch. At the same time, a decaffeinated variant was introduced in a red packaging. The design with its bright red label self-confidently stood out from what consumers were used to seeing in the coffee aisle. It is what looks different that sticks in the mind: the colour red is still today the brand's characteristic brand feature. In communication, it is represented by a red cup (variety "Nescafé Classic), which is offered as a free gift with the product as an on-pack promotion at retail. In the 1950s, besides the patented tin, a handy small pack also was common. A directly printed aluminium half tube offered coffee powder for two cups. In the advertisements of the 1950s, Nescafé saw itself as a companion of modern times. "For the breakfast break!" it called out to the targeted female consumer and, for instance, showed a smiling secretary enjoying her cup of Nescafé at the typewriter. Women were conquering the working world now, and Nescafé accompanied them to the work place.

Then in 1962, the patented tin had served its time and was replaced by glass jars in shapes that followed the zeitgeist of the period. Important features of the premium glass packaging was its confidence-building transparency and "high-end" feel.

| III. | „DRAUSSEN ZUHAUSE": MARKENFÜHRUNG – AM POINT OF SALE | "AT HOME OUTDOORS": BRAND MANAGEMENT – AT THE POINT OF SALE |

dem Produkt selbst als Zugabe im Handel angeboten wird. In den 1950er Jahren war neben der Patentdose auch eine conveniente Kleinpackung gebräuchlich: Eine direkt bedruckte Aluminium-Halbtube bot Kaffeepulver für zwei Tassen. In der Werbung der 1950er Jahre stellte sich „Nescafé" als Begleiter des modernen Lebens dar. „Für die Frühstückspause!", rief die Marke ihren Konsumentinnen zu und zeigte beispielsweise eine genießerisch lächelnde Sekretärin mit Nescafé an der Schreibmaschine. Frauen eroberten nun die Berufswelt, und Nescafé begleitete sie an den Arbeitsplatz.

Dann hatte 1962 die Patentdose ausgedient. Seit diesem Jahr wurde der lösliche Kaffee in Gläser verpackt, deren Form sich dem jeweiligen Zeitgeist anpasste. Wichtig war der Vertrauen spendende Einblick auf das Produkt und die „gehobene" Haptik und Aufmachung der gläsernen Premium-Verpackung.

Nescafé am Point of Sale

Der Innovationskraft der Marke entsprach die moderne Umsetzung der Markenkommunikation am Point of Sale. Schon 1952 wurde die „Nescafé"-Tube in einem kleinen, Waren tragenden Thekendisplay angeboten. Und 1960 – also noch vor Einführung der Selbstbedienung – wurden Schaufensterdisplays eingesetzt, beispielsweise zur Weihnachtszeit in der Art einer Bühnen-Kulisse. Eine weihnachtliche, schneebedeckte Kleinstadt ist hier samt Sternenhimmel zu sehen.

Nur ein Jahr später wurden als „Hingucker" für den Handel optische „Störer" konzipiert, die als Aufsteller die Blicke der Besucher aufs Regal lenken sollten. Hier wurden bereits 1961 dreidimensionale Packungsnachbildungen mit großflächiger Werbemotivik kombiniert.

Draht war zunächst das stabilisierende Konstruktionselement bei einem Waren tragenden Bodendisplay, das für „Nescafé" in den frühen 1960er Jahren eingesetzt wurde. Ein zusammenlegbarer (von Nestlé für unterschiedliche Werbemotive nutzbarer) Ver-

Schaufensterdisplays (mit „Störer" von 1961 und Weihnachten 1960)
Shop window displays (with "eye-catcher" in 1961 and at Christmas in 1960)

Thekendisplay für Aktivumsatz mit den Portions-Tuben, Deutschland 1952
Counter display to boost sales of the one-portion Nescafé "tubes", Germany 1952

Bodendisplay mit Drahtkonstruktion, um 1960
Wire based floor stand display, around 1960

Bodendisplay mit Drahtkonstruktion, frühe 1960er Jahre
Wire based floor stand display, early 1960s

Wellpappe-Verkaufsaufsteller der 1960er Jahre zur Aufnahme eines Versandkartons (beidseitig begehbar)
Corrugated cardboard floor stand holding double-sided shipping boxes, 1960s

„Der neue Nescafé", Bodendisplay aus Wellpappe, 1968
"The new Nescafé", corrugated cardboard floor stand display, 1968

III. | „DRAUSSEN ZUHAUSE": MARKENFÜHRUNG AM POINT OF SALE | AT HOME OUTDOORS": BRAND MANAGEMENT - AT THE POINT OF SALE

Vorsteck-Regaldisplay als Zweitplatzierung, Wellkiste in Metalldraht-Konstruktion, Deutschland 1973
Display tray used as secondary placement. The corrugated cardboard box could be attached to shelves by its metal hooks, Germany 1973

Necafé Gold, Anzeige mit Bodendisplay, Deutschland 1979
Nescafé Gold, advertisement featuring floor stand display, Germany 1979

---

kaufsaufsteller bot seitlich und frontal großen, aus offsetbedruckter Wellpappe gefertigten Werbeschildern Aufnahme. Darüber thronte in der Höhe das damals obligatorische Aufsteckplakat.

Ein anderer Verkaufsaufsteller der 1960er Jahre war als einteiliger Verkaufssockel aus Wellpappe für die Aufnahme eines Versandkartons mit Nescafé geeignet. Die perforierten Teile des Versandkartons wurden herausgetrennt, um den Inhalt gut präsentieren zu können. Beworben wurde die Portionspackung von Nescafé in der Tube, indem beim Kauf einer Glaspackung eine Gratis-Tube beigegeben wurde. Schon zum Zeitpunkt der Einführung der Selbstbedienung wurde mit derartigen ersten Bodendisplays der Promotion-Absatz angekurbelt, um die Kundschaft mit dem damals noch erklärungsbedürftigen Produkt des löslichen Kaffees in persönlicher Ansprache vertraut zu machen. Beachtung fand auch ein Bodendisplay, mit dem – offenbar nach einer Produktverbesserung – 1968 der „neue Nescafé" angekündigt wurde. Diesem Display bescheinigte „Die Absatzwirtschaft" (Heft 21, 1968), dass sich „neue Produkte nicht nur durch Insertion, Rundfunk- und Fernsehwerbung, sondern auch durch gute Präsentation im Verkaufslokal einführen lassen".

Eine Innovation waren 1973 die aus Metalldraht gefertigten Vorsteck-Regaldisplays mit eingesetzter, bedruckter Wellkiste, in der sechs Packungen „Nescafé Gold" im Markt an fremder Stelle als Zweitplatzierung ihre Käufer suchen konnten, so z. B. am

Nescafé at the POS

The brand's innovative force was reflected in its modern presentation at the POS. As early as 1952, the so-called Nescafé tube was offered to customers on a small counter display. And before the introduction of self-service in 1960, shop window displays were used for the presentation of Nescafé products, for instance in a kind of stage setting in the run-up to Christmas that showed a small, festive looking, snow-covered town under a starlit sky.

Only a year later, floor stand displays were designed as eye-catchers for retail that were meant to direct the customer's eye to the shelf. As early as 1961, three-dimensional product replicas were used together with large images of the Nescafé product.

At first, wire was the stabilising element of the floor stand display used for Nescafé in the early 1960s. A foldable floor stand was designed that could be used by Nescafé to promote various product varieties. Advertising posters made of offset printed corrugated cardboard could be attached to the front, back and sides of the display. At its top, there was always the header card typical for the times.

Another display typical of the 1960s was a one-piece corrugated cardboard pedestal suitable for holding a shipping box full of Nescafé packs. The perforated parts of the shipping box were torn off to present the contents in an effective way. Nescafé in the tube was pro-

Regaldisplay, 2000
Shelf display, 2000

Regaldisplay aus der „italienischen" Phase, 2001
"Italian phase" shelf display, 2001

„Nescafé Eiskaffee", Bodendisplay als Palettenmantel, 2002
"Nescafé Eiskaffee" iced coffee, open wrap-around display for pallets, 2002

Kombiniertes Bodendisplay für die Marken „Nescafé" (Regal) und „Orion" (Schütte), 2003
Floor stand display for the brands "Nescafé" (shelf) and "Orion" (bin), 2003

Kühlregal bei der Milch. Für „Nescafé Gold" fanden später auch praktische Stapeldisplays aus Wellpappe Anwendung, beispielsweise 1979, als dem Handel in einer Werbeaktion die Aufstellung des neuen „Maxi Kartons" nahegebracht wurde.

„Nescafé" sollte in der Folge zu einer der am stärksten werbende Marken am Point of Sale werden. Im Jahre 2001 erschien unter der Headline „typisch italienisch" der italienische Kaffeegenießer, der sehnsüchtig die „Crema" seines „Nescafé Cappucino" betrachtet. Es ist dies die „italienische Phase" der Marke. Unvergessen sind die TV-Spots mit dem italienischen Nachbarn „Alberto", der seine hübsche, offenbar jedoch wegen Parkproblemen erboste Nachbarin schmeichlerisch erst einmal mit einer Tasse Nescafé beruhigt, um ihr dann zu beichten: „Isch abe gar keine Auto!"

Die Marke „Nescafé" wurde dann bis in den Bereich der Kalt-Mischgetränke ausgebaut. Für den in Getränkedosen vertriebenen „Nescafé Eiskaffee" warb 2002 ein attraktives Bodendisplay, das als halbrunder, fast zylinderförmiger Palettenmantel gefertigt war. Die Ware wird auf Palette innerhalb dieses bewusst an die Getränkedose erinnernden Displayrahmens präsentiert.
In allen europäischen Ländern werden Nescafé-Produkte am POS in Szene gesetzt. Die Gestaltung und Art der Warenpräsentation ist dabei abhängig von den Vorlieben der Verbraucher in den einzelnen Ländern auf der einen und den Handelsanforde-

moted by giving a free sample to customers who bought a glass jar. In the early days of self-service, this new type of floor stand display was used to drive promotional sales and make customers familiar with the then rather unfamiliar instant coffee through a personal approach. Another floor stand display became popular, which, apparently after a product improvement, was used in 1968 to present the "new Nescafé". The magazine "Absatzwirtschaft" (issue 21, 1968) said of this display that it demonstrated how "new products can be launched not only by means of print ads and radio and TV commercials, but also by a good presentation in the store".

Another innovation introduced In 1973 was a metal wire shelf display with an inserted, printed corrugated cardboard box for six packets of "Nescafé Gold". It was used in unusual places in the store, like in the chill cabinets with the milk, to attract customers. Later, practical stacking displays of corrugated cardboard were also used to present "Nescafé Gold", for instance in 1979, when retailers were made familiar with the new "Maxi carton" in an advertising campaign. After that, Nescafé became one of the brands with the highest level of POS promotion activity. In 2001, under the slogan "typical Italian" the Italian coffee gourmet was born, who lovingly contemplated the "crema" of his "Nescafé Cappucino". That was the brand's Italian phase. The commercials with the Italian Alberto and his pretty, but angry neighbour are unforgettable. She is furious about an evident parking problem she blames him for, he calms her with a cup of coffee, only to later confess, with a heavy

III. „DRAUSSEN ZUHAUSE": MARKENFÜHRUNG – AM POINT OF SALE | "AT HOME OUTDOORS": BRAND MANAGEMENT – AT THE POINT OF SALE

rungen auf der anderen Seite. Dies führte dazu, dass beispielsweise die Zahl der für Nestlé in Frankreich eingesetzten Displays ein fast unüberschaubares Ausmaß annahm.

Im Jahre 2008 wurde daher ein modulares Konzept entwickelt, das die Anzahl der Varianten von zehn auf zwei Displaytypen reduzieren konnte – und zwar als Multidisplay für „Nescafé", „Ricoré" und „Nesquik", den drei Getränkemarken des „Nestlé Département Boissons Instantanées" in Frankreich. Mit dem Relaunch der eingesetzten Displaymaterialien sollte gleichzeitig die Sichtbarkeit der Produkte im Handel verbessert und eine wahlweise bestückte oder flachliegende Anlieferung der Displays ermöglicht werden.

Nach wie vor ist für Nestlé die persönliche Begegnung mit dem Kunden am Point of Sale von herausragender Bedeutung für die Markenpolitik. Peter Brabeck-Letmathe, Vorsitzender des Verwaltungsrates Nestle S.A., stuft heute den Direktkontakt mit den Konsumenten gar als stärkstes Element der Markenkommunikation ein.

Italian accent, that he did not steal her parking place, because: "I don't even have a car!"

The brand "Nescafé" was extended as far as to cold mixed drinks. In 2002, „Nescafé Eiskaffee" iced coffee in beverage cans was promoted on an attractive floor stand display in the style of a half round, almost cylindrical cardboard floor stand display. Goods were presented on a pallet inside the display, which had been deliberately designed to resemble a beverage can. Nescafé products are strongly promoted at the POS in all European countries. The design and form of product presentation depends on the particular preferences of the customers in the individual countries on the one hand and on retailers' requirements on the other hand. In France, this led to an almost uncontrollable number of displays used at retail.

Modularisierte Zweitplatzierung für diverse Nestlé-Getränke, Frankreich 2008
Modular displays for the secondary placement of various Nestlé drinks, France 2008

In 2008, a modular concept was developed, which reduced the number of display variants from ten to two. These variants were multiple displays for "Nescafé", "Ricore" and "Nesquik", the three drink brands of "Nestlé Département Boissons Instantanées" in France. The idea behind relaunching the display materials was to increase product visibility at retail and allow displays to be delivered to stores either pre-stocked or flat-packed.

Customer approach at the POS is still a prominent aspect of Nestlé's brand policy. For Peter Brabeck-Letmathe, Chairman of the Board of Directors, Nestlé S.A., direct contact with the customer is the strongest of all elements of brand communication.

POS-Dekoration für eine Inselplatzierung 2009
POS decoration for an island display, 2009

NESQUIK – Der Kakao mit dem lustigen Hasen

Das Unternehmen Nestlé hatte sich mit Produkten wie Milchpulver und Kondensmilch eine hervorragende Marktstellung erarbeitet. Was lag näher, als sich nun auch mit einem Geschmackszusatz für Milch zu beschäftigen? Der klassische Kakao wurde ja nur mit heißem Wasser aufgebrüht.

Die Idee eines Geschmackszusatzes für die Milch wurde 1941 zum ersten Mal in der Nestlé-Fabrik in Fulton, USA, diskutiert. Schon 1942 griffen Dr. McCloskey und sein Team diese Idee auf und führten erste Testreihen durch. Im April 1948 konnte man dann in den USA erste Marktversuche mit einem Produkt starten, welches nun „NES-QUIK" hieß. Noch im September dieses Jahres wurde „NES-QUIK" in den USA als erstes Instant-Schokoladengetränk am Markt eingeführt. Der Markenname ist eine Verbindung der ersten Silbe des Herstellers Nestlé mit dem Eigenschaftswort „quick" für schnell. Er deutet auf die Leichtigkeit der Zubereitung und damit den Convenience-Aspekt des modernen Produkts hin.

So ganz sicher war man sich jedoch mit dem Markennamen nicht. Im Juni 1949 erfolgte eine Umbenennung in „NESTLÉ'S QUIK". Im Dezember dieses Jahres nahm dann die Fabrik in Fulton die Produktion von „NESTLÉ'S QUIK" auf. Der kürzere Name „NESQUIK" war jedoch nicht mehr aus der Welt zu kriegen, und bald wurde das Kakaopulver unter verschiedenen Markenbezeichnungen vermarktet.

Eine erste große Marketing-Aktion war eine breit angelegte Werbekampagne in den USA im Frühjahr 1952: die „Nestlé's Quik Spring Promotion". In Deutschland und in der Schweiz wurde das Kakaopulver 1959 eingeführt, in Frankreich 1961. In Europa hatte sich – insbesondere im französischsprachigen Raum – eine andere, traditionelle Variante des Kakaos bereits etabliert, den Nestlé als „NESCAO" herausgebracht hatte. Hier lag es also nahe, das moderne Instantprodukt als „NESQUIK" zu benennen. Und dieser Name setzte sich durch. In den USA wurde erst 1999 der „NESTLÉ'S QUIK" offiziell in „NESTLÉ'S NESQUIK" umbenannt, um eine Angleichung herbeizuführen.

NESQUIK – the cocoa with the funny bunny

The Nestlé group has gained an outstanding reputation for products like milk powder and condensed milk. What could have been more logical than to turn its attention to flavour additives too? Remember: the classic cup of cocoa was prepared with boiling water only.

The idea of adding flavours to milk was discussed in the Nestlé factory in Fulton in the US for the first time in 1941. The idea was picked up by Dr McCloskey and his team as early as 1942 and led to first experiments. In April 1948, Nestlé was ready to start the trial of a product in the US called "Nes-Quik" at the time. In September of the same year, "Nes-Quik" was launched onto the US market as the first instant chocolate drink. The brand name is a portmanteau word combining the first syllable of producer Nestlé's name and the adjective "quick". It stresses the easy preparation of the drink and the convenience aspect of the product.

But there was uncertainty about the brand name. So it was renamed "Nestlé's Quik" in 1949. The factory in Fulton started to produce the drink under the name of "Nestlé's Quik" in December the same year. But the shorter name "Nesquik" had stuck in the minds of customers and soon the cocoa powder was sold under various brand names.

One of the first major marketing steps was an extensive advertising campaign in the US in spring 1952: the "Nestlé's Quik Spring Promotion". The cocoa powder was launched in Germany and Switzerland in 1959, France followed in 1961. Another, traditional cocoa variant Nestlé had launched under the name "Nescao", had already been established in Europe, in particular in France. So it made sense to call the modern instant product "Nesquik". And the name stuck. In the US, "Nestlé's Quik" was officially renamed "Nestlé's Nesquik" to make sure that the product was sold under the same name in all markets.

A company circular revealed as early as 1959 that the flavour variant "Strawberry Quik" was being tested in the US market. This means that the product has existed in the US in the flavours chocolate and strawberry since the 1960s.

In Germany, there was no likeable mascot featured on the pack at the beginning that was able to make the product popular at the POS.

Eine der sympathischsten Werbefiguren ist der Hase „Quiky".
Er fungiert seit 1972/73 als Begleiter der Marke Nesquik
(Tray, Deutschland 2008–2009).
*One of the most likeable advertising characters was the
„Quiky" bunny. He has accompanied the Nesquik brand since
1972/73 (tray, Germany 2008–2009).*

III. „DRAUSSEN ZUHAUSE": MARKENFÜHRUNG AM POINT OF SALE | "AT HOME OUTDOORS": BRAND MANAGEMENT – AT THE POINT OF SALE

Mit „Nestlés Quik" nahm die Marke in den USA ihren Anfang. Hier erscheint bereits ein Schokoladehase zur Auslobung, den Bruce Kellet 1972/73 entwickelt hatte (dieser ist gleichwohl noch kein Bestandteil des Labels). Anzeige, USA 1975.
The brand started in the US as "Nestlés Quik". The packaging already features the chocolate bunny created by Brunce Kellet between 1972 and 1973 (the bunny is not yet part of the label). Advertisement, US 1975.

Am Anfang stand die vornehme Marke „Nescao". Dieser Kakao konnte gleichwohl nur in warmer Milch gelöst werden (Packung um 1930).
At the beginning, there was the refined brand "Nescao". The cocoa could be prepared only with warm milk (packaging around 1930).

Schon 1959 wird in einem Zirkular der Firma erwähnt, dass sich als Geschmacksvariante das Produkt „STAWBERRY QUIK" in einer Testphase auf dem amerikanischen Markt befand. Schon seit den 1960er Jahren gibt es also in den USA das Produkt in zwei Geschmacksvarianten: Erdbeer und Schokolade.

Auf der deutschen Verpackung war zunächst kein Maskottchen abgebildet, das die Marke sympathiestark an den Point of Sale hätte begleiten können. In Frankreich und in Griechenland dagegen besaß – noch vor der Ära des Hasen – die Marke ein eigenes Maskottchen. Dies war ein sanftmütiger gelber Riese, der – auf den Namen „Groquik" getauft – auf einer populären Zeichentrickfilm-Figur der 1940er und 1950er Jahre aufbaute. Anfang der 1990er Jahre ersetzte der lustigere, „leichtere" und unbekümmerte Hase namens „Quiky" den gutmütigen Riesen. Er sollte den Kindern ein „aktiveres" Image der Marke vermitteln.

Die Geburt des Hasen

Die Anfänge des beliebten Hasen finden sich auf einer amerikanischen Produktverpackung von „NESTLÉ'S QUIK STRAWBERRY": Auf dem Label der Packung von 1966/67 erscheint der so genannte „Erdbeerhase", eine Figur, die von Gene Kolkey entwickelt wurde. Er sollte auf Packungen und in TV-Spots für „NESTLÉ'S QUIK STRAWBERRY" Werbung machen. Der Name „Erdbeerhase" leitet sich von seinem Hut her, auf dem er Erdbeeren hatte. In ei-

France and Greece had their own mascot, even before the times of the bunny. It was a gentle yellow giant baptised "Groquik". The mascot was based on a popular cartoon character of the 1940s and 1950s. In the early 1990s, the gentle giant was replaced by the funny, "less heavy" and untroubled bunny "Quiky". Quiky was supposed to convey a more "active" image to children.

The bunny's birth

The birth of the popular bunny goes back to a US product pack of "Nestlé's Quik Strawberry". The label of the packs of 1966 and 1967 featured the so-called "strawberry bunny", a character created by Gene Kolkey. The strawberry bunny's task was to promote "Nestlé's Quik Strawberry" in TV commercials. The name "strawberry bunny" is derived from the bunny's hat, which had strawberries on top of it. The bunny appeared in an advertising campaign in 1965 and 1966. And from 1967 at the latest, it had become a integral feature of the strawberry flavour variant's brand image.

Naturally, after the strawberry bunny's big success, the main chocolate flavour needed its own bunny too – exactly, the "chocolate bunny". The bunny appeared as a feature of the brand's image for the first time on a product label in November 1976, a fact that was recorded in the Archives Historiques Nestlé (Vevey). The "chocolate bunny" character was created by Bruce Kellet in the US

Nestlés Quik, Packungsdesign (noch ohne den Hasen), USA um 1965
Packaging design for Nestlés Quik (still without the bunny), US around 1965

Nestlés Quik, Packungsdesign mit dem „Erdbeerhasen", dem Vorläufer der späteren „Quiky"-Figur (Sorte Erdbeergeschmack), Wickler, USA 1966/67
Packaging design for Nestlés Quik featuring the "strawberry bunny", the predecessor to the "Quiky" (for the strawberry flavour), wrapper, US 1966-67

ner Werbekampagne erscheint der Hase 1965/66. Und spätestens ab 1967 ist er Bestandteil des Markenbilds der Erdbeer-Sorte.

Natürlich musste – nach dem großen Erfolg des „Erdbeerhasen" – nun auch für die Hauptsorte ein eigener Hase entwickelt werden, ein „Schokoladehase" eben. Er erscheint erstmals als Bestandteil des Markenbilds auf einem Verpackungslabel vom November 1976, das sich in den Archives Historiques Nestlé (Vevey) erhalten hat. Die Figur des „Schokoladehasen" wurde 1972/73 von Bruce Kellet in den USA entwickelt. Erste Werbekampagnen mit ihm wurden im Jahr 1974 durchgeführt.

Im Zuge der Marken-Umbenennung erhielt in den USA 1999 auch der als „Quik Bunny" bekannte Hase den stärker „europäisch" verankerten Namen „Nesquik Bunny". Zierte bis dato seine Brust noch ein „Q" (für „Quik"), so musste dieses nun in ein „N" umgeändert werden.

Nesquik am Point of Sale

Eine hübsche Schaufensterdekoration kam bereits um 1959/60 zum Einsatz, die als Werbung noch nicht mit einer direkten Absatzfunktion verbunden war. Sechs Schaupackungen der Marke „Nesquik" – damals natürlich noch ohne Maskottchen – konnten zu einem „Sockel" zusammenmontiert werden, auf dem sich wirkungsvoll „thronend" eine siebte Packung niedergelassen

between 1972 and 1973. The first advertising campaigns featuring the chocolate bunny were run in 1974.

As part of a brand renaming campaign in 1999, the bunny known as "Quik Bunny" adapted the name "Nesquik Bunny", which had established itself in Europe. The "Q" that was on his chest until then had to be changed to an "N".

Nesquik at the POS

As early as sometime around 1959 or 1960, a nice shop window decoration was used at a time when advertising was not yet linked to direct sales promotion. Six "Nesquik" dummy packs, at the time naturally without the mascot, could be assembled to form a pedestal that was "crowned" by a seventh pack, which effectively drew the attention to the product. Hidden behind this "product building" was a little boy who wanted nothing else but to drink his Nesquik in peace. Designed as a cut-out figure, only his head and hands were visible. In one hand he held a glass with a straw, with the other one he pointed to the packs behind him, with a meaningful grin. Advertising at its easiest! Customers later encountered the same boy with the straw again in the counter display of 1960, this time together with a girl drawn in a similar way.

In the late 1960s, Nesquik products were promoted on bright red displays. The idea to add a dispenser for lottery tickets to the back

III. „DRAUSSEN ZUHAUSE": MARKENFÜHRUNG AM POINT OF SALE | "AT HOME OUTDOORS": BRAND MANAGEMENT – AT THE POINT OF SALE

Thekendisplay mit integriertem Strohhalmspender, Deutschland 1960
Counter display with integrated drinking straw dispenser, Germany 1960

Thekendisplay mit trinkendem Jungen, Deutschland um 1959/60
Counter display featuring a boy drinking Nesquik, Germany around 1959-60

hatte. Hinter diesem „Gebinde" versteckt, zeigt sich ein kleiner Junge, der ungestört nichts als seinen Nesquik genießen möchte. Als Stanzfigur gefertigt, sind nur sein Kopf und seine Hände zu sehen. In der einen Hand hält er das Glas mit dem Strohhalm, mit der anderen verweist er (mit vielsagendem Grinsen) auf die hinter ihm aufgebauten Leckereien in den Schaupackungen. Einfacher kann Werbung nicht sein. Derselbe Junge mit Strohhalm begegnet uns – nun gemeinsam mit einem ähnlich gezeichneten Mädchen – in einem Thekendisplay des Jahres 1960.

Bodendisplays werben in den späten 1960er Jahren in leuchtendem Rot für die Nesquik-Produkte. Beachtung fand vor allem die Idee, an dem über der klassischen Schütte angebrachten Aufsteckplakat durch einen einfachen Gestaltungswechsel der Grafik eine Mitnahmemöglichkeit für Lose eines Glücksspiels anzubringen. In „Die Absatzwirtschaft" (Heft 21/1968) hieß es: „Preisausschreiben sind ein beliebtes Mittel der Verkaufsförderung. Mit diesem Bodenaufsteller werden neben der Ware Lose angeboten. Der Kunde wird dieser Verkaufshilfe seine Aufmerksamkeit nicht versagen."

Ebenfalls noch in den 1960er Jahren wurde für Nesquik ein braungrundiger (kakaofarbener) Bodenaufsteller in schmaler, rechteckiger Form gestaltet, der nur eine sehr kleine Aufstellfläche benötigte, trotzdem jedoch eine überraschende Vielzahl von Verkaufsverpackungen aufnehmen konnte. Er wird flachliegend angeliefert und ließ sich schon damals sehr leicht aufstellen.

Wenig später wurde – ähnlich wie beim Schwesterprodukt „Nescafé" – auch für „Nesquik" ein Waren tragendes Display aus Draht entwickelt, das außen am Kühlregal direkt bei der Milch eingehängt werden konnte. Zweitplatzierung – ein Thema für diese Marke schon im Jahre 1970.

Ein ganz neues Produkt war der „Nesquik Schokosirup", eine Art „Kakao-Soße", die in einer figürlichen Kunststoffpackung in Form

card of the classic bin, by means of the simple change in the graphical design, attracted particular interest. "Die Absatzwirtschaft" (issue 21, 1968) wrote that "Prize draws are a popular sales promotion method. This floor stand display offers not only goods, but lottery tickets as well. The customer will not pass this sales promotion tool without noticing."

Also still in the 1960s, a small, brown (cocoa-coloured) rectangular floor stand display was designed for Nesquik that required only a small floor space, but could carry an astonishingly large number of product packs. It was delivered flat-packed and was very easy to assemble, even for those times.

A short time later, as it was in the case of its sister product "Nescafé", a wire product carry case display was developed for "Nesquik". It could be attached to the side of the chilled cabinet where the milk was. Secondary placements were an issue for the Nesquik brand as early as 1970.

A completely new product was "Nesquik Schokosirup", a chocolate syrup resembling a sort of "chocolate sauce", which was offered in a plastic bottle shaped like the "Quiky" mascot. Attractive yellow floor stand displays with a bin for goods were designed in 2002 to promote the product at retail. The solid pedestal was designed to support great weight and featured colourful images of the "Quiky" bunny character on both sides. The graphical design strongly resembled the cocoa powder's classic, yellow pack, but also aimed to transition to the brown form pack of the new product.

In 2005, a further floor stand display was designed that brought the "Quiky" bunny to the POS in stores in France. The shelf display was held in the brand's typical yellow and had four bins stacked on top of each other. That resulted in high product turnover on a small floor space. In the summer of the same year, an effective advertising aid was added to the simple and quick assembly pallet display. It consi-

Bodendisplay aus Wellpappe mit ausladender Schütte und
Aufsteckschild, Deutschland 1960er Jahre
*Corrugated cardboard display with protruding bin and header
card, Germany in the 1960s*

Display in Kakaofarbe, Wellpappe, Schütte mit Regalaufbau,
Deutschland 1960er Jahre
*Cocoa-coloured corrugated cardboard display with shelf
structure, Germany in the 1960s*

Bodendisplay aus Wellpappe, Gewinnspielaktion,
Deutschland um 1967/68
*Corrugated cardboard display with integrated prize draw,
Germany around 1967-68*

Nesquik, Packungsdesign mit „Quiky" für den englischsprachigen Markt, von (oder nach) 1991
Nesquik packaging design for English-speaking markets featuring "Quiky", in (or later than) 1991

Sockelgestaltung mit „Quiky" für ein stabiles Bodendisplay (Schütte), Deutschland 2002
"Quiky" pedestal decoration for a solid floor stand display (dump-bin), Germany 2002

des „Quiky"-Maskottchens eingeführt wurde. Zur Unterstützung im Handel wurden 2002 attraktive gelbe Bodendisplays herausgebracht, die eine Warenschütte trugen. Der massive Sockel war für eine hohe Gewichtsbelastung ausgelegt und trug auf beiden Ansichtsseiten bunte Werbemotive mit der Figur des Hasen „Quiky". Die Grafiken waren eng dem klassischen, gelben Packungsbild des Kakaopulvers entlehnt, sollten zugleich aber den Transfer auf die braune Formpackung des neuen Produkts herstellen.

In Frankreich wurde dann 2005 ein weiteres Bodendisplay herausgebracht, das dem Hasen „Quiky" seinen Auftritt am Point of Sale verschaffte. Durch seine vier übereinander gestapelten Schütten sorgte das – in markentypischem Gelb gehaltene – Regaldisplay dafür, dass auf kleiner Grundfläche viel Warenumschlag erfolgen konnte. Im Sommer desselben Jahres wurde zur einfachen, schnellen Palettendekoration in Deutschland eine wirksame Werbeunterstützung aufgelegt: Ein einfaches Papprohr (auf einen Metallfuß montiert) transportierte als „Standee" das Motiv des beliebten Hasen „Quiky", der mit einem winkenden Eis in der Hand, das durch einen batteriebetriebenen Motor bewegt wird, für zusätzliche Aufmerksamkeit am POS sorgt. Als Gratiszugabe bewirbt dieser hier praktische Eisförmchen, die den Kakao in ein leckeres Schokoladeneis verwandeln. So konnte auch in der Sommersaison der Kakao-Umsatz erhöht werden

Im Rahmen der Display-Modularisierung, die bei Nestlé Frankreich im Jahre 2008 durchgeführt wurde, erreichten die am Beispiel von „Nescafé" bereits behandelten Neuerungen auch die Marke „Nesquik". Streben nach Nachhaltigkeit und ökologisches Verantwortungsbewusstsein äußerten sich in dem Wunsch des Schweizer Lebensmittelherstellers, seine Displays am Point of Sale aus besser recyclebaren Monomaterialien herstellen zu lassen und zugleich unnötige Doppelungen in Lagerbestand und Logistik durch den Einsatz multifunktionaler Standards und Module zu reduzieren.

sted of a simple cardboard tube (on a metal base) featuring the image of the popular bunny "Quiky" in the form of a "standee". The bunny held an ice cream in his waving, motor-driven hand, thus drawing even more attention to the POS. This display also promoted ice cream moulds that turned cocoa into a tasty chocolate ice cream and were given away for free as part of the promotion. That helped increase cocoa sales even in the summer season.

Nestlé France increased the use of modular displays in 2008. As a result, the new kinds of displays tested with "Nescafé" were also used for the brand "Nesquik". The trend towards sustainability and ecological responsibility prompted the Swiss food supplier to use displays at the POS, which were made of mono materials that were easier to recycle. Nestlé also used standardised multifunctional display elements and modules to reduce unnecessary surplus stock.

Palettendekoration als „Standee" für eine Sommer-Promotion, Deutschland 2005
"Quiky" standee for pallet displays in a summer promotion, Germany 2005

Nesquik Bodendisplay mit Stapelschütten, Frankreich 2005
Nesquik floor stand display with stackable bins, France 2005

Ricoré, Nescafé, Nesquik etc., modulares (ökologisch nachhaltiges) Displaykonzept mit veränderbaren Modul-Standards, Frankreich 2008
Ricoré, Nescafé, Nesquik etc., modular (ecologically sustainable) display concept with exchangeable standardised modules, France 2008

NIVEA – Die schneeweiße Creme in der blauen Dose

Ein echter „Markenklassiker" ist die Hautcreme „NIVEA" der Firma Beiersdorf aus Hamburg. Das technisch revolutionäre Produkt war 1911 die erste „Wasser in Öl"-Emulsion der Welt. Das Zusammenspiel dreier Männer hatte die grundlegende Neuerung im Bereich der Hautpflege erst möglich gemacht. Das von Paul C. Beiersdorf in Hamburg 1882 gegründete Unternehmen war schon 1890 an Dr. Oscar Troplowitz verkauft worden, einen Forscher und Geschäftsmann. Er entwickelte bei Beiersdorf vor der Entstehung der „NIVEA" zunächst medizinische Pflaster und Kautschuk-Heftpflaster (Vorläufer von „Hansaplast") sowie technische Klebebänder (Vorläufer der späteren Marke „tesa"). Beide Marken konnten später eine ähnliche Berühmtheit erlangen wie „NIVEA".

Der Unternehmer Troplowitz erkannte in Professor Paul Gerson Unna einen wissenschaftlichen Berater mit einem untrüglichen Instinkt für die Entwicklung fortschrittlicher Produktideen. Professor Unna war es, der den Inhaber mit einem umwälzenden Forschungsergebnis konfrontierte: der Entwicklung eines völlig neuen Emulgators, „Eucerit" genannt. Endlich verfügte man über einen Wirkstoff, der Wasser und Fett zu einer stabilen Salbengrundlage verbinden konnte.

Nun galt es, aus der medizinischen Entdeckung ein erfolgreiches Markenprodukt zu entwickeln. Troplowitz entwickelte mit seinen Chemikern unter tatkräftiger Anleitung von Dr. Isaac Lifschütz, dem eigentlichen Entdecker von Eucerit, die erste stabile Fett- und Feuchtigkeitscreme der Welt. Seine „NIVEA"-Creme bot völlig neue Anwendungspotenziale.

Zur Verbindung der zarten Öle mit Wasser diente ihr das Eucerit. Daneben enthielt sie noch Glyzerin, ein wenig Zitronensäure sowie – zur zarten Parfümierung – etwas Rosen- und Maiglöckchenöl. Ein Welterfolg war geboren.

Frühzeit des Marketings

Zu den beeindruckenden Produkteigenschaften zählte auch jene hygienische Sauberkeit, welche die weiße Farbe des Produkts aus-

NIVEA – the snow-white cream in the blue jar

Beiersdorf's "NIVEA" skin cream is a true "brand classic". In 1911, NIVEA was the first-ever "water-in-oil" emulsion and a technical revolution. This fundamental innovation in skin care was possible only through the joint work of three men. The company founded by Paul C. Beiersdorf in Hamburg in 1882 was sold to Dr Oscar Troplowitz, a researcher and businessman, in 1890. In the "pre-NIVEA days", he developed medical plasters and rubber plasters (the predecessor to "Hansaplast") and technical adhesive tapes (the predecessor of the sellotape brand "tesa") at Beiersdorf. Both brands were to become as famous as "NIVEA".

The businessman Troplowitz appreciated Professor Gerson Unna as a scientific consultant with a remarkable instinct for the development of advanced product ideas. It was Professor Unna who presented the company's owner with a revolutionary research result: the development of a completely new emulsifier called "Eucerit". At last, a substance had been found that could combine water and oil to form a stable base for ointments.

The task now was to turn the medical discovery into a successful branded product. With the active support of Dr Isaac Lifschütz, the original discoverer of Eucerit, Troplowitz and his chemists produced the first stable fatty and moisturising cream in the world. His "NIVEA" cream offered completely new application potentials.

Eucerit helped combine the fine oils with water. Glycerine was added as well as a little citric acid and some rose and lily of the valley oil to give NIVEA a slight perfume. A world success was born. It marked the beginning of a global success story.

Early marketing days

One of the most impressive features of the product was the hygienic cleanness associated with its white colour. The name "NIVEA" was a fortunate choice in 1911 because it could be used without any problem in all languages and markets. The choice of the name was influenced by the cream's white colour, which was its most visually striking feature. "Nix", the Latin word for snow (gen.: nivis), was turned into

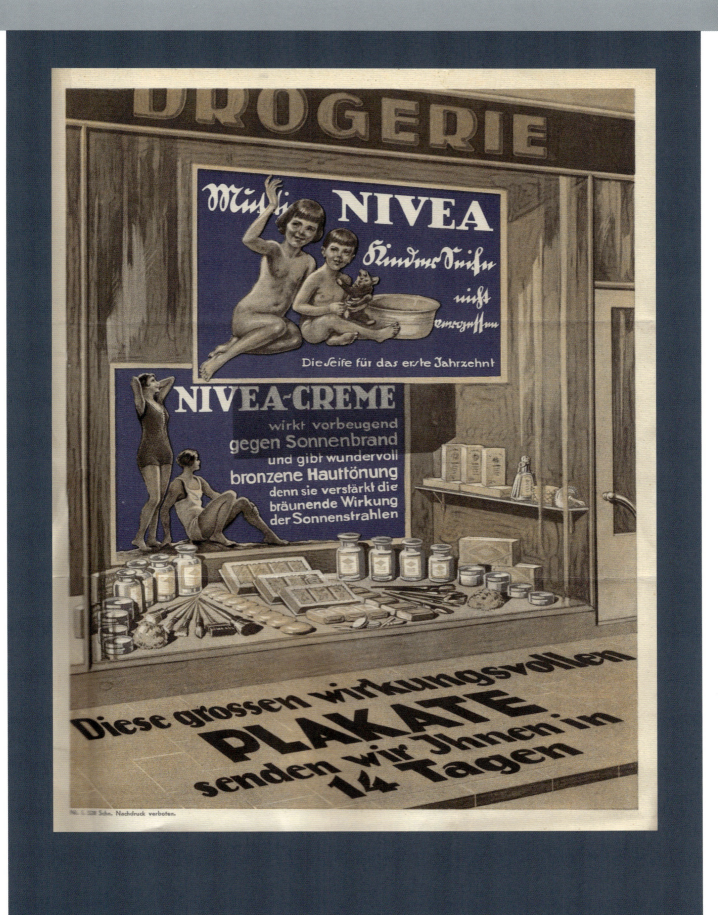

Markenwerbung am Point of Sale. Vorschlag zur Schaufenster-Dekoration, 1928
Brand advertising at the point of sale. Suggestion for window shop decorations, 1928

III. „DRAUSSEN ZUHAUSE": MARKENFÜHRUNG – AM POINT OF SALE | "AT HOME OUTDOORS": BRAND MANAGEMENT – AT THE POINT OF SALE

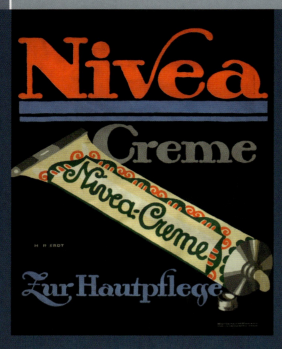

NIVEA war immer „schneeweiß", aber die Packung war anfangs noch nicht blau. Werbeplakat 1912, Entwurf Hans Rudi Erdt.
NIVEA has always been "snow-white", but its packaging was not always blue. Advertising poster designed by Hans Rudi Erdt in 1912.

NIVEA Creme, Anzeige von 1912
NIVEA creme, advertisement from 1912

strahlte. Ein Glücksgriff für die Marke war schon 1911 der in allen Sprachen und Märkten problemlos einsetzbare Name „NIVEA". Bei seiner Entwicklung hatte man sich vom weißen Charakter der Creme, der ersten optisch hervorstechenden Eigenschaft, leiten lassen. Vom lateinischen Wort „nix" (Gen.: nivis) für „Schnee" hatte man ein weibliches Eigenschaftswort abgeleitet, das übersetzt so viel bedeutet wie „die Schneeweiße". „NIVEA" – auch dieser wohlklingende Name sollte die Marke zum Welterfolg führen.

Schon bald nach ihrer Entwicklung im Dezember 1911 wurde die Creme in einer gelben Dose verkauft. Noch war die Dose keineswegs blau. Vielmehr zierten grün-rote Rankenornamente in der zeittypischen Optik des Jugendstils das damals noch vergleichsweise verspielte Markenbild. Auf der Packung waren damals die Begriffe „NIVEA" und „CREME" noch typografisch in gleicher Weise gestaltet und gewichtet.

Passend zum revolutionären Produkt wählte man für dessen Vermarktung einen der modernsten und progressivsten Werbekünstler und Plakatgrafiker der damaligen Zeit. Hans Rudi Erdt (1882–1925) erhielt schon 1912, also direkt nach der Einführung, den Auftrag, der Markenkommunikation ein visuelles Bild zu geben. Sofort gestaltete er erste Plakat- und Anzeigenmotive.

Hier sei daran erinnert, dass das in Europa damals wirtschaftlich stark aufstrebende Deutschland nicht zufällig zur Geburtsstätte

a feminine adjective, which can be translated as "snow-white". The nice sound of the name "NIVEA" was to contribute to the product's worldwide success.

Soon after its creation in December 1911, the cream was sold in a yellow jar. The jar was still far from being blue. Instead, green and red art nouveau arabesques typical of the time adorned the brand's still rather playful image on the jar. At the time, the words "NIVEA" and "cream" both had the same size and design.

For the promotion of this revolutionary product, Beiersdorf hired one of the most modern and progressive commercial and graphic artists of the time. As early as 1912, only shortly after the product launch, Hans Rudi Erdt was asked to give the brand's communication a visual image. He immediately started to design first posters and advertisements.

It should be noted that it was no coincidence that the then strongly growing economy of Germany produced so many major global brands. In Europe, Germany was known as the home of scientific research and leading "agency competence". Progressive artists like Hans Rudi Erdt, Julius Gipkens or Lucian Bernhard were globally recognised as leading brand communications experts around 1910. As early as 1907, they formed the association "Deutscher Werkbund". It was directly linked to the later "Bauhaus" movement, which would revolutionise the world of graphic style once more. Hans Rudi Erdt, who had the chance to

NIVEA Creme, Puder, Seife. Grafisch anspruchsvolle Anzeige, 1922
NIVEA creme, powder and soap. Graphically sophisticated advertisement, 1922

Das Jahr 1925 war die Geburtsstunde der weiß-blauen Dose.
1925 marked the birth of the blue and white jar.

vieler großer Weltmarken geworden ist. Hier war nicht nur wissenschaftliche Forschung, sondern auch tonangebende „Agentur-Kompetenz" zuhause. In der Markenkommunikation waren progressive Künstler, wie Hans Rudi Erdt, Julius Gipkens oder Lucian Bernhard, um 1910 weltweit führend. Schon 1907 hatten sich die Progressiven zum „Deutschen Werkbund" zusammengeschlossen. Von hier geht eine direkte Linie zum späteren „Bauhaus", das erneut den grafischen Stil revolutionierte.

Hans Rudi Erdt, der die Chance hatte, dem späteren Welterfolg „NIVEA" das erste Gesicht zu geben, war einer der Protagonisten der „neuen Richtung". Sein Name stand exemplarisch für den „neuen Stil". Von der mutigen Entscheidung, gerade diesen Grafiker für das neue Produkt heranzuziehen, sollte „NIVEA" enorm profitieren. Alles, einfach alles, passte in der Phase der Markengeburt perfekt zusammen.

Die Farbe Blau

Einen zweiten Anschub erfuhr die Marke, als die blaue Farbe eingeführt wurde. Heute ist NIVEA so untrennbar mit der blauen Blechdose verbunden, dass es für manchen Leser überraschend sein mag, zu erfahren, dass das Markenbild dieser Hautcreme eben nicht immer blau gewesen war. Erst im Jahre 1924 entwickelte das Haus Beiersdorf einen neuen Werbestil. Juan Gregorio Clausen war damals Werbeleiter des Unternehmens. Er erkannte, dass sich das Lebensgefühl nach dem Ersten Weltkrieg in der

give a first face to the success NIVEA would later experience, was one of the protagonists of the "new direction". His name was synonymous with the "new style". NIVEA was to benefit immensely from the courageous decision to hire exactly this graphic artist for the new product. Everything, simply everything worked out perfectly for the brand in its starting phase.

The colour blue

There was a second boost for the brand when its colour was changed from yellow to blue. Think of NIVEA and you think of the blue jar. The brand is so inseparable from its blue jar that some readers may be surprised to learn that the colour of this skin cream brand has indeed not always been blue. It was only in 1924 that Beiersdorf switched to a new advertising style. At the time, Juan Gregorio Claus was in charge of the company's advertising. He realised that the way people in the "Weimar Republic" felt about their lives had changed completely after the first world war. New media like radio, sound film and records was changing people's lives. The 1920s were called the "roaring twenties". Soberness seemed to be the order of the day. "Art nouveau frills" were no longer in vogue. Clausen used photos in a campaign he launched in 1925, which was very successful and laid the foundation for the brand's modern and sporty image.

The shift to a blue jar with no decoration at all was a revolution. The body of the jar was now completely plain, reading only the two

Verkaufshilfe für den Point of Sale: NIVEA-Verkaufsschränkchen, 1925
Sales promotion at the point of sale: NIVEA display cabinet, 1925

NIVEA, Verkaufsschränkchen, 1927
NIVEA display cabinet, 1927

NIVEA, drehbares Verkaufsschränkchen, gemischte Sortierung, 1932
Rotating display cabinet for various NIVEA products, 1932

„Weimarer Republik" völlig verändert hatte. Mit dem Rundfunk, dem Tonfilm und der Schallplatte hatten neue Medien im Leben der Menschen Einzug gehalten. Man sprach von den „Roaring Twenties". Versachlichung schien das Gebot der Stunde. Weg mit den „Jugend-Schnörkeln". Eine erfolgreiche Kampagne mit Fotomotiven wurde von Clausen 1925 ins Leben gerufen, die das moderne, sportliche Image der Marke schon damals begründete.

Revolutionär war die Veränderung des Markenkörpers, der nun gänzlich undekoriert blieb und eine blaue Farbe annahm. In unerreichter Simplizität nahm der Korpus der Dose nur zwei Worte auf: NIVEA CREME. Anfangs war auch das Worte „Creme" noch in Majuskeln geschrieben. Später erst verloren die Buchstaben ihre Serifen, und die Schreibweise der „Creme" erfolgte in einer weicheren Kursivschrift. Neu war 1925 auch die veränderte Auffassung der Zielgruppen. An die Stelle der eleganten Dame und ihrer auf den häuslichen Schminktisch beschränkten Anwendung trat nun die sportliche Frau, die – sei es zum Beruf oder zur Freizeit – das Haus häufiger verließ und nun für die Herausforderungen durch Luft, Licht und Sonne vor allem eines benötigte: NIVEA. Mit dieser Erkenntnis, von der der Weg nicht mehr weit war zum legendären „NIVEA-Ball" (1930er Jahre), konnte NIVEA sich in neue Räume ausdehnen. Nun fand die Marke Platz in der Sporttasche, im Schwimmbad, am Strand, in der Sauna etc.

words NIVEA CREAM. At the beginning, the word "cream" was also written in capitals. It was a while before a non-seriffed style was adopted and a softer italic lettering was used for the word "cream". In 1925, the company also changed its definition of the product's target group. The focus was no longer on the elegant lady at her dressing table, but on the sporty woman who increasingly left her home to work or enjoy herself. What she needed first and foremost to master the challenge of air, light and sun was: NIVEA. This new approach, which would soon lead to the creation of the legendary "NIVEA ball" in the 1930s, allowed the brand to extend its reach. It could now be found in people's sports bags, in the swimming pool, at the beach, in the sauna etc.

A pioneer of sales marketing

The brand's successful extension into new areas of life also expanded its product portfolio. Soon, sun cream, facial care and many more products were launched for sale under the umbrella brand "NIVEA". To promote the sale of all these products, Beiersdorf developed various types of displays. As early as the 1920s, the company provided good business partners with displays containing NIVEA products, a procedure that required some explanation at the time. Until the late 1930s, the majority of these wooden displays were box-shaped. The first "NIVEA display cabinet" was introduced to retail in 1925 and

NIVEA, Theken-Holzdisplay (auch hängbar), 1954
Wooden NIVEA counter display (that could also be hung on the wall), 1954

NIVEA, Theken-Holzdisplay, 1960
Wooden NIVEA counter display, 1960

Ein Pionier des Sales Marketings

Mit der erfolgreichen Ausdehnung der Marke in neue Lebensbereiche ging auch eine frühe Ausdehnung des Portfolios einher. Schon bald gab es unter der Dachmarke „NIVEA" auch Sonnencreme, Gesichtspflege und viele weitere Produkte zu kaufen. Um den Absatz all dieser Erzeugnisse sicherzustellen, etablierte die Firma Beiersdorf unterschiedliche Formen von Displays. Schon in den 1920er Jahren wurden – damals ein noch höchst erklärungsbedürftiger Vorgang – guten Geschäftskunden Waren tragende Absatzhilfen bereitgestellt. Bis Ende der 1930er Jahre waren diese aus Holz gefertigt und meist kastenförmig. Schon 1925 war der erste „NIVEA-Verkaufsschrank" einsetzbar, dem 1927 ein verbessertes Modell folgte. Und schon 1927 wurden Drogisten und Einzelhändler mit gezielter Werbung regelrecht „bearbeitet", diese Waren tragenden Verkaufshilfen auch einzusetzen. „Warum NIVEA-CREME so versteckt?" lautet der Slogan über der Abbildung einer typischen Apotheke, in der das Produkt (farbig herausgehoben) an unterschiedlichen Stellen und Ablageorten „versteckt" und unbeachtet sein Dasein fristet. Den Verkauf aktiv zu gestalten, diese klare Botschaft sendete der Markenartikler seit 1927 an seine Vertriebspartner. „So wirbt und verkauft er!" heißt es 1929 euphorisch auf einer Broschüre über den Verkaufsschrank, der angeblich den „NIVEA-Verkauf verdoppelt und verdreifacht"

improved in 1927. Chemists and retailers were virtually "belaboured" with targeted advertising, urging them to actually use these product holding displays. "Why hide NIVEA Cream like that?" an image of a typical pharmacy reads, where the product, highlighted in colour in the image, is "hidden away" and languishes unnoticed in various places of the pharmacy. Since 1927, the message the branded goods supplier sent to his retail partners was clear: actively control the sales process. "That's how it promotes and sells!" a 1929 brochure enthusiastically says of the display cabinet, which is said to have "helped double and triple NIVEA's sales". In the war years, production of the cream was reduced drastically and so was all advertising activity.

NIVEA's path to a modern display

In the 1950s, decorators used a lot of imagination to make shop window design as impressive as possible. The priority was to be noticed by passers-by rather than sell to them. "Don't forget your NIVEA!" the shop window said, another one reminded the potential holiday-maker to go on his journey "naturally with NIVEA". Posters with photos were placed next to the product in the shop window below colourful buntings and next to other amusing "show pieces" like the "NIVEA balloon" (an inflatable blue captive balloon with a gondola full of NIVEA sun care products. And the classic wooden "NIVEA cabinet" was used and developed further until 1964. Then everything changed. NIVEA's shift

III. | „DRAUSSEN ZUHAUSE": MARKENFÜHRUNG – AM POINT OF SALE | "AT HOME OUTDOORS": BRAND MANAGEMENT – AT THE POINT OF SALE

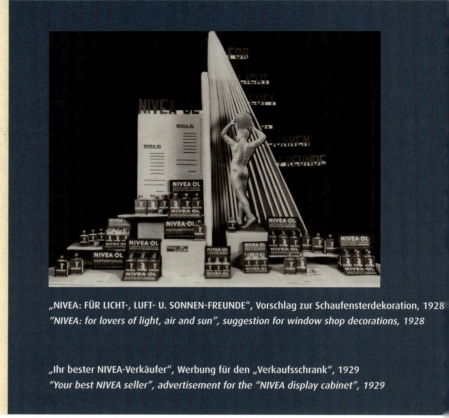

„NIVEA: FÜR LICHT-, LUFT- U. SONNEN-FREUNDE", Vorschlag zur Schaufensterdekoration, 1928
"NIVEA: for lovers of light, air and sun", suggestion for window shop decorations, 1928

„Ihr bester NIVEA-Verkäufer", Werbung für den „Verkaufsschrank", 1929
"Your best NIVEA seller", advertisement for the "NIVEA display cabinet", 1929

habe. Die Kriegsjahre, in denen die Creme schließlich nur noch als Notstandsprodukt gefertigt wurde, unterbrachen dann natürlich solcherlei Werbetätigkeit weitgehend.

Der Weg zum modernen Display

In den 1950er Jahren fokussierte sich die Phantasie der Dekorateure auf eine möglichst imposante Gestaltung der Schaufenster. Ziel war es noch immer, eher das Straßenbild zu beeindrucken, als direkt zu verkaufen. „NIVEA nicht vergessen!" hieß es hier, oder (zum Thema „Urlaub") „Natürlich mit NIVEA". Hier wurden neben der Ware Plakate mit Bildern eingesetzt, bunte Wimpel gespannt, heitere „Schaustücke" einmontiert wie der „NIVEA-Ballon" (ein aufblasbarer blauer NIVEA-Fesselballon, in dessen Gondel die Sonnenschutz-Produkte Platz genommen hatten) und dergleichen. Und bis 1964 wurde noch immer der klassische „NIVEA-Schrank" aus Holz fortgeführt und weiterentwickelt. Dann aber änderte sich alles. Bei „NIVEA" erfolgte die Geburt des direkt verkaufenden Displays absolut parallel zur Einführung der ersten Selbstbedienungsmärkte, also in der Mitte der 1960er Jahre.

Nun waren auffällige Veränderungen zu beobachten: Größere bunte Bodendisplays wurden erstmals eingesetzt, um Produkte im Markt zu positionieren. Hier taucht plötzlich die Wellpappe erstmals als neues Material für die Displayherstellung auf. Zur

to displays that needed no salesperson to sell the product coincided exactly with the opening of the first self-service stores in the mid-1960s.

Now was the time of striking changes. For the first time, larger colourful floor stand displays were used to launch products onto the market. Suddenly, corrugated cardboard was discovered as a new material in display production. Images of the "NIVEA ball" were used to decorate the displays. A typical model of the time was a two-tier floor stand display. It had a strong pedestal of offset printed corrugated cardboard, and its trays were big enough for a large number of small bottles and cans of "Zeozon" branded sun care and "NIVEA" products. The very large header card showing a "NIVEA ball" was an effective eye-catcher.

NIVEA launched its first real promotional campaigns in 1970. In order to remind consumers that they needed NIVEA products for their holidays the company installed an inflatable floating island in stores in the summer and a blue plastic bobsleigh in the winter of 1972. The island and the sleigh were surrounded by display stands or dump bins as well as plastic and metal baskets. In 1978, an inflatable blue canoe went into stores. which was more than three metres long and filled to the brim with NIVEA jars. All around it were different types of display stands and dump bins. What was also new was that NIVEA gave customers decorating tips, thus entering in strategic dialogue with retail marketing.

"NIVEA nicht vergessen!", Sommer-Schaufenster, Dekorationsvorschlag, 1955
"Don't forget your NIVEA!", suggestion for a summer shop window decoration, 1955

"8 x 4" und NIVEA, Sommer-Schaufenster, Dekorationsvorschlag, 1955
"8 x 4" and NIVEA, suggestion for a summer shop window decoration, 1955

Dekoration erscheint der „NIVEA-Ball" als Motiv auf den Displays. Ein typisches Modell dieser Ära war ein Bodenaufsteller: Auf einem stabilen Sockel aus offsetbedruckter Wellpappe waren zwei stufenförmige Tabletts aufgesetzt, die eine Vielzahl kleiner Flaschen und Dosen der Marken „Zeozon" (Sonnenschutzmittel) und „NIVEA" aufnehmen konnten. Das sehr große Aufsteckplakat mit dem Motiv des „NIVEA-Balls" war ein wirksamer Blickfang.

Ab den 1970er Jahren fanden dann richtige Verkaufsförderungsaktionen statt. NIVEA baute 1972 im Markt eine aufblasbare Bade-insel auf („Sommer") oder einen blauen Schnee-Bob aus Plastik („Winter", 1973), um an den Bedarf beim Urlaubsvergnügen zu erinnern. Um diese Themen-Inseln herum wurden dann Verkaufsständer oder Schütten aufgestellt, Körbe aus Kunststoff oder Metall. Ein blaues aufblasbares Kanu, das über drei Meter lang und randvoll mit Dosen befüllt war, wurde 1978 mit allerlei Verkaufsständern und Schütten kombiniert in den Märkten aufgebaut. Neu war auch, dass NIVEA seinen Kunden erstmals Dekorationsvorschläge anbot, also in einen strategischen Dialog mit dem Handelsmarketing eintrat.

Seit Ende der 1970er, Anfang der 1980er Jahre wurde der Absatzgedanke nochmals verstärkt. Nun wurden die neuen Stapelschütten eingesetzt, die einen raschen Abverkauf ermöglichen sollten. Sonderaktionen sollten die Produkte am Point of Sale weiter hervorheben. So wurde 1985 eine Sonderplatzierung mit

At the end of the 1970s and the beginning of the 1980s, the focus on sales promotion increased. New stackable trays were used to speed up the sale of NIVEA products. Special promotions aimed at drawing more attention to the product at the POS. 1985 saw the introduction of the "double deckchair" (and pallet displays) at retail. And in 1987, an amazingly realistic-looking pair of corrugated cardboard roofed beach chairs were set up in stores and filled with bottles of sun cream. From now on, promotional campaigns were designed to target the "impulse buyer". In 1994, a "cosmetically" white shelf display on rolls was specially designed for pharmacies to promote the young sub-brand "NIVEA Visage".

With the help of extensive POS campaigns, NIVEA and its sub-brands took the whole of Europe by storm. Small two-tier counter displays were designed for the launch of sub-brand "NIVEA Beauté" in 1999. A plastic tray kept the small nail polish bottles and slim powder compacts from falling over. If the store had no counter, a floor stand display for "NIVEA Beauté" was provided alternatively, which presented the counter display on an elegantly curved pedestal.

It was in the spirit of sustainability and economical and environmentally-friendly advertising that NIVEA designed in 2000 a multi-use prototype display, which could be used for various NIVEA brands. The four-tier display in the brand's typical blue read NIVEA on the front and had four trays, which were tilted slightly backwards. It could be used for various NIVEA products. Standardized header cards with images of sub-

III. | „DRAUSSEN ZUHAUSE": MARKENFÜHRUNG – AM POINT OF SALE | "AT HOME OUTDOORS": BRAND MANAGEMENT – AT THE POINT OF SALE

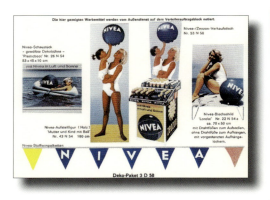

NIVEA-Ball, Hinweise zum Werbemittel-Einsatz, 1965
NIVEA ball, help for the use of advertising material, 1965

Bodendisplay mit doppelter Schütte, Wellpappe, um 1965
Two-tier corrugated cardboard floor stand display, around 1965

Bodendisplay, Drahtkonstruktion mit schwebendem NIVEA-Ball, 1964
Wire based floor stand display with levitating NIVEA ball, 1964

Ein Kajak als Schütte: Displays und Werbemittel (T-Shirts etc.) für den POS, 1978
Display with a canoe instead of a bin. Display and POS advertising material such as T-shirts, 1978

---

dem „Doppel-Liegestuhl" (und Palettendisplays) aufgelegt. Und 1987 wurde ein Pärchen von zwei täuschend echt als Strandkörben gestalteten Displays aus Wellpappe eingesetzt, die mit Sonnencreme befüllt waren. Spätestens jetzt war der „Impulskauf" das erklärte Ziel der Gestaltungen. 1994 wurde die junge Sub-Marke „NIVEA Visage" mit einem rollbaren Regal-Display in „kosmetischem" Weiß beworben, das speziell auf die Bedürfnisse der Apotheken zugeschnitten war.

NIVEA und ihre Sub-Marken traten, von umfangreichen POS-Kampagnen unterstützt, den Siegeszug in ganz Europa an. Für die erfolgreich gestartete Sub-Marke „NIVEA Beauté" waren dann 1999 als Thekendisplay zweistufig gearbeitete Displays im Dienst. Ein Kunststoff-Einsatz verhinderte das Umfallen der kleinen Nagellack-Fläschchen sowie der flachen Puderdosen. Stand keine Theke für einen solchen Aufbau zur Verfügung, dann konnte als Alternative ein Bodendisplay für „NIVEA Beauté" zum Einsatz kommen, das auf einem elegant geschwungenen Sockel das Thekendisplay präsentierte.

Ganz im Zeichen nachhaltiger und ökologisch sparsamer Markenwerbung stand 2000 die Entwicklung eines stabilen Universaldisplays, das mehrfach und vor allem auch für unterschiedliche Marken des Konzerns eingesetzt werden konnte. Das im typischen NIVEA-Blau gehaltene und frontal mit dem NIVEA-Schriftzug versehene

Palettendekoration mit NIVEA-Bällen, 1977
NIVEA balls for pallet displays, 1977

NIVEA-Marktstand als „Pflegecenter", Zweitplatzierung 1978
NIVEA "care centre" market stall, secondary placement 1978

Beispiel für Aktionsplatzierung, 1985
A NIVEA promotional campaign display, 1985

Verkaufsförderung mit der Strandkorb-Palette, 1987
Sales promotion with beach chair pallet displays, 1987

NIVEA Visage, rollbares Regaldisplay, 1994
NIVEA Visage shelf display on wheels, 1994

NIVEA (und Atrix), Universaldisplay mit auswechselbaren Aufsteckschildern, 2000
Universal display with exchangeable header cards for NIVEA and Atrix, 2000

Regal hält vier leicht nach hinten gekippte Regalebenen zur Warenaufnahme bereit. Die Befüllung kann mit unterschiedlichen Produkten erfolgen. Hierfür stehen standardisierte Aufsteckschilder zur Verfügung, die mit Fotomotiven diverse Sub-Marken bewerben, wie „NIVEA Hair Care", „NIVEA Bath Care", „NIVEA For Men", „NIVEA Soft" und sogar die eigenständige Handcreme-Marke „Atrix". Der Gedanke, durch Standardisierung die Zahl der Einsatzmöglichkeiten für ein Display zu erhöhen, zielt in die Richtung verminderter Aufwendungen für Transport, Lagerung, Logistik und die angestrebte Verminderung der damit verbundenen Emissionen von CO_2. Dem Recycling-Gedanken trägt darum die Konstruktion aus Monomaterialien Rechnung.

Im Jahre 2002 wurde dann das 1999 gefertigte Regaldisplay mit den vorstehenden Seitenwangen maßgeblich weiterentwickelt. Es blieb ein Palettendisplay mit dem markant-dynamischen Flankendesign des Regalaufbaus, der sich ja für unterschiedlichste NIVEA-Produkte bewährt hatte. Nun aber

brands like "NIVEA Hair Care", "NIVEA Bath Care", "NIVEA For Men", "NIVEA Soft" and even the independent hand cream "Atrix" could be attached to the display according to which product it promoted. A standard multi-use display was created that reduced transport, storage and logistical costs and thus contributed to reducing the company's CO_2 emissions. The use of mono-materials facilitated the recycling of displays.

A shelf display with protruding side panels designed in 1999 was substantially improved in 2002. It was still a pallet display with the typical distinctive and dynamic design of the shelf structure that had proved successful for selling all kinds of NIVEA products. But now, the display had an additional fold-out case in its base that held products for refill. And now posters with illuminated dimensional structures were attached to the displays. A warm "real light" shined out of a cosy ski hut that lit up the cold alpine scenery.

In 2002, a new type of display was designed for the entire range of "NIVEA Beauté" products. It was made of strong plastic and had

Regaldisplay (Weiterentwicklung) mit ausklappbarem Fach (Nachbestückung), oben: vorgeblocktes Motiv mit integriertem Licht-Effekt (Fenster leuchtet), 2002
Advanced shelf display variant with fold-out case for refill. Above: posters with illuminated dimensional structures (light shining through the window), 2002

NIVEA Beauté, zierliches Bodendisplay mit Aufsatz, der auch als Thekendisplay verwandt werden kann, 1999
Petite NIVEA Beauté floor display with attachment that could also be used as counter display, 1999

NIVEA Beauté, Verkaufshilfe für das gesamte Sortiment, Langzeitplatzierung, schwenkbar, Schweiz 2002
Display for the entire NIVEA Beauté product range, swivelling permanent display, Switzerland 2002

diente zusätzlich ein ausklappbares Gefach im Bodenbereich zur Entnahme von Waren zum Nachbestücken. Und das Plakat wurde nun mit einem vorgeblockten Motiv ausgestattet, das von innen illuminiert wurde. Stimmungsvoll leuchtete nun das Fenster der gemütlichen Skihütte mit „wirklichem Licht" aus der kalten Bergwelt der Alpen heraus.

Kaum mehr als Display zu bezeichnen war eine aus stabilem Kunststoff gefertigte Verkaufshilfe, in der 2002 das gesamte „NIVEA Beauté"-Sortiment als Langzeitplatzierung Platz fand. Die einzelnen Trays konnten während des Transportes in den Korpus integriert werden. Zur Beratung und Anwendung wurden dann einfach die entsprechenden Sortimente seitlich herausgeklappt. Zum einfacheren Handling in Drogeriemärkten und Kosmetikstudios dienten die integrierten Rollen.

Speziell für den Schweizer Markt wurde 2005 eine Langzeitdisplay-Platzierung „NIVEA Beauté" entwickelt, deren Etagenböden sich seitlich herausziehen ließen. Dekorative Kosmetik muss

little in common with a regular display. Its trays could be integrated individually into the display during transport. During consultation and demonstration, the tray with the chosen assortment could be simply pulled out from the side of the display. Wheels were integrated for the easy handling in chemist's stores and beauty parlours.

In 2005, a permanent "NIVEA Beauté" display was specially designed for the Swiss market. The lower trays pulled out sideways, because decorative cosmetics call for a decorative presentation. The display had a mirror, a box of "Kleenex" and an integrated light to allow customers to try the products right there in the store without a problem.

Co-branding – an issue also at the POS

Occasionally, strong brands get together for promotions. In 2009, the world famous lingerie designer Chantal Thomass created a make-up collection for NIVEA that stands for beauty and seduc-

eben auch dekorativ präsentiert werden. Spiegel, „Kleenex"-Box und eine integrierte Beleuchtungseinheit sorgten dafür, dass die Verbraucherinnen die Produkte im Handel problemlos ausprobieren konnten.

Co-Branding – Ein Thema auch für den Point of Sale

Starke Marken treten auch gelegentlich gemeinsam im „Doppel" auf. Zusammen mit der weltbekannten Dessous-Designerin Chantal Thomass hat NIVEA 2009 eine Make-up-Kollektion geschaffen, die für Schönheit und Verführung steht. Das Design der aus Wellpappe gefertigten Displays musste einerseits den Marken-Richtlinien der Dachmarke „NIVEA" voll entsprechen. Andererseits wurde die Gestaltung aber auch an das Design der Lingerie-Shops von „Chantal Thomass" angepasst. Mit seinen geschwungenen Formen und dem integrierten Spiegel griff das Display unverkennbar den Boudoir-Stil der Partner-Marke auf. Für kleinere Kaufhäuser und Drogeriemärkte wurde zusätzlich ein hierzu passendes Thekendisplay entwickelt. Mit viel Kreativität ließ sich für den Auftritt am Point of Sale eine anspruchsvolle, ästhetisch überzeugende Design-„Ehe" gestalten, eine gelungene Kombination des klassischen NIVEA-Auftritts mit dem Lingerie-Shop-Design von „Chantal Thomass". So konnte das Make-up auch im Handel zum sinnlichen Objekt der Begierde werden.

tion. The corrugated cardboard displays used to promote the collection needed to fully meet NIVEA's brand guidelines and at the same time adapt the design of the "Chantal Thomass" lingerie shops. With its rounded shape and integrated mirror, the display unmistakably reflected the boudoir style of NIVEA's new partner brand. A dedicated counter display was developed for small department stores and chemists. A great deal of creativity was involved in setting up an aesthetically convincing "design marriage" for the brands and their joint presentation at the POS. It successfully combined the classic NIVEA presentation with the lingerie shop design of "Chantal Thomass". Make-up thus became a sensual object of desire also at retail.

Pieter Nota

„Der Point of Sale ist die wichtigste Möglichkeit, direkt mit den Verbrauchern in den Dialog zu treten. Es ist wichtig, Marken am POS erlebbar zu machen und ein markengerechtes und in unserem Fall kosmetisches Umfeld zu schaffen. Neben einer emotionalen Ansprache muss sich der Verbraucher gut beraten fühlen. Mit unserer Marke NIVEA erreichen wir das im Handel mit übersichtlichen Produktpräsentationen, die auf die unterschiedlichen Verkaufskanäle abgestimmt sind und schnelle und einfache Orientierung bieten: Shop- in-Shop Systeme, unsere NIVEA Blue Wall oder NIVEA Themenplatzierungen."

Pieter Nota, Mitglied des Vorstands der Beiersdorf AG (Marketing / Forschung und Entwicklung / Vertrieb)

"The point of sale is the key opportunity to enter into direct dialogue with the customer. It is important to offer the customer a brand experience at the POS and create the right, in our case cosmetic, environment. The customer needs an emotional approach and the right assistance. We are doing that with our brand NIVEA by offering clearly arranged product presentations that are tailored to the needs of the individual retail formats and offer quick and easy orientation: shop-in-shop systems, our NIVEA Blue Wall or NIVEA displays that follow dedicated themes."

Pieter Nota, member of the executive board of Beiersdorf AG (Marketing, Research & Delelopment, Sales)

NIVEA Beauté, Langzeit-Display-Platzierung,
seitlich herausziehbare Böden, Schweiz 2005
*Permanent NIVEA Beauté display, its trays
pulled out sideways, Switzerland 2005*

NIVEA Beauté, Co-Branding mit „Chantal Thomass",
Theken- und Bodendisplay im Boudoir-Stil, 2009
*NIVEA Beauté, co-branding with Chantal Thomass,
boudoir style counter and floor stand displays, 2009*

NIVEA Visage, Pop-Up-Store, 2009
NIVEA Visage pop-up store, 2009

PHILIPS – Eine der ersten Design-Marken der Welt

Im niederländischen Eindhoven wurde am 15. Mai des Jahres 1891 von Gerard Philips die Firma Philips & Co. gegründet. Die ersten Produkte des jungen Unternehmens waren Glühlampen, die 1892 mit zehn Arbeitern hergestellt werden konnten. Das Geschäft mit dem elektrischen Licht, das damals noch gegen die Gasbeleuchtung konkurrierte, schien aussichtsreich. Die Firma expandierte, und Gerards Bruder Anton Philips trat 1895 in das Unternehmen ein. Im Zuge wachsenden Kapitalbedarfs wurde der Glühlampenhersteller dann 1912 in eine Aktiengesellschaft (niederländisch: Naamloze Vennootschap, N.V.) überführt. Von nun an hieß er „N. V. Philips' Gloeilampenfabrieken".

Der Weg von der einfachen Glühlampe zum Hersteller von elektrischen Geräten, Systemen, Unterhaltungs- und Medizintechnik war naheliegender, als man heute zunächst vermuten würde. Das Bindeglied war ein kleiner, aber elementarer „Baustein" der frühen Unterhaltungselektronik: die Radioröhre. Da Radioröhren damals auf der Grundlagentechnik der Glühlampe aufgesetzt waren, war die Glühlampenindustrie der vorgezeichnete Hersteller der weitaus komplexeren Röhrentechnik. Philips brachte schon 1918 seine erste Radioröhre auf den Markt. Damit war der Eintritt in die Welt der Unterhaltungselektronik erfolgt. Zu diesem Zeitpunkt arbeiteten bereits 4.000 Mitarbeiter für Philips. Das Unternehmen baute Vertriebsorganisationen in allen bedeutenden Absatzmärkten der Erde auf.

Nach dem Ersten Weltkrieg ging es mit dem Unternehmen rapide bergauf. In Berlin wurde 1926 die Deutsche Philips G.m.b.H. gegründet. Nur ein Jahr später konnte 1927 das Hamburger Unternehmen C. H. F. Müller übernommen werden, ein Hersteller von Röntgenröhren. Damit rundete sich nicht nur das Spektrum der Röhrenfertigung erfreulich ab, sondern es gelang damals bereits der Einstieg in das Feld der modernen Medizintechnik. Und „nebenbei" konnte man mit dieser Akquisition den eingeführten Markennamen „Valvo" übernehmen, der sich für Elektronenröhren etabliert hatte. Im gleichen Jahr 1927 präsentierte Philips dann auch das erste Philips-Radio und trat damit als kompletter Gerätehersteller in den neuen Markt der Unterhaltungselektronik ein.

PHILIPS – one of the world's first design brands

On 15 May 1891, Gerard Philips founded a company called Philips & Co. in the Dutch city of Eindhoven. Light bulbs were the first products that were produced by the young company and its ten workers back in 1892. The electric light business, at the time still competing with gas lighting, seemed to be a promising business. The company expanded, and Gerard's brother Anton Philips joined the business in 1895. To fund increasing capital requirements, the company was turned into a public limited company, or Naamze Vennootschap (NV) in Dutch. From then on, the company was called "NV Philips' Gloeilampenfabrieken.

The company's development from a light bulb manufacturer to a supplier of electrical appliances, systems, entertainment and medical technology was more obvious than one might initially think. The connecting link was a small, but fundamental component of early consumer electronics: the radio valve. Considering that at the time the idea of the radio valve was based on bulb technology, it was only logical that it should be the bulb industry to produce the much more complicated valve technology. Philips launched the first radio valve as early as 1918. That marked the company's entry into the world of consumer electronics. At the time, 4,000 people were already working for Philips. The company set up distribution companies in all key markets worldwide.

After the first world war, the company experienced rapid growth. In 1926, Deutsche Philips GmbH was founded in Berlin. A year later in 1927, the company succeeded in acquiring x-ray tube manufacturer C.H.F. Müller from Hamburg. That had the positive effect of rounding off the company's tube-producing range while at the same time marking its entry into modern medical technology. And, "en passant", the takeover allowed the company to acquire the existing brand name "Valvo", which had established itself as the name for electronic tubes. Also in 1927, Philips presented the first Philips radio, making the company the first comprehensive equipment producer to enter the new consumer electronics market.

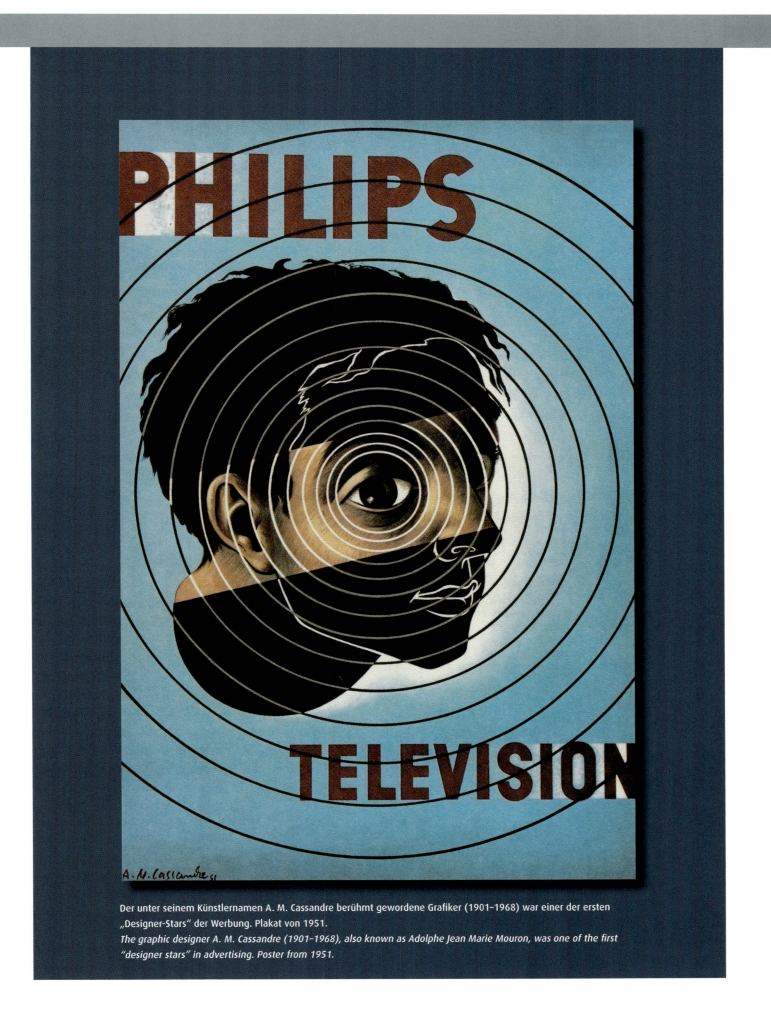

Der unter seinem Künstlernamen A. M. Cassandre berühmt gewordene Grafiker (1901–1968) war einer der ersten „Designer-Stars" der Werbung. Plakat von 1951.
The graphic designer A. M. Cassandre (1901–1968), also known as Adolphe Jean Marie Mouron, was one of the first "designer stars" in advertising. Poster from 1951.

III. „DRAUSSEN ZUHAUSE": MARKENFÜHRUNG – AM POINT OF SALE | "AT HOME OUTDOORS": BRAND MANAGEMENT – AT THE POINT OF SALE

Plakatgestaltung von Mathieu Clement, unter der künstlerischen Leitung von Louis Kalff, Holland 1928
Commercial poster created by Mathieu Clement under the creative direction of Louis Kalff, Holland 1928

Werbeplakat, 1958
Advertising poster, 1958

Marketing für eine neue Produktkategorie

Schon 1928 bewies Philips bereits sein Selbstverständnis als Markenartikler und Pionier der künstlerischen Produkt-Kommunikation. Ein Plakat, stilistisch von Kubismus und dem aktuellen „Art Déco" beeinflusst, wurde 1928 von Mathieu Clement gestaltet. Philips suchte in der Markenkommunikation schon damals spürbar die Nähe zur künstlerischen und gestalterischen Avantgarde. Kein biederes Glück im wohligen Heim ist das Thema, sondern Urbanität und der elegante Chic im puristischen Ambiente des (über die Stadt blickenden) Großstädters. Der Apparat (Typen 2501 und 2502) und seine Bauart treten hier bereits in den Hintergrund gegenüber einer emotionalisierten Aussage über einen zeitgemäßen Lebensstil.

Markenwerbung – Eine „künstlerische" Aufgabe bei Philips

Derartige Plakate spiegeln den prägenden Einfluss des damaligen Werbechefs Louis Christiaan Kalff (1897–1976), der 1925 zu Philips gekommen war. Kalff leitete damals die „Reclameafdeling" (Reklameabteilung) und hatte als „künstlerischer Leiter" ein gutes Gespür für Zeitströmungen. Schon 1926 brachte Kalff das erste Corporate Design für Philips heraus, das damals bereits die Sterne und die Äther-Wellen enthielt und zur Grundlage des legendären Philips-Logos wurde.

Und im Dezember 1928 hatte Kalff sich mit seinem Anliegen durchsetzen können, ein eigenes Kommunikationszentrum für

Marketing a new product category

As early as 1928, Philips demonstrated that it was exactly what it considered itself to be: a supplier of branded goods and pioneer of artistic product communication. That year, Philips asked Mathieu Clement to design a poster in the style of cubism and the "Art Déco" of the time. The company's brand communication was clearly already influenced by avant-garde art and design. Its communication centred around urbanity and the elegantly chic surroundings of the city slicker (and his view over the city) rather than on conventional happiness in the comfort of people's home. The Philips radio itself, and its design (types 2501 and 2502), were second to the emotionalised statement on a modern lifestyle.

Brand advertising – an "artistic" issue for Philips

Posters of the kind reflect the lasting influence the then advertising chief Louis Christiaan Kalff (1897–1976) had on the company's advertising. Kalff joined Philips in 1925 to head the "Reclameafdeling" advertising department. In his role as "artistic director" he proved to have a good feel for prevailing trends.

As early as 1926, Kalff developed the first corporate design for Philips, which featured the well-known ether waves and stars and became the basis for the famous Philips logo.

Then in December 1928, Kalff succeeded in persuading Philips to build a communications centre. The new centre was intended to have four

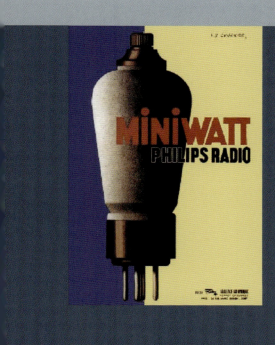

„Miniwatt", Design für Plakat und Produktverpackung (Radioröhren), A. M. Cassandre 1931
"Miniwatt", design for posters and product packs (radio valves), A. M. Cassandre 1931

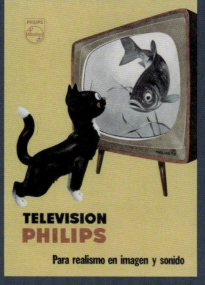

Anzeige für Fernsehgeräte, Apparatus Design Gruppe, 1950er Jahre
Advertisement for televisions, Apparatus Design Group, 1950s

Philips einzurichten. Das neue Zentrum sollte vier Abteilungen haben, jeweils eine für kommerzielle, literarische, technische und künstlerische Werbung.

Kalff war der Chef der künstlerischen Abteilung und dort für Plakatschöpfungen, Anzeigengestaltung, Broschüren sowie Messe-Auftritte und den damals bereits aufkommenden Bereich der Displays im Handelssektor verantwortlich. Seine Aufgabe war es, die verschiedenen Bereiche des Hauses durchgängig mit pointierten künstlerischen Grafikdesigns auszustatten und auch als eine Art „Wächter" für die generellen ästhetischen Aspekte der neuen Philips-Produkte zu fungieren. Dieses Aufgabenfeld war 1928 extrem fortschrittlich definiert.

Da sich Kalff – typisch für einen Kommunikationsmann in der Glühlampenindustrie – von Beginn an sehr für das Feld der neuartigen Leuchtreklame interessierte und hier mit Philips-Produkten auch erfolgreich aufzutreten beabsichtigte, wurde 1929 auch das „Lichtadvies Bureau", kurz „LIBU" aufgelegt.

Unter dem Eindruck des Crashs an der Wall Street 1929 schmolzen dann auch bei Philips die Budgets der Abteilungen deutlich zusammen. Und 1932 wurden die beiden Kommunikationsabteilungen wieder zusammengelegt. Erst 1966, als Philips unter dem Eindruck des anstehenden 75-jährigen Jubiläums sein Design analysierte und die Notwendigkeit der Einführung einheitlicher Design-Standards erkannte, wurden unter Knut Yran wieder ähnlich ambitionierte Anstrengungen in Richtung der Designentwicklung unternommen.

departments for commercial, literary, technical and artistic advertising. Kalff was the chief of the artistic department, where he was in charge of poster and advertisement design, brochures and exhibition appearance as well as the display business, which was starting to gain importance for retail. It was his task to develop outspoken artistic graphical designs for all of the company's divisions and act as a kind of "guardian", who made sure that new Philips products were designed according to the brand's basic aesthetic requirements. His job had an extremely avant-garde claim in 1928.

As one would expect from a communications expert of the light bulb industry, right from the beginning, Kalff was very much interested in the innovative field of illuminated signage and planned to successfully use the new form of advertising to promote Philips products. In 1929, he set up the "Lichtadvies Bureau", or "LIBU" for short.

In view of the Wall Street crash in 1929, budgets at the individual Philips departments were slashed. And in 1932, the company's two communications departments were consolidated into one again. It was only in 1966, after analysing its logo in view of the company's upcoming 75th anniversary, that Philips realised the need to introduce design standards. As a result, Philips once again invested ambitious efforts in the design of its products under the leadership of Knut Yran.

The first displays in the 1930s

One of the most famous artists to have worked with Philips is surely French avant-gardist A. M. Cassandre (1901–1968). And of course, as

III. „DRAUSSEN ZUHAUSE": MARKENFÜHRUNG – AM POINT OF SALE | "AT HOME OUTDOORS": BRAND MANAGEMENT – AT THE POINT OF SALE

Live-Marketing am Point of Sale: Philips setzte bereits 1937 beleuchtbare Holzdisplays ein.
Live marketing at the point of sale: Philips used illuminated wooden displays as early as 1937.

Die ersten Displays in den 1930er Jahren

Zu den berühmtesten Künstlern, die für Philips tätig wurden, zählt wohl insbesondere der französische Avantgardist A. M. Cassandre (1901–1968). Und natürlich – wie könnte es unter der Ägide eines Innovators wie Louis Kalff anders sein – wurden damals auch bereits erste Displays für den Handel gestaltet.

Historisch gesichert ist der Einsatz komplex gestalteter Holzdisplays, die bereits 1937 in den Elektro-Fachgeschäften aufgestellt wurden. Auf einer nach hinten ansteigenden „Tischplatte" waren dreißig Fassungen für Philips-Glühbirnen eingearbeitet, die unterseitig am Strom angeschlossen waren und einen eindrucksvollen, „lichtstarken" Testbetrieb an diesem „Manual" ermöglichten. Ein als Rückwand des Aufstellers angebrachtes Werbeschild pries die Vorteile des „Lichts", das man sich mit den Glühlampen nach Hause holen konnte. Der unterhalb der Präsentationsebene verbleibende Platz wurde genutzt, um hier Informationsbroschüren und Drucksachen unterzubringen. Philips suchte also schon in den 1930er Jahren den direkten Kontakt mit den Konsumenten.

Natürlich war damals – lange vor Einführung der Selbstbedienung – der Einsatz solcher Werbemittel sehr personalintensiv. Verbraucher durften damals erwarten, dass sie von am Produkt geschulten Fachkräften persönlich in den Gebrauch der neuartigen Glühbirnen eingewiesen wurden.

one should expect it would happen under the leadership of an innovator like Louis Kalff, the first displays for retail were designed as early as the 1930s.

In 1937, the first elaborately designed wooden displays were set up in electrical stores. The display consisted of a "tabletop", its front lower than the back, with thirty sockets for Philips light bulbs, powered by an electrical connection underneath the tabletop. The testing of bulbs at this "manual" had an "enlightening" effect. A promotional poster on the display's back card highlighted the advantages of the "light" customers could take home with them together with the light bulbs. The space underneath the tabletop was used to store information brochures and printing material. This shows that Philips sought direct contact to costumers already in the 1930s.

Naturally, at a time long before the introduction of self-service, using advertising means of the kind required a lot of personnel. Consumers could expect that trained staff that was familiar with the product would instruct them on how to use the new light bulbs.

Philips makes light bulb history

Later, trained retail staff was replaced by the proverbial "cardboard characters" for promotions in all stores. These characters, sometimes wrongly described as "silent salespersons", in truth provided retailers with a very eloquent way to efficiently evoke emotions and trust for the brand on a large space.

Display für eine der ersten Mikrowellen, späte 1970er Jahre
Display for one of the first-ever microwaves, late 1970s

Philips schreibt Display-Geschichte

Später sollte dann an die Stelle der verkaufsgeschulten Beratungskräfte bei den Promotions der flächendeckende Einsatz jener sprichwörtlichen „Pappkameraden" treten. Diese Figuren, die zu Unrecht auch als „stumme Verkäufer" bezeichnet wurden, waren in Wahrheit ein sehr beredtes Mittel, um effizient auf großer Fläche Emotionen und Vertrauen auf die Marke zu lenken.

Philips ist dafür ein gutes Beispiel. Erinnern wir uns: Ende der 1970er und zu Beginn der 1980er Jahre war die Zeit des großen Booms einer neu entwickelten Geräte-Kategorie: Die „Mikrowelle" eroberte sich ihren Platz in den modernen Küchen. Philips war von Anfang an dabei. Vielen Kunden, die sich um die Qualität der Speisen, den Erhalt der Vitamine oder sogar die Genießbarkeit des in der Mikrowelle erwärmten Essens sorgten, mussten Ängste genommen werden. Philips erkannte dies und setzte damals ein Bodendisplay ein, neben dem als Stanzfigur ein sympathischer „Chefkoch" zum Einsatz kam, der die wattstarke Leistung des beworbenen Geräts als professionell, ja meisterlich herausstellte: „Meisterleistung! 900 Watt. Für uns Chefköche schon lange selbstverständlich. Mit Philips jetzt auch im Haushalt." Nebenbei bewarb der Koch-„Meister" auch noch ein Preisausschreiben, das für Philips-Kunden eine zweiwöchige Fernreise in die USA auslobte. Im Mittelpunkt der Aufmerksamkeit stand jedoch das Produkt selbst, das mit Hilfe eines Displays in Szene gesetzt wurde.

Später wurden für Philips in den 1980er Jahren attraktive Bodendisplays eingesetzt, die beispielsweise als Sekundendisplay

Philips is a very good example for this. Let's remember: the late 1970s and the early 1980s witnessed the boom of a new category of electronic appliances. The "microwave" conquered the modern kitchens. Philips was involved in the movement right from the start. Customers were anxious about the quality and the preservation of vitamins of food that was warmed up in the microwave. Some even feared that it could not be eaten at all. These fears had to be calmed, and Philips was aware of that. A floor stand display was designed with the cut-out figure of a likeable chef praising the strong watt power of the promoted appliance as professional, fit even for a "maître de cuisine": "A masterpiece! 900 watt. A given for us chefs for long. Now brought by Philips to all households." At the same time, the "master" chef also promoted a contest offering a two-week journey to the USA as a prize for Philips customers. The spotlight, however, was on the product itself, promoted effectively by means of the display.

Later on, in the 1980s, Philips used attractive floor stand displays like a quick assembly cardboard display with an inclined bin. The display's

III. „DRAUSSEN ZUHAUSE": MARKENFÜHRUNG – AM POINT OF SALE | "AT HOME OUTDOORS": BRAND MANAGEMENT – AT THE POINT OF SALE

Bodendisplay, 1980er Jahre
Floor stand display, 1980s

Home Cinema, Manteldisplay für ein (interaktives) Originalgerät, 1998
Home Cinema, display for a real (interactive) Philips Home Cinema device, 1998

mit schräger Schütte gestaltet sein konnten. Die schwarze Grundfarbe und die raffiniert abgesetzte Farbgestaltung der weinroten Trays verraten bereits den gestalterischen Anspruch von Philips als „Design-Marke".

Für das „Philips Home Cinema" wurde dann in der Mitte der 1990er Jahre eine Sonder-Promotion auf die Fläche gebracht. Eine mehrteilige Displaystellwand, die eine gewisse Abschirmung herstellen konnte, fungierte als eine Art „Manteldisplay", in das dann ein Originalgerät eingebracht wurde. In gewisser Weise war diese Form des Displays bereits eine Art Vorläufer der „multisensorischen Konsumenten-Ansprache", wie sie 2008 zum Aufbau der PC-Peripheriegeräte zur „amBX"-Spieleserie von Philips eingesetzt wurde.

Attraktiv war 2008 die neue Verknüpfung von On- und Offline-Inhalten für die Test-Spieler. Licht, Sound, Vibrationen und sogar Ventilatoren, die Wind machen konnten, sorgten in der Spielkabine für ein authentisches Spielerlebnis. Ziel war es, den Kunden bereits beim wichtigen Erstkontakt mit dem Produkt nachhaltig zu faszinieren. So fängt die Haube des Bodendisplays den Sound auf, bildet einen guten Schallraum und ausreichend Platz für den integrierten Subwoofer-Lautsprecher. Eine mit dem Spielgeschehen gekoppelte Lichttechnik sorgt für ein variantenreiches Ambiente. Sogar die Handauflage der Tastatur vibrierte passend zum Streckenverlauf, und zwei integrierte Ventilatoren kühlten die erhitzten Fahrer. Das Display, das in allen großen Elektromärkten platziert wurde, lud zum Ausprobieren ein und machte Kunden zu echten Fans.

black ground colour and the cleverly contrasting colour of the wine-red trays already reflected Philips's graphical claim of being a "design brand".

A special promotion for retail was developed for the "Philips Home Cinema" in the mid-1990s. A multi-piece display wall worked as a display stand for a real Philips Home Cinema device, its side frames shielding the home theatre system from its surroundings. In a way, this display was a kind of forerunner of the "multi-sensory consumer approach" Philips took in 2008 to display the gaming peripherals needed for the "amBX" games at retail.

The combination of on and offline content was very attractive for test players in 2008. Light, sounds, vibrations and wind that was produced by ventilators in the games cabin created an authentic experience. Philips used this method to make a lasting impression on the customer at the important moment of initial contact with the product. The floor stand display's roof was designed to collect the sound, act as a sound chamber and offer sufficient room for the integrated subwoofer loudspeaker. Lighting effects linked to the game changed the atmosphere in the cabin according to the course of action. Even the keyboard's handrest vibrated according to the course of the game, and two integrated ventilators cooled the heated drivers. The display, which could be found in all major electronics stores, invited customers to try the game out and managed to turned them into real fans.

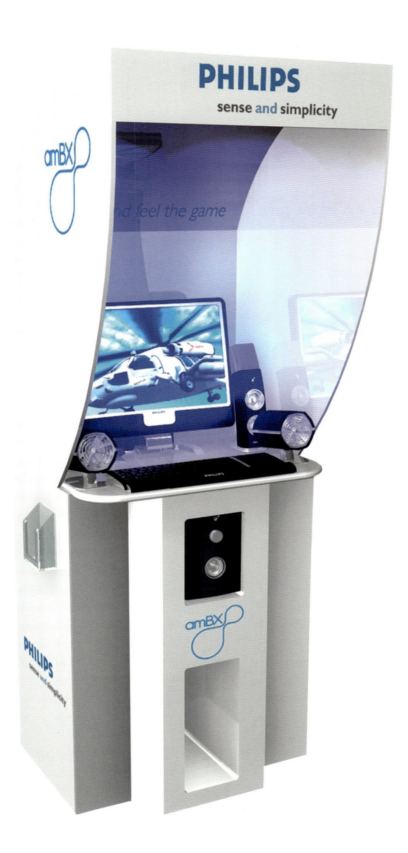

Spielserie „amBX", Multimediadisplay zur multisensorischen Konsumentenansprache (inklusive Ventilatoren und Boxen), 2008
The "amBX" games series, multimedia display offering a multi-sensory customer approach (including fans and speakers), 2008

Philips als Innovator des Sales Marketings

Bei einem Unternehmen, das die Geschichte des elektrischen Lichts und seiner Leuchtmittel begleitet und mitgeschrieben hat, verwundert es nicht, dass Philips nicht beim Einsatz attraktiver Displays stehen blieb, sondern neue, radikalere Konzepte einsetze, um die Marke nicht nur medial, sondern eben auch in der wirklichen Welt „ins rechte Licht" zu setzen und zu inszenieren. Die Welt der Features lässt die Marke bewusst hinter sich, setzt auf Emotionalisierung und dominante Gestaltung des „First Moment of Truth".

So wurde 1994 eine ambitionierte Ausstellung zum Thema „Fernsehen" auf die Beine gestellt, die die Prototypen aller Modelle hinaus in die Welt sandte, um eine Markenbotschaft zu positionieren. Eingeladen waren außer der Presse zu Diskussionsforen auch Designer und Design-Experten, um gemeinsam über die Zukunft des Fernsehens zu reden. Auf Großleinwänden wurden die Konzepte erläutert durch die Einspielung von Mission Statements namhafter Star-Designer wie Alessandro Mendini und Andrea Branzi oder des Philips-Designchefs Stefano Marzano. Gezeigt wurde „Television" auf der „Crossroads" in Wien (Museum für Angewandte Kunst), reiste 1994/95 durch halb Europa und hatte als dreidimensionale Inszenierung Auftritte in Mailand (Magna Pars), Paris (Centre Georges Pompidou) und Eindhoven (Evoluon).

Unter dem doppeldeutigen Motto „a brandnew shopping experience" bemühte sich Philips später noch stärker um die Gestaltung innovativer Erlebniswelten, die Markenwerbung und Shop-Erlebnis unter einem Dach zusammenführen konnten. Die Antwort war der „PHILIPS experience showroom", den Philips Singapur eröffnete. Hierzu wurde 2004 der bisherige Mitarbeiter-Shop umgebaut und völlig neu gestaltet.

Der alte Shop war in die Jahre gekommen. „It was also a location where customers could bring their products for service and redeem items connected with promotional activities. Nothing remarkable. It stayed the same for many years, obviously out-of-sync with the evolving Philips brand values." So der mit dem Redesign beauf-

Philips as an innovator of sales marketing

It is not surprising that a company that has accompanied and contributed to the history of electrical light with its lighting solutions would not stop at the use of attractive displays, but continue with new, more radical concepts that help create a setting that shows the brand "in the right light" not only in the media, but also in the real world. The brand deliberately neglects the world of features to focus on creating an emotional and lasting "First Moment of Truth".

In 1994, Philips organised an ambitious "television" exhibition that presented the prototypes of all models and delivered the brand's message to the world. Apart from the press, designers and design experts had been invited to take part in panels that discussed the television's future. The mission statements of famous star designers like Alessandro Mendini and Andrea Branzi as well as Philips design chief Stefano Marzano were shown on screens to explain the company's concepts. The "Television" exhibition was staged at the "Crossroads" in Vienna (the museum of arts "Museum für Angewandte Kunst"), toured half of Europe between 1994 and 1995 and included three-dimensional events in Milan (Magna Pars), Paris (Centre Georges Pompidou) and Eindhoven (Evoluon).

Under the ambiguous motto "a brand new shopping experience", Philips later increased efforts to create innovative experiences and events that combined brand promotion and shopping experience. These efforts produced the "PHILIPS experience showroom", which opened in Singapore in 2004 in the completely refurbished and remodeled Philips employee shop.

The former shop had become a bit long in the tooth. „It was also a location where customers could bring their products for service and redeem items connected with promotional activities. Nothing remarkable. It stayed the same for many years, obviously out-of-sync with the evolving Philips brand values," design director Cheaw Hwei said, who was in charge of the redesign of the shop. He had a new vision to change the way the shop was divided into what seemed to be five or six different brand shops in one. „It was almost like stepping into

„Television", Marken-Präsentation u. a. auf der „Crossroads" Wien, 1994/95
"Television", brand presentation as staged at the "Crossroads" in Vienna, 1994/1995

tragte Design-Director Cheaw Hwei. Seine Vision war es, vor allem die heterogene Aufteilung des alten Shops in separate Markenwelten zu verändern. „Es war fast als ob man in einen Laden von fünf oder sechs unterschiedlichen Marken getreten wäre. Man hatte sich sehr wenig Mühe gegeben, eine Markenwelt zu schaffen, wie sie der Marke gebührt. Es war höchste Zeit, etwas zu tun. „Wir waren der Meinung, dass der Shop die Entwicklung der Marke Philips und des Unternehmens als Ganzes zeigen müsse. So bot sich die ideale Gelegenheit, das gesamte Philips-Produktangebot auf eine gleichförmige Art zu zeigen, so wie es der ‚One Philips'-Philosophie entspricht."

Das Experiment war interessant. „Das Wichtigste was wir dabei lernten, war, dass es bei einer starken Markenwelt nicht darum geht, wie gut die mit der Markenwelt verbundenen physikalischen Merkmale reproduziert werden, sondern wie selbstähnlich die Touch Points grundsätzlich sind, die dieser Markenwelt zugrunde liegen. Versäumt man es, die Touch Points in Einklang zu bringen und zu inszenieren, kommt es zur ‚Fragmentierung der Markenwelt' und damit, letztendlich, zur ‚Marken-Schizophrenie'", sagt Cheaw Hwei. „Wenn sich die Marke jedoch erfolgreich durch die verschiedenen Touch Points ausdrückt, wird dem Konsumenten eine selbstähnliche und gesamtheitliche Markenwelt geboten."

Cheaw Hwei beschreibt den Raum der Handelsfläche metaphorisch als jenen Ort, wo der Konsument und die Marke sich entscheiden, miteinander eine Ehe einzugehen – oder eben nicht.

a shop of five or six different brands. There was a very little effort to create an experience befitting the brand." It was high time the shop was remodeled. "We felt that the shop should reflect the evolution of the Philips brand and of the company as a whole. It was also an ideal opportunity for us to showcase the Philips portfolio in a seamless fashion, in line with the One Philips philosophy."

It was an interesting experiment. „The most important thing it taught us is that a strong brand experience is not about how well we duplicate the physical elements linked to the experience, but about how essentially consistent the touch points that underpin that experience are. Failing to harmonize and orchestrate these leads to 'experience fragmentation' and, ultimately, 'brand schizophrenia,'" Cheaw Hwei said. "In Contrast, successfully articulating the brand through the various touch points means a consistent and total brand experience for the consumer".

Cheaw Hwei, metaphorically, describes the store as a place where the consumer and the brand decide to get married, or not.

Präsentationsdisplay der PHILIPS LIGHTING „Podium for the home" Leuchtenserie, Frankreich 2009
Display PHILIPS LIGHTING "Podium for the home" lamp series, France 2009

„Der Kunde ist da, weil die Marke schon irgendwie seine Aufmerksamkeit erregt hat und ihn in ihren Bann gezogen hat. An dieser Stelle wollen wir hören, wie der Kunde ‚Ja, ich will' zur Marke sagt, und es gibt eine Reihe von Dingen, die wir tun können, um den Kunden dazu zu ermutigen, genau diese Antwort zu geben."

Low Cheaw Hwei, senior account and design director Philips

„The customer is there because, in some way, the brand has already caught their attention and 'wooed' them. This is where we want to hear customers say 'I do' to the brand, and there are a number of things we can do to encourage that response."

Low Cheaw Hwei

Low Cheaw Hwei, senior account and design director Philips

Philips Experience Showroom (Singapur), konzeptioneller Flagship-Store für ein totales Marken-Erlebnis, Design von Low Cheaw Hwei, errichtet ab 2004
Philips Experience Showroom in Singapore, a concept flagship store for a complete brand experience, designed by Low Cheaw Hwei and opened in 2004

REXONA – Die weltweit größte Deo-Marke

Bei jüngeren Konsumenten schon wieder in Vergessenheit geraten ist die einst weltberühmte Markenseife, die unter dem Namen „Sunlicht" (im angelsächsisch geprägten Absatzraum „Sunlight" benannt) eine ganze Kategorie prägen und dominieren konnte. „Sunlicht" war einer der ersten globalen Markenartikel der Welt. Die Sunlicht Seifenfabrik AG wurde 1899 vom Briten William Hesketh in Mannheim/Rhein gegründet, nahm also in Deutschland ihren Anfang und entwickelte sich zu einem der führenden Seife-Hersteller weltweit. Die Unternehmensgeschichte ist wechselhaft. Sunlicht war ein wichtiger Nukleus der aufstrebenden Lever-Gruppe (England). Dann wurde die Firma im Zuge von Zoll- und Beschaffungsnöten zunächst ausgegliedert, 1924 aber von Lever Brothers Ltd. wieder zurück erworben. Von nun an berichtet Sunlicht Mannheim wieder nach London und wird in die sich zunehmend erweiternde Firmengruppe integriert, die wir heute als Konzern mit dem Namen „Unilever" kennen.

Die Marke „Rexona" wurde von diesem „Seifen-Riesen" zunächst als Seife eingeführt. Sie erblickte 1953 das Licht der Welt, herausgebracht von dem feinen Tochterunternehmen „Elida", das bereits 1932 von „Sunlicht" übernommen und in die Gruppe integriert wurde. Für das konzeptionell neuartige Produkt erwies es sich von Anfang an als Vorteil, dass mit „Elida" eine noble Dachmarke zur Verfügung stand, die alle Verwechslungen und Überschneidungen mit der preiswerten „Sunlicht"-Seife, einem Massenprodukt, ausschloss. Denn die luxuriöse „Rexona" war keine „normale" Seife. Sie war von Beginn an als kosmetisches Produkt mit desodorierendem Zusatznutzen ausgelegt. Dieser jedoch war damals noch höchst erklärungsbedürftig.

„Man selber merkt es nicht": die Entdeckung des „Körpergeruchs"

Gibt es hygienische Probleme, von denen man vielleicht selber gar nichts weiß? Aber sicher, sagte man sich im Hause Elida, nämlich das Problem mit dem Körpergeruch. Als 1953 die „Rexona"-Seife eingeführt wurde, war sie eine der ersten desodorierenden Seifen überhaupt. Noch, daran sei erinnert, stand das Thema des Körpergeruchs so direkt nach den Schrecken des Weltkriegs nicht

REXONA – the world's number one deodorant brand

A once world-famous soap brand unlikely to be remembered by younger customers is the "Sunlicht" soap (called "Sunlight" in the English-speaking markets), which has influenced and dominated an entire product category. "Sunlicht" was one of the first global branded products in the world. Founded by British born William Hesketh in Mannheim on the Rhine in 1899, soap maker "Sunlicht Seifenfabrik AG" had its beginnings in Germany and grew to become one of the world's leading soap makers. The company's history, however, is chequered. Sunlicht was a key part of the growing Lever Group in England. Due to customs and sourcing problems, the company was spun off only to be bought back by Lever Brothers Ltd in 1924. From then on, Sunlicht Mannheim once again reported to London and was reintegrated into the strongly expanding group known today as "Unilever".

This "soap giant" first used the brand "Rexona" for a soap. The soap was launched in 1953 by the group's subsidiary "Elida", which had been acquired and integrated by "Sunlicht" in 1932. Being a product with a new concept, it was an advantage for "Rexona" from the beginning to be part of the up-market brand "Elida". That ruled out any confusion or clash with the inexpensive mass product "Sunlicht" soap. The luxury "Rexona" soap was not any kind of "normal" soap. From the beginning, it was designed to be a cosmetic product with a deodorising effect. At the time, that was a complete novelty that called for some explanation.

"We ourselves don't notice" – the discovery of body odour

Are there unpleasant smells we are so accustomed to that we do not notice? For "Elida", body odour was clearly a problem. When "Rexona" soap was launched in 1953, it was one of the first soaps ever to have a deodorising effect. In times when the horrors of the world war were still present, body odour was not a big issue yet. Hygiene and cleanness were foremost on the minds of people in post-war Europe, which was still largely in ruins. For large parts of the population on both sides of the channel, to have an own bathroom was a pie in the sky.

That's why simple soaps like the reputable "Sunlicht" ("Sunlight") soap were needed. There was a market for the many soaps of that

Rexona war als erste desodorierende Seife im Markt eine absolute Innovation. Mit vollen Segeln ging die Marke von Beginn an auch am Point of Sale ins Rennen.
Bodendisplay, um 1960.
Rexona was the first deodorising soap and a complete novelty. Right from the beginning the brand sailed through the retail race, also at the point of sale. Floor stand display, around 1960.

III. | „DRAUSSEN ZUHAUSE": MARKENFÜHRUNG – AM POINT OF SALE | "AT HOME OUTDOORS": BRAND MANAGEMENT – AT THE POINT OF SALE

Rexona, Entwicklung des Packungsdesigns von 1953 bis um 1980.
How the Rexona soap's packaging changed between 1953 and 1980

im Mittelpunkt der hygienischen Ansprüche und Bedürfnisse. Vielmehr ging es im Schmutz des großenteils ja noch in Trümmern liegenden Europa um Sauberkeit und Hygiene. Ein eigenes Badezimmer – das war für weite Bevölkerungskreise auf beiden Seiten des Ärmelkanals damals noch Zukunftsmusik.

Einfache Seifen wie die althergebrachte „Sunlicht" („Sunlight") waren damals also notwendig und hatten ihren Markt. Davon jedoch gab es genügend Marken im Angebot. Warum sollten Kunden eine ganze Deutsche Mark für eine Seife wie „Rexona" ausgeben? Hier kam die Sache mit dem „Körpergeruch" ins Spiel. Auf jeder Seifenpackung stand wortreich zu lesen: „Diese zart duftende milde Toiletteseife enthält einen speziellen Wirkstoff, der nachhaltig desodoriert. Regelmäßiges Waschen mit Rexona gibt Ihnen den ganzen Tag die Sicherheit, frisch zu sein von Kopf bis Fuß, frisch – und frei von Körpergeruch."

Tatsächlich war die euphemistische Wortschöpfung vom „Körpergeruch" fast ebenso wertvoll wie die Erfindung der Seife selbst. Beides wurde ungefähr zeitgleich im Markt eingeführt und bekannt gemacht.

Elida schaltete Print-Anzeigen, in denen ab 1953 junge moderne Frauen gezeigt wurden, die als Trendsetter angesehen werden konnten. Eine junge Sekretärin an der Schreibmaschine war als Frau bereits emanzipiert genug, um ihr eigenes Geld zu verdienen.

kind. Why should customers spend a whole Deutsch Mark on a soap like "Rexona"? That is where the thing with the "body odour" came into play. The eloquent message on every pack of soap was: "This gently scented mild toilet soap contains a special deodorising substance for a lasting effect. Washing every day with Rexona will keep you fresh overall all day, fresh and free from body odour". Basically, the coining of the euphemistic term "body odour" was just as valuable as the invention of the soap itself. Both the term and the soap were introduced into the market and popularised more or less at the same time.

In 1953, Elida started to run advertisements in magazines and papers that showed young women considered as trend setters. A young secretary at her typewriter was emancipated enough to earn her own money. The advertisement featured a woman's arm pointing threateningly at the alarming headline: "You are still fresh now, but..." then it continues menacingly: "...are you sure you will stay fresh? Body odour can come at any time – you don't notice, but the others do. Better play safe and wash with Rexona, the mild toilet soap."

Those who did not wash risked isolation and social impoverishment. The phenomenon of deodorising still required aggressive advertising at the time. The intention was to highlight the problem with unrestrained candour. The launch of man-made fibre textiles like "Trevira" and "Nylon" (remember that Nylon shirts went down in history for making men sweat) then finally raised the public awareness for the

Zwei Anzeigen mit ermahnend-direkter Konsumenten-Ansprache, beide um 1955
Two advertisements taking a menacingly direct consumer approach, both around 1955

Ein in das Motiv hineinragender Frauenarm zeigt mahnend auf die bedrohlichen Worte der Headline: „Noch bist du frisch, aber..." Der Text mahnt dann eindringlich: „... aber bist du sicher, dass Du so frisch bleibst? Körpergeruch kann jederzeit auftreten – du selbst merkst es nicht, aber die anderen. Darum geh sicher – wasch dich mit Rexona, der milden Toiletteseife."

Dem Ungewaschenen drohte also Einsamkeit und soziale Verarmung. Noch musste für das Phänomen der Desodorierung massiv geworben werden. Es galt, das Problem mit hemmungsloser Offenheit in den Fokus zu stellen. Doch spätestens mit dem Aufkommen von Textilien aus Kunstfasern wie „Trevira" und „Nylon" (die „Nylon"-Hemden gingen ja als „schweißtreibend" in die Geschichte ein) rückte das spezifische Leistungsprofil der desodorierenden Seife auch beim Publikum in den Mittelpunkt. Rexona war nun ein Spezialist für diesen Punkt der Körperpflege geworden. In der Printwerbung hieß es nun: „Wenn ich ein Problem mit Körpergeruch habe, dann hilft nur Rexona." Fast zwangsläufig entwickelte sich aus dieser Kernkompetenz auch das erste Deodorant.

Ein Innovator des Deodorants

Die Deodorants sollen übrigens auf die chemische Entwicklung eines australischen Pharmazeuten zurückgehen, der „Rexona" gemeinsam mit seiner Frau erfunden habe. Sie wurden im Jahre 1960

specific benefits of the deodorising soap. Rexona had now become a specialist for this particular aspect of grooming. The print advertisement now said: "Whenever I have a body odour problem, Rexona helps". The brand's core competence was to almost inevitably produce the first deodorant.

An innovator of deodorants

Deodorants, by the way, are said to go back to the chemical development of an Australian pharmacist who is claimed to have invented "Rexona" together with his wife. Deodorants launched for the first time in 1960. In 1965, "Rexona" for women was launched in Europe on a large scale. The brand was first sold as a deodorant spray (aerosol technology), but was available also as roll-on and squeeze spray. By 1968, deodorant sprays came in three different fragrances. Anti-perspirants were added in 1971. In 1977, the first glass roll-ons were launched. Their bigger roller "balls" offered higher reliability. The deodorant stick was added to the product range in 1984. As a result of the aerosol spray debate, Rexona extended the product range to include environmentally-friendly pump sprays in 1988. At the same time a roll-on was launched for the men's line "Original for men". The brand, which had become somewhat "old-fashioned" in the 1980s, was successfully relaunched with a harmonised image across Europe in 1995. Rexona's sales have increased fivefold since then.

"Deo-Lotion", Anzeige 1971
"Deo-Lotion", advertisement 1971

herausgebracht. Im Jahre 1965 gab es für Rexona für Frauen einen umfassenden Launch in Europa. Die Marke wurde nun erstmals als Deo-Spray (Aerosoltechnik), daneben aber auch als Roll-on und als Squeeze-Spray angeboten. Das Deo-Spray wurde schon 1968 auf drei Duftvarianten erweitert. Ab 1971 folgten dann die Anti-Transpirantien. Schon 1977 wurden die ersten Roll-on-Packungen aus Glas eingeführt, die mit ihren neuen, größeren Deo-„Bällen" eine höhere Anwendungssicherheit boten. Der Deo-Stick wird 1984 in die Range integriert. Schließlich wurde die Produktpalette von Rexona 1988 im Zuge der Debatte um die Aerosol-Sprays durch umweltfreundliche Pump-Sprays erweitert. Gleichzeitig wird als Herrenlinie „Original for men" als Roll-on gelauncht. Die Marke, die dann in den 1980er Jahren etwas „in die Jahre gekommen" war, wurde 1995 europaweit erfolgreich harmonisiert und re-launcht. Seitdem haben sich Umsätze mit Rexona verfünffacht.

Die Marke mit den vielen Markennamen

„Rexona", so heißt das größte Deodorant der Welt, allerdings: nur in Europa und Lateinamerika. In Großbritannien nämlich lautet der Markenname des Produkts „Sure", verspricht also Sicherheit. In Nordamerika dagegen heißt die gleiche Marke „Degree",

The brand and its many brand names

The world's leading deodorant was called "Rexona", but only in Europe and Latin America. In the UK, the brand name was "Sure", promising reliability. In North America, the same brand was called "Degree", possibly because it prevented sweating even at high temperatures. In Asia Pacific, the brand freed customers of sweat and body odour under the name of "Quest". Using different brand names in different markets is not unusual in marketing. Even though marketers may see this practice as a hindrance, it respects the developments in the world's culturally distinct regions.

The "Rexona" brand is split not only into geographic regions, but also into different target groups. Several sub-brands cater to the distinct

Der „Tick" ist weltweit identisch, der Markenname variiert.
The "tick" is worldwide identical, the brand name changes.

vielleicht weil sie auch bei heißeren Temperaturgraden vorm Schwitzen bewahrt. Im asiatischen und pazifischen Teil der Welt hingegen bewahrt dieselbe Marke unter dem Namen „Quest" ihre Kundschaft vor Schweiß und Körpergeruch. Derlei Splits sind in der Welt des Markenartikels nicht ungewöhnlich. Auch wenn das Marketing sie oft als hinderlich empfindet, zollen sie den kulturellen Entwicklungen in unterschiedlichen Weltgegenden Respekt.

Die Marke „Rexona" ist indessen nicht nur nach Weltregionen, sondern auch nach Zielgruppen aufgeteilt. Unterschiedliche Sub-Brands greifen das Lebensgefühl verschiedener Alters- und Geschlechtergruppen auf. Darum gibt es heute getrennte Auftritte von „Rexona women", „Rexona men" und „Rexona girl".

Marketing

Seit 1970 arbeitet Rexona mit dem Line: „It won't let you down" („Rexona lässt Dich nicht im Stich"). In der Grafik etablierte sich als Markenkennung 1990 europaweit der so genannte Rexona-„tick", ein grafisches Symbol, das einem Haken ähnelt.

Die Themen der Markenkommunikation von Rexona spiegeln die gesellschaftliche und soziale Entwicklung im Umgang mit Körperhygiene wider. In den 1970er Jahren stand immer noch das Thema der gesellschaftlichen Sicherheit im Fokus. Die Werbung stellte heraus, wie man sich mit Rexona auch bei hochstehenden gesellschaftlichen Anlässen sicher fühlen kann. Akteure in den

lifestyle needs of various age and gender groups. Today there are sub-brands like "Rexona women", "Rexona men" and "Rexona girl", each with its own presentation.

Marketing

Since 1979, Rexona has been working with the line: "It won't let you down". The so-called Rexona "tick", a mark used to check off or call attention to an item, was added to the graphics in 1990 as a brand characteristic across Europe.

Rexona's brand communication reflects the changing social and societal attitudes towards personal care. In the 1970s, the focus was still on social acceptance. The brand's advertising conveyed the message that Rexona allowed people to feel at ease even at important social events. The protagonists in the TV commercials are self-confident, independent women. The first TV commercial for deodorant sprays in Germany was broadcast in 1971, while a dinner party spot was shown on English televisions as early as 1960. In the 1980s, advertising focused on sweat-inducing physical exertion and sports, a line that was continued in the early 1990s.

From now on, the Rexona "tick" appeared in all brand design and advertising. Steffi Graf became the face of the Rexona campaign. Two commercials featuring the German tennis star were broadcast. Then in the mid-1990s, the so-called "tick test" became part of the brand's communication and proved to be a highly effective promotional tool

III. „DRAUSSEN ZUHAUSE": MARKENFÜHRUNG – AM POINT OF SALE | "AT HOME OUTDOORS": BRAND MANAGEMENT – AT THE POINT OF SALE

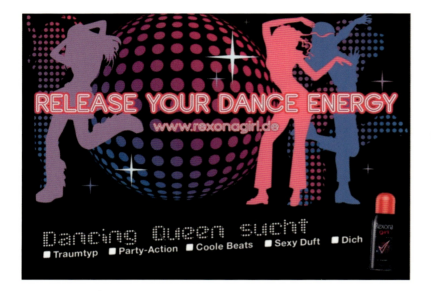

ABBA lässt grüßen: Rexona Girl ließ 2008 disco-begeisterte „Tanz-Königinnen" nach dem „perfekten Typ" und einem „Sexy Duft" suchen…
Almost like ABBA: in 2008, Rexona Girl sent disco-loving "dancing queens" out to find the "perfect guy" as well as a "sexy scent"…

„Fan Pack" zur Weihnachtszeit (mit Beach Bag), abgestimmt auf die Tanz-Promotion der Sub-Marke „Rexona Girl"
The "Fan Pack" (with beach bag) launched for Christmas that accompanied the "Rexona Girl" sub-brand's dance promotion campaign

---

TV-Spots sind selbstsichere, unabhängige Frauen. In Deutschland geht 1971 der erste TV-Spot über den Äther („Deo Spray"), während in England bereits 1960 ein Spot (zum Thema „Dinner-Party") lief. In den 1980er Jahren wurde dann das Schwitzen aufgrund von körperlicher Anstrengung und bei Sport-Aktivitäten aufgegriffen und zu Anfang der 1990er Jahre weitergeführt.

Im Markendesign und in der Markenwerbung erscheint ab nun als grafisches Symbol der Rexona-„tick". Als Testimonial für Rexona wird Steffi Graf gewonnen. Zwei TV-Spots mit dem deutschen Tennis-Star wurden ausgestrahlt. Ein nachhaltig werbewirksames Motiv war der so genannte „Tick-Test", der ebenfalls Mitte der 1990er Jahre in der Kommunikation eingeführt wird. Die Idee: Unter Verwendung einer Schablone wird der Protagonistin des TV-Spots ein „Tick" aufgesprüht. In der Wüste schwitzt die Protagonistin, jedoch der mit Rexona eingesprühte „Tick" auf ihrer Haut ist gänzlich trocken und blieb ohne Schweißtropfen. (Diese Werbung ist bis heute eine der am besten wieder erkannten TV-Spots dieser Marke).

Innovativ war dann der am Ende der 1990er Jahre allmählich inszenierte Übergang zu einem neuen Thema, nämlich dem „men-

with a lasting effect. This was the idea: a woman is sweating heavily in the desert, but the Rexona-sprayed "tick" on her skin is completely dry and without a single drop of sweat. (This commercial is still one of the brand's best-remembered TV commercials).

An innovation in the late 1990s was the brand's gradual shift to the new topic "mental sweat" as a result of stress and fears. A print advertising campaign for men was run in Germany in 2000 that included the sexually evocative advertisement about "90 minutes".

In 2001 and 2002, Rexona found yet another way to talk about sweating. This time "emotional sweating" is integrated into its brand communication. As part of its sponsorship of the TV series "POPSTARS on Stage", Rexona chose dancing trainer Detlef D! Soost as the face of the "Rexona girl" campaign. And when the casting mania reached its peak in Germany in 2008, a female contestant from the casting show "Germany's Next Topmodel" was featured in Rexona advertisements together with Heidi Klum.

Many famous tennis stars were among the faces of Rexona campaigns in several international markets. In Australia, tennis players like Björn Borg and Ivan Lendl appeared in the campaigns as well as

Für die Sub-Marke „Rexona Girl" wurden 2007 unter der Ägide des Tanz-Trainers Detlef D! Soost junge Mädchen für einen Werbe-Tanzspot gecastet. Und „Hello Kitty" drückte „ganz fest die Daumen".
For the sub-brand "Rexona Girl", dancing trainer Detlef D! Soost casted young girls for a dance commercial in 2007. And "Hello Kitty" "kept fingers crossed" for the contestants.

talen" Schwitzen als Folge von Stress und Ängsten. So startet im Jahr 2000 die Printwerbung für Männer in Deutschland mit dem erotisch-anspielungsreichen Print-Motiv „90 Minuten".

Einen neuen, nochmals anderen Weg, über das Schwitzen zu sprechen, findet Rexona in den Jahren 2001 bis 2002. Nun wird das Thema „emotionales Schwitzen" in die Kommunikation integriert. Im Rahmen des Sponsorings der TV-Staffel „POPSTARS on Stage" wurde 2007 für „Rexona girl" der Tanz-Trainer Detlef D! Soost als Testimonial verpflichtet. Und als die Casting-Welle in Deutschland ihren Höhepunkt erreichte, wurde 2008 eine Kandidatin aus der Casting-Show „Germany's Next Topmodel" mit Heidi Klum zum Modell eines Rexona-Printmotivs.

Für Rexona wurden in zahlreichen internationalen Märkten zumeist die bekannten Sport-Stars als Testimonials aktiv: In Australien Tennisspieler wie Björn Borg oder Ivan Lendl oder der Leichtathlet Carl Lewis. In Europa Tennis-Stars wie Guy Forget (1987) oder in den 1990ern Steffi Graf. Und in Südamerika (Brasilien) 2006 – im Jahr der Fußball-Weltmeisterschaft – der beliebte Fußballer Ronaldinho.

track athlete Carl Lewis. In Europe, tennis stars like Guy Forget (1987) and Steffi Graf (in the 1990s) acted as spokespersons for the brand. And in South America, the popular footballer Ronaldinho was the Rexona face in the World Cup year 2006.

Rexona – a pioneer of sales marketing

Rexona was one of the very first branded goods suppliers to go into stores with attractive floor stand displays. The brand started with a display that consisted of a bin on top of a massive pedestal featuring the typical "Rexona wave". A header card was attached to the back of the bin that promoted the elegant soap.

In the early sales marketing years, the issues free time and boats dominated the brand's advertisements for years. In the 1960s, various floor stand displays centred around boats. Rexona once attracted a large amount of attention by putting a real boat into stores. A plastic boat with the Rexona logo was simply placed on top of a two-piece corrugated cardboard pedestal so that it could be used as a bin for Rexona products. A sail-like poster was attached to the boat's wooden paddle. In its brand communication, Rexona said at

| III. | „DRAUSSEN ZUHAUSE": MARKENFÜHRUNG – AM POINT OF SALE | "AT HOME OUTDOORS": BRAND MANAGEMENT – AT THE POINT OF SALE |

Bodendisplay als Segelschiff, am Mast gab eine echte Blinkleuchte Signal, 1960er Jahre
Sailing boat floor stand display, a real flashing light on its mast sending out signals, 1960s

Bodendisplay als einfache Schütte, 1960er Jahre
Simply dump-bin, 1960s

Bodendisplay mit aufblasbarem Paddelboot auf Wellpappe-Sockel, 1960er Jahre
Floor stand display with an inflatable canoe on a corrugated cardboard pedestal, 1960s

„New Rexona", Live-Marketing auf
dem schwarzen Kontinent, Bodendisplay,
1970er Jahre
*Live marketing for "New Rexona" on
the black continent, floor stand display,
1970s*

Rexona – Ein Pionier des Sales Marketings

Rexona gehört zu den frühesten Markenartiklern, die mit attraktiven Bodendisplays die Supermärkte betraten. Den Anfang machte ein massiver, von der typischen „Rexona-Welle" geschmückter Sockel, der eine Warenschütte trug. Hinter diesem wurde ein Aufsteckplakat angebracht, das die elegante Seife bewarb.

Eine über Jahre durchlaufende Werbe-Idee kreiste dann in der Frühzeit des Sales Marketings um das Thema Freizeit und Boot. Man realisierte hierzu in den 1960er Jahren verschiedene Bodenaufsteller mit einem Boot. Aufmerksamkeit garantierte beispielsweise der Einsatz eines echten Boots im Handel. Dafür montierte man einfach ein wassertaugliches, aber werblich bedrucktes Kunststoff-Boot auf einen zweiteiligen Sockel aus offsetbedruckter Wellpappe, so dass es als Warenschütte dienen konnte. Das Holzpaddel hält ein als Segel ausgebildetes Plakat. „Diese Konstruktion", so hieß es in der damaligen Werbekommunikation, „hat einen besonders hohen Werbewert, da das Boot später in den Bädern usw. weiterhin für das Produkt wirbt."

Später konnte man auf das Kunststoffboot verzichten. Nun gestaltete man auf elliptischem Grundriss einen schnittigen, vom Boden aufragenden Aufbau, der unter einem Segelboot auch die plätschernden Wellen illustrierte. Das Boot besteht nun aus offsetbedrucktem Karton. Die Spitze bildete eine rote, batteriebetriebene Blinkleuchte.

Modern und ansprechend präsentiert sich fast ein halbes Jahrhundert später die Deo-Range. Als vor eine Rückwand montierte halbrunde Tonne präsentierte sich 2008 ein schwarzes Bodendisplay für „Rexona girl". Dessen Form war ein Zitat des Verpackungs-designs der Deo-Packung. Die Grafik zeigte ein junges Mädchen, das als Schattenriss beim Tanzen zu sehen war. Die Markenbotschaft, die die Girls an ihre (möglicherweise „schweißtreibenden") abendlichen Auftritte in der Disko erinnern sollte, lautete: „Release your Dance Energy!".

Rexona blieb im Einsatz von Dipslays immer innovativ. Im Jahre 2008 brachte man zur Unterstützung des Launchs von Rexona „Roll-ons" ein ovales Palettendisplay in die Märkte, das optisch an die ovale

the time that "this construction has a particularly strong advertising effect because the boat will later continue to promote the product in bathrooms etc.".

Later, Rexona could do without the plastic boat. A racy superstructure was designed that towered over an elliptical pedestal holding a sailing boat and presenting an imitation of splashing waves underneath it. This time the boat was made of corrugated cardboard. Right at the top was a battery powered flashing light.

Almost half a decade later, Rexona chose a modern and attractive way to present its deodorants range. A black floor stand display for "Rexona girl" was designed that had a back panel with a half-round barrel in front. It repeated the design of the deodorant's package. The pack featured the silhouette of a dancing young girl. The brand's message to the girls during their (possibly sweat-inducing) visits to the clubs was: "Release your Dance Energy!"

Rexona was also innovative in its use of displays. To support the launch of Rexona "roll-ons" in 2008, an oval pallet display was introduced into stores that mimicked the product's oval pack and had three trays. A key advantage of the inverted roll-on was that it could be used immediately and "smoothly". The clever bit was a battery powered rotating roll-on that was positioned at the top of the display to visually illustrate the important "upside down" effect. The 118 shape display could be used for roll-ons from both the men's and the women's lines.

Another creative "shape display" was designed in 2009. It supported the "Rexona Women" line by representing the shape of a dress up paper doll that had been used in media advertising. The animated dress up doll is the protagonist of an international TV spot for the Rexona "Women Skin Care" product. The dress up doll was created by an agency in Argentina. The doll seemed to be the right vehicle to talk about "skin irritations in the armpit area". The dress up doll that women around the world know from their childhood days and stands for "sensitivity" and "fragility" was used to communicate with customers. With the dress up paper doll the agency created a feminine world all of its own.

The dress up doll then became the hero of a special display introduced by the brand's POS agency in Germany to promote the new range at

Packungsform erinnerte und zugleich drei Trays zu tragen vermochte. Ein zentraler Vorteil des auf dem Kopf stehenden Roll-ons ist die sofortige und „geschmeidige" Anwendbarkeit. Der Clou: Um den wichtigen „Upside-Down"-Effekt anschaulich darzustellen, ist im oberen Bereich des Displays ein Roll-on angebracht, der sich batteriegetrieben dreht. Das 118er Shape-Display konnte sowohl mit Roll-ons für Männer als auch mit solchen der Frauen-Linie befüllt werden.

Ein anderes kreatives „Shape-Display" stammte aus dem Jahre 2009. Es unterstützte die Serie „Rexona Woman", indem es die Gestalt einer in der medialen Werbung bereits eingeführten Anzieh-Puppe aus Papier annahm. Eine solche Anziehpuppe wird, zeichentricktechnisch animiert, zur Protagonistin eines internationalen TV Spots für das Produkt Rexona-„Women Skin Care". Die Anziehpuppe wurde von der argentinischen Kreativagentur ins Leben gerufen, weil sie als besonders geeignet erschien, über das Problem der „Hautirritationen im Achselbereich" zu sprechen. So gelangte man zur Kommunikation über jene Anziehpuppe, die „Frau" aus eigener Kindheit überall in der Welt kennt und die für „Empfindlichkeit" und „Zerbrechlichkeit" steht. Über die Anziehpuppe aus Papier schuf die Kreativagentur eine feminine Welt.

Die deutsche POS-Agentur machte die Anziehpuppe dann zur Heldin des Sonderdisplays, das zum Launch der neuen Range bei einem Handelspartner platziert wurde. Angeboten wurde hier ein spezieller „Duo-Pack" mit einer Gratis-Beigabe (einem „Post-it"-Block im Design der Anziehpuppe). Verzahnung von medialer Werbung mit dem Point of Sale: Diese Kampagne zeigte, wie es optimal gelingen kann, die Verbraucherinnen zu emotionalisieren. Längst können Marken wie Rexona mit attraktiven Displays auch komplexe Emotionen und subtile Gestaltwelten hinaus zum Kunden an den Point of Sale tragen. Das Display hat sich damit eine neue Rolle erobert. Es ist längst nicht mehr nur der „rohe" Absatz-Dynamo, der die Vertriebsmaschine beim Handel „motorisch" zum Laufen bringt. Längst hat das Display gelernt, auch komplexe, emotionale Aussagen konform zum Wording der Markenkommunikation zu formulieren. Das Display liefert heute nicht nur Waren, sondern auch Bilder und Gefühle an den Point of Sale. Es hat damit seine Rolle als gleichwertiges, je teilweise sogar überlegenes Werkzeug im „Marketing-Mix" neben den etablierten Medien (Print, Internet, TV) unter Beweis gestellt. Der sinnliche Kontakt mit dem Produkt, die physische Nähe zu dessen Verkauf, aber auch das stimulierende Wettbewerbsumfeld machen das Display (und überhaupt alle Ansätze einer markentypischen Regalgestaltung im Handel) zu einem unverzichtbaren Partner von Marken, dessen Bedeutung gar nicht überschätzt werden kann. Aus der einstmaligen „Nebenleistung" des Marken-Vertriebs ist so über die Jahre ein echtes „Medium of Excellence" geworden.

the stores of one of the brand's retail partners. Customers could buy a special "duo pack" that offered a post-it note pad giveaway with a dress up doll design. This campaign shows how to perfectly integrate media advertising at the POS while at the same time offering customers an emotional experience. It is matter of fact for Rexona today to convey even complex emotions and subtle design arrangements to customers with its attractive displays.

The display has taken on a new role. It has long shed its image of being a mere "rough" sales "motor" engine that kick-starts the machinery of selling at retail. Today, the display knows how to transport even complex emotional statements that conform with the wording of brand communication. Today's displays offer not only goods, but also ideas and feelings at the POS. The display has proved to be an equally important, in cases even superior, "marketing mix" tool next to established media like print, Internet and TV. By offering direct physical contact with the product, the display appeals to the customer's senses. It also creates a stimulating competitive environment at retail. This shows that the importance of the display as an indispensable partner of brands can simply not be overestimated. Once a mere "side effect" of brand distribution, the display today is a true "medium of excellence".

> „Rexona ist eine Marke, die mit dem Leistungsversprechen von Körperpflege und Hygiene ihre Kunden ganzheitlich anspricht. Darum legen wir im Marketing auch besonderen Wert darauf, dem Kunden im realen Leben in einer realen Kaufsituation zu begegnen, statt unsere Kommunikation nur Brechung durch einzelnen Medien zu überlassen. Wir sind uns unserer Ro als Pionier des Displays voll bewusst und werden weiterhin mit Innovatio den Point of Sale zum Ort der emotionalen Verbraucheransprache mache
>
> *Harry Brouwer, Chairman Unilever Deutschland, Österreich und Schweiz*

Harry Brouwer

> "The Rexona brand with its commitment to personal care and hygiene tak an holistic approach towards the customer. That is why we place particul emphasis on meeting and engaging the customer in real life, in a real sho ping situation, instead of leaving our communication to the abstract app rance in the different media. We are very much aware of our role as a dis pioneer and will continue to drive innovation to make sure the point of sa a place that offers the customer an emotional experience."
>
> *Harry Brouwer, Chairman Unilever for Germany, Austria and Switzerland*

Rexona Girl, Bodendisplay 2006
Rexona Girl, floor stand display 2006

Rexona Girl, „Dance Energy", Bodendisplay 2008
Rexona Girl, "Dance Energy", floor stand display 2008

Rexona, ovales Shape-Regaldisplay in Form der Packung mit rotierendem Deo im Plakat, 2008
Rexona, oval shelf display repeating the product pack's oval shape, with a rotating roll-on on the back card

Shape-Regaldisplay in Form der Packung, 2009
Shelf display repeating the product pack's shape, 2009

Shape-Regaldisplay in Form der Packung, 2009
Shelf display repeating the product pack's shape, 2009

Rexona Woman, Bodendisplay mit Konturfigur einer nostalgischen Anzieh-Puppe, passend zur Promotion 2009
Rexona Woman, floor stand display featuring the cut-out figure of an old-fashioned dress up paper doll, 2009

RICOLA – Vom Nischenprodukt zum Weltmarktführer

Im kleinen Örtchen Laufen bei Basel ist ein weltweit erfolgreicher „Global Seller" zuhause, ein Produkt, das Attribute wie „Bio" oder „Öko" schon lange für sich reklamieren konnte, bevor die Kategorie hierfür überhaupt geboren war. Eines der meistverkauften Bonbons der Welt kommt aus der Schweiz: Ricola.

In Laufen kaufte Emil Richterich im Jahre 1924 eine Bäckerei, die auf Confiseriewaren spezialisiert war. Über hundert süße Leckereien umfasste damals schon das Angebot dieser „Bäckerei Bleile". Darunter war auch der beliebte „Fünfermocken", ein in der Schweiz bekanntes Karamellbonbon, das von Kindern für fünf Rappen pro Stück erworben werden konnte, sowie ein Kräuterbonbon gegen Husten und Heiserkeit. 1930 gründete Richterich die Confiseriefabrik Richterich & Co. in Laufen. Aus ihrem Namen (Ri-Co-La) leitete sich später der Markenname „Ricola" ab.

Richterich hatte mit der Bäckerei ein bereits eingeführtes Halsbonbon übernommen, begann aber schon früh, dessen Rezeptur zu verbessern und experimentierte mit Kräutern und Zutaten. Das Ergebnis ist der Geschmack des legendären Ricola „Schweizer Kräuterzucker", das er im Jahre 1940 aus 13 Kräutern entwickeln konnte. Der „Schweizer Kräuterzucker" wird zum Grundstein für den weltweiten Erfolg seines Unternehmens.
Die Rezeptur ist bis heute ein streng gehütetes Geheimnis. Bekannt sind nur die dafür verwendeten Kräuter.

Markenauftritt und Verpackung

Das Bonbon selbst sah bereits damals aus wie heute: Das eigenwillige, viereckige Kräuterbonbon mit seiner geriffelten Struktur ist ein echter Klassiker der Markenwelt und pflegt seit Jahrzehnten einen auch in Sachen Konsistenz und Selbstähnlichkeit des Marketings vorbildlichen Markenauftritt. Leitfarbe ist ein leuchtendes Gelb.

Begonnen hat der Welterfolg in einer bescheidenen Bonbon-Tüte aus Papier. Sie war anfangs sehr schlicht gehalten, aus einfachem braunem Packpapier mit unbuntem Aufdruck gefertigt. Bald wurde sie zum ersten Träger des Markenlogos. In den 1950er

RICOLA – from niche product to global market leader

A small village near Basel is the home of a successful "global seller", a product that could assert the claims "eco" or "green" for itself long before these terms were born. One of the best-selling sweets in the world is from Switzerland: Ricola.

In 1924, Emil Richterich bought a bakery in Laufen that was specialised in confectionery. At the time, the "Bleile bakery" offered more than a hundred sweet treats including the popular "Fünfermocken", a familiar Swiss toffee that children could buy for five centimes each. It was also a herbal sweet that eased coughs and a hoarse throat. In 1930, Richterich founded Confiseriefabrik Richterich & Co in Laufen. The brand name "Ricola" was derived from the company's name (Ri-Co-La).

Along with the bakery, Richterich had acquired an established throat lozenge, but he soon started to improve its formula and experimented with herbs and ingredients. The result was the taste of the legendary Ricola "Schweizer Kräuterzucker" he succeeded in developing from a blend of 13 herbs in 1940. The "Swiss herbal sugar" laid the foundations for his company's global success. The lozenge's formula is still today a well kept secret. Only the herbs used in the sweet are known.

Brand presentation and packaging

The sweet itself looks the same as it did more than 60 years ago: the unconventional, rustic, rock-hard drop with its rectangular shape and ribbed structure is a true brand classic, and its marketing has been competent and consistent for decades. The brand's colour is a bright yellow. Ricola's global success started in a modest paper sweets bag. At the beginning, the bag was very simple, made of brown paper with a black and white print. Soon it became the first bag to bear the brand's logo. In the 1950s, a tin with a wrap around label was the pack with the strongest advertising effect. The tin was later joined by the soft bag that offered a lot of print surface for the brand's image. Today, the brand comes in all kind of different varieties and packs. There are special editions like the company's own "Ricola Kräutertee" tea and "tea sticks". The classic lozenge is mainly sold in bags as well as the "Böxli", a kind of flip top box.

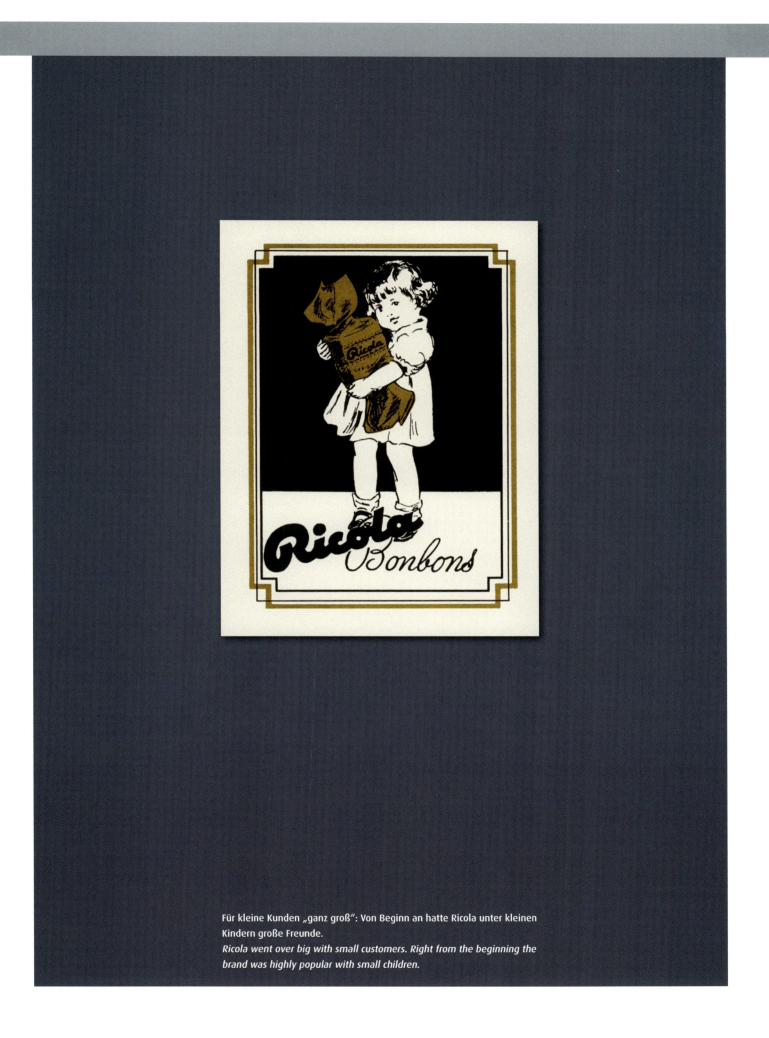

Für kleine Kunden „ganz groß": Von Beginn an hatte Ricola unter kleinen Kindern große Freunde.
Ricola went over big with small customers. Right from the beginning the brand was highly popular with small children.

III. "DRAUSSEN ZUHAUSE": MARKENFÜHRUNG – AM POINT OF SALE | "AT HOME OUTDOORS": BRAND MANAGEMENT – AT THE POINT OF SALE

Am Ursprung der Marken-Kommunikation stand die klassische Bonbon-Tüte. Hier Ausführungen aus der Anfangszeit um 1940 sowie Designs aus der Zeit um 1954, um 1960, um 1970, 1980 bis Mitte 1990er Jahre, ab der Mitte 1990er Jahre, ab 2005.
Ricola's brand communication started with the traditional sweets bag. See variants from the brand's early days around 1940 as well as designs from around 1954, 1960, 1970, 1980 to the mid-1990s, from 1990 and 2005.

Jahren war die Blechdose, bald mit einem Rundum-Etikett gelabelt, das werbewirksamste Packmittel der Marke gewesen. Ihr trat später der Weichbeutel zur Seite, der dem Markenbild eine große Druckfläche bot. Heute dagegen stellt sich der Markenauftritt variantenreich dar. Neben Spezialitäten wie einem eigenen „Ricola Kräutertee" und „Tea sticks" wird das klassische Bonbon vor allem in Beuteln sowie in dem praktischen „Böxli" vertrieben, einer Flip-Top-Faltschachtel.

In der Markenkommunikation liegt der Fokus auf den Heilkräutern der Schweizer Hochalmen und der Unberührtheit ihres Lebensraums. Gerade hier ist die positive Herkunftsenergie der Schweizer Berge unverzichtbar. Ein in der Werbung eingesetztes „Key visual" vereinigt die Elemente der Erlebniswelt der Marke: Aus dem Motiv der Berge (dem Matterhorn), bestimmten Kräutern und der Kernfarbe Gelb setzen sich hier die Bausteine der Markenwahrnehmung zusammen. Als Sinnbild der Schweiz ziert seit einigen Jahren manche der zylindrischen Blechdosen ein Bild des Matterhorns. Die sortendifferenziert gestalteten Weichbeutel dagegen, die mehr Bildfläche bieten, zeigen ganze Alpenpanoramen.

Die Frühzeit des Marketings

In den Anfangsjahren gehörte das Marketing zu den Aufgaben des Unternehmers Emil Richterich, der selbst sein bester Verkäufer war. Mit einem auf seinem Velo festgeschnallten Vertreterkoffer bereiste er persönlich Kunde um Kunde und bewarb im Handel seine Zuckerbonbons. Insbesondere die Tankstellen an

Ricola's brand communication focuses on the medicinal herbs of the Swiss mountain pastures and the unspoilt landscape they grow in. The positive original energy of the Swiss mountains is an essential element of Ricola's marketing. A "key visual" used in advertising brings together the typical characteristics of the brand's world: the mountain motif (the Matterhorn), certain herbs and the typical colour yellow are the basis of Ricola's brand perception. For many years, some of the cylindrical tins have featured the Matterhorn as a symbol of Switzerland. The soft bags, each variety with its own design, featured entire panoramic alpine sceneries on a larger surface.

Early marketing

In the brand's first years, entrepreneur Richterich was responsible for marketing and he was his best salesperson. His sample case strapped on the back of his bike, he visited every customer personally and promoted his lozenges to retailers. They sold particularly well at the petrol stations of motorway service stations. The company could afford the first machine in 1954. In 1960, the range was reduced to two products, the established "Fünfermocken" and "Ricola Schweizer Kräuterzucker", which was becoming increasingly popular.

The "export success story" of "Ricola Schweizer Kräuterzucker" started in 1960 when more and more rich North Italians crossed the Swiss border with their cars to buy petrol. They bought "Ricola Kräuterzucker" at the petrol station kiosk and took it home with them together with Maggi cubes and Swiss chocolate. Soon it became clear that the successful product

  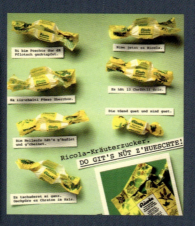 

Schon 1981 wurde die neue „Böxli-Packung" beworben (Anzeige, Schweiz 1981).
The new „Böxli pack" was promoted as early as 1981 (Advertisement, Switzerland 1981).

Zur „Entfaltung" der Marke trägt der klassische Wickler des Bonbons bei (Anzeige, Schweiz 1981).
The sweet's classic wrapper contributes to the brand's "unfolding" (Advertisement, Switzerland 1981).

„Wer hat's erfunden?" – TV-Spot mit Kult-Faktor. Das Konzept begann 1998 mit der Finnen-Sauna – und wurde im Laufe der Jahre auf viele andere Länder übertragen. So behaupten immer mehr Nationen, die Erfinder der originalen Schweizer Ricola-Bonbons zu sein: Ende 1999 postulierten dies die Australier, im Jahr 2000 die Engländer, dann 2001 die Mexikaner, 2004 wurde der Spot in Rio gedreht, bis 2005 auch die Chinesen und Ende 2009 gar die Eskimos ihre Ansprüche anmeldeten.
„Who invented it?" – A TV commercial that achieved cult status. The concept started with the Finnish sauna in 1998 and was later applied to many other countries. More and more nations came to claim to have invented the original Ricola lozenge: in late 1999 it was the Australians, in 2000 the English and the Mexicans in 2001. The spot was then filmed in Rio in 2004, and in the end even the Chinese claimed to have invented Ricola in 2005 and the Eskimos in 2009.

den Raststätten erwiesen sich als gute Vertriebsorte. Im Jahre 1954 konnte sich das Unternehmen die erste Maschine leisten, seit etwa 1960 wurde die Angebotspalette nur noch auf zwei Artikel, nämlich auf den etablierten „Fünfermocken" und den aufsteigenden „Ricola Schweizer Kräuterzucker", begrenzt.

Die ersten „Exporterfolge" konnte der „Ricola Schweizer Kräuterzucker" in den 1960er Jahren verbuchen, als zunehmend reiche Norditaliener zum Tanken über die Schweizer Grenze fuhren und am Tankstellen-Kiosk dann neben Maggi-Würfeln und der Schweizer Schokolade auch die „Ricola Kräuterzucker" über die Grenze mitnahmen. Schon bald erwies sich die universale Einsetzbarkeit dieses Erfolgsprodukts. Ab 1963 exportierte Ricola in die Nachbarländer der Schweiz: Italien, Deutschland, Luxemburg und Frankreich. Die Umbenennung der Firma Richterich & Co. in Ricola erfolgte im Jahr 1967. Sie war nun eine Aktiengesellschaft und erhielt schon 1967/68 eine Fabrikation nach modernster Technik. Längst ist aus dem kleinen Familienunternehmen eine Weltmarke geworden. Ricola exportiert nicht nur in 50 Länder Europas, sondern auch nach Asien und Nordamerika, Singapur, Hongkong und Hawaii. Ricola „Schweizer Kräuterzucker" ist heute das weltweit führende Halsbonbon auf Kräuterbasis.

Ricola-Displays im Handel

Schon seit den 1960er Jahren verhalfen unterschiedliche Formen von Displays der Marke zu einem stimmungsvollen Auftritt am Point of Sale. Zu Beginn stand noch der klassische „OTC-Vertrieb" als Apotheken-Artikel (im sprichwörtlichen

could be sold everywhere. In 1963, Ricola started to export its sweets to Switzerland's neighbouring countries Italy, Germany, Luxembourg and France. Richterich & Co changed its name to Ricola in 1967. Ricola was now a public limited company and started to produce with the latest technology in 1967/68. Today, the small family-owned company has long become a global brand. Ricola exports to 50 countries in Europe as well as cities and states in Asia and North America such as Singapore, Hong Kong and Hawaii. Today, Ricola is the world's leading herb-based throat lozenge.

Ricola displays at retail

As early as the 1960s, Ricola used various forms of displays to create an atmospheric and effective presentation at the POS. At the beginning, Ricola was sold mainly face-to-face, over the counter in pharmacies. A creative counter display for the classic Ricola soft bags was developed in 1975. Paper strips printed with images of herbs on the side of the display could be folded open to stand up, thus creating the impression that the "Kräuterzucker" were offered for sale on a meadow with herbs. The advertising claim "Does you good. Tastes good." aimed at taking away the fear of a "medical", thus negative, taste experience. The same claim was used in 1975 to promote the

Thekendisplay für Ricola (Beutel), um 1975
Ricola counter display (bag), around 1975

Achteckiges Thekendisplay für Kräutertee, 1978
Octagonal herbal tea counter display, 1978

Sinne: „Over the Counter") im Fokus. Ricola wurde also „über die Theke" verkauft. Kreativ war um 1975 ein Thekendisplay für die klassischen Ricola-Weichbeutel. Durch mit Kräutern bedruckte Motiv-Streifen, die seitlich der Produkte aufgeklappt wurden und auftragten, entstand der Eindruck, die „Kräuterzucker" würden auf einer Kräuterwiese präsentiert. Der Claim „Tut gut. Schmeckt gut." sollte die Angst vor einem „medizinischen" (also negativen) Geschmackserlebnis nehmen. Unter dem gleichen Claim wurden 1975 in einem Thekendisplay, das an ein altmodisches Holzregal erinnern sollte, auch die Kräutertees der Marke angeboten.

Ein großer Schritt war es von hier zu einem echten Bodenaufsteller, der Ende der 1970er Jahre entwickelt wurde. Der offsetbedruckte Sockel war in Form einer (standfesten) Ricola-Tüte gestaltet. Der Sockel trug eine doppelte (beidseitige) Warenschütte. Die Konstruktion war sehr leicht aufstellbar und benötigte kaum Platz. Die Rückseite der Schütten bildete ein Aufsteckplakat („Gesundheit, die schmeckt."). Da sich dieser Displaytyp bewährte, blieb er auch 1978 im Einsatz. Nun zeigte das Motiv eine offene Ricola-Tüte, aus der die alpine Bergwelt samt ihren Heilkräutern heraus zu „strömen" schien.

Ebenfalls 1978 wurde das erste Sortimentsdisplay eingesetzt: Kräutertees und Kräuterzucker wurden in einem Display platziert, ein achteckiges Thekendisplay löste 1978 bei den Kräutertees das Regalschränkchen im „Oma-Stil" ab.

Da die Distribution immer stärker auch den Lebensmitteleinzelhandel einbezog, wurden neue Angebotsformen wie die „Böxli"-Kartonverpackung entwickelt. Parallel dazu hielten in den 90er Jahren auf Chep-Paletten platzierte Logistikdisplays im Handel Einzug. Sie ermöglichten eine effiziente Bestückung in der Produktion von Ricola und gleichzeitig eine einfache Logistik für den Handel.

Perfekt wieder aufgegriffen wurde die Idee des Bodendisplays mit der Almhütte vor dem konturgestanzten Matterhorn dann im Jahr 2000. Das Palettendisplay erhielt durch das hervorstehende Dach nicht nur eine schöne 3D-Wirkung, raffiniert war auch die Idee

brand's herbal teas in a counter display supposed to look like an old-fashioned wooden shelf. There was a big step between the counter display and the proper floor stand display that was developed in the late 1970s. The offset printed pedestal had the shape of a (rigid) Ricola bag. It had trays on both sides. It was easy to assemble and took up hardly any space. A header card attached to the back of the display read "Good health tastes good". This type of display proved successful and was used at retail until 1978. Now the display featured an open Ricola bag that seemed to release the alpine mountains into the store with all of its medicinal herbs.

Also in 1978, the first full-range display was introduced into stores. Herbal teas and Kräuterzucker were placed in the same display. An octagonal counter display for herbal teas replaced the small "granny style" cupboard with shelves.

As Ricola was now selling its products at a growing number of food retailers, new packs like the "Böxli" carton pack were designed for sale at these stores. At the same time, logistical displays on Chep pallets became common use in stores in the 1990s. They increased efficiency of key processes like stocking at the production sites and made it easier for retailers to get the product to the sales floor.

The idea of the floor stand display featuring the alpine hut in front of a cut-out Matterhorn was revived in 2000. The protruding roof of the pallet display created a nice three-dimensional effect. The display's back panel that was covered in mountain flowers and herbs was artful. Gradually, as the packs were sold off the pallet, more and more of the attractive back panel unveiled to the customer's eye.

An aesthetic appearance and design also characterised the quick assembly displays with concave and convex pedestals that were introduced into stores in 2007. The unusual shape nicely fitted the "chunky" shape of the Kräuterzucker. In the case of Ricola, in terms of branding, the shape was, so to say, "self-similar".

A counter display that went into stores in 2007 added a third level for free taste samples to the standard trays carrying "Böxli" packs. It

Bodenaufsteller, Ende 1970er Jahre
Floor stand display, late 1970s

Sortimentsdisplay (Kräutertee und Kräuterzucker), 1978
Display for herbal tea and Kräuterzucker lozenges, 1978

Stapelschütten auf Chep-Palette vor Matterhorn-Motiv (Konturstanzung, dreidimensionales Dach), 1997
Stacking bins on a Chep pallet, its back card featuring a die-cut image of the Matterhorn (three-dimensional roof), 1997

Palettendisplay, Almhütte vor konturgestanztem Matterhorn, 2000
Pallet display, mountain hut in front of a cut-die image of the Matterhorn, 2000

III. | „DRAUSSEN ZUHAUSE": MARKENFÜHRUNG – AM POINT OF SALE | "AT HOME OUTDOORS": BRAND MANAGEMENT – AT THE POINT OF SALE

Sechseckiges Bodendisplay, 1998
Hexagonal floor stand display, 1998

Thekendisplay für „Böxli"- und Probepackungen, 2007
Counter display for "Böxli" and sample packs, 2007

Thekendisplay für „Böxli"-Packungen, um 2007
Counter display for "Böxli" packs, around 2007

Sekundendisplay mit konkav-konvexem Sockel, 2007
Quick assembly display with concave and convex pedestal, 2007

---

der mit Almblumen und -kräutern bedeckten Rückwand. Je mehr sich durch fortschreitenden Abverkauf der Warenaufbau „lichtete", desto mehr wurde von der attraktiven Rückwand sichtbar.

Ästhetik und Design strahlten die 2007 eingeführten Sekundendisplays mit konkav-konvexem Sockel aus. Die außergewöhnliche Formgebung fügte sich gut in die Formwelt des „klobigen" Kräuterzuckers ein; sie war im Falle von Ricola also, markentechnisch gesehen, „selbstähnlich".

Ein Thekendisplay aus dem Jahre 2007 kombinierte die herkömmlichen Aufbauten der „Böxli"-Packungen in Trays mit einer dritten Ebene, wo Geschmacksmuster und kostenlose Proben entnommen werden können. Verkaufsware und kostenlose „Give-aways" in einem einzigen Display, auch das war nun möglich.

Unter dem Motto „Jetzt schlägt's drizäh (13)!" wurde 2009 ein Wettbewerb ausgelobt, in dem man „eine von 13 hochwertigen Victorinox-Uhren" gewinnen konnte. Ricola blieb also ganz „schwyzerisch".

Ebenfalls als Verlosungsaktion in Apotheken konzipiert war ein Bodendisplay, das anstelle einer Schütte einen aufgeklappten Hartschalen-Trolley in Ricola-Gelb präsentierte. Die Botschaft hinter der Kampagne: Ricola ist der optimale Reisebegleiter. Dieses Beispiel zeigt, dass Displays in der Lage sind, ganze Geschichten zu erzählen.

was now possible to offer Ricola sales packs and giveaways in the same display.

A competition was launched in 2009 under the motto "Jetzt schlägt's drizäh!" (That's the last straw). "Drizäh" meaning 13, Ricola promised to give away "one of 13 high-end Victorinox watches". In using Swiss-German and Swiss watches, Ricola remained true to its Swiss heritage.

Another event was a raffle organised in pharmacies. In this promotion, a floor stand display was used that had an open hard shell suitcase instead of a bin. The suitcase was yellow, like all of Ricola's products. The message of the campaign was that Ricola is the perfect travelling companion. This example shows that displays can tell a whole story.

To increase the time the customer stays in the store and secure the right in-store location for the product while also taking into account sustainability, Ricola started to increase the number of permanent displays in the 21st Century. These displays in part were designed to present the brand's entire product range.

In 2009, a smart display on wheels was designed as a permanent display that had hangers for hanging packs like the Ricola bags as well as trays for the classic "Böxli" boxes and tins.

Different sales channels require different display solutions. Ricola has set standards here by using constructions and designs tailored to the needs of the individual distribution channels.

Bodendisplay mit Hartschalen-Trolley, 2009
Floor stand display with hard shell suitcase, 2009

Rollbares Langzeitdisplay, 2009
Wheeled permanent display, 2009

III. „DRAUSSEN ZUHAUSE": MARKENFÜHRUNG – AM POINT OF SALE | "AT HOME OUTDOORS": BRAND MANAGEMENT – AT THE POINT OF SALE

Um eine längere Verweildauer im Handel zu erreichen, gute Platzierungsflächen zu sichern und auch nachhaltig zu handeln, setzte Ricola ab dem 21. Jahrhundert verstärkt auf Langzeitdisplays, die zum Teil eine Präsentation des gesamten Sortimentes ermöglichen. Als Langzeitdisplay wurde in 2009 eine rollbare Verkaufshilfe entwickelt, die sowohl hängende Packungen (wie die Ricola-Beutel) als auch die klassischen „Böxli"-Faltschachteln und Dosen optimal aufnehmen kann.

Unterschiedliche Vertriebskanäle ziehen unterschiedliche Anforderungen an Displays mit sich. Ricola setzt hier Maßstäbe, indem jeweils vertriebskanalspezifische Konstruktionen und Designs zum Einsatz kommen.

Speziell für den Lebensmitteleinzelhandel entwickelt wurden dreieckige Displays aus gesteckter Wellpappe, mit denen die Seitenwangen der Regale dekoriert und im vertrieblichen Sinne genutzt werden kann. Innovation und Ideenreichtum bescheren dieser Marke unterschiedliche, auf die jeweilige Vertriebsschiene abgestimmte Auftrittsmöglichkeiten. Gemeinsam ist allen Display-entwicklungen dieser Marke die starke Verankerung in der Herkunftsenergie der Alpenwelt. Über die Jahre ist Ricola so zu einem bedeutenden Innovator des Handelsmarketings geworden.

Food retailers were offered a specially-designed assembled triangular corrugated cardboard display that was used to decorate the sides of shelves, where it not only looked nice, but was also able to generate sales. Ricola is a brand that uses innovation and inventiveness for the different forms of presentation each distribution channel requires. Despite the variations, however, all types of displays have one thing in common: the energy of the brand's strong roots in its original alpine home.

Felix Richterich

„Ricola ist eine Traditionsmarke, die mit ihrer Verbindung von Werten wie Natürlichkeit, Geschmack, Funktionalität und Schweizer Herkunft ihren Kunden einen hohen emotionalen Mehrwert bietet. Wir legen darum im Marketing großen Wert darauf, den Kunden nicht nur medial anzusprechen, sondern ihm auch am Point of Sale physisch in einer realen Situation zu begegnen. Dort können wir alle Sinne ansprechen und ein umfassendes Markenerlebnis von Ricola inszenieren."

Felix Richterich, Präsident des Verwaltungsrates der Ricola AG

"Ricola is a traditional brand that offers customers strong emotional surplus value by combining values like naturalness, good taste, functionality and Swiss heritage. That is why our marketing approach places great emphasis on appealing to the customer not only in the virtual world, but to make a real physical impact at the point of sale. There we can stimulate all of the customer's senses and create a complete brand experience."

Felix Richterich, Chairman of the Ricola AG administrative board

Bodendisplay mit Alpenpanorama, 2007
Floor stand display featuring view of the Alps, 2007

Dreieckiges Display für Regalseiten, 2009
Triangular display for shelf sides, 2009

Thekendisplay als echter Flechtkorb (mit Konturschild), 2009
Counter display with real wicker basket (and embossed back card), 2009

Bodendisplay, 2009
Floor stand display, 2009

Display-Säule für „Böxli"-Packungen, um 2007
Display column for "Böxli" packs, around 2007

Verkaufsförderungsaktion mit Paletten- und Sortimentsplatzierung, 2009
Sales promotion with pallets and various Ricola products, 2009

IV. SHOPPER INSIGHTS: WAS KUNDEN BEWEGT | SHOPPER INSIGHTS: HOW CUSTOMERS TICK

SHOPPER INSIGHTS:
WAS KUNDEN BEWEGT
SHOPPER INSIGHTS:
HOW CUSTOMERS TICK

Hendrik Schröder

Point of Purchase-Marketing im Einzelhandel – Weniger Shopper Confusion, mehr Shopper Convenience

1. Ausgangssituation und Problemstellung

Tagtäglich sind wir unzähligen Reizen ausgesetzt, zuhause, bei der Arbeit, beim Einkauf, in der Freizeit und auf den Wegen zwischen den Orten, wo wir wohnen, arbeiten, einkaufen und uns vergnügen.

Es gibt mehrere Gründe, warum die Zahl der Reize sprunghaft gestiegen ist. Da sind zunächst die vielen neuen Techniken, die die Information und die Kommunikation unterstützen. Spitz formuliert: Wenn wir es zulassen, sind wir zu jeder Zeit und an jedem Ort in einen Informations- oder Kommunikationsprozess eingebunden, sei es durch Printmedien, sei es durch persönliche Gespräche, sei es durch elektronische Medien.

Die Industrien aller Branchen bringen in den letzten Jahren zunehmend neue Produkte auf den Markt, nutzen neue Kommunikationskanäle sowie zusätzliche Absatzkanäle – dazu zählen auch eigene Flagship-Stores – und widmen sich vermehrt der personalisierten Kommunikation mit ihren Endkunden. Ähnlich sieht die Entwicklung im Einzelhandel aus: neue Betriebsformen (z. B. Live-Shops, Factory Outlet Center oder Ein-Euro-Shops), die Zunahme des Multi-Channel-Retailing, der Anstieg der Verkaufsfläche, die Nutzung zusätzlicher Kommunikationskanäle und die Differenzierung der Werbemaßnahmen.

Auch das Kunden- und Konsumentenverhalten hat sich verändert. Die räumliche Mobilität und die Akzeptanz neuer Kommunikations- und Einkaufskanäle steigen. Das Wissen, die Unabhängigkeit und die Emanzipation nehmen zu: Viele Kunden erobern mittlerweile die Informationshoheit gegenüber den Anbietern. Mehr denn je streben die Kunden nach der Erfüllung ihrer individuellen Wünsche. Hierfür stehen Begriffe wie hybrides, multioptionales und paradoxes Kaufverhalten. Auf die zahlreichen Informationen ihrer Umwelt reagieren die Kunden unterschiedlich. Teilweise suchen sie gezielt nach Informationen, teilweise nehmen sie aus ihrem Umfeld selektiv Informationen auf, und teilweise schirmen sie sich gegenüber den vielen Informationen ab, insbesondere dann, wenn sie sich durch eine Flut an Reizen überfordert fühlen.

Hendrik Schröder

Point of purchase marketing at retail – Less shopper confusion, more shopper convenience

1. Introduction and problem definition

Every day we are exposed to a flood of information and stimuli, at home, at work, while shopping, in our free time and on our way from and to the places we live, work, shop and enjoy ourselves.

The number of stimuli has jumped for various reasons. First of all, there is a large number of new techniques that promote information and communication. Put bluntly, if we allow it, we are involved in an information and communication process at any time, and in any place, whether by print media, private conversations or electronic media.

In the past years, manufacturers of all industries have launched an increasing number of new products onto the market. They are taking advantage of new communication and additional distribution channels like flagship stores, and are dedicating more efforts to communicate directly and personally with end consumers. More or less the same is happening at retail: new distribution formats are emerging like live shops, factory outlet centres and one-euro shops, multi-channel retailing is expanding, and retail space is growing. Retailers are discovering new communication channels and are differentiating their advertising activity.

Customer and consumer behaviour has also changed. There is greater geographical mobility and acceptance of new communication and buying channels. The knowledge, independence and emancipation of consumers is increasing. Today, costumers are often better informed than suppliers. More than ever, costumers are striving to fulfil their personal desires. Terms like hybrid, multi-optional and paradox buying behaviour prove this. Customers react in different ways to the vast information around them: sometimes they look for specific information, other times they selectively pick up information from their surroundings, or fend off an information overload, especially when the flood of stimuli becomes too much.

Suppliers aware of this customer behaviour are likely to try to draw the attention to their products and services, engage the customer's interest and convince the customer of the quality of their products. That applies to both the manufacturers of consumer goods and the retailers, who

In diesem Umfeld dürfte jeder Anbieter das Ziel verfolgen, auf sich und seine Leistungen aufmerksam zu machen, das Interesse des Kunden zu wecken und ihn von seinen Angeboten zu überzeugen. Das gilt für die Hersteller von Konsumgütern ebenso wie für die Einzelhändler dieser Güter. Der Unterschied ist: Dem Hersteller ist es egal, mit welchen Händlern er seinen Umsatz macht, dem Händler ist es egal, mit welchen Herstellern, insbesondere mit welchen Herstellermarken, er seinen Umsatz tätigt.

In den letzten Jahren ist zu beobachten, dass die Einzelhändler weithin sichtbare Anstrengungen unternehmen, sich klar im Wettbewerb zu positionieren und bei den Kunden zu profilieren. Besonders deutlich wird das an den Beispielen von EDEKA („Wir lieben Lebensmittel"), Rewe („Jeden Tag ein bisschen besser.") und real („Einmal hin. Alles drin.") im Lebensmittelhandel, bei OBI („Wie wo was weiß OBI") und Hornbach („Hornbach. Es gibt immer was zu tun.") im DIY-Bereich und bei Media-Markt („Ich bin doch nicht blöd.") und Saturn („Wir hassen teuer!") im Markt für Consumer Electronics. Das zentrale Ziel besteht darin, die Händlermarke (auch: Storebrand, Retailbrand) zu fördern, wenn nötig auch dadurch, dass Hersteller- durch Handelsmarken ersetzt werden. Die Erreichung dieses Ziels spiegelt sich wider in allen Marketing-Maßnahmen, die außerhalb der Einkaufsstätte und in der Einkaufsstätte, d.h. am Point of Purchase, eingesetzt werden. Eine Anmerkung: Der Begriff Point of Purchase drückt die Sichtweise der Kunden besser aus als der Begriff Point of Sale.

In diesem Beitrag widmen wir uns dem POP-Marketing, also solchen Maßnahmen, die das Informations-, das Such- und das Entscheidungsverhalten der Kunden im Sinn der Zielsetzungen des Einzelhändlers unterstützen sollen. Damit sind folgende Fragestellungen verbunden:

- Wie kann sich ein Einzelhändler mit seiner Einkaufsstätte von der Konkurrenz abheben?
- Welche Bedürfnisse haben die Kunden beim Einkaufen?
- Welche Entscheidungen treffen die Kunden erst in der Einkaufsstätte?
- Welche Voraussetzungen sind zu erfüllen, um die Entscheidungen der Kunden zu deren Zufriedenheit (d.h. Bedürfnisbefriedigung) und im Sinne der Zielsetzungen des Einzelhändlers zu unterstützen?

2. Am Anfang steht das Ziel

Gerade angesichts der großen Komplexität und Dynamik, die den Einzelhandel kennzeichnen, muss der Einzelhändler am Anfang und dann in regelmäßigen Abständen seine Ziele formulieren und ihre Erreichung überprüfen. Ziele sind Aussagen mit normativem Charakter, die einen von einem Entscheidungsträger gewünschten

sell them. The difference is that the manufacturer does not care what retailer helps to generate sales, and the retailer does not care what manufacturers or manufacturer's brands help generate sales.

It has become obvious in recent years that retailers everywhere are making visible efforts to position themselves clearly against competitors and raise their profile with their customers. This is particularly evident in the cases of food retailers EDEKA ("we love food"), Rewe ("a bit better every day") and real ("go once, get all"), DIY retailers Obi ("where, how, what, Obi knows") and Hornbach ("Hornbach. There's always work to do") and consumer electronics retailers Media Markt ("I'm not that stupid") and Saturn ("we hate expensive!"). The main goal is to strengthen the retail brand (also store brand) even if this means replacing manufacturer's brands with private labels. All marketing measures in or outside the shopping location, i.e. the point of purchase, are aimed at achieving that goal. Note: the term point of purchase represents the customer's view better than the term point of sale.

In this paper, we will focus on POP marketing, meaning those measures that support retailers in their goal of assisting the customer in his searching for information and products and the decision whether or not to buy a product. The following questions must be considered in this context:

- *How can retailers distinguish themselves clearly from competitors?*
- *What are the customer's shopping needs?*
- *What decisions do customers make in the store?*
- *What conditions must be met to make sure customers are satisfied with their decision (i.e. satisfaction of needs), while taking into account the objectives of retailers?*

2. Everything starts with a goal

It is the greatly complex and dynamic nature of retail that should remind retailers of defining their goals and assessing whether or not these goals were achieved, not only once, but regularly. Goals are purposes with a normative character that represent a particular future situation decision makers' endeavour is directed to and which they want to achieve through their actions (see Hauschildt 1977, page 9). The theory of goal setting deals with the definition and arrangement of the activity's system of goals. Theoretical goal research focuses on the goal's differentiation and content as well as the structure of the goal-setting system and the changes it undergoes. This is based on empirical goal research that covers the kind and scale of goals, the correlation with goals currently in practice in relation to time and target groups, the relative meaning they have for activity, its changes over time and the group of people involved in the goal setting process (see Heinen 1976, p. 30ff).

Informationsverhalten der Kunden	Suchverhalten der Kunden	Entscheidungsverhalten der Kunden
■ Verringerung von Shopper Confusion ■ Vermittlung von Shopper Convenience ■ Verringerung der Informationsüberlastung Anregungen für Einkäufe ■ etc.	■ Verringerung von Shopper Confusion ■ Vermittlung von Shopper Convenience ■ Unterstützung von Plankäufen Vermittlung einer angenehmen Atmosphäre ■ Reduktion der Unsicherheit bei Kaufentscheidungen ■ etc.	■ Verringerung von Shopper Confusion ■ Vermittlung von Shopper Convenience ■ Verbesserung der Orientierung ■ Verringerung von Suchzeiten Erhöhung der Suchzufriedenheit ■ etc.
Customer's information behaviour	**Customer's search behaviour**	**Customer's decision behaviour**
■ reducing shopper confusion ■ providing shopper convenience ■ reducing information overload ■ giving shopping inspiration ■ other	■ reducing shopper confusion ■ providing shopper convenience ■ improving orientation ■ reducing search time ■ increasing search satisfaction ■ other	■ reducing shopper confusion ■ providing shopper convenience ■ supporting planned purchases ■ creating a pleasant atmosphere ■ reducing uncertainty about buying decisions ■ other

Abbildung 1: Vorökonomische Zielinhalte des POP-Marketings

Figure 1: The pre-economic goals of POP marketing

zukünftigen Zustand beschreiben, den er durch seine Aktivitäten zu erreichen anstrebt (vgl. Hauschildt 1977, S. 9). Mit der Formulierung und der Gestaltung des Zielsystems der Unternehmung befasst sich die Theorie der Zielsetzungslehre. Gegenstand der theoretischen Zielforschung sind die Abgrenzung und die inhaltliche Ausfüllung des Zielbegriffs sowie die Strukturierung des Zielsystems einschließlich ihrer Veränderungen. Als Basis hierfür dient die empirische Zielforschung, welche die Art, das Ausmaß, den zeitlichen und den zielgruppenspezifischen Bezug der in der Unternehmungspraxis anzutreffenden Ziele, die relative Bedeutung der Ziele für die Unternehmung, deren Veränderung im Zeitablauf sowie den am Zielbildungsprozess beteiligten Personenkreis untersucht (vgl. Heinen 1976, S. 30 ff.).

So wichtig es ist, es reicht nicht aus, allein Ziele wie Umsatz, Wertschöpfung, Gewinn und Rentabilität zu definieren. Vielmehr ist das Zusammenspiel von solchen ökonomischen Inhalten und den ihnen kausal vorausgehenden vorökonomischen Inhalten zu beachten: An welcher Stelle im psychologischen Wahrnehmungsraum will ein Einzelhändler wahrgenommen werden? Versteht er sich als Versorger oder als Problemlöser? Sieht er sich im Niedrigpreissegment oder im Premiumbereich oder irgendwo dazwischen? Welche Zielgruppen will er erreichen? Wie zufrieden sollen die Kunden mit dem in der Einkaufsstätte Erlebten sein? Mit welchen Merkmalen und Assoziationen soll die Händlermarke in den Köpfen der Kunden verankert werden? Wenn solche und weitere damit zusammenhängenden Fragen nicht oder nicht hinreichend geklärt und in entsprechende vorökonomische Ziele transformiert werden, dann fehlt der Maßstab, um geeignete Maßnahmen zu identifi-

Even though this may be very important, it does not suffice to define goals like sales, added value, profit and profitability. Attention must in fact be paid to the interaction between these economic aspects and the causally linked pre-economic aspects preceding the economic aspects. Where exactly in the psychological space of perception do retailers want to be noticed? Do retailers consider themselves as suppliers, or as solvers of problems? Do they consider themselves as discount or high-end retailers, or somewhere in between? What target groups do retailers want to reach? Just how satisfied does the retailer want customers to be with their experience at the store? What are the features and associations retailers want their retail brand to evoke in the customer? If these questions, and further related questions, are not sufficiently answered and translated into appropriate pre-economic goals, the retailer will have no yardstick to identify and introduce the adequate measures. All too often, retail practice has made deficits evident.

Considering the phases information, search and decision as starting points, then the following pre-economic goals can be defined for POP marketing (figure 1). In all three phases, reducing shopper confusion and providing shopper convenience are the overriding goals.

3. Category management – a holistic view of the customer

It makes sense, at this point, to talk about the concept of category management and the part it plays in the concept of Efficient Consumer Response. Category management is nothing other than the management of product groups that are created according to the customer's needs (see Schröder 2003). If this principle is taken

zieren und einzuleiten. Der Test in der Handelspraxis zeigt allzu häufig, dass hier Defizite bestehen.

Wenn man die drei Phasen Information, Suchen und Entscheiden der Kunden als Anknüpfungspunkt verwendet, dann lassen sich für das POP-Marketing entsprechende vorökonomische Zielinhalte nennen (Abbildung 1). Die Verringerung von Shopper Confusion und die Vermittlung von Shopper Convenience sind in allen drei Phasen übergeordnete Ziele.

3. Category Management – Eine ganzheitliche Perspektive auf den Kunden

Es ist sinnvoll, an dieser Stelle über das Konzept des Category Managements und seine Einbettung in das Konzept des Efficient Consumer Response zu sprechen. Category Management ist nichts anderes als die Bewirtschaftung von Warengruppen, die nach Kundenbedürfnissen zusammengesetzt werden (vgl. Schröder 2003). Wer dieses Prinzip ernsthaft verfolgt, denkt und handelt nicht mehr in einzelnen Marken und Artikeln, d.h. anbieterorientiert und damit oft partikulär, sondern in Bedürfnissen und Problemlösungen, d.h. nachfragerorientiert und damit ganzheitlich.

Dieser nachfragerorientierte und ganzheitliche Ansatz drückt sich in mehreren Punkten aus. Da ist erstens die Verbindung der Supply Side mit der Demand Side, d.h. des Supply Chain Managements mit dem Category Management als Teilbereiche des Efficient Consumer Response-Konzeptes. Die Verzahnung besteht darin, jene Waren effizient am Point of Purchase bereitzustellen, die vom Endkunden gewünscht sind. Gewünscht ist, was nachgefragt wird. Damit steuert ein Pay on Scan-Customer-Konzept die Wertkette im Sinne des Pull-Prinzips unternehmungs- und wirtschaftsstufenübergreifend (vgl. Swoboda/Janz 2002). Der Nachteil des Push-Prinzips, d.h. Waren zu ordern, weil sie besonders

seriously, the focus of thoughts and actions will be on needs and problem solving rather than on individual brands and products. That leads away from a supplier-oriented and often isolated approach to one that is demand-oriented and holistic.

A demand-oriented and holistic approach is characterised, firstly, by the interaction between the supply side and the demand side, i.e. between supply chain management and category management, both part of the Efficient Consumer Response concept. The interaction of these two sides makes sure that end customers find the products they want at the POP, presented in an effective way. Customers want what is currently in demand. This means that a pay on scan concept commands the value chain across all stages of the economic and corporate process according to the

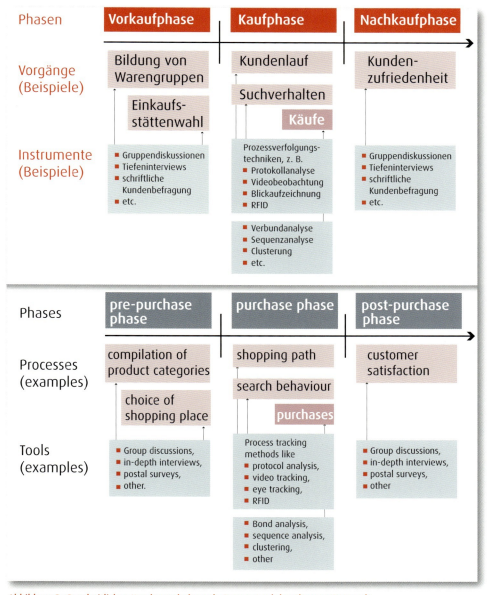

Abbildung 2: Ganzheitliches Kundenverhalten als Gegenstand des Shopper Research
Figure 2: Holistic customer behaviour as the focus of shopper research

günstig im Einkauf sind mit dem Ergebnis, dass diese sich dann aber nicht in der bestellten Menge verkaufen lassen und zu kapitalintensiven Überbestände führen, wird verringert, wenn nicht sogar vermieden. Ebenso sollte die am Nachfrageverhalten ausgerichtete Disposition von Waren dazu beitragen, Fehlmengen (Out of Stocks) zu vermeiden.

Das ganzheitliche Denken und Handeln des Category Managements äußert sich zweitens darin, dass man sich nicht auf die quantitativen Größen des Kaufverhaltens beschränkt, wie z. B. Absatz, Umsatz, Kosten und Roherträge, sondern sich eingehend mit den qualitativen Aspekten befasst. Diese qualitativen Aspekte beziehen neben dem Kauf auch die Phasen vor und nach dem Kauf ein (Abbildung 2). Es interessieren die Entscheidungen des Kunden über die Wahl einer Einkaufsstätte und sein Denken in Kategorien (Problemlösungen) ebenso wie sein Verhalten in der Einkaufsstätte, seine Zufriedenheit und sein Empfehlungsverhalten nach dem Kauf. Erst mit diesen Kenntnissen lässt sich verstehen, was wieviel wann und wo ein Kunde einkauft. Man erhält ein ganzheitliches Bild vom Kunden: von seiner Planung über seinen Einkauf bis zur Verwendung seiner Produkte.

Drittens sind die aus dem Kundenverhalten gewonnenen Erkenntnisse umzusetzen in Marketing-Maßnahmen. Die Ganzheitlichkeit des Marktbearbeitungs-Konzepts drückt sich darin aus, dass die Maßnahmen außerhalb und innerhalb der Einkaufsstätte ebenso aufeinander abzustimmen sind wie die Maßnahmen der Industrie und des Einzelhandels. Auch wenn das Category Management die ureigene Aufgabe des Handels ist, so kann der Händler Teile davon, wie z. B. die Zusammensetzung von Warengruppen, ihre Platzierung in den Regalen sowie ihre Bewerbung, ganz oder teilweise einem Hersteller übertragen, der in diesem Fall als Category Captain, Category Advisor oder Category Consultant bezeichnet wird (vgl. Schröder 2004). Kein Handlungsspielraum besteht bei der Entscheidung, wer die Endverbraucherpreise festlegt. Sie liegt im Fall von Eigengeschäften (Geschäfte im eigenen Namen und auf eigene Rechnung) allein beim Händler. Wer auch immer welchen Bereich zu verantworten hat, Industrie und Handel haben darauf zu achten, dass sie

pull principle (see Swoboda/Janz 2002). This also helps prevent, or at least reduce, the negative effect of the push principle, meaning that goods are ordered for their low wholesale price, but can later not be entirely sold, which leads to capital-intensive excess stock. A demand-oriented approach will also help retailers prevent out-of-stocks.

Secondly, holistic category management will not limit its thinking and acting to quantitative aspects of buying behaviour like selling, sales, costs and gross profits, but will also take into account qualitative aspects. Apart from the purchase itself, these aspects include the pre-purchase and post-purchase phases (figure 2).

Shopper research takes into account where customers decide to shop, their thinking in categories (solution-oriented), their degree of satisfaction and whether or not they recommend a product after buying it. Only this knowledge allows us to understand, what, when, where and how many products the customer buys. It gives us a holistic view of customers and their needs, from the planning of the shopping journey and the actual purchase to the use of the product.

Thirdly, the insights won about the customer's behaviour must be translated into marketing measures. Holistic marketing means that in-store measures and those taken outside of the store must be just as well coordinated as the measures taken by manufacturers and retailers. Even though, traditionally, category management is the domain of retailers, the retailer may decide to leave some aspects, such as the compilation of product groups and the placement of products on shelves, entirely, or partially, to the manufacturer, who, in this case, is referred to as category captain, category adviser, or category consultant (see Schröder 2004). There is no room for manoeuvre, however, when it comes to retail prices. The price of products sold in company-owned stores (stores run under the name and on the account of the retailer) are established by the retailer alone. Regardless of who is in charge of what, both retailers and manufacturers must assume a customer-oriented approach and avoid duplications and uncoordinated and counter-productive actions.

die Maßnahmen an den Bedürfnissen der Kunden ausrichten und dass sie unabgestimmte, doppelte sowie kontraproduktive Anstrengungen vermeiden.

4. Wie viel entscheidet der Kunde am Point of Purchase?

Wir greifen aus den vielen Bedürfnissen und Verhaltensweisen der Kunden einen Ausschnitt heraus: geplante und ungeplante Käufe. Ein Blick in die Lehrbücher sagt uns, dass die Kunden ihre Entscheidungen extensiv, limitiert, habitualisiert oder impulsiv treffen. Bei extensiven Kaufentscheidungen werden zahlreiche Kriterien, Produkte und Anbieter in den Entscheidungsprozess einbezogen, bei limitierten ist der Kreis der in Frage kommenden Anbieter und Produkte beschränkt, man spricht dann von dem so genannten Evoked Set oder Relevant Set; bei habitualisierten Entscheidungen greift der Kunde auf eine bewährte Lösung zurück, das Evoked Set besteht aus einem Anbieter oder einem Produkt. Diese Arten von Kaufentscheidungen sind mit einer mehr oder weniger hohen kognitiven Beteiligung und Planung der Käufer verbunden, bei extensiven am höchsten, bei habitualisierten am geringsten.

Etwas anders verhält es sich mit dem, was man unter impulsiven Kaufentscheidungen versteht. Wir möchten diesen Begriff zurückstellen und zunächst über die Abgrenzung von geplanten und ungeplanten Käufen sprechen. Denn: Oftmals werden ungeplante Käufe mit Impulskäufen gleichgesetzt und Impulskäufe als emotional, nicht aber kognitiv gesteuert bezeichnet. Zur Beantwortung der Frage, worüber der Kunde am Regal entscheidet und wie der Einzelhändler diese Entscheidung unterstützen kann, ist das wenig hilfreich.

Hilfreich ist es vielmehr zu verstehen, worüber und wann Kunden entscheiden. Sie haben vor allem über die Wahl der Einkaufsstätte, den Einkaufszeitpunkt, Produkte, Marken, Packungsgrößen und die Ausgabenhöhe zu entscheiden. Zwei Extrempunkte sind möglich:

1. Alle Entscheidungen werden außerhalb der Einkaufsstätte getroffen.
2. Alle Entscheidungen – außer über die Einkaufsstätte und den Einkaufszeitpunkt – werden innerhalb der Einkaufsstätte getroffen.

Nicht ausgeschlossen, hier aber nicht weiter betrachtet, wird die Möglichkeit, dass Kunden auch zu einem ungeplanten Zeitpunkt eine ungeplante Einkaufsstätte aufsuchen. Zwischen den beiden Extrempunkten gibt es eine Reihe von Abstufungen. Zwei Beispiele: Das Produkt und die Marke sind geplant, nicht aber die

4. What is decided at the POP?

We will highlight one of the many aspects relating to the customer's needs and behaviour: planned and impulse purchases. Relevant literature shows that the customer's buying decision is either extensive, limited, habitualised, or impulsive. When making an extensive decision, customers decide extensively what product to buy and where to buy it. When making a limited decision, the choice and number of products and suppliers is limited, reference is made here to the so-called evoked set, or relevant set. A customer making a habitualised buying decision will opt for a proven solution, in this case, the evoked set consists of one product, or one supplier. These types of buying decisions are characterised by a varying degree of cognitive involvement and planning, which is highest in extensive decisions and lowest in habitualised decisions.

Things are different for what are called impulsive buying decisions. We will return to this term later, after taking a closer look at the difference between planned and unplanned purchases. This is important because unplanned purchases are often equated with impulse purchases, while defining impulse purchases as emotional, but not cognitive. That is unhelpful in finding an answer to the question what the customer decides at the shelf and how this decision can be encouraged by the retailer.

It is more helpful to understand what customers decide and when they make their decisions. Their decisions focus on what store to shop at, the time of purchase, products, pack sizes and spend. The following two extremes are possible:

1. *All decisions are made outside of the store.*
2. *All decisions, apart from where and when to shop, are made in the store.*

Another possibility that is not ruled out, but not taken into consideration here, is that customers may enter a store they had not planned to go to, at an unplanned time. In between the two extremes are a number of graduations as demonstrated by the following examples: The customer has decided what product and what brand to buy, but not what pack size; the customer has decided what product to buy, but not what brand and pack size. Empirical research on unplanned purchases is not consistent in its differentiation. But that is not the only reason why the results of empirical research should be treated with caution. Research on the customer's plan that is based only on shopping lists and notes neglects the possible existence of unwritten plans. Customers often make "mental notes" of their shopping lists and shopping journeys. They know where they want to buy a certain product. But measuring mistakes can occur even when examining written plans. Not necessarily will the customer plan to buy "Nutella" if "Nutella" has

Packungsgröße; das Produkt ist geplant, nicht aber die Marke und die Packungsgröße.

Diese Unterscheidungen treffen empirische Untersuchungen zu ungeplanten Käufen keineswegs konsequent. Aber nicht nur aus diesem Grund sind die Ergebnisse mit Vorsicht zu genießen: Die Planung ausschließlich über einen Einkaufszettel oder über einen Handzettel zu messen, vernachlässigt, dass Planungen auch nicht schriftlich verfasst sein können: Die Kunden haben den Einkaufszettel oder die Laufwege „im Kopf". Sie wissen, was sie an welcher Stelle kaufen wollen. Messfehler können sich aber auch bei schriftlicher Planung einschleichen: Die Angabe einer Marke, z. B. Nutella, muss keineswegs dafür stehen, dass diese Marke geplant ist. Vielmehr kann die Marke stellvertretend für ein Produkt stehen, in diesem Fall Nussnougatcreme. Welche Marke der Kunde tatsächlich kauft, kann sich erst am Regal entscheiden. Umgekehrt kann es sein, dass nur das Produkt auf dem Einkaufszettel steht, der Kunde aber bereits auf eine Marke festgelegt ist.

Wenn also Untersuchungsergebnisse über ungeplante Käufe sagen: „Rund 50 Prozent der Deutschen, vor allem Frauen und jüngere Konsumenten, bleiben beim Lebensmitteleinkauf trotz Einkaufszettel offen für Spontankäufe." (www.focus.de vom 18.3.2005) oder: „Etwa 70 Prozent der Kaufentscheidungen werden von den Kunden direkt vor dem Regal getroffen. Nur jeder Dritte hat einen Einkaufszettel." (www.gfk.com vom 27.3.2009), dann sollte man darauf achten, worauf sich die Planung bezieht und wie gemessen worden ist.

Kommen wir zurück zu den impulsiven Kaufentscheidungen und ordnen sie in die ungeplanten Käufe ein. Sehr häufig werden ungeplante Käufe ausschließlich als Impulskäufe bezeichnet und Impulskäufe mit Spontankäufen gleichgesetzt. Führt man sich aber vor Augen, welche kognitiven und emotionalen Prozesse bei den Kunden ablaufen, die einen ungeplanten Kauf tätigen, dann ist es sinnvoll, ungeplante Käufe in solche mit höherer und niedriger kognitiver Beteiligung zu unterscheiden. So unterteilt Baun ungeplante Käufe in (vgl. Baun 2003, S. 47 f.):

been written on the shopping list. The brand may simply be used as a generic term for a certain product, in this case hazelnut spread. Customers might decide only at the shelf what brand to buy. It may, however, also be the other way round: possibly, the customer has written the product on the shopping list, but has already decided to buy a certain brand.

This means that we should be alert when considering research on unplanned purchases stating that "approximately 50 % of German customers, in particular women and younger customers, remain open to spontaneous food purchases, despite having a shopping list" (www.focus.de, 18.3.2005), or "roughly 70 % of buying decisions are made directly at the shelf. Only one in three customers has a shopping list" (www.gfk.com, 27.3.2009). It is important to know what the customer's plan refers to and how these findings have been measured.

Returning to the issue of impulse buying decisions, we will consider impulse decisions as unplanned decisions. Very often, unplanned purchases are considered entirely as impulse purchases, with impulse purchases being equated with spontaneous purchases. If we take the customer's cognitive and emotional involvement into account, however, it makes sense to distinguish between unplanned purchases with a high cognitive involvement and unplanned purchases with a low cognitive involvement. Baun (see Baun 2003, p. 47 f.) distinguishes between four types of unplanned purchases:

- *Reminder purchases: stimuli at the POP remind customers to buy a product they need and should have planned, but did not plan to buy.*
- *Bargain purchases: a product considered by the customer to be a bargain triggers an unplanned purchase.*
- *Substitute purchases: customers are not satisfied with a product, or the product is not available and is replaced by a product they had not planned to buy.*
- *Planned pleasure purchases: the customer plans to reward himself with a special treat, but has not decided what to buy. The stimuli at the POP and the mood the customer is in decide on whether the customer will "give in to temptation".*

- Erinnerungskäufe: Stimuli am Point of Purchase erinnern den Kunden daran, ein Produkt zu kaufen, das er benötigt und das er hätte planen sollen, aber nicht geplant hat.
- Sonderangebotskäufe: Ein dem Kunden günstig erscheinendes Sonderangebot löst einen ungeplanten Kauf aus.
- Ersatzkäufe: Der Kunde ist mit dem geplanten Produkt nicht zufrieden oder das geplante Produkt ist nicht vorhanden und er ersetzt es durch ein anderes Produkt, das er nicht geplant hatte zu kaufen.
- Käufe geplanter Verführung: Der Kunden nimmt sich vor, etwas zu kaufen, etwa weil er sich belohnen möchte, hat aber kein konkretes Produkt geplant und überlässt es den Stimuli am Point of Purchase und seiner Stimmung, sich zu einem Kauf „verführen zu lassen".

Diese vier Arten von Spontankäufen zeichnen sich durch eine spürbare kognitive Beteiligung aus, d.h., es werden Bewertungen und Abwägungen vorgenommen. Anders ist dies bei dem Impulskauf: Ihn zeichnet aus, dass emotionale Kaufmotive dominieren, so bewirkt z. B. die Freude an einem Produkt den Wunsch, das Produkt zu besitzen. Kognitive Prozesse finden kaum statt. Umgangssprachlich kann man sagen, die Lust, der Impuls überwiegt, der Verstand ist ausgeschaltet. Die verschiedenen Arten ungeplanter Käufe verlangen verschiedene Maßnahmen, um sie am Point of Purchase zu fördern.

1	Nicht kommunizierte Neuerungen	▪ Regale und/oder Produkte werden im Geschäft zu häufig umgestellt. ▪ Liebgewonnene Produkte werden oft viel zu schnell durch neue Produkte ersetzt.
2	Mangelnde Überprüfbarkeit vertrauensbildender Eigenschaften	▪ Ich bin mir teilweise nicht sicher, was die vielen Produktaufmachungen bedeuten. ▪ Ich kenne mich bei den verschiedenen Produktbezeichnungen teilweise nicht so gut aus (z.B. Bio, lactosefrei). ▪ Preise ähnlicher Produkte lassen sich nur mühsam vergleichen.
3	Störende Angebotsvielfalt	▪ Es stehen aus meiner Sicht in den Geschäften zu viele Produkte zur Auswahl. ▪ Es ist nicht einfach, sich zwischen den Produkten zu entscheiden. ▪ Aus meiner Sicht gibt es in den Geschäften zu viele Informationen (z.B. Aktionstafeln).
4	Störende Einkaufsatmosphäre	▪ Zu starker Kundenandrang im Geschäft verhindert ein angenehmes Einkaufen. ▪ Beim Einkauf stören mich Kunden, wie lärmende Kinder, hektische Erwachsene usw. ▪ Wenn ich schon beim Eintreten ins Geschäft lange Warteschlangen an den Kassen sehe, gehe ich am liebsten wieder.
5	Mangelnde Differenzierung	▪ Ich bin mir manchmal nicht sicher, ob ein teureres Produkt wirklich besser ist als das billigere Produkt. ▪ Produkte sehen häufig ähnlich aus und sind doch nicht gleich.
1	Customers are not informed about changes	▪ Shelves, or products, are moved to new locations in the store too often ▪ Favourite products are replaced too often by new products
2	It is difficult to verify confidence-building features	▪ I am not sure what the product presentations all mean ▪ I am not familiar with many of the product specifications (e.g. organic and lactose-free products) ▪ Comparing the prices of similar products is tiresome
3	Too many products in the store	▪ In my opinion there are too many products in the store ▪ It is difficult to decide what product to buy ▪ In my opinion there is too much information in the store (e.g. advertising boards)
4	Customers feel disturbed in the store	▪ The store is too crowded. Shopping is no longer enjoyable. ▪ I feel disturbed in my shopping by noisy children, frantic adults etc. ▪ When I enter the store and see long queues at the check-out, I feel like turning on my heel.
5	The store lacks differentiation	▪ Sometimes I am not sure if the expensive product is really better than the cheaper one ▪ Products often look alike, but are not the same

(Quelle/Source: Liebmann 2006)

Abbildung 3: Zentrale Auslöser für Shopper Confusion
Figure 3: Central factors causing shopper confusion

5. Was Kunden am Point of Purchase erwarten

Aus dem Wissen darüber, wie Kunden ihre Käufe planen und wann sie zu ungeplanten Käufen neigen, lassen sich die Erwartungen der Kunden an die Einkaufsstätte und damit die Voraussetzungen für das POP-Marketing ableiten. Diese Voraussetzungen lassen sich unterteilen in das, was es zu vermeiden gilt, in diesem Beitrag am Thema Shopper Confusion verdeutlicht, und das, was es zu fördern gilt, hier am Thema Shopper Convenience veranschaulicht. Diese Betrachtung knüpft an den Zielen des POP-Marketings an (Abbildung 1).

These types of spontaneous purchases are characterised by marked cognitive involvement, i.e. the customer rates the product and considers its benefit. This does not apply to impulse purchases. Impulse purchases are emotionally-driven purchases. If a product appeals to customers, they simply want to have it. Cognitive control and elaboration are not constituent attributes of impulsive buying behaviour. In simply terms, the desire to have the product, the impulse, triumphs over reason. Different kinds of unplanned purchases call for different kinds of promotion measures at the POP.

5. What customers expect from the POP

Knowing how customers plan their shopping and when they are most inclined to making unplanned purchases means knowing what their

Abbildung 4: Shopper Confusion: Zu viele Stimuli und zu viele Menschen machen für den Kunden das Einkaufen anstrengend.
Figure 4: Shopper confusion: information overload and a crowded store turn shopping into an exhausting experience.

Shopper Confusion ist ein emotional geladener, dysfunktionaler Gemütszustand, der es dem Kunden erschwert, effizient und effektiv Stimuli zu selektieren und zu interpretieren (vgl. Schweizer 2004, S. 34). Daraus resultieren zwei Kernprobleme:

- Die Beeinträchtigung kognitiver Prozesse: Die Anzahl und die Qualität der Informationen verhindern oder erschweren es, dass die Kunden sie als kauffördernd wahrnehmen und entsprechend verarbeiten. Der Kauf bleibt aus.
- Die Beeinträchtigung emotionaler Prozesse: Die Kunden nehmen das Einkaufsumfeld als unangenehm wahr und verlieren die Lust am Einkaufen.

Beide Probleme können sowohl geplante als auch ungeplante Käufe verhindern. Es gibt mittlerweile eine Reihe empirischer Untersuchungen, die sich mit den Ursachen und den Folgen von Shopper Confusion befassen. So kommt Liebmann zu fünf zentralen Auslösern (Abbildung 3).

Viele dieser Aspekte betreffen die Anzahl, die Gestaltung und die Platzierung der Produkte. Daneben findet sich eine Rubrik „zu viele Informationen". Hält man sich einmal vor Augen, wie viele Möglichkeiten es gibt, in einer Einkaufsstätte Informationen zu verbreiten, wir denken hier z. B. an Durchsagen, Laden-TV, Verköstigungen, Displays, Deckenhänger, Dispenser,

expectations at the POP are and what the conditions must be for POP marketing to help customers with their buying decisions. We can distinguish between conditions that should be avoided, defined as shopper confusion in this article, and conditions that should be furthered, defined here as shopper convenience. These observations tie in with the goals of POP marketing (figure 1).

Shopper confusion is an emotionally charged, dysfunctional state of mind, which makes it difficult for the customer to efficiently and effectively select and understand stimuli (see Schweizer, 2004, p. 34). Shopper confusion creates two central problems:

- *Cognitive processes are adversely affected: There is too much, or poor information at the POP. It makes it difficult for customers, or prevents them from perceiving information as helpful and from using it for their purchase. No purchase is made.*
- *Emotional processes are adversely affected: The customer feels uncomfortable in the store and is put off shopping.*

Both problems can prevent planned as well as unplanned purchases. Extensive empirical research is available now that looks at the reasons and consequences of shopper confusion. Liebmann mentions five key factors causing shopper confusion (figure 3).

Many of these aspects regard the number, presentation and display of products. There is also the aspect "too much information". Bearing

Bodenaufkleber und Wobbler (ein Begriff aus dem Angeln, der einen künstlichen Köder beschreibt, der für das Angeln von Raubfischen verwendet wird), dann wird deutlich, dass die menschlichen Sinne auf vielfältige Weise angesprochen werden. Die Folge kann sein: Die Kunden haben Schwierigkeiten, Stimuli effizient und effektiv zu selektieren und zu interpretieren, es entsteht Shopper Confusion, sie wenden sich von den Stimuli und damit von einem möglichen Kauf ab. Die Kunden verhalten sich als Reizabschirmer.

Umfragen unter Handelsmanagern, wie sie regelmäßig von der Unternehmensgruppe Wiesbaden durchgeführt werden (zuletzt: POS-Marketing-Report 2008/2009), zeigen, dass die Akzeptanz gegenüber diesen Maßnahmen des POP-Marketings sehr hoch ist. Industrie und Handel sollten aber überlegen, ob sie mit dem intensiven Einsatz solcher Maßnahmen nicht das Gegenteil von dem erreichen, was gewollt ist, nämlich dem Kunden ein Umfeld zu verschaffen, in dem er erstens kaufrelevante Informationen aufnehmen kann und will und in dem er zweitens die Einkaufsatmosphäre als angenehm empfindet. Es muss das Ziel sein, ihn zum Reizsucher zu entwickeln.

Nähert man sich der Förderung von Käufen über das Thema Shopper Convenience, so geht es darum, den Kaufprozess vom Zugang zu und in dem Geschäft über die Entscheidungen des Kaufs, die Abwicklung des Einkaufs bis zu der Nachkaufphase zu unterstützen. An dem Beispiel der Zugangs-Convenience, und hier greifen wir die Kundenfreundlichkeit der Verkaufsräume heraus, lassen sich die Anforderungen eines Kunden an das POP-Marketing verdeutlichen (vgl. Reith 2007, S. 124 ff.):

in mind the almost endless possibilities of providing information in the store, for instance through announcements, in-store TV, tastings, displays, hangers, dispensers, floor graphics and wobblers (wobbler is a term used in fishing to describe a lure that resembles fish prey used to catch fish) it quickly becomes clear that there are many ways of stimulating people's senses. Loaded with too much information, customers may experience difficulties in efficiently and effectively selecting and understanding stimuli, which leads to shopper confusion. They turn away from the stimuli and abandon possible buying plans. This situation produces indolent buyers.

Surveys among retail managers like those carried out by Unternehmensgruppe Wiesbaden (most recently: POS Marketing Report 2008/2009) show that these POS marketing measures are largely accepted. Manufacturers and retailers should be careful, however, not to over-use these measures, because they might achieve the opposite of what was intended. The intention is to create an environment, which, firstly, makes it easy for customers to take in information that supports them in their purchase, and, secondly, offers an enjoyable shopping experience. The objective is to turn the customer into a sensualist.

Sales promotion that focuses on the concept of shopper convenience picks customers up when they enter the store, accompanies them on their journey through the store and provides assistance in their buying decision, during the purchase as well as after the purchase. Shopper convenience starts at the beginning of the customer's shopping journey. In terms of store access convenience, in order to be considered as customer-friendly, stores must meet the following customer needs (see Reith 2007, p. 124 ff.):

Abbildung 5: Im Raiffeisen-Markt in Borken zieht ein Traktor oder ein lebensgroßer Gartenzwerg die Aufmerksamkeit der Kunden auf sich.
Figure 5: A tractor or life-size garden gnome attracts the customer's attention in the Raffeisen store in Borken.

Abbildung 6: Die Zweitplatzierung in diesem Beispiel kann zu Missverständnissen beim Kunden führen.
Figure 6: The secondary placement in this example could be misleading and might confuse the customer.

- Ich kann mich im Markt einfach orientieren, z. B. durch Hinweisschilder.
- In den Verkaufsräumen kann man sich bequem bewegen, z. B. durch breite Gänge.
- Die Wege zu den Regalen mit den gewünschten Produkten kosten wenig Zeit.
- Ich kann die gewünschten Produkte im Markt einfach finden.
- Die Waren können mit wenig Anstrengung aus den Regalen genommen werden.
- Die Umfeldbedingungen, z. B. Temperatur, Musik, Beleuchtung, sind in den Verkaufsräumen angenehm.
- In den Verkaufsräumen fühle ich mich nicht gestresst.

- *I can easily find my way around the store, signs make orientation easy.*
- *Moving around in the store is comfortable, aisles are wide.*
- *Finding the shelf with the desired product takes little time.*
- *I can easily locate the product I am looking for in the store.*
- *Taking the product from the shelf is easy.*
- *Overall conditions in the store, including temperature, music and lighting are good.*
- *I do not feel stressed in the store.*

Manche Kunden empfinden beim Einkaufen an verschiedenen Stellen und in verschiedenen Situationen Stress. Häufig genannte Bereiche sind die Bedienungstheken und die Kasse. Hier ist es sinnvoll, die Kunden durch die Verringerung der Reizmenge und durch klare Hinweise zu entlasten. In vielen Einkaufsstätten muss man jedoch den Eindruck gewinnen, dass Händler das Motto „Viel hilft viel" verfolgen. Viel an Schildern jeglicher Art, viel an Farben, viel an Formen, viel an elektronischen Medien, die die Kunden informieren sollen. Werden diese Mittel nicht gezielt an Kaufphasen und Orten höherer Empfänglichkeit ausgerichtet, verkehren sich die beabsichtigen Wirkungen in ihr Gegenteil. Die Kunden wenden sich den Informationen nicht zu, sondern von ihnen ab. In diesen Fällen gilt also: Weniger ist mehr. Demgegenüber ist es an anderen Stellen in der Einkaufsstelle sinnvoll, den Kunden Abwechslung, Neues, Interessantes und Aufregendes zu bieten. Man kommt denjenigen Kunden entgegen, die bewusst eine solche Abwechselung suchen, hierzu zählen die so genannten Variety Seeker als auch solche Kunden, die empfänglich sind für neue emotionale und kognitive Anspannungen. In diesen Fällen gilt also: Es darf ein bisschen mehr sein.

Es ist aber darauf hinzuweisen, dass ein zu hohes Maß an Abwechslung zur Desorientierung führen kann, nämlich dann, wenn die für die Orientierung wichtigen inneren Landkarten zerstört

Some customers consider shopping at the store as stressful at certain stages of their shopping journey. Customers often feel stressed at the serving counter or in the checkout area. It is useful to limit the amount of stimuli in these areas and offer customers helpful information that is easy to understand. Many retailers, however, seem to act according to the motto "the more the better" in their stores. The more signs, colours, shapes and electronic media informing the customer the better. If information and measures are not targeted and used at the relevant times and places in the store, retailers are likely to achieve the opposite of what they had intended. Customers do not welcome, but turn away from the information. In this case the motto is: less is better.

On the other hand, it can be useful to surprise customers and offer them new, interesting and exciting experiences in the store. This is in the interest of all customers seeking a new experience in a store, including the so-called variety seekers, as well as customers who are open to emotional and cognitive exertion. Here the motto is: a little more won't hurt.

It should be mentioned, however, that too much variety can lead to disorientation if the customer's mental maps are destroyed, for instance by frequently changing secondary placements (see Kroeber-Riel/Weinberg/Gröppel-Klein 2009, p. 472). So the order of the day is to strike the right balance between exertion and relaxation.

werden, etwa durch den häufigen Wechsel von Zweitplatzierungen (vgl. Kroeber-Riel/Weinberg/Gröppel-Klein 2009, S. 472). Daher ist das richtige Maß zwischen Anspannung und Entspannung zu finden.

Das gilt auch vor dem Hintergrund, dass viele Kunden ihre Wege durch den Laden in verschiedenen Geschwindigkeiten zurücklegen, am Anfang schnell, dann langsam, zum Schluss wieder schnell. Entsprechend sollten die Reizmengen darauf abgestimmt sein. Somit schließt sich hier der Kreis zu dem zuvor Gesagten: Das Verhalten der Kunden ist ganzheitlich zu betrachten, nicht alle Kunden haben dieselben Verhaltensweisen, die POP-Maßnahmen sind darauf auszurichten.

6. Konsequenzen für die Gestaltung des POP-Marketings

Jede Einkaufsstätte wird wegen ihrer Positionierung und der von ihr angesprochenen Zielgruppen ein gewisses Maß an Individualität aufweisen, wenn es um die Planung und Umsetzung geeig-

This should be born in mind when considering that customers change pace during their shopping journey in the store. They tend to start off quickly, then slow down only to pick up pace again towards the end of the shopping journey. The amount of stimuli should vary accordingly. This brings us full circle to what has been said before: a holistic view of the customer is needed, not all customers have the same habits, and all POS measures must take this into account.

6. Implications for POP marketing

Due to its position in the market and the target groups it caters for, every store will plan and introduce more or less individually tailored POP marketing measures. In view of the goal of reducing shopper confusion and increasing shopper convenience, however, we can make the following basic recommendations:

1. *The core statement is that a concept must be developed that takes into account the overall appearance of the store, the location of its departments and all dedicated areas. Measures are required that create alternating phases of exertion and relaxation*

Abbildung 7: Das Frischecenter EDEKA-Zurheide kombiniert geschickt eine ansprechend gestaltete Ruhezone mit der Möglichkeit, Produkte auszuprobieren.
Figure 7: EDEKA cleverly uses the attractively designed rest area in its store in Zurheide as a demonstration area where customers can test-taste its products.

neter POP-Maßnahmen geht. Vor dem Hintergrund der Ziele, die Shopper Confusion zu verringern und Shopper Convenience zu vermitteln, lassen sich gleichwohl einige grundsätzliche Empfehlungen aussprechen.

1. Die Kernaussage: Mit Blick auf die gesamte Einkaufsstätte, die Lage der Abteilungen und die verschiedenen Funktionsflächen sowie auf die Laufwege die Kunden ist ein Konzept von Maßnahmen zu entwickeln, bei dem sich Anspannung und Entspannung abwechseln, bei dem auf der einen Seite Überraschungen geboten, auf der anderen Seite die vorhandenen kognitiven Strukturen, d.h. das Gelernte, wie innere Lagepläne, gewohnte Wege und zusammengehörige Produkte, unterstützt werden.
2. Warenferne Funktionszonen einrichten: Diese Bereiche sprechen z.B. das Bedürfnis der Erholung (Sitzgelegenheit) und das Stillen von Hunger und Durst (Handelsrestaurants, Kaffee-Ecken etc.) an. Viele Einzelhändler bieten ihren Kunden bislang kaum Raum für Entspannung. Positive Beispiele sind das Frischecenter EDEKA-Zurheide (Abbildung 7), das Bekleidungskaufhaus von P&C in Köln, die Buchgeschäfte von Thalia sowie die Sitzgelegenheiten, wie sie im Drogeriemarkt von dm zu finden sind.
3. Warennahe Funktionszonen einrichten: Diese Bereiche kommen vor allem dem Bedürfnis der Kunden entgegen, Produkte auszuprobieren. Dazu zählen Umkleidekabinen im Bekleidungseinzelhandel, die den Kunden auch genügend Raum, Sitz- und Ablagegelegenheiten bieten, und Flächen zum Ausprobieren von Produkten. So hat der französische Sporthändler Décathlon durch die Ausweitung von Testflächen seinen Umsatz um 10% steigern können (vgl. Kreutz 2000, S. 179 f.). „Mehr Testflächen" lautet auch das Motto der 2009 neu eröffneten Filialen von Karstadt Sport.
4. Warenvielfalt reduzieren: Die Zahl der Artikel in einer Warengruppe ist überschaubar zu halten. Weniger vorrätig gehaltene Artikel (Stock Keeping Units) und mehr Platz (Facings) für die vorhandenen Artikel nehmen viele Kunden als ein umfangreicheres (sic!) Angebot wahr, aus dem sie dann auch auswählen. Daher werden sich viele Einzelhändler auf die stärksten Herstellermarken sowie – sofern in der

and offer surprise moments while at the same time respecting existing cognitive structures, i.e. acquired knowledge like mental maps, familiar itineraries and products that belong together.

2. *Set up service areas where customers can, for instance, rest (seating) and eat and drink (store restaurants, cafes etc.). Many retailers fail to offer customers spaces where they can relax. EDEKA in Zurheide (figure 7), the Cologne store of clothing retailer P&C, the Thalia bookshops and the sitting areas of drug store chain dm can be cited as positive examples.*
3. *Set up service areas where customers can try products. These areas include changing rooms in clothing stores that offer sufficient space for customers and their belongings as well as appropriate seating, as well as areas where customers can touch, try or test-taste products. The decision of French sporting goods retailer Decathlon to expand its demonstration areas has contributed to a 10% increase in sales (see Kreutz, p. 179 f.). Karstadt Sport has also dedicated more space to demonstration areas in stores that were opened in 2009.*
4. *Be more selective in the choice of products. Every category should be limited to a manageable number of articles. Less stock-keeping units on more space is often perceived by customers to be a larger (sic!) range on offer, from which they will then actually choose a product. Retailers are therefore likely to focus on the strongest brands as well as on private label that are possibly part of the category.*
5. *Arrange categories and items according to how customers look for products. Extensive research has been carried out, (see, e.g. Schröder/Möller/Zimmermann 2007) finding that sub-categories are arranged on the shelves according to a vertical order of meaning. Brands are displayed horizontally, products vertically. Furthermore, the different sub-categories are separated by vertical signs that feature one product representing an entire sub-category. This way of displaying products promotes planned purchases in particular, because they are conform with the customer's cognitive structures.*
6. *Use targeted information. Media that provides too much information about products on shelves and the shelf's adjacencies can lead to an overload that confuses customers. In simple words, be sure to avoid a forest of signs. Information must make sense to the customer. That is the only way to encourage*

Warengruppe vertreten – ihre Handelsmarken konzentrieren.

5. Warengruppen und Artikel nach der Suchlogik der Kunden anordnen: Hierzu sind in den letzten Jahre viele Untersuchungen durchgeführt worden (vgl. z. B. Schröder/Berghaus 2005, Schröder/Berghaus/Zimmermann 2005, Schröder/Möller/Zimmermann 2007). Das Ergebnis ist, dass die Subwarengruppen als vertikale Sinneinheiten platziert werden, Marken horizontal, Produkte vertikal. Zudem werden die Subwarengruppen optisch durch vertikale Schilder getrennt, auf denen z. B. ein Produkt stellvertretend für eine Subwarengruppe abgebildet ist. Die Maßnahmen unterstützen vor allem geplante Käufe, weil sie den kognitiven Strukturen der Kunden entgegenkommen.
6. Informationen gezielt einsetzen: Die Medien, die im Regal und im näheren Umfeld des Regals Informationen über die Produkte vermitteln, dürfen nicht zu einem reizabschirmenden Verhalten der Kunden führen. Salopp formuliert: Schilderwälder sind zu vermeiden. Vielmehr müssen die Informationen als sinnvoll wahrgenommen werden. Nur so lassen sich Erinnerungskäufe, Sonderangebotskäufe und Ersatzkäufe wie auch Impulskäufe fördern.
7. Zonen für wechselnde Platzierungen von Waren festlegen: Diese müssen sich in die gesamte Abfolge von Anspannung und Entspannung einfügen. Die immense Ansammlung vieler Displays und Zweitplatzierungen wird diesem Prinzip ebenso wenig gerecht wie die übermäßige Anhäufung medialer Instrumente. Was die Kunden als immens oder übermäßig wahrnehmen, lässt sich nur in Abhängigkeit von den jeweiligen Gegebenheiten ermitteln, wie z. B. der Größe des Geschäftes, der Art der Waren sowie der Breite und Tiefe des Sortimentes. Kaufimpulse können sowohl von großen Stückzahlen eines Artikels („Masse zieht an.") als auch von Artikeln ausgehen, die unter einem Thema präsentiert werden. So präsentiert z. B. der Sportfachhändler Globetrotter die Waren in einer Umgebung, die an die Verwendungsorte erinnern (vgl. Hurth 2006, S. 135).
8. Die Ladengestaltung und die Warenpräsentation als Teil der Markenführung betrachten: Alle Gestaltungsmittel in der Einkaufsstätte, von der Ware über die Instore-Medien bis hin zum Verkaufspersonal, sollen dem Kunden zu erkennen geben, bei welchem Händler er sich befindet und für welches Verkaufsversprechen dieser Händler steht. Wer dieses Prinzip konsequent verfolgt, wird weniger starke Herstellermarken durch Handelsmarken ersetzen, wird auf Werbematerialen der Hersteller verzichten und wird statt dessen Displays, Hinweisschilder und sonstige Medien benutzen, die den Händler mit seiner Marke, der Händlermarke, als Absender erkennen lassen.

reminder purchases, bargain purchases and impulse purchases.

7. *Settle on permanent areas for changing product presentations. These areas must take into account the alternating phases of exertion and relaxation. Too many displays and secondary placements and too many marketing tools are not conducive to this principle. What customers perceive as huge or excessive can be established only by taking into account the particularities of the situation like, for instance, the size of the store, the type of goods on offer as well as the variety and number of products. The impulse to buy can be triggered by large numbers of a particular product ("mass attracts mass") as well as by product presentations that follow a particular theme. Outdoor retailer Globetrotter, for instance, presents products in surroundings that look like the places they are normally used in (see Hurth 2006, p. 135).*
8. *Consider store design and product presentation as an integral part of brand management. All of the store's attributes, from the product to in-store media and sales staff should be recognised by the customer as being characteristic of the store. Customers know exactly where they are and easily identify the retailer's product claim. Retailers who follow this principle will replace not-so-strong brands with private labels and will abandon using promotional material supplied by the manufacturer to instead use displays, signs and other media that is identified by the customer to belong to the retailer, the retailer's brand and brand message.*

Hendrik Schröder

Louise Spillard

Der neue „Wettbewerb um Preis und Qualität" – Wie Käufer in Europa ihre Kaufentscheidungen verändern

Jüngste Untersuchungen der IGD zeigen, dass als Folge eines starken „Wettbewerbs um Preis und Qualität" unter Lebensmitteleinzelhändlern und -herstellern überall in Europa neue Formen der Kundenbindung entstehen, der Markt ist derzeit in Bewegung. Als Director of Research bei IGD untersuche ich mit meinem Team, wie Käufer in Frankreich, Deutschland, Spanien und Großbritannien auf das Wirtschaftsklima reagieren.

Vor der Finanzkrise verfügten die Kunden in der Regel über eine hohe Kaufkraft und wenig Zeit. Die Industrie entwickelte Strategien, Sortimente und Kommunikationsformen, um diesen Bedürfnissen zu entsprechen. Die globale Krise wirkte sich jedoch schon bald auf die Budgets der Käufer aus und führte zu einer rapiden Veränderung des Konsumverhaltens: Bargeld wurde jetzt zunehmend knapper und die Kunden waren bereit, für ihren Einkauf mehr Zeit zu investieren.

Bald entstanden neue Gewohnheiten, man aß jetzt häufiger zuhause und seltener im Restaurant, es wurde gekocht, was noch vorrätig war, und man widmete dem Einkauf und den Entscheidungen über die Wahl eines Produkts mehr Zeit und Aufmerksamkeit. Die Industrie sah sich mit einem neuen Käufertypus konfrontiert, der sich in seinem Kaufverhalten dem Wirtschaftsklima angepasst hatte.

In unserer jüngsten Untersuchung analysieren wir das Kaufverhalten in den Hauptmärkten Westeuropas: in Frankreich, Deutschland, Spanien und Großbritannien. Wir befragten eine große Anzahl von Käufern in diesen Märkten, begleiteten sie bei ihren Lebensmitteleinkäufen und diskutierten in kleinen Gruppen über die Kaufgewohnheiten. Außerdem führten wir eine europaweite Lieferantenbefragung durch, um herauszufinden, mit welchen Maßnahmen Hersteller auf diese Veränderungen reagieren.

Reaktionen auf das Wirtschaftsklima – Preis und Qualität sind entscheidend für den Käufer

Mehr als ein Viertel (27 %) der Käufer in diesen Märkten kaufen angesichts der veränderten Wirtschaftslage Nahrungs- und

Louise Spillard

The 'contest for value' – how shoppers in Europe are making their buying decisions

Latest research from IGD reveals new shopper loyalties are emerging across Europe as food retailers and manufacturers engage in an intense 'contest for value.' Louise Spillard, Director of Research at IGD, looks at how shoppers in France, Germany, Spain and Britain are responding to the economic climate.

Before the recent credit-crunch, shoppers were considered to be 'cash rich and time poor' and industry had developed strategies, ranges and communications designed to meet these needs. However, as the global crunch filtered down to shoppers' budgets, consumer behaviour quickly changed, and shoppers began trading time back for cash.

New habits such as eating at home instead of out at restaurants, cooking more from scratch, shopping around more and taking more time over product choices quickly emerged, and industry was faced with a new type of shopper, adapting to the economic climate.

Our research looks at shopper behaviour in the key western European markets of France, Germany, Spain and Britain. We've spoken to thousands of shoppers in these markets, joined them as they shop for groceries, and spent time discussing their shopping habits with them in small groups. We've also conducted a pan-European supplier poll, to see what actions manufacturers are taking in response to the economy.

Reacting to the economic climate – price and value key for shoppers

Over a quarter (27 %) of shoppers in these markets are making changes to their food and grocery shopping in response to the economy and nearly three quarters of these (70 %) intend to make the change permanent. The new shopping habits, developed out of economic need, are working for them, and shoppers are unlikely to swiftly change back as soon as the situation changes.

IGD shopper research revealed that price was a key driver of product choice and we are now seeing shoppers increasingly willing

Lebensmittel anders ein als zuvor, davon beabsichten fast drei Viertel (70%), ihr verändertes Kaufverhalten beizubehalten. Die aus wirtschaftlichen Gründen veränderten Kaufgewohnheiten haben für die Käufer positive Konsequenzen, denn oft ist ein in der Qualität gleichwertiges Produkt zu einem günstigeren Preis erworben worden – es ist somit unwahrscheinlich, dass der Käufer die neuen Gewohnheiten direkt wieder ablegen wird, sobald die wirtschaftliche Situation sich wieder verbessert.

Eine IGD-Studie zeigt, dass der Preis eine wesenliche Rolle bei der Entscheidung für oder gegen den Kauf eines Produkts spielt. Hinzu kommt eine größere Experimentierbereitschaft der Käufer, was das Produkt oder die Einkaufsstätte betrifft. Um Geld zu sparen, ist man bereit, auf günstigere Produkte und Anbieter umzusteigen.

Ein einheitliches Bild

In allen vier Ländern war die Tendenz ähnlich: Veränderung oder Einschränkung des Kaufverhaltens, Erwägung weiterer Konsequenzen im Falle einer Verschlechterung der Situation und eine gewisse Beharrlichkeit, an den neuen Gewohnheiten festzuhalten. Deutsche Käufer brachten dabei im Gegensatz zu Käufern in Großbritannien und Frankreich ihre dauerhaft veränderten Einkaufsgewohnheiten eher nicht mit der wirtschaftlichen Krise in Zusammenhang. Das lässt sich möglicherweise durch den geringeren Anstieg der Arbeitslosenquote im Vergleich zum restlichen Europa zur Zeit der Untersuchung erklären.

Einschneidende Veränderungen in unserer Industrie stehen unmittelbar bevor, die jüngsten Veränderungen im Einkaufsverhalten und die Absicht der Käufer, neue Gewohnheiten beizubehalten, haben neue Bedingungen für die Zukunft der Industrie geschaffen.

Wie gut sind wir vorbereitet?

Nur 14% der Lebensmittelhersteller hatten sich schon im Vorfeld mit entsprechenden Plänen auf die Krise vorbereitet – und einige dieser Firmen planen jetzt für die Zukunft. Allen schlechten Prognosen zum Trotz eröffnen sich durch die veränderten Kaufgewohnheiten auch neue Geschäftsmöglichkeiten, und die Experimentierbereitschaft des heutigen Käufers birgt Chancen für alle Marktteilnehmer.

Veränderte Schwerpunkte im Lebensmitteleinzelhandel

Studienübergreifend ließen sich zwei bedeutende Schwerpunkte für Käufer und Industrie erkennen: Private Label-(Handelsmarken)-Trends und das wachsende Niedrigpreissegment.

to experiment how they shop, where they shop and what they buy – seeking every opportunity to save some money.

A consistent picture

Across the four markets we surveyed, general trends of relative current inertia, the potential for more widespread change should the situation worsen, and the 'stickiness' of the new behaviours, were fairly consistent. German shoppers, however, were less likely to identify permanent changes to their shopping habits as a specific result of the downturn compared to their British and French counterparts. This may be explained by the lower rate of unemployment growth experienced in Germany compared to the rest of Europe during the time of the research. Our industry is on the cusp of major change but the recent shift in shopper behaviour and the fact that shoppers intend to stick to newly formed habits, gives us useful indications of what our industry's future might look like.

How well prepared are we?

Just 14% of businesses in the food and grocery industry had a plan in place to tackle the downturn prior to it happening – and now many of these organisations are planning for the future. Despite

Käufer in allen vier untersuchten Märkten gaben an, mehr Private Label-Produkte zu kaufen, unabhängig davon, wie die bisherige Verbreitung und Akzeptanz von Private Label in den einzelnen Märkten war. Mehr als ein Viertel gaben zudem an, mehr bei Discountern, wie Aldi, Lidl, Norma, Penny, Netto und Plus, einzukaufen.

Die Übereinstimmung zwischen den verschiedenen Nationen ist angesichts der unterschiedlichen Marktanteile der Discounter in den vier Märkten beachtlich. In Großbritannien haben Aldi, Lidl und Dansk Netto zusammen einen Marktanteil von 6 %, in Deutschland beträgt der Anteil nach Angaben von IGD mittlerweile 39 %.

Auch wenn ein gewisser Anteil von Käufern angibt, unabhängig von der Wirtschaftskrise mehr Private Label-Produkte (16 %) und mehr bei Discountern (14 %) zu kaufen, hat die globale Krise diesen Trend ganz klar verstärkt – sowohl aus Sicht der Nachfrage als auch des Angebots.

Private Label

Handelsmarken bieten dem experimentierfreudigen Käufer ein Produkt mit einem guten Preis-Leistungs-Verhältnis, und die jüngsten Untersuchungsergebnisse zeigen, dass die Mehrheit der Käufer in diesem Segment eine Verbesserung der Qualität festgestellt hat.

Diese Veränderung kam nicht über Nacht – Einzelhändler haben sich mit einem innovativen Lieferantenkreis umgeben, der sich über technische Hindernisse hinwegsetzt und komplett neue Produktkategorien entwickelt.

Die weitreichendste Verbesserung hat in Deutschland stattgefunden – Initiativen wie der komplette Relaunch des Private Label-Sortiments bei EDEKA 2007 und die kontinuierlichen Investitionen in das Private Label-Geschäft von Rewe haben dazu geführt, dass 73 % der Käufer eine Verbesserung der Qualität von Private Label-Produkten wahrgenommen haben.

potential challenges, plenty of business opportunities still exist and the experimental nature of current shopper behaviour creates prospects for everyone.

Two areas of focus

Across IGD's pan-European research, two significant areas of focus for both shoppers and the industry emerged; trends in private label and the growth of the discount channel.

Shoppers across all four countries surveyed said they were buying more private label products, regardless of the different level of private label penetration in each country. There was also a consistent trend across the countries when we asked shoppers if they were purchasing more or less from discount stores, with over a quarter claiming to be shopping more at discounters (such as Aldi, Lidl, Norma, Penny, Netto and Plus).

The level of consistency between nations is striking when we consider the variation in the discounters' market share across these four coun-

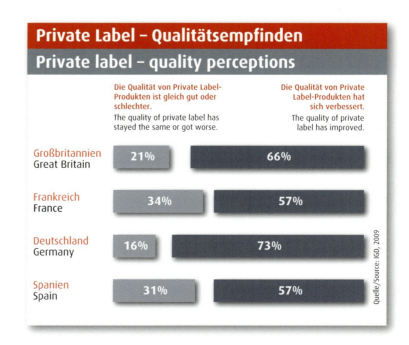

In Großbritannien glauben zwei Drittel der Käufer, dass sich die Qualität von Private Label-Produkten in den vergangenen Jahren verbessert hat. Britische Supermärkte entwickeln, erneuern und erweitern kontinuierlich ihr Private Label-Angebot, was zu einem „Drei-Stufen"-System bei allen führenden Unternehmen führt. Angeboten werden auch spezielle Sortimente, wie gesundheitsbewusste Produkte, Bioprodukte oder kindergerechte Erzeugnisse. Darüber hinaus investieren Einzelhändler auch in die Verbesserung der Rezeptur und Verpackung von Produkten bestehender Sortimente.

Die Hauptstärke von Private Label-Produkten bleibt jedoch nach wie vor das bessere Preis-Leistungsverhältnis gegenüber dem Markenartikel. 77 % der deutschen und 69 % der britischen Käufer sind sich darin einig. Die entscheidende Frage, die sich der Markenindustrie derzeit stellt, ist, wie die Preislücke zwischen Private Label-Produkten und Eigenmarkenprodukten geschlossen werden kann und – falls dies nicht realisierbar ist – wie die Preisdifferenz vor dem Kunden gerechtfertigt werden kann.

Discounter

Der Einkauf beim Discounter bietet Käufern eine zusätzliche Möglichkeit, gute Qualität für wenig Geld zu bekommen, und die Erfahrungen der Käufer mit dem Sortiment sind sehr positiv.

Da die deutschen Käufer die Qualität der Produkte von Discountern schätzen, ist es nicht verwunderlich, dass mehr als drei Viertel (77 %) der Käufer, die regelmäßig bei Discountern einkaufen (d.h. Stammkäufer), die Qualität der Produkte als gleichwertig oder besser als die etablierter Marken einstufen. Deutsche Käufer, die nur gelegentlich bei Discountern einkaufen, bewerten die dort gekauften Produkte weniger gut als Käufer in Spanien, wobei fast sechs von zehn (58 %) die Qualität von Discounter-Produkten und Markenprodukten gleichstellen.

Selbst in Großbritannien wird die Produktqualität der Discounter als hoch eingeschätzt, wobei die Hälfte der regelmäßigen Käufer die beim Discounter gekauften Produkte als gleich gut oder besser als bekannte Marken bewerten. Einige britische Käufer betrachten Produkte von Discountern eher als Exklusivmarken denn als Private Label-Marken, für andere sind bestimmte Discounter-Produkte typisch kontinental. Käufer, die nicht bei Discountern einkaufen, schätzen die Qualität dieser Produkte nied-

tries. In the UK, Aldi, Lidl and Dansk Netto hold a combined market share of 6 %, while in Germany market share has now reached 39 %, according to IGD.

Although a proportion of shoppers claim to be buying more private label (16 %) and shopping more at discounters (14 %) irrespective of the credit-crunch, the global downturn has clearly accelerated these trends – from both demand and supply perspectives.

Private label

Private label provides a route for the experimental shopper to seek value, and our latest research reveals that the majority of shoppers feel quality has been improving.

This hasn't happened overnight - retailers have encouraged a very sophisticated base of suppliers, doing things differently, pushing back technical boundaries and developing entirely new categories.

We've seen the most dramatic improvement in Germany, where initiatives from German grocers, such as the complete re-launch of EDEKA's private label range in 2007 and the continued investment in private label by Rewe, has led 73 % of German shoppers to agree that private label quality has improved.

In Britain, two-thirds of shoppers think that private label quality has improved in recent years. British supermarkets have continued to develop, refresh and extend their private label ranges, ensuring all major operators have a 'three tier' proposition and adding specialist ranges, such as healthy eating, organic or children's

Discounter-Produkte werden gleichwertig oder besser bewertet als etablierte Marken.

Discounter products perceived to be similar to or better than 'well known' brands.

Quelle/Source: IGD, 2009

riger ein, was gleichzeitig für Discounter das Potenzial birgt, die Erwartungen derer zu übertreffen, die einem Discounter-Produkt dennoch eine Chance geben.

Markenstärke

IGD hat auch Lebensmitteleinzelhändler dazu befragt, wo sie die Stärke von Herstellermarken sehen. In der Vergangenheit stand die Marke in erster Linie für Qualität und Innovation. Heute gehören aus Sicht des Käufers diese Eigenschaften nicht mehr alleine zu den primären Vorzügen von Markenprodukten.

Für deutsche Käufer ist Vertrauen in den Hersteller das Wichtigste, Produktkompetenz und Qualität werden jedoch ebenfalls als Schlüsselmerkmale von Markenstärke genannt. Für britische Käufer ist Tradition besonders wichtig. In Frankreich spiegelt das Merkmal „Breite Distribution" den regionalen Fokus von vielen Lebensmittelhändlern wider, während Spanien das Land ist, in dem Käufer sich am meisten durch die Sonderangebote von Herstellerprodukten angesprochen fühlen.

Eine solche Bandbreite von unterschiedlichen Ansichten in den einzelnen Ländern unterstreicht, wie länderspezifisch die Struktur unserer Industrie aufgebaut ist und wie wichtig es ist, sich bei der Einführung eines Produktes an den individuellen Anforderungen des jeweiligen Marktes zu orientieren.

Es ist jedoch auch ein gewisser Grad an Übereinstimmung zwischen den vier europäischen Märkten festzustellen. Für alle Käufer ist die Verlässlichkeit auf ein Produkt, auf seinen Geschmack und seine Qualität in einer bestimmten Produktkategorie bei der Beurteilung von Markenstärke ausschlaggebend. Im Gegensatz hierzu werden Anspruch und Internationalität selten als Merkmale für Markenstärke genannt.

Wie es weitergeht

Ein Drittel der Käufer in Deutschland (33%) und Großbritannien (31%) sowie ein Viertel der Käufer in Frankreich (25%) und Spanien (24%) haben ihr Kaufverhalten als Folge der Finanzkrise

ranges. Furthermore, retailers continue to invest in existing ranges through product reformulation and packaging redesigns.

However, the clear primary strength of private label for European shoppers is the fact it is cheaper than brands for the equivalent quality. Seventy-seven per cent of German shoppers and 69% of British shoppers were in agreement. Our industry must pose the question: can the price gap between private label and own-brand products be closed, and if not, can the difference be justified?

Dicounters

Shopping at discounters provides another opportunity for those seeking value and shoppers are very positive about the products they find there.

As German shoppers are attracted by the quality of products at discounters, it is not surprising that over three quarters (77%) of regular (i.e. primary and secondary) discounter shoppers in Germany rate discounter products at parity with or better than well know brands. Occasional discounter shoppers in Germany are less favourable than their Spanish counterparts, although almost six in ten (58%) do place them alongside well known brands.

Even in Britain, perceptions of product quality are high, with half of regular shoppers rating discounter products as equally good as well known brands, if not better. Some British shoppers view discounter products as exclusive brands rather than private label and others regard certain products as being authentically continental. Those not shopping at discounters have lower quality perceptions of discounter products, although this does demonstrate the potential for discounters to exceed expectations having persuaded someone to give them a go.

Strength of brands

IGD also asked grocery shoppers what they see as the key strengths of manufacturer branded goods. Historically, brands have been about "aspiration and innovation", so it was interesting to find that this is not what shoppers are currently giving brand owners credit for.

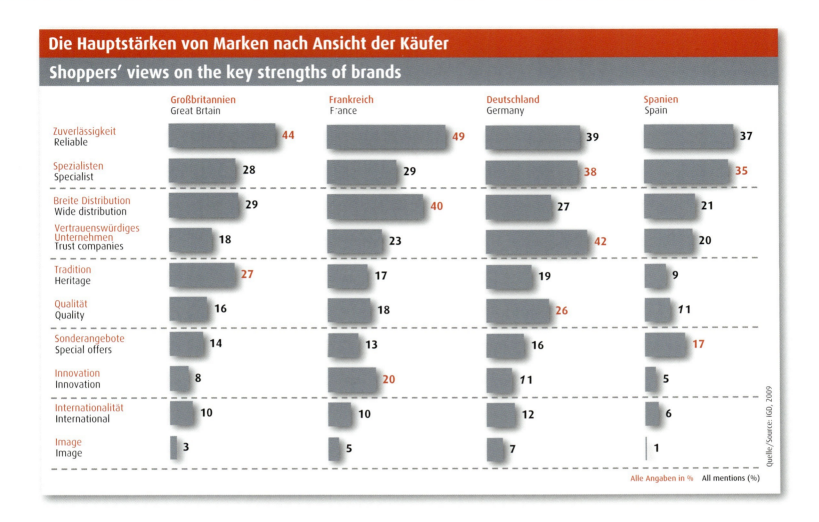

noch nicht wesentlich verändert, erwarten jedoch, dass sich die Situation verschlechtern wird. Während viele Käufer schon dabei sind, ihre Gewohnheiten zu verändern, experimentierfreudiger werden und Qualität und Wert neu einschätzen, werden so manche Käufer erst längerfristig ihr Kaufverhalten verändern.

Die veränderten Gewohnheiten werden die Kunden nicht so schnell wieder ablegen, was die Unternehmen, die neue Marktanteile gewonnen haben, vor die Aufgabe stellt, dem Kunden langfristig ein gutes Preis-Leistungsverhältnis zu bieten, um ihn auf Dauer an ihr Produkt zu binden.

Hersteller von Markenartikeln müssen sich im Klaren darüber sein, dass „Wahrnehmung gleich Realität ist", und die Käufer haben Private Label- und Discounter-Produkte positiv bewertet. Marken haben zwar immer noch viele Stärken aus Sicht des Käufers und spielen damit eine Schlüsselrolle. Die Markenhersteller müssen sich dabei aber bewusst machen, was Käufer motiviert, Markenprodukte zu kaufen. Eine Marke lebt nicht nur von ihrem über Jahrzehnte gefestigten Image, sondern wird zunehmend im direkten Vergleich mit anderen Produkten gemessen werden.

For German shoppers, trust in manufacturers ranks as the most important factor, with product expertise and quality also more widely viewed as strengths in brands. For British shoppers the importance of brand heritage is clear. In France, the wide distribution of brands reflects the regional focus of many grocers, while in Spain more shoppers are drawn to manufacturer brands by promotions than in any other market.

Such a spread of shopper views supports the intrinsically local nature of our industry, and the importance of country-by-country tailoring of your route to market.

There is also a degree of consistency between these four European markets. Offering reliable taste/quality and demonstrating category expertise were perceived by shoppers as key strengths for brands, whereas an aspirational image and international reach are rarely regarded as strengths for brands.

The road ahead

A third of shoppers in Germany (33 %) and Britain (31 %) and a quarter of shoppers in France (25 %) and Spain (24 %) have yet to make major changes to their grocery shopping during the downturn,

In solch einem bewegten Markt, in dem sich neue Formen der Kundentreue bilden, müssen Einzelhändler und Lebensmittelhersteller schnell auf die neuen Herausforderungen reagieren, vor die sie die wirtschaftliche Lage gestellt hat. Der Wettbewerb um die Käufer zielt darauf ab, Wert zu bieten, und die Erfolgreichsten profitieren schon davon. Es gibt noch großen Spielraum angesichts der großen Zahl der Käufer, die ihre Gewohnheiten erst noch ändern werden. Eine genau Beobachtung der Kaufgewohnheiten und eine schnelle Reaktion auf Veränderungen werden für den zukünftigen Erfolg der Branche ausschlaggebend sein.

but expect to if conditions worsen. Although many shoppers are changing their habits, experimenting and forming new perceptions about quality and value, there are also many shoppers who have yet to respond. Shopper behaviours that have already developed will be sticky so businesses must be prepared to keep apace with shoppers and continue to offer value, and values, even when the economy recovers. Branded manufacturers need to recognise that 'perception is reality' and shoppers have given positive feedback about the quality of private label ranges and discounters. Brands also have many perceived strengths and a key role to play, but they must be aware of what motivates shoppers to buy them.

In such a vibrant marketplace, in which new shopper loyalties are emerging, retailers and food manufacturers are responding rapidly to the challenges presented by the economic climate. The competition for shoppers is based on delivering value, and the most effective are reaping the rewards. There remains a great deal to play for with many shoppers yet to change their habits and keeping a close eye on shopper behaviour and reacting quickly to changes will be key to our industry's future success.

Louise Spillard

Jon Kramer

Solving for Shoppers

Most of the marketing world, I fear, views retail promotion as a tactic. A place where a disparate assortment of displays and other merchandising is sent - along with hopes and wishes for a short-term sales lift. The recent study of display visibility reported by Goliath Solutions in a major drugstore chain highlighted several issues, all of which are all too familiar:

- 25 percent of displays had less than five-percent impact on sales
- Many displays are poorly targeted
- Missed opportunities of building market basket and "retailer brand" by not offering category/cross category solutions

One of the greatest missed opportunities became clear in this additional point: 50 percent of all shoppers who come into the store to fill a prescription do not buy anything else.

Turn shoppers into buyers

There is a serious lack of strategic procedure when it comes to marketing through stores. If only 25 percent of displays have less than a five percent impact on sales, we need to take a very hard look at how we are planning and evaluating retail as media.

Both retailers and brand marketers are suffering from a misconception about the very meaning of the term, "Shopper Marketing." Yes, we all agree that it's about in-store and the "first moment of truth." But many have yet to realize that it's the retailer — not the brand marketer — who is in charge.

Too many brand marketers are making the mistake of adopting the definition of Shopper Marketing offered by Deloitte & Touche: "All marketing stimuli developed based on a deep understanding of shopper behaviour designed to build brand equity, engage the shopper and lead him/her to purchase."

This is a flawed definition because it disregards the retailer as the key decision-maker. It also ignores the retailer's key objective, which is to provide shopper solutions and drive sales by category, not by brand.

Retailers aren't thinking about brand equity; they care only about their shoppers and providing them with solutions — in health care, pet care, household, meals, entertainment.

Design und Farbe der Wal-Mart-Displays sind im Style-Guide genau definiert.
The design and colour of Wal-Mart displays is clearly defined in the company's style guide.

Diese Definition ist fehlerhaft, da sie den Einzelhändler als Hauptentscheidungsträger ausschließt. Sie vernachlässigt zudem dessen Hauptanliegen, nämlich die Wünsche und Bedürfnisse des Kunden zu erkennen und das Angebot daraufhin auszurichten. Das vordergründige Ziel des Einzelhändlers ist es, den Umsatz einer bestimmten Produktkategorie zu steigern, ohne dabei eine bestimmte Marke zu bevorzugen.

Nicht der Markenwert ist demnach für den Handel entscheidend, sein Interesse gilt allein dem Kunden und dessen Bedürfnissen, unabhängig davon, ob es sich um den Bereich Gesundheit, Tierbedarf, Haushalt, Nahrungsmittel oder Unterhaltung handelt.

Tatsächlich geht es beim Shopper-Marketing, wenn es richtig umgesetzt wird, gar nicht um Marketing im üblichen Sinne. Traditionell zielt Marketing hauptsächlich auf die Vermittlung von Botschaften an den Konsumenten.

Im Handel ist das Ziel, nicht nur mit dem Kunden zu kommunizieren, sondern diesem auch kundenorientierte Lösungen zu bieten. Das verhilft dem Kunden zu einer größeren Zufriedenheit beim Shopping-Erlebnis. Der Einsatz von Werbung hat dabei in der Regel eine gegenteilige Wirkung, weil dadurch der Kaufprozess meist verlangsamt anstatt gefördert wird.

The reality is: Shopper Marketing, done correctly, isn't even about marketing in the conventional sense. Traditionally, marketing is mainly about communicating messages to consumers – mostly advertising of one kind or another.

At retail, the goal is not just to communicate to – it is to offer solutions for – shoppers. That's what helps shoppers have a more satisfying shop-

Das zeigt, dass traditionelles Marketing bei der Zielsetzung von Shopper-Marketing keinerlei Rolle spielt. Stattdessen dreht sich alles ausschließlich darum, kundenorientierte Lösungen aufzuzeigen. Das ist eine ganz andere Zielsetzung. Der Kunde ist meist nicht auf der Suche nach einer bestimmten Marke, sondern auf der Suche nach einem Produkt, das seinen Vorstellungen entspricht.

Das Wal-Mart-Blau

Einzelhändler verstehen das durchaus, allen voran Wal-Mart. Jeder, der in letzter Zeit mit den Merchandising- und Marketing-Teams von Wal-Mart gesprochen hat, weiß, dass es ihr Anliegen ist, Kunden kategoriespezifische Lösungen zu bieten.

Wal-Mart hat den Anspruch an seine Lieferanten, dass sie als Partner zusammenarbeiten und neue und innovative Wege finden, um kundenorientierte Lösungen zu entwickeln und zu optimieren. Dies bedeutet eine radikale Veränderung.

Wal-Mart hat einen „Style-Guide" herausgegeben, um sicherzustellen, dass Displays das Wal-Mart-spezifische Aussehen und Image haben. Wird Wal-Mart ein Display angeboten, das nicht in der für Wal-Mart typischen Farbe Blau gehalten ist, kann es durchaus passieren, dass es direkt in der Recycling-Tonne landet.

Das Beispiel Wal-Mart belegt: Die Marktmacht der Einzelhändler hat sich im vergangenen Jahrzehnt vergrößert. Wer diese Entwicklung schon länger verfolgt hat, ist heute nicht weiter verwundert über die aktuelle Situation. Einzelhändler nutzen schon länger gezielt ihre Immobilien, um ihre Handelsmarken aufzubauen. Auch ihr Anspruch an die für sie akzeptablen Formen des Merchandisings ist höher geworden.

Die Tage einer isolierten Betrachtung unserer Marken im Handel sind gezählt – eigentlich sind sie schon vorbei. Wenn Wal-Mart heute signalisiert, dass Markenhersteller ihre verkaufsfördernden Maßnahmen auf die Wal-Mart-Displays hin ausrichten sollten, so ist das der Beginn einer Entwicklung, die auch den Rest der Branche bald erreichen wird.

ping experience. Interrupting them with ads usually has just the opposite effect because it tends to slow them down instead of help them out.

So, the objective of Shopper Marketing really is not about traditional marketing at all. It is about delivering shopper solutions. And that's a very different objective. We need to stop treating shoppers as if they are consumers in search of brands. They are not. They are shoppers in search of solutions.

The Wal-Mart Blues

Retailers certainly understand this, most notably Wal-Mart. Anyone who has spoken with the merchandising and marketing teams at Wal-Mart lately knows that their directive to brands is to offer shopper solutions by category.

Wal-Mart wants its suppliers to get together with each other as partners and come back with new and innovative ways to provide shoppers with better solutions. This is a radical shift.

In case its intentions are not clear, Wal-Mart has also issued a style guide that suggests displays conform to the Wal-Mart look and feel. If you come to them with a display idea that is not done up in Wal-Mart "blue," you might find yourself taking it straight to the back and tossing it in their recycling bin.

This should come as no shock to anyone who has been following the power shift to retailers - from Wal-Mart on down - over the past decade or more. Retailers have been chasing a "solutions" approach for quite some time now, utilizing their real estate to build their brands. They've also become far more demanding when it comes to the kinds of merchandising they will accept.

The difference is, the days of thinking of our brands in isolation at retail are ending – in fact, we might as well assume those days are over. If Wal-Mart is now saying that it wants brands to collaborate to create solutions - which it will present in Wal-Mart branded displays - then you can be sure that the rest of the retail industry is not far behind.

Entwicklung handelsnaher Lösungen

Mit Wal-Mart oder einem anderen Einzelhändler zusammenzuarbeiten heißt, Marken aus deren Perspektive betrachten. Letztendlich bedeutet es, Marken im Zusammenhang mit ihrem Point of Difference zu sehen und somit aus der Perspektive des Kunden.

Dies hat enorme Auswirkungen, denn wir müssen anfangen, unsere Marken als Lösungen zu betrachten und zu erkennen, wie diese im Vergleich zu Marken anderer Hersteller dastehen. Wir müssen uns aufrichtig bemühen, verstehen zu lernen, wie Kunden unsere Marken im Vergleich mit ähnlichen Produkten sehen und wie sie unsere Marken miteinander kombinieren können, und um zu einer ganzheitlichen Lösung zu gelangen.

Ziel ist es, das Warenangebot lösungsorientiert zu präsentieren. Wenn wir beispielsweise an eine Erkältung oder einen Husten denken, werden wir vielleicht Purell Hand Sanitizer-Händedesinfektionsmittel, Kleenex-Tücher und NyQuil-Erkältungssaft zusammen in einem Display präsentieren. Das wäre eine wirkliche Unterstützung der Kunden, die oftmals keinen aufeinander abgestimmten Rundum-Vorrat an Produkten für Erkältungskrankheiten in ihrem Badezimmer haben. In der Regel kaufen die Kunden diese dann ein, wenn sie krank und nicht in der Stimmung sind, den gesamten Laden nach allen Produkten abzusuchen.

In einigen Fällen wird der Händler diese Art der ganzheitlichen Versorgungslösung inszenieren. Aber wenn wir Wal-Mart als Maßstab nehmen, können wir davon ausgehen, dass Wal-Mart und andere Einzelhändler sich von uns wünschen werden, dass wir mit unseren Ideen zu ihnen kommen. Die Zusammenarbeit von verschiedenen Markenherstellern wird zu Komplikationen führen, was aber deutlich mehr Wert ist, als die Chance einer effektiven und ganzheitlichen Markenpräsentation bei Wal-Mart oder anderswo zu verpassen.

Vereinzelt mögen Marken auch für sich alleine Lösungen dazu in der Lage sein. Aber die Zukunft liegt in ganzheitlichen Lösungen verschiedener Markenhersteller: Lösungen für Schüler-Mahlzeiten beispielsweise könnten von einer bestimmten Anzahl von Unternehmen als eine Marke angeboten werden. Mehrere Hersteller könnten beispielsweise Mundpflegeprodukte für Diabetiker innerhalb ihres Produktangebots gestalten. Generell sind wir in einer neuen Zeitrechnung angekommen, in der es nicht nur um die Zusammenarbeit mit Einzelhändlern geht, sondern auch um die mit anderen Marken.

Engineering Solutions

Working with Wal-Mart, or any other retailer, means viewing brands from their perspective. Ultimately, that means viewing brands in the context of their point-of difference - that is, from the shopper's perspective.

The implications of this are huge. It means we have to start thinking about our brands as solutions, as such, and how they relate to brands made by other manufacturers. We need to dig in and really understand how shoppers view our brands in combination with related products – how they might combine and recombine our brands to come up with a total solution.

We need to become solutions engineers. For example, you're thinking about cough/cold, then maybe you've got Purell hand sanitizer and Kleenex tissues and NyQuil bundled nicely in a single display. That would be a real service to shoppers who rarely keep a stash of cold-care items in the bathroom. Usually, when we're sick we go out and buy them, and are in no mood to navigate the entire store to find all the products we need.

In some cases, the retailer may orchestrate this type of total-solution delivery. But if Wal-Mart is setting the standard, we can expect that they and other retailers will want us to come to them with ideas. The idea of brands working together in this way will have its complications, but such complications obviously pale by comparison to the prospect of losing the exposure opportunity at Wal-Mart or anywhere else.

It is possible that some brands may be able to provide solutions on their own. Back-to-school meal solutions probably could be handled by a number of companies as a single brand. Diabetes oral-care could be handled by several manufacturers within their own portfolios, for example. But by and large it is a brand new day and one that calls not only for collaboration with retailers but also with other brands.

Adjacencies, Insights & Investments

Understanding adjacencies at retail is a major part of this, because adjacencies can drive solutions. Sometimes a very simple, but insightful placement can yield a remarkable result. For example, one major brand put a display of its antibacterial soap in the petfood aisle and drove sales substantially. Apparently people associate pet care with dirty hands. This points directly at another imperative - we need to invest more heavily in research that provides the kind of shopper insights required to arrive at the most complete and compelling solutions.

It is absolutely essential that we invest in tools that can tell us who lives in each store's trading area and what their problems might

Umfeld, Einblicke und Investitionen

Das Umfeld von Produkten im Einzelhandel zu analysieren, ist ein wesentlicher Schritt, um Lösungen zu generieren. Zuweilen kann eine sehr einfache, aber weitsichtige Platzierung zu erstaunlichen Resultaten führen. So platzierte zum Beispiel eine führende Marke antibakterielle Seife in der Abteilung für Tiernahrung, was zu einer bedeutenden Abverkaufssteigerung führte. Offensichtlich assoziieren viele Menschen Tierpflege mit schmutzigen Händen. Folglich sollten wir mehr in eine Forschung investieren, die diese notwendigen Erkenntnisse über den Kunden liefern kann, um zu einer möglichst umfassenden und attraktiven POS-Platzierung zu gelangen.

Entscheidend sind Investitionen in statistische Erhebungsmethoden, mit denen festgestellt werden kann, wer in der jeweiligen Umgebung eines Ladens wohnt und was für Wünsche und Bedürfnisse diese Menschen haben. Nur so kann man ihnen relevante Lösungsvorschläge anbieten und das Merchandising entsprechend darauf abstimmen. Häufen sich in diesem Gebiet Herzprobleme? Diabetes? Gibt es viele Senioren? Familien mit Kleinkindern? Haustiere?

Das müssen wir wissen, um zu verstehen, wie der Kunde beim Einkauf gezielt unterstützt werden kann. Das müssen wir auch wissen, um keine Ressourcen zu verschwenden. Nehmen wir an, eine landesweite Einführung eines Produkts ist geplant, und in jedem Laden sollen die gleichen Materialien benutzt werden. Auch wenn im besten Fall eine Übereinstimmung von 70 % erreicht wird, werden dabei Hunderttausende von Euro vergeudet werden, ganz zu schweigen von den Folgen für die Umwelt.

Mit Kunden sprechen

Wenn wir aber unsere Hausaufgaben machen und es schaffen, genau die richtigen Lösungen für genau die richtigen Läden anzubieten, werden wir das Wirtschaftswachstum fördern und unsere Ausgaben durch wirklich effektive Investitionen verringern. Und diese Hausaufgaben verbessern ganz nebenbei auch

be so that we can offer them relevant solutions and build our merchandising plans accordingly. Is there a high incidence of heart issues? Diabetes? Seniors? Families with young children? Pets?

We need to know so we know how to help them when they go shopping. We also need to know so we don't waste resources. Suppose you're planning a national introduction and you expect to put the same materials in every store. Say that in a best-case scenario, you might get 70 percent compliance - you'll be wasting hundreds of thousands of dollars (not to mention the environmental impact).

Speaking with Shoppers

But if we do our homework and can target just the right stores with just the right solutions, we'll drive growth and save money. And, by the way, that homework also includes boning up on how to communicate effectively to shoppers. The most common mistake is simply transferring the creative from television commercials to in-store media.

While it's obviously important to keep a brand's identity consistent, it's equally important to keep it coherent. Too many times, displays assume that the shopper remembers your advertising. Even if recall is at a healthy level today — say, 25 percent — that means 75 percent of shoppers might have no idea what your slogan or tagline means.

A brand marketer would no more consider putting an ad on television without research to prove it works than jump out of the Empire State Building. And yet, they will spend a lot more money putting a display in store without testing it. That's just wrong and has to change.

Shopper Marketing is not about individual brands - it's not even about marketing in the usual sense. It's about communicating in a way that shoppers understand and appreciate, because it helps them find a solution to their needs and get the most out of their shopping trips. The good news is, the result is increased category sales, increased basket load - and growth for brands.

die effektive Kommunikation mit den Kunden. Der häufigste Fehler, der gemacht wird, ist die Übertragung von Fernsehwerbung auf Instore-Medien.

Es ist zweifelsohne wichtig, Markenidentität konsistent zu halten. Genauso wichtig ist es aber auch, dass sie kohärent bleibt. Nur zu oft geht man bei der Gestaltung von Displays davon aus, dass der Käufer sich an die Werbung eines bestimmten Produkts erinnert. Auch wenn die Werbeerinnerung beim Konsumenten heute relativ hoch ist – sie liegt bei etwa 25 % –, bedeutet es, dass 75 % der Kunden keine Vorstellung davon haben, was ein Slogan oder Werbespruch eigentlich bedeutet.

Der Markenanbieter wird genauso wenig in Erwägung ziehen, eine Fernsehwerbung zu schalten, nur um deren Wirkung zu testen, wie er vom Eiffelturm springen wird. Und dennoch werden Unsummen ausgegeben, um ein Display im Handel zu platzieren, ohne es vorher getestet zu haben. Das ist ein großer Fehler und muss in Zukunft vermieden werden.

Beim Shopper-Marketing geht es nicht um einzelne Marken – es geht noch nicht einmal um Marketing im üblichen Sinne. Es geht vielmehr um eine Art der Kommunikation, die der Kunde versteht und schätzt, weil sie ihm hilft, eine Lösung zur Erfüllung seiner Bedürfnisse zu finden und das Beste aus seinem Einkauf herauszuholen. Die gute Nachricht ist, dass das Resultat daraus steigende Umsätze und ein größerer Warenkorb sowie Markenwachstum sind.

„The Project Place" macht Elektrowerkzeuge für Frauen anziehend

Beispielsweise hat The Home Depot eine andere Sicht auf Marken und sieht sie mit den Augen des Kunden, wie ein mit Black & Decker zusammen gestaltetes Marketing-Programm zeigt. Es ist deswegen bemerkenswert, weil es die Erkenntnisse aus der Marktforschung in eine strategische Produktpositionierung umsetzt. Diese Erkenntnis war, dass Frauen zwar mehr als die Hälfte aller Elektrowerkzeuge bei The Home Depot kauften, jedoch durch eine Werkzeugabteilung eingeschüchtert wurden, deren Gestaltung auf die Bedürfnisse von Baufirmen ausgerichtet war. Die Strategie bestand darin, ein lösungsorientiertes Modul in Form einer attraktiven, interaktiven Dauerplatzierung für Kundinnen zu gestalten, das mit einer breiten Auswahl an Elektrowerkzeugen und Zubehör bestückt war.

Unter dem Namen „The Projekt Place" wurde das Display in der Nähe von Abteilungen wie „Teppiche und Bodenbeläge" und „Haushaltsgeräte" platziert, beides Abteilungen, die von Frauen besonders stark frequentiert werden. Das Ergebnis war eine bedeutende Steigerung der Umsätze mit den präsentierten Produkten.

„The Project Place" ist ein POP-Konzept speziell für Frauen: Das lösungsorientierte Modul für Black & Decker führte zu einer bedeutenden Steigerung der Umsätze mit den präsentierten Produkten.

"The Project place" is a POP concept especially designed for women: The shopper solution center for Black & Decker led to a significant sales lift for the featured products.

"The Project Place" attracts power tools to women

The Home Depot® looks at brands differently - and through the eyes of its shoppers – as demonstrated by a program created with Black & Decker® power tools. The program was noteworthy because it was resulted in an insight and based on a strategy. The insight was that while women purchased more than half of all power tools at The Home Depot, many felt intimidated by the tool department presentation that was geared for contractors. The strategy was to create a shopper solution center, in the form of a beautifully designed, interactive, permanent display, stocked with a broad assortment of power tools and accessories.

Dubbed "The Project Place" it was located in proximity to departments such as flooring and appliances, high-traffic areas for women shoppers. The result was a significant sales lift for the featured products.

Der 3M Post-it® Notes Marken-Shop
The 3M Post-it® Notes Brand Shop

3M Post-it® Notes Marken-Shop

Mit dem 3M Post-it® Notes Marken-Shop hat die Marke Post-it eine dauerhafte Präsenz in 2000 Staples-Läden erreicht. Von Staples durchgeführte Studien zeigen, dass Kunden es schätzen, den Marken-Shop leicht lokalisieren zu können, die gesuchten Produkte schnell zu finden und neue, interessante Produkte im Shop zu erkennen. Das System bietet auf eine intelligente und effektive Weise die gesamte Produktlinie zum Verkauf an, optimiert das Sortiment und spricht den Kunden mit relevanten Botschaften an. Modulkomponenten bieten eine Vielzahl von Kombinationsmöglichkeiten im Standaufbau und in der Ladengestaltung.

Abschließend lässt sich im Hinblick auf Ladendisplays sagen, dass es wichtig ist, eine markenübergreifende Lösung in Blick zu haben, anstatt sich isoliert mit einer einzelnen Marke zu befassen. Die Lösungsfindung für den Kunden erfordert eine strategische, ganzheitliche Herangehensweise.

3M Post-it® Notes Brand Shop

The 3M Post-it® Notes Brand Shop establishes a permanent home for Post-it Brand at 2,000 Staples stores. Staples research confirmed that shoppers appreciated being able to easily locate the Brand Shop, quickly find their products and identify new products of interest. The system effectively merchandises the entire product line, optimizes product assortment and "speaks to shoppers" with relevant messaging. Modular components accommodate a variety of fixture set-ups and store layouts.

In conclusion, when considering in-store displays, it's important to think about the total solution not just your brand in isolation. Solving for shoppers requires a strategic, holistic approach.

Jon Kramer

V. DIE EFFIZIENZ VON POS-MASSNAHMEN | THE EFFECTIVENESS OF POS ACTIVITY

WAS VERKAUFSFÖRDERUNG BEWEGT:
DIE EFFIZIENZ VON POS-MASSNAHMEN
DRIVING SALES PROMOTION:
THE EFFECTIVENESS OF POS-ACTIVITY

Susanne Czech-Winkelmann

Was Verkaufsförderung bewegt: Die Effizienz von POS-Maßnahmen

Von Shopper-Insights zu betriebswirtschaftlichen Erfolgskennziffern

1. Shopper entscheiden am POS

Bis der Konsument in das Geschäft des Lebensmittelhändlers kommt, hat er viele Gelegenheiten, sich über das Angebot im Markt und die wichtigsten Produkte, die per Werbung oder Redaktionsbeiträgen aktuell forciert werden, zu informieren. Dafür stehen ihm in Deutschland immerhin 3.122 Publikumszeitschriften zur Verfügung, möglicherweise ist er Leser einer Fachzeitschrift - von denen 4.170 am Markt sind – oder er interessiert sich für eine der 1.524 Zeitungen. Mit Sicherheit hat er eines oder zwei von insgesamt 1.374 Anzeigenblättern in seinem Briefkasten, abends wird er mehrere der 24 TV-Sender einschalten, wenn nicht sogar sich durch alle durchzappen, von den 341 Rundfunksendern sind sicher höchstens zehn auf seinem Radio eingespeichert, und im Lauf des Tages ist er an mehreren der 341.159 Plakatierungsstellen vorbeigekommen (GWA 2008). Was uns zudem an Produktinformationen durch das Internet geboten wird, ist nicht mehr zählbar und kommt natürlich noch hinzu.

Wie schön ist es daher für den Shopper – wie die Konsumenten, die sich in einem Handelsgeschäft befinden, bezeichnet werden – sich angesichts dieses „kommunikativen Grundrauschens" im Laden in aller Ruhe inspirieren zu lassen!

Nicht ohne Grund werden bis zu 70 % der Kaufentscheidungen für Fast Moving Consumer Goods (FMCG) erst vor Ort im Geschäft getroffen. Dafür geben die Hersteller jährlich mehr Geld aus, und auch die aktuelle Tendenz ist, die Werbeetats für Verkaufsförderung, so genannte VKF-Maßnahmen, weiter zu steigern. Eine Aussage darüber zu treffen, inwieweit Ausgaben für Werbung im Fernsehen, in Zeitschriften/Zeitungen und im Radio bzw. Kino vom klassischen so genannte Above-the-line-Etat zunehmend auf den Below-the-line-Bereich – womit alle anderen kommunikativen Maßnahmen, insbesondere aber VKF-Aktivitäten gemeint sind – verschoben werden, ist derzeit nicht eindeutig machbar.
Dieser Beitrag bezieht sich auf die Verkaufsförderungsaktivitäten des Herstellers am „Verkaufspunkt", dem Point of Sale

Susanne Czech-Winkelmann

Driving sales promotion: the effectiveness of POS activity

From shopper insights to economic success indicators

1. Shoppers decide at the POS

Before entering the grocery store the consumer has various opportunities to obtain information about the product offer in the market and the key products that are promoted by advertising or the media. In Germany, consumers can get information from a total of 3,122 popular magazines, possibly as a reader of a trade magazine or one of the 1,524 newspapers. Surely, the consumer will find one or two of Germany's 1,374 advertisers in the letter box and in the evening is likely to watch more than one of the 24 television channels or even zap through all of them. Probably customers will have programmed not more than ten of the existing 341 radio channels on the radio and at the end of the day will have passed by several of the 341,159 permanent advertising posters and signs (GWA 2008). Of course we must also add the vast information available online.

How nice it is therefore for the shopper, as the consumer in a store is called, to take all the time needed to find inspiration in a retail environment without that "communication ambient noise".

It is not without reason that up to 70 % of buying decisions for Fast Moving Consumer Goods (FMCG) are made inside the store. Manufacturers spend an increasing amount of money on that every year and recent trends show that advertising budgets for sales promotion, or so-called sales promotion activity, are continuing to rise. Presently, it is not possible to make a definite statement on whether spending on television, radio and cinema commercials and print advertising is shifting from the traditional so-called above-the-line budget to below-the-line, which includes all other communication activity, in particular sales promotion activity.

This article relates to the sales promotion activity of manufacturers at the point of sale, or POS for short, sometimes also referred to as point of purchase, or POP. The terms POS activity and sales promo-tion activity are used alternatively. I would like to point out here that in theory there are three levels of sales promotion rather than only the POS:

1. *The company's own field sales force that makes sure the POS is fit and powerful.*

oder kurz POS, manchmal auch POP, Point of Purchase, also „Einkaufspunkt" genannt. Die Begriffe POS-Aktivitäten und VKF-Aktivitäten werden hier alternativ verwendet. Ich möchte an dieser Stelle darauf hinweisen, dass die Theorie drei Ebenen der Verkaufsförderung kennt, nicht nur den Point of Sale:

1. Den eigenen Außendienst, um diesen fit und schlagkräftig zu machen.
2. Den Handel mit Maßnahmen zum Hineinverkauf (Push) und Aktivitäten, die den Herausverkauf (Pull) am POS durch den Shopper fördern.
3. Den Verbraucher, um die Kaufentscheidung – auch außerhalb des POS – zu stimulieren.

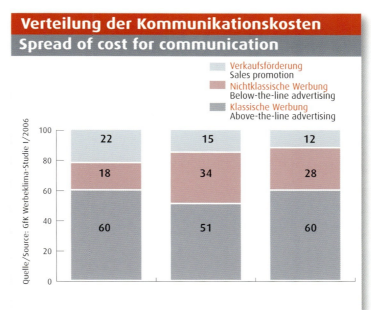

Aufteilung der Kommunikationskosten auf klassische Werbung, nicht-klassische Werbung und Verkaufsförderung

The share of above-the-line advertising, below-the-line advertising and sales promotion

2. Supporting retailers with Push measures as well as Pull activity by the shopper.
3. The consumer to stimulate the buying decision outside the POS.

2. Shopper-Insights: Welche POS-Aktivität ist „richtig"?

Den Shoppern begegnen POS-Aktionen in den vielfältigsten Formen: Bereits außerhalb eines Marktes in Form von Plakaten am Parkplatz, am Eingang und zum Teil in den Fensterflächen, in Form von Bodenaufklebern oder Werbung an Einkaufswagen.

Im Geschäft selbst wird der Kunde animiert, wenn er zur Decke schaut, vor dem Regal steht, sich im Gang bewegt, an der Kasse wartet. Gängige Werbemedien sind dabei Deckhänger, Ladendurchsagen, Zweitplatzierungen, Handzettel, Proben, Coupons, Aktionen mit und ohne Personal usw.

Welche VKF-Maßnahmen die Hersteller von Gebrauchsgütern in Bau- und Gartenmärkten für „richtig" halten und einsetzen zeigt die Abbildung auf der nächstren Seite.

Für FMCGs gibt die Studie der GfK, Nürnberg, über „POS-Maßnahmen im Verbrauchermarkt" (GfK 2006) gute Shopper-Insights. Die Studie zeigt, wie Marktleiter und Verbraucher die unterschiedlichen POS-Maßnahmen beurteilen. So werden Hand- und Werbezettel von den rund 1.500 befragten Verbrauchern als die werbewirksamste Maßnahme angesehen, 71 % der Konsumenten sagen, dass ihre Kaufentscheidung dadurch beeinflusst wird. Von Proben ist fast die Hälfte der befragten Verbraucher überzeugt. Auch Produkthinweise am Regal und der Einsatz von Werbedamen

2. Shopper insights: what is the ‚right' POS activity?

Shoppers are confronted with various forms of POS activity: Promotion starts outside the store, where the consumer encounters advertising posters in the parking lot, at the store entrance and partly in the shop windows, floor decals and trolley advertisements.

In the store, the customer is surrounded by advertising on the ceiling, in front of the shelves, in the aisles and at the cash desk. Familiar advertising tools are danglers, in-store announcements, secondary placements, flyers, giveaways, vouchers, promotions with or without staff, etc.

The illustration on the following page shows what forms of sales promotion manufacturers of consumer goods for DIY and gardening markets use and consider as "right".

For FMCGs, the "POS-Maßnahmen im Verbrauchermarkt" survey from GfK in Nürnberg on POS measures in hypermarkets provides valuable shopper insights. The survey shows how store managers and consumers rate different POS activity. The 1,500 consumers covered by the survey state that flyers and advertising leaflets are the most effective advertising tools, with 71 % saying they influence their buying decision. Almost half of respondents appreciate giveaways. Many consumers also appreciate product information on shelves and female promoters. But there is often a great divide

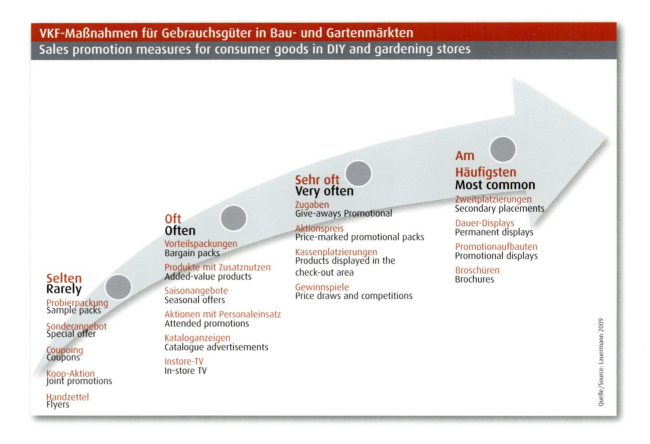

sind sehr akzeptiert. Allerdings liegt zwischen dem Kennen einer Aktion und dem Handeln oftmals eine große Kluft. Während die Verteilung von Warenproben sehr positiv beurteilt wird, entschließt sich nur etwa jeder Vierte zum Kauf des Produktes.

Die Studie untersucht weiterhin, was Kunden als positiv empfinden, was sie eher nervt und welche Aktivitäten wirklich zum Kauf anregen. Sie trennt bei den Ergebnissen nach Männern und Frauen sowie nach verschiedenen Altersklassen.

Ohne entsprechende Marktforschung und Shopper-Befragung „tappt" der Hersteller im Dunkeln und kann nur aus den Ergebnissen einer Aktion ableiten, ob er den „Nerv" der Shopper getroffen hat oder nicht.

3. POS-Promotions verfolgen Herstellerziele – Handelsziele – Shopperziele

Befragt man Hersteller, so ist Verkaufsförderung sehr oft nur auf kurzfristige Marktreaktionen ausgerichtet, also die Erreichung von mehr Absatz, Umsatz und auch mehr Marktanteilen. Obwohl letztere oft genannt werden, werden sie in der Praxis nur relativ selten auch tatsächlich erhoben!

Der POS kann aber auch zur Erreichung weiterer kurzfristiger quantitativer Ziele genutzt werden, wie

between knowing and responding to a promotion activity. Most consumers think positively of product giveaways, but only one in four decides to buy the product.

The survey further looks at what activity customers appreciate and what irritates them and what kind of activity actually moves customers to buy. The survey distinguishes between men and women and various age bands.

Without the help of relevant market research and shopper surveys manufacturers end up groping in the dark and can only judge from the results of single promotions whether they have their finger on the pulse of what shoppers respond to.

3. POS promotions target manufacturers, retailers or shoppers

When asking manufacturers about promotions it emerges that sales promotion is very often limited to short-term objectives like increasing selling, sales and market share. Even though these factors are often mentioned, they are very rarely actually ascertained in practice!

The POS can also be used to achieve other short-term objectives like
- *generating additional sales*

- Zusatzabsätze schaffen,
- Erstkäufer gewinnen,
- eine Ausweitung der POS-Präsentation ermöglichen,
- und die erfolgreiche Platzierung von Sonderprodukten.

Diese Ziele werden von Herstellern aber wesentlich seltener formuliert!

Mit Verkaufsförderungsaktivitäten können darüber hinaus auch langfristige qualitative, imageforcierende (Koinecke und Großklaus 1985) Marketingziele erreicht werden, wie

- das Image einer Marke im Markt aufzubauen,
- Produkt-Präferenzen beim Konsumenten zu erzeugen,
- Markentreue zu stützen,
- die Bekanntheit einer Marke auszubauen,
- den Markenwechsel von Konsumenten zu forcieren,
- oder auch die Einstellung des Handels zum Unternehmen, und seinen Produkten (positiv) zu beeinflussen.

Nebenstehende Grafik zeigt, welche Ziele von POS-Aktionen in einer empirischen Studie bei Zulieferern von Bau- und Gartenmärkten genannt wurden. Auffallend ist, dass – befragt nach den Zielen von POS-Aktionen – von Seiten der Hersteller fast ausschließlich herstellerspezifische Ziele genannt werden. Für die Akzeptanz und Durchsetzung dieser Maßnahmen beim Handel ist es zunehmend notwendig, Ziele zu formulieren, die den Händler selbst und die Shopper in seinen Geschäften in den Mittelpunkt stellen. Hier ist also ein Umdenken erforderlich!

4. „Efficient Promotion" muss geplant werden!

Die Durchführung von POS-Maßnahmen bedarf einer sorgfältigen Planung. Erfolgreiche Unternehmen planen ihre Promotions strategisch, d.h., die Promotionplanung ist fester Bestandteil des jährlichen Kundenplanungsprozesses.

Folgende Schlüsselfragen müssen für eine effiziente Promotionplanung geklärt werden:

- Welcher Handelskunde?
- Welche Vertriebslinie?
- Welche Warengruppe? Welche WG-Rolle?
- Welche Promotionziele? Welche Strategie?
- Welches Budget? Welcher Zeitraum?

Für eine effiziente Promotion ist bezüglich der Vertriebslinie (VL), in der sich das zu promotende Produkt befindet, Folgendes zu untersuchen:

- *win first time buyers*
- *expand presence at the point of sale*
- *successfully launch special offers*

But, much more rarely, these objectives are mentioned by manufacturers!

Sales promotion activity is designed to go beyond short-term targets to achieve long-term value and image creating objectives (Koinecke und Großklaus 1985) like

- *building brand image in the store*
- *encourage product preferences*
- *maintain brand loyalty*
- *increase brand awareness*
- *move consumers to change brands*
- *or (positively) influence retailers' views of a company and itsproducts*

The figure below shows manufacturers' objectives of POS promotions mentioned by suppliers of DIY and gardening stores. It is remarkable that when asked about their objectives for POS promotions manufacturers cited almost entirely manufacturer specific objectives. But for retailers to accept and apply this activity at retail it is of increasing importance to set objectives that focus on the retailer and the shoppers in his store. Manufacturers need to completely rethink their approach!

Ziele von POS-Aktionen bei Zulieferern von Bau- und Gartenmärkten
Manufacturers' objectives of POS promotions among suppliers of DIY and gardening stores

Umsatzwachstum / Sales growth	100 %
Erhöhen der Marktanteile / Market share growth	91 %
Präsenz am Ort des Verkaufs / Presence at the point of sale	64 %
Aufbau des Images / Image building	55 %
Generierung von Erstkäufern / Winning first time buyers	45 %
Erhöhung der Markenbekanntheit / Increasing brand awareness	36 %
Aufbau von Markentreue / Building brand loyalty	36 %
Markenwechsel / Brand change	27 %
Durchsetzung von Angeboten / Launching successful special offers	18 %
Bekanntheit für Produktkategorie erhöhen / Increasing the awareness of a product category	9 %

Quelle/Source: Lauermann 2009

Auswahl wichtiger handelsbezogener Ziele
Select key retailer specific objectives

Steigerung der Abverkäufe
Increase sales volumes

Verbesserung der Flächenproduktivität
Improve retail space productivity

Erhöhung der Umschlagshäufigkeit
Increase stock turnover

Reduzierung des Lager- und Regalbestandes
Reduce inventory

Abbau von Out-of-Stocks
Avoid out-of-stocks

Verbesserung der Spannenkalkulation
Improve margin calculation

Besseres Regalbild usw.
Improve shelf presentation, etc.

Auswahl wichtiger shopperbezogener Ziele
Select key shopper specific objectives

Erhöhung der Ausgabenintensität
Increase intensity of spending

Erhöhung der Käuferpenetration
Increase buyer penetration

Verbesserung der Kundenpotentzialausschöpfung
Improve the exhaustion of customer potential

Steigerung der Shopperloyalität
Increase shopper loyalty

Erhöhung der Bedarfsdeckung
Improve the covering of customer requirements

Erhöhung der Share of Customer
Increasing the share of customer wallet

Steigerung der Shopperzufriedenheit usw.
Increase shopper satisfaction, etc.

---

1. Welche Stärken und Schwächen hat die Vertriebslinie des Handelskunden in seinem Wettbewerbsumfeld?
2. Wie ist das Shopperprofil in der Vertriebslinie?
3. Durch welche Charakteristika zeichnet sich die Warengruppe aus?
4. Welche Bedeutung spielen Wettbewerber in der Warengruppe?
5. Welche Bedeutung haben Handelsmarken?
6. Welche Rolle spielt die Warengruppe im Sortiment des Handelsunternehmens? Handelt es sich aus Sicht des Handelsunternehmens um eine Pflichtkategorie, eine Profilierungskategorie, eine Ergänzungskategorie oder ist es eine Impuls- bzw. Saisonkategorie?
7. Welche Preis- und Vermarktungsaktivitäten wurden bisher in der Vertriebslinie durchgeführt und sind sie für die Planung von neuen Aktivitäten relevant?

Diese Vorgehensweise führt zu vertriebskanalspezifischen und handelskunden-individuellen Promotionaktivitäten, die den Shopper im Fokus haben. Promotionplanung, die auf diese Weise durchgeführt wird, entspricht dem Gedanken von „Efficient Consumer Response" (ECR) und der Basisstrategie „Efficient Promotion". ECR ist eine gemeinschaftliche Initiative zwischen Groß- und Einzelhandelsunternehmen und Herstellern sowie weiteren Partnern in der Versorgungs- und Wertschöpfungskette, der die Idee einer effizienten Reaktion auf die Kundennachfrage zugrunde liegt. Diese partnerschaftliche Zusammenarbeit ist erforderlich, um das gemeinsame Ziel einer kostenoptimalen, bedarfsgerechten und kontinuierlichen Warenversorgung und einer an der Nachfrage orientierten Angebotssituation zu erreichen. Der Grund-

4. "Effective promotion" requires planning!

POS activity needs to be carefully planned. Successful companies are strategic in their planning, i.e. the planning of promotions plays a key part in their annual customer planning processes. The following key issues must be considered for effective promotion planning:

- *Which retail customer?*
- *Which distribution channel?*
- *Which product category? Which product category role?*
- *Which promotion objectives? Which strategy?*
- *Which budget? Which time frame?*

The following issues must be considered to ensure effective promotion of the product to be promoted within a determined retail format:

1. *What are the strengths and weaknesses of the client's retail format compared to competitors?*
2. *What is the retail format's shopper profile?*
3. *What are the product category's characteristics?*
4. *How strong is competition within the product category?*
5. *How important are retail brands?*
6. *What role does the product category play in the retailer's assortment? Does the retailer consider the product category as a compulsory, image, additional or impulse or seasonal category?*
7. *What have the retail format's pricing and promotional activities been so far, and are they of importance for future activities?*

This approach leads to shopper-oriented promotion activity that is tailored to the needs of a specific retail format and a specific retail

gedanke ist: „Working together to fulfill consumer wishes better, faster and at less cost." (ECR Europe Board 1997). Eine der vier Basisstrategien, die die ECR-Zielerreichung unterstützen soll, ist „Efficient Promotion". Sie soll dazu beitragen, die Zusammenarbeit von Handel und Industrie im Bereich der Vermarktung und der Verkaufsförderung der Waren effizienter zu gestalten. „Efficient Promotion" zielt auf sämtliche Aktivitäten ab, die zu einer Aktivierung und Belebung am POS beitragen. Im Ergebnis wird durch Efficient Promo-tion als Wettbewerbsinstrument die Kundenfrequenz erhöht, als Wertschöpfungsinstrument kann zusätzliches Einkaufsvolumen in ertragsstarken Produktgruppen erzeugt werden, und als Kundenbindungsinstrument führt Efficient Promotion zu einer Erhöhung der Kundentreue für Handel und Industrie.

Für marktführende Hersteller ist das Denken in ECR-Anforderungen mittlerweile schon fast eine Selbstverständlichkeit geworden. Kleinere Lieferanten müssen sich hierum zukünftig verstärkt bemühen, um für den Handel als Partner am POS interessant zu bleiben.

Abschließend soll noch ein wichtiger operativer Aspekt angesprochen werden: POS-Promotions müssen in jedem Fall vor dem Einsatz zwischen Hersteller und Händler (Handelszentrale) inhaltlich, bezüglich des Distributionsumfangs in den Filialen und auch zeitlich abgestimmt werden. Der Zeitpunkt der Abstimmung ist in der Praxis unterschiedlich. Untersuchungen zeigen, dass die zeitliche Spannweite von kurz vor Beginn der Aktion bis einmal pro Jahr zu Jahresbeginn reicht. Hier ist, bei

client. This form of promotion planning is conform with the "Efficient Consumer Response" (ECR) idea and fundamental "Efficient Promotion" strategy. ECR is a joint initiative of large companies, retailers and manufacturers as well as other partners in the supply and value chain that is based on an effective response to customer demand. This kind of cooperation is necessary to achieve the joint objective of optimising the costs of a continuous demand-oriented supply of goods and product offer. The basic idea is "Working together to fulfill customer wishes better, faster and at least cost". (ECR Europe Board 1997). One of the four fundamental strategies for achieving the ECR objective is "Efficient Promotion". The objective of "Efficient Promotion" is to increase the effectiveness of joint marketing and sales promotion activity of both retailers and manufactures. "Efficient Promotion" is directed at all activity that activates and stimulates the POS. As a result, Efficient Promotion as a competitive tool increases store traffic, as a value creating tool it can generate additional sales volume in profitable product categories and as a customer loyalty tool it will drive shopper loyalty to retailers and manufacturers.

For leading manufacturers, thinking in terms of ECR is meanwhile accepted as being almost self-evident. Smaller suppliers will have to make greater efforts in the future to make sure retailers do not lose their interest in them as a POS partner.

As a last important aspect the coordination and timing of joint promotions should be mentioned. Manufacturers and retailers (the retailer's head office) need to agree on the time and extent of the promotion before execution of the promotion. The time of coordination in practice differs. Research shows that everything happens, some

DIE EFFIZIENZ VON POS-MASSNAHMEN | THE EFFECTIVENESS OF POS ACTIVITY

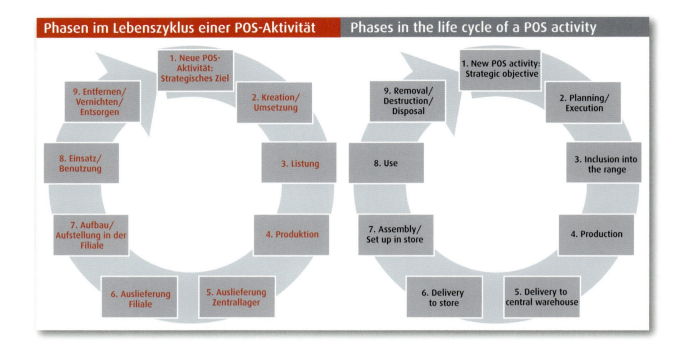

Phasen im Lebenszyklus einer POS-Aktivität | Phases in the life cycle of a POS activity

genauerer Betrachtung und unter Berücksichtigung der vielfältigen Planungsaktivitäten, sicher noch Verbesserungspotenzial vorhanden!

5. Am Anfang steht das Ziel – Am Ende muss die Durchführung klappen!

In einer Prozessbetrachtung ist der „Lebenszyklus" einer POS-Aktivität durch folgende Phasen in einem kontinuierlich fortlaufenden Kreislauf gekennzeichnet:

- Phase 1: Die Zielformulierung erfolgt durch den Hersteller, dabei meist durch die Abteilung Trade-Marketing und/ oder Vertrieb.
- Phase 2: Die Kreation und die Umsetzung durch Agenturen und/oder Lieferanten
- Phase 3: die Produktion durch die Lieferanten
- Phase 4: die Listung durch den Vertrieb / das Key Account Management
- Phase 5: Für die Auslieferung in das Zentrallager sind Speditionsunternehmen des Herstellers oder des Co-Packers verantwortlich
- Phasen 6 und 9: die Auslieferung in die Filiale und die Entsorgung/Vernichtung übernimmt das Handelsunternehmen. Diese Prozesse sind normalerweise gut organisiert und etabliert.
- Phase 7: Soweit der Hersteller über einen Außendienst bzw. Merchandiser verfügt, sollte auch der Abruf der Aktion vom Zentrallager des Handels und der Aufbau der Aktion in der Filiale geregelt und überwacht sein.
- Phase 8: In der Praxis weisen die POS-Aktivitäten bei Einsatz und Benutzung eine Reihe von Mängeln auf.

promotions are planned shortly before their execution, in other cases, promotion planning takes place at the beginning of the year for the whole year. On closer inspection, and considering all possible planning activity, there is surely potential for improvement.

5 First comes the objective – in the end execution counts!

When analysing a process, the "life cycle" of a POS activity is characterised by the following phases of a continuous cycle:

- *Phase 1: The manufacturer, in most cases the trade marketing and/or sales department, sets the objective*
- *Phase 2: The promotion is planned and carried out by agencies and/or suppliers*
- *Phase 3: Production by the supplier*
- *Phase 4: Inclusion into the product range by the sales department/key account management*
- *Phase 5: Freight services companies or co-packers are in charge of the delivery to the central warehouse*
- *Phases 6 and 9: The retailer is responsible for the delivery to the store and the destruction/disposal. Normally these processes are well organised and established processes*
- *Phase 7: If manufacturers have a field sales force or merchandising team, they should also handle and control the delivery from the central warehouse and the assembly in the store*
- *Phase 8: Several problems occur during POS activity*

Considering the large amount of sales promotion activity the store manager is confronted with, it becomes more than clear

POS-Aktivitäten/Bewertung durch Marktleiter		POS activities, experienced by store managers	
Deckenhänger	Schwierige Anbringung erschwert die Überwachung	Danglers	difficult to set up difficult to control
Regalstopper	Verdeckte Informationen Schlechte Befestigung	Shelf wobblers	hide information difficult to put up
Displays	Aussehen nach Abverkauf Erhöhung der Bestände	Displays	unattractive after use increases inventory
Instore-Radio	Artikel nicht im Markt vorhanden Kein Einfluss auf das Programm	Instore radio	the product is not in stock no influence on the programme
Floor Graphics	Schnell verdreckt Beseitigung ist schwer	Floor graphics	get dirty easily difficult to remove
Verkostung	Schlechte Promotermengen Hohe Abnahmemengen	Tastings	unqualified promotional staff, large quantities of product must be purchased
Gewinnspiel	Hohe Abnahmemengen	Prize draws and competitions	large quantities of product must be purchased

Quelle/Source: Schmidt 2009

Schwächen bei Einsatz und Nutzung von POS-Aktivitäten aus der Sicht von Marktleitern

Problems occurring during POS activity as experienced by store managers

Vergegenwärtigt man sich die Flut von VKF-Aktivitäten, die auf einen Marktleiter zukommen, wird verständlich, dass Aktionen, die problemlos aufstellbar sind, gut aussehen, das Budget der Filiale nicht belasten und bestens entsorgbar sind, bevorzugt werden – auch hinsichtlich der Platzierung und der Präsenzdauer im Geschäft. Hier bestehen Optimierungsmöglichkeiten, die Hersteller ausschöpfen können. POS-Aktionen müssen konsequent nicht nur strategisch, sondern auch operativ durchgeplant werden. Der letztendliche Erfolg entscheidet sich in der Umsetzung und der Akzeptanz am Point of Sale.

6. Die Erfassung der Effizienz von POS-Maßnahmen

Um es vorwegzunehmen: Im Vergleich zu der verfügbaren Literatur zur Verkaufsförderung oder zur Führung von Verkaufsgesprächen gibt es zu diesem wichtigen Thema äußerst wenig zu lesen, obwohl bereits vor mehr als 25 Jahren Klaus Birkigt darauf hinwies, dass es wichtig zu wissen sei, welchen Erfolg eine Verkaufsförderungsmaßnahme bewirkt (Birkigt 1983). Birkigt wies aber auch schon damals auf die Schwierigkeiten bei der Erfolgsmessung für Verkaufsförderung hin: Ein Ertragszuwachs muss nicht zwingend das Resultat der Verkaufsförderung sein, er kann durch Werbung, Preisgestaltung oder z.B. auch Maßnahmen der Konkurrenz beeinflusst werden.

Fuchs und Unger (Fuchs/Unger 2003) systematisieren Messinstrumente in der Verkaufsförderung erstmals in die Kategorien: qualitativ – quantitativ und intern – extern.

Gedenk (Gedenk 2002) weist darauf hin, dass es für Hersteller und Händler indes unerlässlich ist, den Erfolg der Verkaufsförderung zu analysieren. Das Hauptproblem besteht in der empirischen

that retailers will prefer promotions that are easy to set up, look good, do not financially burden the store and can be disposed of without problems. They will prefer such promotions both in terms of display location and time of presentation. Here, there is leeway for manufacturers to optimise their promotions. POS activity requires consistent and thorough strategic, but also operational planning. In the end, the execution and acceptance at the POS will be decisive for the promotion's success.

6. Evaluating the effectiveness of POS activity

Compared to literature available about sales promotion in general, or literature about how to conduct sales conversations, to come straight to the point, there is hardly anything to read in this important matter, even though it was 25 years ago that Klaus Birkigt stressed the importance of knowing how successful a promotion was (Birkigt 1983). At the time, Birkigt also pointed out that it is difficult to establish the success of sales promotion: increased profits are not necessarily the result of sales promotion, they can also be influenced by advertising, pricing policies or possibly by competitors' activity.

Fuchs and Unger (Fuchs/Unger 2003) were the first to establish a sales promotion evaluation system divided into the categories: qualitative – quantitative and internal – external:

Gedenk (Gedenk 2002) notes that it is essential for manufacturers and retailers to analyse the success of sales promotion. The main problem is the empirical evaluation of the selling effect: "Evaluation of sales promotion is like driving in the dark with your headlights on: you can't see everything, but why switch off the light altogether?" (Gedenk 2005)

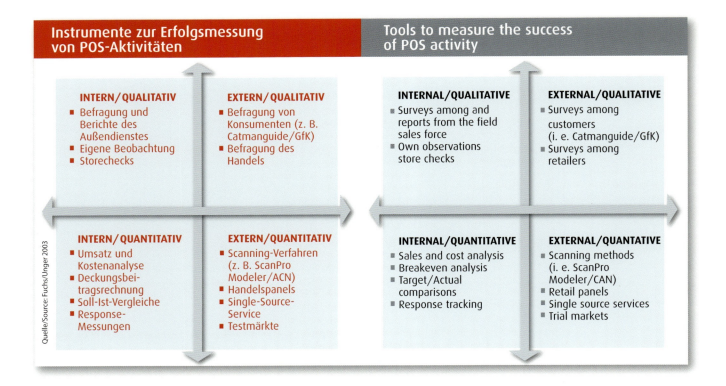

Quelle/Source: Fuchs/Unger 2003

Messung der Absatzwirkungen: „Die Evaluierung der Verkaufsförderung ist wie Autofahren im Dunkeln mit Scheinwerfern: Man sieht nicht alles – aber soll man deswegen das Licht ausmachen?" (Gedenk 2005).

Es bieten sich verschiedene Methoden zur Messung auf Handels- und Konsumentenebene an. Bei der Messung auf Handelsebene steht der Hersteller vor der Frage, ob er die Liefermengen an den Handel (Hineinverkauf) verwendet oder ob der Absatz des Handels an den Konsumenten (Abverkauf/Offtakes) ebenfalls berücksichtigt werden soll. Bei der Analyse auf Konsumentenebene besteht die Wahl, so Gedenk, zwischen aggregierten Handelsdaten, wie z.B. Abverkaufszahlen des Handels oder Scanner-Handelspanels, und disaggregierten Kaufverhaltensdaten zu Geschäftswahl, Kaufzeitpunkt, Markenwahl, Kaufmenge usw., wie sie z.B. in Verbraucherpanels oder Single-Source-Panels erhoben werden. Aggregierte Daten sind leichter zu beschaffen, ermöglichen aber nur begrenzt eine Untersuchung des kurzfristigen Mehrabsatzes. Zudem lassen sie kaum Aussagen über langfristige Wirkungen auf Marken- und Geschäftstreue zu. Hierzu sind disaggregierte Daten nötig, um eine Verzerrung der Modellparameter zu vermeiden. Der dabei notwendige Aufwand, insbesondere der finanzielle, ist allerdings wesentlich größer.

Gerade auch für mittelständische Hersteller ist der Erwerb dieser Daten von Marktforschungsinstituten finanziell nicht (immer) möglich. Zudem sind einige Handelsorganisationen auch nicht bereit, die entsprechenden Abverkaufsdaten aus der Hand zu

There are various evaluation methods for retail and consumption. In terms of retail, the manufacturer will have to decide whether to use only the quantities delivered to the retailer, or also consider the retailer's sales to the customer. On the consumer level, manufacturers can choose between aggregated retail data like retail sales figures or scanner retail panels, and non-aggregated buying behaviour data concerning the choice of the store, time of purchase, choice of brand, the amount of products bought etc., as recorded by consumer panels or single source panels. Aggregated data is easier to collect, but is useful for a evaluation of short-term additional sales only to a limited extent. It also provides little information about the long-term effects on brand and store loyalty. Non-aggregated data is needed in order to avoid the distortion of model parameters. Collecting non-aggregated data, however, is substantially more expensive.

Medium-size companies in particular cannot (always) afford to acquire this kind of data from market research companies. Furthermore, some retail companies are not willing to provide information, especially when it comes to their own retail brands or information about competitors.

Manufacturers, however, always have the possibility to collect their own data in an own promotion data base. They can keep a record of their POS activity in that systematic data base that includes information about:

- *Type of activity*
- *Distribution channel*

geben, vor allem nicht die Daten zu den eigenen Handelsmarken und auch nicht die Daten der Wettbewerber.

Es besteht für den Hersteller aber immer die Möglichkeit, sich eine eigene Promotion-Wissensdatenbank aufzubauen. In dieser Wissensdatenbank erfasst er seine POS-Aktivitäten systematisch mit z. B. folgenden Daten:

- Art der Maßnahme
- Vertriebslinie
- Zeitpunkt
- Zeitdauer
- Zielsetzung
- Platzierungsqualität
- Ergebnis

Dies führt zu einer gewissen Disziplin hinsichtlich der Zielformulierung und der Erfassung der Ergebnisse. Im Laufe der Zeit ergibt sich eine recht umfangreiche Informationssammlung, aus der man Tendenzen ablesen kann über das, was für das eigene Produkt „arbeitet" und was eher nicht so effizient ist.

7. Betriebswirtschaftliche Erfolgskennziffern – Von den Besten lernen!

Was machen die Besten in den Branchen anders, wenn sie besonders erfolgreich POS-Aktivitäten durchführen und sich diese Ergebnisse im wirtschaftlichen Erfolg dieser Unternehmen niederschlagen? Aktuell ist es eine Studie von McKinsey, die dazu zurate gezogen werden kann (Wellhöfer/Weng o. J.). Die Best Practices von erfolgreichen Unternehmen, wie Colgate, Unilever, Procter & Gamble, beim Kundenmanagement wurden detailliert untersucht. Fünf Erfolgshebel kristallisierten sich heraus:

- Transparenz über die Kundenprofitabilität
- Leistungsorientiertes Konditionenmanagement und Systematisches Preismanagement
- Aktive Promotion-Steuerung
- Kundengerechte Gestaltung von Supply-Chain-Management
- Exzellenz in der Durchführung der In-Store-Aktivitäten

Die Studie gibt also auch viele Hinweise, wie es die Besten schaffen, ihre POS-Aktivitäten erfolgreicher zu gestalten. Insbesondere sind hier nachfolgende „Erfolgshebel" wichtig:

1. Transparenz über Kundenprofitabilität

Best-Practise-Unternehmen erfassen alle Kosten, die ein Kunde verursacht bzw. die diesem zugeschrieben werden können, und führen eine kundenbezogene Gewinn- und Verlustrechnung. Diese Berechnung gibt viele Anhaltspunkte, welche Ziele bei

- *Time*
- *Duration*
- *Objectives*
- *Display position quality*
- *Results*

This allows for a certain degree of discipline regarding the objectives and the evaluation of the results. Over time, the manufacturer will be able to collect a rather extensive amount of information that indicates what generally "works for" the own product and what is less effective.

7. Economic success indicators – learn from the best!

What distinguishes the particularly successful POS activity of market leaders that is reflected in their economic success? Answers can be found in a recent McKinsey study (Wellhöfer/Weng, undated) that took a close look at the best practices of companies like Colgate, Unilever and Procter & Gamble for customer management. It identifies five success factors:

- *Transparency on customer profitability*
- *Performance oriented management of conditions and systematic cost control*
- *Active promotion management*
- *Customer oriented supply chain management*
- *Excellent execution of in-store activity*

Promotion-Wissensdatenbank eines Herstellers / Manufacturer's promotion data base

welchen Kunden mit Priorität bezüglich der POS-Aktivitäten verfolgt werden sollten, um die eigene wirtschaftliche Situation sinnvoll zu gestalten.

2. Aktive Promotion-Steuerung

Best-Practise-Unternehmen werten mindestens einmal pro Quartal alle verfügbaren Daten zu ihren Promotions aus und errechnen auf Basis von realen Kosten und Erlösen, welche Promotion den höchsten ROI erzielt. Ausgehend von dieser Wissensbasis entwickeln sie dann individuelle Promotion-Pläne, die exakt auf Produktsegment, Kunden und Vertriebskanäle abgestimmt sind.

3. Exzellenz in der Durchführung der In-Store-Aktivitäten

Hervorragende Unternehmen bewerten ihre Artikel nach deren Leistung in Bezug auf Drehgeschwindigkeit, Absatzwachstum und Deckungsbeitrag. Zudem kümmern sie sich aktiv um Listungsentscheidungen des Handels. Die besten Unternehmen arbeiten mit einem exzellenten Außendienst, dessen Einsatzzeiten beim Kunden z. B. am Umsatzvolumen und Ertragspotenzial des Händlers ausgerichtet sind. Best-Practise-Unternehmen holen den Konsumenten am POS mit attraktiven Platzierungen und Inszenierungen ab und machen Shopper-Marketing zum integralen Bestandteil ihrer Strategien.

8. Ausblick

Von Shopper-Insights zu betriebswirtschaftlichen Kennziffern? Effiziente Verkaufsförderungsmaßnahmen machen das möglich! Unter Beachtung von frühzeitiger und abgestimmter Planung, Zielformulierungen, die nicht nur den Hersteller, sondern auch den Handel und den Shopper einschließen, sorgfältiger Umsetzung und Realisation bis zum Point of Sale, Controlling der erreichten Ergebnisse zusammen mit einem exzellenten Außendienst, Abstimmung mit dem Handelsunternehmen und einer hohen Attraktivität des Promotion-Angebotes ist das für jedes Unternehmen erreichbar.

The study also gives many clues about how these market leaders manage to be more successful with their POS activity than others. The following "levers for success" are of particular importance:

1. Transparency on customer profitability

Best practice companies keep record of all the costs a retailer creates, or are assigned to the retailer, and draw up a retailer specific profit and loss account. That shows the company what objectives it should focus on in a promotion cooperation with a customer in order to draw financial benefits from the situation.

2. Active promotion management

Best practice companies analyse all available promotion data at least once every quarter and, on the basis of real costs and sales, calculate which promotions generate the highest return on investments. Based on this knowledge, the companies make individual promotion plans that are tailored to the individual needs of the product, retailer and retail format in question.

3. Excellent execution of in-store activity

Outstanding companies judge their products according to their stock turnover, sales growth and gross margin performance. They also play an active role in deciding what products should be included in the retailer's offer.

8. Outlook

From shopper insights to economic indicators? Efficient sales promotion activity makes that possible! Any company can achieve that if it plans early and coordinates planning, set its objectives in view of both retail's and shoppers' requirements, carefully handles processes up to the POS, keeps track of achievements together with a qualified field sales force, coordinates activities with retailers and offers high-quality promotions.

Susanne Czech-Winkelmann

Bram Nauta

Der Wirkungsgrad von Marketingaktionen im Handel

Marktuntersuchungen in niederländischen Supermärkten nach der Vision Tracking-Methode

1. Einleitung

POPAI Benelux hat es sich zur Aufgabe gemacht, das Verhalten von Shoppern und die Möglichkeiten, deren Verhalten zu beeinflussen, zu erforschen.
Eine der Zielsetzungen ist es dabei, die Wirkung unterschiedlicher Instore-Maßnahmen und Medien messbar zu machen, so dass einerseits Werber und Medienplaner auf einer einheitlichen Basis ihre Marketingbudgets planen können und andererseits POS-Dienstleister Know-how und Einblicke in die Wirkungsweise von Marketingmaßnahmen erhalten.

Wir wissen aus früheren POPAI-Untersuchungen, dass durchschnittlich 70 % der Kaufentscheidungen im Geschäft selbst getroffen werden. Dieses Wissen gibt uns Hinweise darauf, wie Instore-Medien in Produktkategorien bzw. Geschäftstypen eingesetzt werden müssen. Die Frage, ob und auf welche Weise jedes Instore-Medium eigentlich zur Kaufentscheidung beigetragen hat, bleibt jedoch unbeantwortet.

Wenn wir eine bestimmte Standardisierung der Verhältnisse (Ratios) erreichen möchten, müssen diese bestimmte Anforderungen erfüllen. Ein messbarer Standard muss

- getestet sein,
- für alle Parteien der Kategorie akzeptabel sein,
- konsistent sein,
- vergleichbar mit anderen Medientypen wie TV und Outdoor-Medien sein,
- für alle Parteien verfügbar sein und
- regelmäßig aktualisiert werden.

Die Marketing At Retail Initiative (MARI)-Untersuchung, die POPAI im Jahre 2007 als Pilotstudie in zwei englischen und vier amerikanischen Geschäften (Supermärkte, Drogerien und Mini-Märkte) durchgeführt hat, hat zur Entwicklung eines Systems zur Messung der Effizienz von Instore-Kommunikation geführt.

Bram Nauta

The effectiveness of marketing at retail

Vision tracking market research in Dutch supermarkets

1. Introduction

POPAI Benelux has researched shopper behaviour and the possibilities of influencing shopper behaviour. One of the objectives was to make the effectiveness of different in-store activity and promotional materials measurable, thus providing advertisers and media planners with a standardised basis for marketing budget allocation on the one hand and POS services companies with knowledge and insights about the effectiveness of marketing on the other hand.

We know from earlier POPAI research that 70 % of buying decisions are made inside the store. This information gives us clues about what in-store promotional materials should be used for what product or business form. The questions if the in-store materials influenced the buying decision and, if yes, what effect they exactly had, however, remain unanswered.

In order to achieve a certain degree of standardisation (ratios), we need to fulfil certain requirements. A measurement standard has to be:

- *tested*
- *accepted by all parties of a category*
- *consistent*
- *comparable to other media forms like TV and outdoor media*
- *available to all parties*
- *updated regularly*

The Marketing At Retail Initiative (MARI) study carried out by POPAI as a pilot study in two British and four US supermarkets, drug stores and minimarkets in 2007, has led to the development of a measuring system of in-store communication effectiveness.

This new measurement method contributes to developing a new business model that measures the impact of communication on the customer and puts it on the par with other media forms. For the first time, we get insight into what grabs the shopper's attention and what motivates the shopper's actions.

Diese neue Messmethode hilft bei der Entwicklung eines neues Geschäftsmodells, das die Auswirkungen der Kommunikation auf die Käufer misst und mit anderen Medientypen vergleichbar macht. Zum ersten Mal können wir uns nun ein Bild davon machen, was die Aufmerksamkeit der Käufer auf sich lenkt und sie zum Handeln bewegt.

Darüber hinaus bietet diese Untersuchung einen Einblick in die vielfältigen Aspekte, die mit dem Verhalten des Käufers, dem Category-Management, den Präsentationstechniken und dem Laden-Layout zusammen hängen. Kurzum: Die Ergebnisse der Studie liefern vor allem Informationen, um taktische und strategische Entscheidungen in Bezug auf Instore-Marketing und eine sinnvolle Verteilung der Marketingbudgets zu fällen.

Vision Tracking (ClipCam®): Die Shopper wurden mit einer Brille ausgestattet, auf der eine winzige Digitalkamera angebracht wurde. Die Kamera beobachtet das Blickfeld des Kunden während seines Einkaufstripps und registriert, wohin er/sie schaut.

ClipCam® vision-tracking technology: Digital micro cameras were fitted to special glasses or the shopper's own glasses. The camera captured the shopper's field of vision during his journey in the store, registering where he looked.

Dieser Beitrag beschreibt die Zielsetzung, die Methodik, das Konzept und die Ergebnisse der ersten MARI-Studie in niederländischen Supermärkten.

Vision Tracking Food

Die Vision Tracking-Studie wurde auf Initiative von POPAI Benelux von der Het Lageveld B.V. unter Leitung von Dr. A. J. Nauta durchgeführt. Die Feldarbeit erfolgte im September 2008.

Insgesamt 13 Unternehmen haben sich an dieser ersten MARI-Studie beteiligt: Albert Heijn, C 1000, Super de Boer, PLUS Retail, Bloemenbureau Holland, Douwe Egberts, Friesland Foods, Heineken, LU, Mars Nederland, Perfetti van Melle, Sanoma und Unilever.

2. Untersuchungskonzept
2.1 Ziel und Problemstellung der Untersuchung
Das Ziel der Untersuchung wurde folgendermaßen formuliert:

The study also gives insight into various aspects like shopper behaviour, category management, presentation techniques and store layout. The findings, in short, deliver information that helps make tactical and strategic marketing at retail and adequate budget allocation decisions.

This paper presents the objectives, methodology, concept and findings of the first MARI study carried out in Dutch supermarkets.

Vision tracking food

The vision tracking study was initiated by POPAI Benelux, carried out by Het Lageveld BV and headed by Drs A. J. Nauta. The field work took place in September 2008.

A total of 13 companies took part in the first MARI study: Albert Heijn, C 1000, Super de Boer, PLUS Retail, Bloemenbureau Holland, Douwe Egberts, Friesland Foods, Heineken, LU, Mars Nederland, Perfetti van Melle, Sanoma and Unilever.

Vision Tracking Food wertet die Instore-Kommunikation in Supermärkten aus und leitet daraus Shopper Insights ab, die später einen Einblick in die Kauffaktoren von Shoppern liefern.

Ausgehend von diesem Ziel wurden folgende Fragestellungen formuliert:

- In welchem Maßhaben die Käufer die verschiedenen Kommunikationsbotschaften im Geschäft wahrgenommen (Auswirkungen von Instore-Promotion-Materialien und deren Fähigkeit, den Kunden einzubinden)?
- Welcher Zusammenhang besteht zwischen „Anschauen" und „Kaufen"?
- In welcher Beziehung stehen Kaufabsicht und tatsächlicher Kauf?

2.2 Untersuchungsmethode

Die Untersuchung selbst bestand aus vier Elementen:

1. **Laden-Audit:** Im Rahmen eines vollständigen Audits wurden die gesamten Instore Werbematerialien und Werbebotschaften in den teilnehmenden Geschäften registriert.
2. **Vision Tracking (ClipCam®):** Die Shopper wurden mit einer Brille ausgestattet, auf der eine winzige Digitalkamera angebracht wurde (bei Kunden, die bereits eine Brille tragen, wird die Kamera auf den Brillensteg gesteckt). Mit dieser Kamera wird das Blickfeld des Kunden während seines Einkauftripps beobachtet und registriert, wohin er/sie schaut.
3. **Entry und Exit Interviews:** Zu Beginn des Einkaufs findet ein kurzes Interview statt, in dem der Kunde unter anderem nach seiner Kaufabsicht in Bezug auf bestimmte Produktkategorien gefragt wird, ebenso werden nach dem Kauf diverse Fragen gestellt (u. a. nach der Wahrnehmung der verschiedenen Instore-Medien).
4. **Registrierung der Einkäufe:** Anhand des Kassenbons wird registriert, welche Produkte tatsächlich eingekauft wurden.

2. Concept

2.1 Objective and questions

The objective of the study: Vision tracking food evaluates in-store communication in supermarkets to derive insights into the factors that influence the shopper's buying decision.

The objective led to the following questions:

- *To what extent were shoppers aware of the various communication messages in the store (what was the impact of in-store promotional materials and their ability to engage the customer)?*
- *What is the correlation between "viewing" and "buying"?*
- *How does the buying intention relate to the actual purchase?*

2.2 Methodology

Four techniques were utilised in the study:

1. *Retail audit: A full audit of all advertising material and messages of each store was undertaken.*
2. *ClipCam® vision-tracking technology: Digital micro cameras were fitted to special glasses or the shoppers' own glasses. The camera captured the shoppers' field of vision during the journey in the store, registering where they looked.*
3. *Entry and exit interviews: at the beginning of the shopping journey shoppers were asked about the products they intended*

3. Erklärungsmodell

Der in der Abbildung auf der vorhergehenden Seite gezeigte Umwandlungstrichter bildet das zentrale Element der Vision Tracking-Methode.

Die einzelnen Begriffe sind dabei wie folgt definiert:
Käufer: Anzahl der Personen in einem Geschäft.
Diese Käufer **kommen an** Instore-Medien **vorbei** bzw. **schauen** sich diese an, treten in **Interaktion** mit dem jeweiligen Produkt und **kaufen** es (oder nicht).

Anhand der Parameter aus dem Umwandlungstrichter lassen sich Kennzahlen berechnen. In der Analyse werden vier Kennzahlen verwendet, um die Werbewirksamkeit eines Instore-Mediums zu bestimmen:

- **Impact Ratio:** Wie oft ist der Käufer an einem Instore-Medium vorbeigekommen und wie oft hat er dieses tatsächlich wahrgenommen. Ein Käufer kann mehrmals an einem Instore-Medium vorbeigehen, ohne es bewusst oder unbewusst wahrzunehmen. Die Impact Ratio gibt an, inwiefern dieses Medium imstande ist, die Aufmerksamkeit auf sich zu lenken.
- **Engagement Ratio:** Wie oft hat eine Interaktion zwischen dem Shopper (beispielsweise in die Hand nehmen, Lesen des Labels, Zurückstellen) und dem jeweiligen Produkt im Verhältnis zur Häufigkeit der Betrachtung des Produktes stattgefunden? Dieser Wert gibt unter anderem an, in welchem Maße das Instore-Medium imstande war, den Käufer zu einer Interaktion mit dem Produkt zu „verführen". Es gibt daher auch einen Hinweis darauf, inwiefern die Botschaft/Gestaltung ausreichend relevant war bzw. den Kunden zur Interaktion angeregt hat.
- **Conversion Ratio:** Wie oft wurde ein Produkt im Verhältnis zur Beachtung der Instore-Werbemaßnahmen tatsächlich gekauft? Dabei geht es nicht um die Art und Weise, wie wir normalerweise "Umwandlung" definieren. Es geht um die Anzahl Käufer, die einen Einkauf tätigen im Verhältnis zur Gesamtzahl der Käufer in dem jeweiligen Geschäft oder in der Abteilung. Bei kommunikativen Effekten geht es darum, wie oft ein Einkauf im Verhältnis zur Beachtung der Instore-Medien erfolgt ist.

Die Ergebnisse für alle Instore-Medien sind der nachstehenden Tabelle zu entnehmen.

Conversion funnel

Buying intention	Entry interview
Shoppers / Passing / Viewing / Interaction / Purchase	Vision Tracking
Shopping	Exit interview

to buy. At the end of the journey shoppers were asked about how aware they were of various in-store promotional materials.

4. *Purchase audit: The shopper's receipt was checked to see what products were actually bought.*

3. Explanatory model

The conversion funnel featured in the figure above is the central element of the vision tracking method.

Definitions:

Shoppers: *the number of shoppers in a store*
These shoppers pass an in-store promotional material, look at it, interact with the product in question and buy it (or not).

Key metrics can be calculated on the basis of the conversion funnel parameters. Four key metrics are used in the analysis to measure the communicative effectiveness of an in-store promotional material:

- ***Impact ratio:*** *how often did the customer pass the in-store promotional material and how often did the shopper actually see it. A shopper can pass an in-store promotional material more than once without consciously or unconsciously noticing it. The impact ratio determines the promotional material's ability to attract the shopper's attention.*
- ***Engagement ratio:*** *how often did the shopper interact with the product (for example picking up the product, reading its labelling and putting it back) in relation to the number of times the shopper looked at the product? The ratio shows, among other things, to which extent the promotional material "tempted" the shopper to interact with the product. In this way, the ratio also shows to which extent the design or message of the promotional material was relevant enough, or encouraged the customer to interact.*

Einzelhändler	Anzahl der Shopper	Anzahl der Promotionmaterialien	Impact	Engagement	Conversion
Total	980	15.961	14.6%	8.4%	5.2%

Retailers	Number of shoppers	Number of promotional materials	Impact	Engagement	Conversion
Total	980	15.961	14.6 %	8.4 %	5.2 %

Die Impact Ratio beträgt 14,6 %

15 % aller Kunden, die an einem Instore-Medium vorbeigekommen sind, haben dies angeschaut. Dieser Prozentsatz differiert von Einzelhändler zu Einzelhändler und liegt zwischen 10 und 17 %.

Wenn wir uns vor Augen führen, dass ein durchschnittlicher Shoppingtrip 20 Minuten dauert, schaut der Käufer sich also alle sechs Sekunden ein Instore-Medium an.

Die Engagement Ratio beträgt 8,4 %

Von allen Fällen, in denen der Kunde ein Instore-Medium angeschaut hat, ist er in 8 % der Fälle in Interaktion mit dem Produkt getreten. Die Streubreite liegt hier zwischen 7 und 14 %.

Die Conversion Ratio beträgt 5,2 %

5 % der Kunden, die ein Instore-Medium angesehen haben, haben zum Schluss das Produkt auch gekauft.

Die Analyse dieser Verhältnisses auf Ladenebene/Kategorieebene und die Art der Instore-Medien liefert zusammen mit der Instore-Marketing-Situation einer Erklärung für diese Ergebnisse und bietet die notwendigen Einblicke, um das Konzept in Bezug auf die Instore-Kommunikation zu optimieren.

Zunächst müssen wir jedoch die unterschiedlichen Arten von Instore-Medien genauer betrachten:

I. Die Werbewirksamkeit digitaler Instore-Medien

Neun der Geschäfte, die an der Studie teilnahmen, setzten in irgendeiner Art Digital Signage ein. Dazu gehörten alle Formen animierter Plakate und Screens, die an der Decke, in Augenhöhe oder als Teil eines Displays oder einer Demo-Unit integriert waren.

Die Impact Ratio betrug 15 %. Zu berücksichtigen ist in diesem Kontext einerseits, dass „Schauen" nicht gleichzeitig „Wahrnehmen" bedeuten muss, und andererseits, dass auch andere Aspekte des Kundenverhaltens diese Kennziffer beeinflussen. Wir haben daher Käufer im Exit Interview gefragt, „ob sie in diesem Geschäft Bildschirme gesehen haben" und „falls ja, ob sie sich an etwas aus dem Programm erinnern konnten".

- *Conversion ratio:* How often did a shopper actually buy a product viewed in a promotional material? Note: we are not referring to the definition of conversion in its usual sense. That would be the number of shoppers that buy a product compared to the total number of shoppers in a store or department. In the evaluation of communicative effectiveness conversion looks at how often shoppers viewed and how often they bought a product.

See the table above for the results for all in-store promotional materials.

The impact ratio was 14.6 %

15 % of all shoppers that passed an in-store promotional material looked at the material. The percentage differs between retailers, ranging from 10 to 17 %.

Considering that an average shopping journey takes 20 minutes, this means that the shopper looked at an in-store promotional material every six seconds.

The engagement ratio was 8.4 %

8 % of all shoppers that looked at in-store promotional material actually interacted with the product. The percentage ranges from 7 to 14 %.

The Conversion ratio was 5.2 %

5 % of shoppers that looked at a product bought the product. Together with the in-store situation, an analysis of these conditions in the store and product category level and the type of in-store promotional material explains these conditions and gives the necessary insights to optimise the in-store communication concept.

But first we need to take a closer look at the types of in-store promotional materials:

I. The communicative effectiveness of digital in-store promotional materials

Nine stores that took part in the study used some kind of digital signage. This included all types of animated posters as well as screens fitted either to the ceiling, placed at eyelevel, or integrated into a display or demo unit.

Auf die erste Frage haben 24 % positiv geantwortet, von diesen 24 % erinnerten sich 28 % an Programm-Details. Eine „Netto Erinnerung" von fast 7 %. Mit anderen Worten: 24 % der Kunden sagen, dass sie einen Bildschirm gesehen haben, während nur 15 % aller Kunden, die an einem Screen vorbeigelaufen sind, auch tatsächlich den Bildschirm angeschaut haben. Eine mögliche Erklärung dafür könnte sein, dass diese Stichprobe relativ viele Stammkunden umfasst, die diesen Supermarkt zweimal in der Woche oder sogar öfter besuchen. Sie wissen daher bereits von früheren Besuchen, dass in dem Geschäft Bildschirme hängen.

II. Die Werbewirksamkeit semi-permanenter Displays

In den Geschäften konnten elf unterschiedliche Arten von semi-permanenten Displays identifiziert werden. Die Impact Ratio zeigt eine Verteilung von 2 bis 34 %. Der erste Wert bezieht sich auf einen Drehständer, der neben der Stirnseite eines Regals aufgestellt wurde, der zweite bezieht sich auf ein Kühldisplay. Es ist nur logisch, dass auch die Engagement Ratio eine große Spannbreite von 0 bis 40 % zeigt.

III. Die Werbewirksamkeit von Promotiondisplays

In den untersuchten Geschäften waren acht unterschiedliche Promotiondisplays platziert. Die Impact Ratio war hier die höchste von allen Instore-Medien und lag zwischen 17 und 55 %.

Die Engagement und Conversion Ratios fielen je nach Art des Displays und des Standortes im Geschäft sehr unterschiedlich aus. Die Ergebnisse unterstreichen einmal mehr, dass Promotiondisplays ein starkes Medium innerhalb der Instore-Medien darstellen.

IV. Die Werbewirksamkeit von POS-Maßnahmen

Auch hier basieren die Werte auf verschiedenen Formen von POS-Maßnahmen, also auf einem Durchschnittswert. Diese reichen von Produktpräsentationen mit multimedialer Unterstützung bis hin zu Verkostungsaktionen, bei denen geschnittene Käsestücke auf einem Tablett präsentiert werden.

Die Impact Ratio betrug hier 22 %, die Engagement Ratio 20 % und die Conversion Ratio 3 %. Bei der Interpretation dieser Zahlen gilt es zu beachten, dass Demo-Units an bestimmten Tagen nur mit einer Person „besetzt" waren und auf Probe-Tabletts manchmal keine Produkte lagen.

V. Die Werbewirksamkeit von Verkaufsförderungsmaßnahmen am Regal

Gerade in dieser Gruppe sind die Maßnahmen im Handel sehr vielfältig, und die Ergebnisse wiesen daher auch große Unterschiede auf. Die Impact Ratio betrug 3 bis 24 %, die Engagement Ratio 0 bis 24 % und die Conversion Ratio 0 bis 13 %.

The impact ratio was 15 %. In this context, it should be pointed out that "viewing" is not the same as "noticing" and that this figure is also influenced by other aspects of shopper behaviour. That is why we asked shoppers in the exit interview "if they saw screens in the store" and "if yes if they remembered anything about the programme".

24 % said they saw screens in the store, 28 % of these 24 % remembered details from the programme. This is a "net remembrance" of almost 7 %. In other words this means that 24 % of shoppers say they saw a screen while only 15 % of all shoppers that passed a screen actually looked at it. A possible explanation could be that the random sample drawn included a rather large number of regular customers that shop at the supermarket in question twice or more a week. They are likely to know from earlier visits that there are screens in the store.

II. The communicative effectiveness of semi-permanent displays

There were 11 different types of semi-permanent displays in the stores. The impact ratio ranged from 2 to 34 %. A revolving stand next to a shelf had an impact ratio of 2 %, a cooler display of 34 %. It is only logical that the engagement ratio varied largely from 0 to 40 %.

III. The communicative effectiveness of promotional displays

There were eight different promotional displays in the stores that took part in the study. The impact was the highest of all in-store promotional materials, ranging from 17 to 55 %.

The engagement and conversion ratios varied greatly depending on the type of display and its position within the store. The results underline once more that the promotional display is one of the most effective in-store promotional materials.

IV. The communicative effectiveness of POS activity

Figures here also refer to various different forms of POS activity and are average figures. POS activity ranges from multi-media product presentations to tastings of cheese that was cut into cubes and offered to shoppers on a tray.

The impact ratio was 22 %, the engagement ratio 20 % and the conversion ratio 3 %. When analysing these figures it has to be considered that on certain days there was only one promotional person at the demo unit and that the trays were sometimes empty.

V. The communicative effectiveness of shelf promotions

There is a large number of different activity in this group and the results therefore differ largely. The impact ratio ranged from 3 to 24 %, the engagement ratio from 0 % to 24 % and the conversion ratio from 0 to 13 %.

VI. The communicative effectiveness of posters

A total of nine different posters were evaluated in this study with the

VI. Die Werbewirksamkeit von Plakaten

Insgesamt neun unterschiedliche Plakate wurden im Rahmen dieser Studie beurteilt, wobei die Impact Ratio sich zwischen 3 und 33 % bewegte. Die Engagement und Conversion Ratio fielen sehr niedrig aus.

VII. Die Werbewirksamkeit von Visual Merchandising

Die in den Geschäften praktizierten sechs unterschiedlichen Formen von Visual Merchandising weisen eine Impact Ratio von 2 bis 28 % auf. Die höchsten Ergebnisse wurden dabei mit dekorierten Tischen erreicht.

VIII. Die Werbewirksamkeit sonstiger Instore-Medien

Aufgrund der Vielzahl der darüber hinaus im Handel platzierten Instore-Maßnahmen haben wir nur einige der wichtigsten herausgegriffen und für diese die Impact Ratio ermittelt, die sich wie folgt darstellt:

	Impact Ratio
Floor Graphics (Bodenplakate)	16 %
Deckenhänger und Plakate	12 %
Eingangsschranke/Gates	27 %
Kassentrennstab	27 %

Auffällig ist, dass auch bei Medien wie der Eingangsschranke oder dem Kassentrennstab, mit denen alle Kunden in Kontakt kommen, die Impact Ratio nicht über einen Wert von 30 % hinauskommt. Die Kunden scheinen sich an diese Form der Werbung „gewöhnt" zu haben. Wirklich herausragende Werte wurden in der gesamten Studie nur von den Promotiondisplays erreicht, da diese aus dem üblichen Raster herausfallen und dem Auge des Kunden Halt bieten.

impact ratio ranging from 3 to 33 %. The engagement and conversion ratios were very low.

VII. The communicative effectiveness of visual merchandising

The six different forms of visual merchandising in the stores had an impact ratio of between 2 and 28 %. Decorated tables had the highest impact ratio.

VIII. The communicative effectiveness of other in-store promotional materials

In view of the large number of in-store promotional materials used at retail, we have calculated the impact ratio of a select number of key materials:

	Impact ratio
Floor graphics (floor posters)	*16 %*
Danglers and posters	*12 %*
Entrance gates	*27 %*
Checkout dividers	*27 %*

What is striking is that even materials all shoppers come in contact with like the entrance gates and checkout dividers have an impact ratio of not more than 30 %. Apparently, shoppers have "got used to" this form of advertising. The only materials that reached a noticeably high impact ratio in this study were promotional displays. They stand out from the usual promotional materials and catch the shopper's eye.

Bram Nauta

VI. DAS DISPLAY DER ZUKUNFT | THE DISPLAY OF THE FUTURE

DAS DISPLAY DER ZUKUNFT:
POS 2.0 – DISPLAY 2.0

THE DISPLAY OF THE FUTURE:
POS 2.0 – DISPLAY 2.0

Günter Bauer

Die Rolle des Displays im Supermarkt der Zukunft

Retaildesigner prägen die Optik der Märkte von morgen: Sie entwickeln dabei nicht nur das Ladendesign, sondern befassen sich auch mit dem Sortiment und der Markenstrategie. Wie verkaufen sich Produkte und Dienstleistungen am besten und wie muss das dazu passende Umfeld inszeniert werden? Bei diesen Überlegungen lassen sie Displays außen vor, weil ein Laden ohne Displays besser aussieht – wohl wissend, dass der Handel den Freiraum nutzen wird, um auf die Schnelle Displays zu platzieren. Und warum platziert der Handel sie trotzdem? Weil Displays ein Umsatzplus generieren – gibt es etwas Wichtigeres für ein Untrnehmen?

Die Geschichte lehrt uns, was wir in der Zukunft finden

Wie sieht das Display der Zukunft in der Handelslandschaft der Zukunft aus? Seine Aufgabe ist unverändert die Positionierung der Marke und das Auslösen von Kaufimpulsen, wobei neben den ästhetischen die logistischen Aspekte an Bedeutung gewinnen. Ästhetik und Logistik bilden dabei Gegenpole wie Nord- und Südpol, doch anders als im Magnetismus gibt es im Handelsalltag die Möglichkeit, diese Spannungen zu überwinden. Verschiedene internationale Super- und Hypermärkte haben dies bereits bewiesen. Sie legen dabei den Fokus nicht auf das Produkt, sondern auf den Shopper und dessen Bedürfnisse – und genau diese Ebene muss das Display zukünftig erreichen.

Lange bevor Neuromarketingkonzepte in das Ladendesign einflossen, hatte Maslow[1] bereits erkannt, dass die menschlichen Bedürfnisse nicht eindimensional, sondern stufenförmig verlaufen. Auf der obersten Stufe strebt der Mensch nach Selbstverwirklichung, wohingegen die physiologischen Bedürfnisse (Wohnen, Nahrung, Sexualität) die unterste Stufe formen. Das höchste Niveau, die Selbstverwirklichung, ist nur zu erreichen, wenn zuvor die Bedürfnisse der tiefer liegenden Ebenen erfüllt wurden. Die oberste Ebene zu erreichen, ist Ziel von Ladendesignern und Händlern.

Günter Bauer

The display in the supermarket of the future

Retail designers will shape the look of tomorrow's supermarkets. They will not only develop the design of the store, but will also be involved in matters of assortment and brand strategy. How do products and services sell best and what must the retail environment look like? Displays will not be on the minds of store designers while they work out answers to these questions, knowing that stores look better without displays. They also know that retailers will put up displays whenever there is free space. But why do retailers insist on displays? Because displays generate sales growth – what is more important for a company?

© Jos de Vries The Retail Company

History tells us what the future will look like

What will the display of the future look like in the retail environment of the future? It will continue to present brands and trigger the shopper's impulse to buy a product, but logistical aspects will gain increasing importance next to the aspect of how nice the display looks. The look and logistical function of a display represent opposite poles like the North Pole and the South Pole, but unlike magnetism, every-day retail life offers possibilities to overcome this tension. Many international supermarkets and hypermarkets have already proved that. Their focus is not on the product, but on the shopper and the shopper's needs – that is exactly what the display will have to do in the future too.

Long before aspects of neuromarketing started to influence store design, Maslow[1] realised that human needs are not one-dimensional but multi-dimensional. At the highest level, the human being strives for self-actualisation, while the lowest level is represented by physiological needs like shelter, food and sexuality. The highest level, self-actualisation, can only be reached if the needs of the lower levels are satisfied. It is the goal of store designers and retailers to reach the highest level.

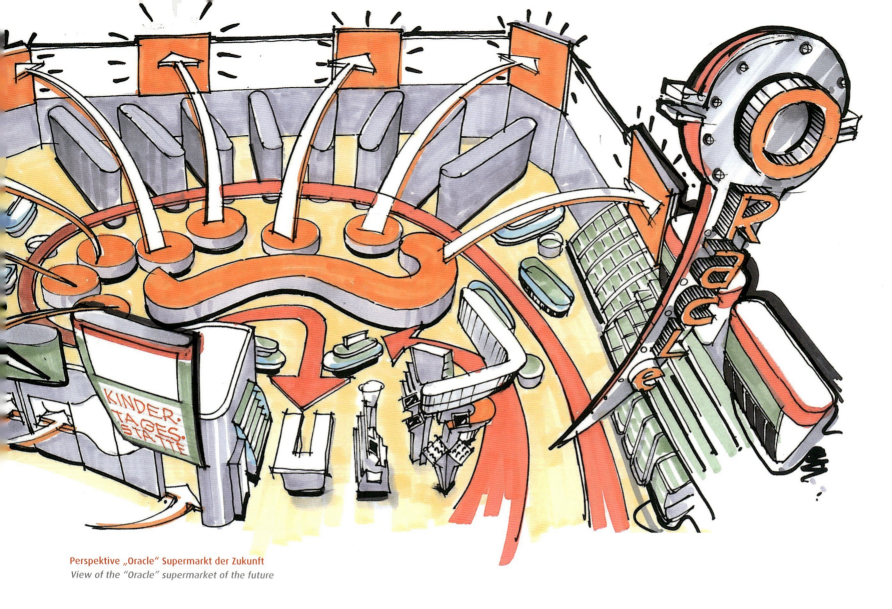

Perspektive „Oracle" Supermarkt der Zukunft
View of the "Oracle" supermarket of the future

Das Konzept Future Store „Oracle"

Der Supermarkt von heute ist das Servicecenter von morgen. Es geht dabei nicht nur mehr um „Food" (Physiologie), „Herkunft" (Sicherheit), „Kochen" (Sozial) oder „Marke" (Anerkennung/Status), sondern um Freiheit. Diese Freiheit bietet Zeit für die eigene Selbstverwirklichung. Vom Zeitalter der Auswahl und Fülle gelangen wir in das Zeitalter der Effizienz. Aufgabe der Marketingstrategen ist es, vorherzusagen, was der Kunde möchte und nicht abzuwarten, was er aus dem Regal nimmt. Basis hierfür bilden die Kundendateien, die unter kundenpsychologischen Aspekten ausgewertet werden.

Das Display in der Zukunft

Das Display der Zukunft ist Teil eines Konzeptes, das zwar in erster Linie als Promotiondisplay konzipiert wurde, jedoch nicht losgelöst, sondern gemeinsam mit dem Handel. Verzichtet man in der Entwicklungsphase auf eine intensive gegenseitige Abstimmung, dann begrenzt man damit nicht nur den Erfolg des neuen Produktes, sondern in letzter Konsequenz den Erfolg der gesamten Warengruppe. Die so genannten „Category Captains", d.h. die

The "Oracle" future store concept

Today's supermarkets will be tomorrow's services centres. Their focus will be not only on "food" (physiological needs), "origin" (safety needs), "cooking" (social needs) or "brands" (esteem and achievements), but also on freedom. This freedom provides the time needed to reach self-actualisation. We will move from times of choice and abundance to times of effectiveness. Marketing strategies will have to focus on predicting what customers want instead of waiting to see what product they pick from the shelf. These predictions will be based on customer data that will be evaluated while taking into account customer psychology.

The display of the future

The display of the future is part of a concept based mainly on the display as a promotional tool, developed not independently, but together with retailers. If manufacturers and retailers fail to thoroughly coordinate the development of displays, the success of the product in particular, and of the entire product group in general, will be limited. The so-called "category captains", i.e. the market leaders in a certain product group, will have the biggest say and

VI.1 DIE ROLLE DES DISPLAYS IM SUPERMARKT DER ZUKUNFT | THE DISPLAY IN THE SUPERMARKET OF THE FUTURE

Marktführer innerhalb einer Warengruppe, haben dabei das größte Mitspracherecht und auch die Chance, ihre Produkte in Langzeitdisplays oder sogar Shop-in-Shop-Systemen zu platzieren.

Der erste Eindruck zählt

Ein Handelskonzept sollte zwei wichtigen Regeln folgen. Erstens: Das Ladenkonzept muss eine Geschichte erzählen, in welcher der Kunde die Hauptrolle spielt, sich wohl fühlt und sich leiten lässt. Zweites: „The product is the hero", das Produkt selbst steht im Zentrum der Warenpräsentation. Wenn das Produkt den Kunden

also the chance to present their products in permanent displays or even shop-in-shop systems.

The first impression counts

A retail concept should follow two important rules. Firstly, the store concept has to tell a story in which the customer plays the leading role, feels good and is easily led. Secondly, "the product is the hero", the product itself has to be at the centre of the product presentation.

Perspektive des Eingangsbereichs
View of the entrance area

© Jos de Vries The Retail Company

nicht angeboten wird, können diese es auch nicht kaufen. Diese Grundregel des Visual Merchandising wird leider allzu häufig vergessen.

Future Store Check-in

Der erste Eindruck ist entscheidend. Dieser beginnt bei der Auffahrt auf den Parkplatz und geht über den Eingangsbereich des Marktes bis zur Gestaltung der einzelnen Warengruppe. Die erste Warengruppe, die nach dem Betreten des Marktes platziert wird, definiert dessen Positionierung. Obst und Gemüse stehen für ein hochwertiges Konzept, Basisartikel, wie Brot und Kaffee, eher für den Discount.

Alle zur Verfügung stehenden „Entwicklungstools", wie Layout, Shopdesign, Kommunikation und Visual Merchandising, müssen aufeinander abgestimmt werden, um ein harmonisches Bild des Handels zu erzeugen und diesen als eigenständige Marke zu etablieren. Die Technik muss dabei zukünftig als weiteres Tool integriert werden. Hierzu zählen beispielsweise variable Leuchten, die sich an Tages- und Jahreszeiten anpassen, oder eine kanalisierte Tageslichtnutzung zur Steigerung des Wohlbefindens und die damit verbundene Reduzierung der Energiekosten. Mehrwegsysteme bei Kisten, Paletten und Dollys mit integrierten RFID-Chips sorgen für eine nachhaltige Logistik und effiziente „Just-in-time"-Lieferungen. Handscanner und Infoterminals unterstützen die Kunden dabei, schneller den Weg zum richtigen Produkt zu finden.

Neue Technik bei Displays

Die gleiche Technik erhöht die Flexibilität und Anwendungsmöglichkeiten von Displays. So wird das Promotiondisplay durch den Einsatz von Touchscreens zum Informationsdisplay. RFID-Chips ermöglichen eine Individualisierung der Displays und den Wandel vom Massenmarketing zur maßgeschneiderten Kommunikation.

Weniger ist mehr

Menschen sehen heute nicht nur anders aus als vor 50 Jahren, sondern haben im Laufe der Zeit auch ihre Gewohn-

If shoppers are not presented with the product they can not buy it. Unfortunately, this fundamental rule of visual merchandising is all too often forgotten.

Future store check-in

The first impression is crucial. It starts when driving into the parking lot, continues in the entrance area of the store ends at the product group's in-store presentation. The store's positioning in the market is defined by the product group that is encountered upon entering the store. Fruit and vegetables are associated with upmarket, basic products like sugar, bread and coffee with discount.

All available "development tools" like layout, store design, communication and visual merchandising have to be coordinated to form a harmonious whole at retail and establish the retailer as a brand. Technology must be included as a future tool. Technology, for example, includes variable lighting that varies according to the time of day or season of the year, or the use of daylight in stores to increase wellbeing and at the same time reduce energy costs. The recycling of boxes as well as pallets and dollies with integrated RFID chips ensure that logistics are sustainable and products are delivered "just in time". Hand scanners and information terminals help the customer to easily and quickly locate the right product.

New display technology

This technology increases the display's flexibility and the number of ways it can be used at retail. In this way, a promotional display with a touch screen, for example, turns into a information display. The use

Perspektive des Conveniencebereichs
View of the convenience area

© Jos de Vries The Retail Company

heiten verändert. Das Gleiche gilt für die Produkte: Nicht nur die Verpackungen verändern sich, sondern auch deren Inhalt. Herkunft und Verarbeitung spielen eine wichtige Rolle. Regionalität, Bio aber auch Nanofood sind wachsende Marktsegmente, da Umweltschutz und effiziente Nutzung der existierenden Ressourcen das gleiche Ziel haben: „Aus weniger mehr machen."

Bedienung versus Selbstbedienung

Die Entwicklung des Handels reicht von der Selbstversorgung über den Tauschhandel und Wochenmarkt bis zum SB-Warenhaus, wie wir es heute kennen. Sie führt dazu, dass wir mehr Freizeit und auch mehr finanzielle Mittel zur Verfügung haben – ein weiterer Schritt auf dem Weg der Selbstverwirklichung. Fachmännisches Können, Authentizität und genussvolles Erlebnis innerhalb des Ladens akzentuieren dies. Allerdings spüren wir aktuell auch den Gegentrend: Verbraucher werden auf Ebay selbst zum Händler, Umweltschutzdiskussionen lassen den Trend zum Selbstversorger wieder aufleben.

Displays bieten Raum für Ideen

In einer Welt der Vielfalt haben Displays einen festen Platz, denn sie dienen als Präsentationsfläche für neue Produkte, inszenieren neue Verpackungen, laden zum Probieren ein oder präsentieren ganze Sortimente unter einem Dach.

Warenwelten

Unattraktive Regale und Gondelköpfe, die wie im Discount bis oben mit Ware befüllt werden, sind heute noch immer eher die Regel als die Ausnahme. Die Händler arbeiten jedoch gemeinsam mit der Industrie an Konzepten, um Sortimente zu optimieren, neue Produkte zu präsentieren oder neue Warengruppen zu entwickeln.

Eine Kommunikation, die auf Erlebnis und Individualität ausgerichtet ist, verwandelt logistisch optimierte Warengruppen in Erlebniswelten.

of RFID chips makes every display unique and contributes to shifting from mass marketing to individually tailored communication.

Less is more

People do not only look different than they did 50 years ago, they have also changed their habits. The same is true for the product: not only the packaging changes, but also the content. Origin and processing play important roles. The markets for regional products and organic food as well as nanofood are growing because concern for the environment and the effective use of existing resources have one and the same objective: "Get more out of less".

Service versus self-service

As it has been described in the previous chapters, retail has changed from self-supply, barter trade and weekly markets to self-service department stores as we know them today. The changes at retail have provided people with more free time and financial resources - which takes them a step closer to achieving self-actualisation. Expertise, authenticity and an enjoyable experience in the store contribute further to this process. But we are also seeing an opposite trend: on ebay, consumers themselves act like retailers and discussions about environment protection are reviving the tendency towards self-supply.

Displays provide scope for ideas

In the world of diversity we live in, displays have a firmly established place because they are a platform for new products and packaging, invite customers to try out a new product or present entire product groups in one place.

"Product worlds"

Today, unattractive shelves and end-of-the-aisle displays crammed with goods are still the rule rather than the exception. But retailers have started to cooperate with manufacturers to work out concepts that improve assortments, present new products or develop new product groups.

Communication that is focused on interaction and individuality builds a truly engaging experience around logistically optimised product groups.

Perspektive der Warenwelt
View of the "product world"

Im Supermarkt der Zukunft herrscht in den Regalen reduzierte Vielfalt

Die Warenpräsentation der Zukunft spricht alle Sinne an. Eintönigkeit ist tödlich, der Kunde soll begeistert sein und den Einkauf als Glücksmoment erleben. Das Sortiment der Zukunft benötigt je Produktgruppe mindestens drei unterschiedliche Ausprägungen: Private Label-Produkte für das Preiseinstiegsortiment, ein mittleres Niveau mit gutem Preis-Leistungsverhältnis sowie ein Premiumprodukt. Zudem sollte es zu der A-Marke eine weitere Alternative geben, und auch Bio- und regionale Produkte dürfen im Sortiment nicht fehlen.

Einen elementaren Beitrag auf diesem Weg leistet die Markenkommunikation, denn wie sonst soll der Kunde den Unterschied zwischen „Gold Premium" und „Pur Natur" erkennen?
Neben einer Reduzierung der „Me-Too-Produkte" ist auch eine Optimierung des Sortimentes erforderlich, um beispielsweise Raum für neue Produkte in anderen Warengruppen zu schaffen. So schmeckt ein gekühlter Orangensaft, der auch im Kühlbereich

Selective diversity will rule in the supermarket of the future

The presentation of goods in the future will appeal to customers and all of their senses. Monotony is deadly, the store and its assortment must provide the customer with a thrilling and blissful shopping experience. Each of the product groups of tomorrow's assortment will have to include products at entry-level prices, mid-market products with a good price/performance ratio and premium products. There should be more than one luxury brand to choose from as well as organic and regional products.

Brand communication will be fundamental in guiding customers on their shopping journey, otherwise how will they know what the difference is between "Gold Premium" and "Pure Nature"?

Apart from reducing the number of "me too products", it will be necessary to optimise the assortment to make space for new products in other product groups. Chilled orange juice taken from the fridge

VI.1 DIE ROLLE DES DISPLAYS IM SUPERMARKT DER ZUKUNFT | THE DISPLAY IN THE SUPERMARKET OF THE FUTURE

angeboten wird, frischer und gesünder als ein ungekühltes Produkt aus dem Saftregal.

Nach einer entsprechenden Optimierung der Sortimentsbreite und -tiefe wird der Kunde mit Cross-Merchandising-Präsentationen zu Zusatzkäufen verführt. Und wo bleibt die Einheitlichkeit? Wichtig ist, dass sich der Handel mit seinem Format von der Masse differenziert und erkennbar spezialisiert. Dies ist die Magie, die den Unterschied zwischen einem guten und einem schlechten Format ausmacht. Das ist heute so und verspricht auch in der Zukunft Erfolg.

cabinet will taste better and healthier than the non-chilled one taken from the shelf in the juice aisle.

When the assortment has been improved in terms of choice and number of products, cross-merchandising presentations will tempt customers to make additional purchases. And what about consistency? The important thing is that the retailer stands out from the crowd with a distinguished and specialist concept. That is the magic that makes the difference between a good concept and a bad concept. This is true for success today and will be in the future.

Perspektive Café und Service-Zone
View of cafe bar and services area
* Oracle's services cover all of your domestic needs

© Jos de Vries The Retail Company

Langzeitdisplays

Für die Verpackungs- und Displayhersteller gibt es eine wichtige Aufgabe zu lösen: ein Präsentationssystem, das multifunktional als Regal- oder Promotioneinheit eingesetzt werden kann. Shelf-Ready-Packaging ist hier eine Möglichkeit, aber nicht die optimale Lösung, da der Präsentationswert der Primärverpackung angesichts der logistischen Dominanz an Kraft verliert. Gesucht wird ein Verpackungsdisplay oder eine Displayverpackung, die sowohl in der Freifläche als auch im Regal platziert werden kann.

Multi-Channel-Vertrieb

Da die Regalflächen im Handel begrenzt sind, wird der Wettbewerb um die verfügbare Regalfläche zunehmend härter. Mit der Ausweitung der Handelsmarken sind die Markenartikelhersteller gezwungen, neue Vertriebskanäle zu erschließen, um eine flächendeckende Distribution sicherzustellen. Auf die Multi-Channel-Kommunikation folgt nun der Multi-Channel-Vertrieb.

Der Markt der Zukunft ist ein Spezialist

Die Kommunikationstechnologie hat es vorgemacht: Der Weg führt von Broadcast über Narrowcast zum Podcast – von der Massenkommunikation zur individualisierten Botschaft. Der Konsument von heute hat einen bestimmten Lebensstandard und eine Weltanschauung, die mit der Identität des Handelskonzeptes übereinstimmen muss. Mit dem Konzept „einmal hin, alles drin" erreicht man heute keinen Kunden mehr. Manche Cash & Carry-Märkte machen es vor: Sie haben den direkten Kontakt zum Profikunden und sind – nicht zuletzt aufgrund der Direktzustellung – sehr dicht an den Kundenwünschen, die sie in ihre Sortimentsgestaltung einfließen lassen.

Die niederländische Warenhauskette HEMA bietet ein „One Brand"-Konzept und hat dafür das Motto „Ein schönes und einfaches Leben muss nicht teuer sein" gewählt. Unter diesem kommunikativen Dach werden dem Kunden unterschiedlichste Lösungen angeboten, die das Leben einfacher machen: Autoversicherungen ohne Kleingedrucktes, (grüne) Energie zum Jahresfestpreis, vorverpackte Wurst für einen Euro usw.

Ein solches Konzept lässt sich auch auf andere Branchen, das Internet oder Netzwerke übertragen. Um Kunden zu erreichen, müssen alle Kommunikationsmedien aufeinander abgestimmt werden, die Homepage darf keine andere Botschaft vermitteln als der Besuch des Ladens.

Das Display als Dienstleistung

Wie bereits beschrieben, bleibt die Verkaufsförderungsfunktion auch in Zukunft die wichtigste Aufgabe des Displays. Durch die

Permanent displays

Packaging and display manufacturers are facing an important task: to create a multi-functional presentation system that can be used for both shelves and promotions. Shelf ready packaging is one solution to the problem, but not an ideal one, because the effect the primary pack's presentation has pales against the dominant role that logistics play. What is needed is a packaging display or display packaging that can be placed both on the shelf and in the middle of the store.

Multi-channel distribution

As shelf space at retail is limited, competition for available shelf space will become increasingly fierce. In view of expanding retail brands, manufacturers of branded goods are forced to open new sales channels to ensure distribution across the whole of the market. Multi-channel communication thus leads to multi-channel distribution.

The supermarket of the future will be a specialist

Communication technologies have shown us that the trend moves from broadcast to narrowcast to podcast - from mass communication to the individualised message. Today, every consumer has an own standard of living and view of the world that has to fit the identity of the retail concept. An "einmal hin alles drin" (Go once. Get all.) concept no longer appeals to customers. Some Cash & Carry stores are setting a good example: they are in direct contact with professional customers and their requirements, not least thanks to their direct supply policy. The product range is developed according to customers' requirements.

Dutch department store chain HEMA has a one-brand concept it promotes under the slogan "A happy and easy life does not have to be expensive". As part of this communication theme, HEMA shows its customers all kinds of ways to make life easier, by offering car insurances without the small print, green energy at a fixed annual fee, pre-packaged sausage for one euro etc.

A concept like HEMA's can also be applied to other industries, the Internet or entire networks. To reach the customer, communication needs to be consistent across all forms of media. The message on the company's homepage and its stores must be the same.

The Display as a service provider

Sales promotion, as indicated before, will continue to be the display's key function in the future. Equipped with audio, video and transmission techniques (UMTS, Bluetooth, NF RFID etc.), displays will go beyond simply presenting products to providing individual information and services to the customer.

Integration neuer Audio-, Video- und Sendetechniken (UMTS, Bluetooth, NF RFID usw.) haben Displays die Möglichkeit, den Kunden individuelle Informationen und Dienstleistungen zu liefern, anstatt nur Produkte zu präsentieren. Durch die Verknüpfung von Online- und Offline-Inhalten lassen sich zusätzliche Vertriebskanäle erschließen, der Kunde erfährt eine ganzheitliche Markenpräsentation. Das Beispiel „Waschmittel" macht dies besonders deutlich, denn die Tatsache, dass ein Waschmittel gut wäscht, ist gemeinhin bekannt. Markenartikel differenzieren sich durch Zusatzleistungen: neue Darreichungsformen, Additive oder Geruchssorten. Displays, die das Produkt erlebbar – weil riech- und fühlbar – machen, runden die Produktpräsentation am POS ab.

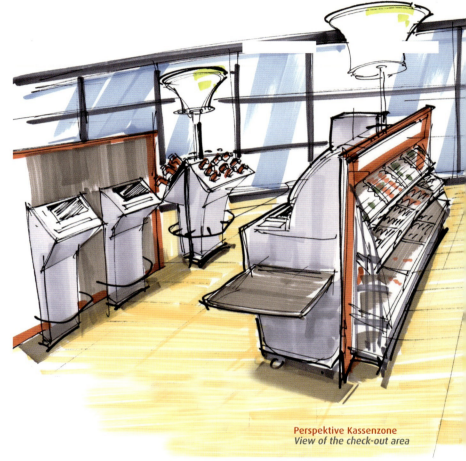

Perspektive Kassenzone
View of the check-out area

Der „letzte Gruß" hinterlässt bleibenden Eindruck

Es ist ein Fehler zu denken, dass die Kasse keinen Umsatz geniert. Die Impulszone im Kassenbereich ist eine wahre Goldgrube, für die sich Kassiererinnen leider nicht verantwortlich fühlen. Unaufgeräumte Kassenzonen und eine wenig einladende Warenpräsentation hinterlassen jedoch einen nachhaltigen Eindruck beim Kunden, da sie den letzten Kontaktpunkt im Markt bilden.

Im Supermarkt der Zukunft macht Bezahlen Spaß

Die „Checkout-Zone" erfährt im Handel derzeit die massivsten Veränderungen. Selfscanning, bargeldloses Bezahlen mit EC-Karte oder aber Handybezahlsysteme verwandeln den passiven Warteprozess an der Kasse in einen aktiven Prozess, der vom Kunden gesteuert und gestaltet wird.

Die zunehmende EU-Regulierung des Angebots von Tabakwaren, Süßigkeiten und Spirituosen führt zudem dazu, dass neue

Linking online and offline content opens new distribution channels and leads to an integrated product presentation. "Washing powder" is a particularly good example for this, because everyone knows that washing powder gets your laundry clean. It's the additional merits like new pack sizes, additives or fragrances that distinguish branded goods from other goods. Displays that allow the customer to experience the product by feeling or smelling it makes product presentation at the POS complete.

The "last impression" makes a lasting impression

It is a mistake to believe that sales cannot be generated at the check-out. Stores could strike gold in the check-out area, where customers can be tempted to make spontaneous purchases, but unfortunately cashiers do not seem to feel responsible for taking care of this area.

© Jos de Vries The Retail Company

Customers will not forget untidy and unattractive check-out areas because they are their last point of contact with the store.

Paying will be fun in the supermarket of the future

Check-out areas are currently undergoing dramatic change. Self-scanning, cashless payment systems or mobile phone payment systems are becoming commonplace. Rather than passively waiting in the queue customers are actively involved in the paying process.

Due to increasing European Union regulation of tobacco, confectionery and alcohol, more and more new products are ending up in the check-out area. Flowers, magazines and special offers sell well in the check-out area as well as services like insurances and event tickets.

Display 2.0 – Motivation for retailers

In the supermarket of the future the display of the future will continue to have the important task that was outlined at the beginning of this article, the task of driving sales! Provided that retailers and manufacturers coordinate communication, the display will also have a firm and at the same time flexible place in the store design of the future.

Produkte die Kassenzone erobern. Impulsbringer auf dem letzten Meter sind Blumen, Zeitschriften und Aktionswaren sowie Dienstleistungen aus dem Bank- und Veranstaltungssektor.

Display 2.0 – Impulse für den Handel

Das Display der Zukunft hat auch im Supermarkt der Zukunft eine wichtige Aufgabe, die bereits zu Beginn des Beitrages beschrieben wurde: Mehr Umsatz generieren! In einer abgestimmten Kommunikation von Händler und Hersteller hat damit auch im Ladendesign der Zukunft das Display seinen festen (flexiblen) Platz.

Günter Bauer

Raphael Stix

The Future of Retail

Zwischen heute und dem Jahr 2015 liegt eine Zeit des Umbruchs im Handel: Das Umfeld wird sich nachhaltig ändern.

Alles wird kleiner und einfacher

Vielleicht sind große Vertriebstypen davon ausgenommen. Für alle anderen wird es ein „Jahrzehnt des Downsizing". Produkte, Verpackungen, Handelsketten, die durchschnittliche Größe von Geschäften: Alles wird kleiner. Der Trend zur Nachhaltigkeit wird alle Dinge bezüglich ihrer ökologischen und sozialen „Erwünschtheits-Bilanz" normieren. Aber auch bei den Menschen und ihrem Verhalten hält dieser Trend Einzug: Die Shopper wollen klare und einfache Lösungen.

Sie schauen auf kleinere (feinere), stärker auf sie eingehende Angebote und Geschäfte. Unendliche Auswahl - besonders durch das Internet und die zunehmende Möglichkeit der Konsumenten, die Angebote einerseits zu vergleichen und andererseits die Leistungen selbst zu definieren - wird so manches etablierte (Handels-)Angebot verschwinden lassen. Es wird zunehmend kleine „Nischen" geben. Am POS wird man zwei Richtungen erleben: Weitere Effizienzsteigerung durch standardisierte (Display-)Lösungen und genau das Gegenteil: kleine, individualisierbare Platzierungen.

Retail is Detail

Der nächste bedeutende Schritt für große Handelsorganisationen ist die Segmentierung und das Eingehen auf „lokale" Bedürfnisse. Retailer werden zunehmend unterschiedliche Formate haben und mit differenzierenden Konzepten versuchen, spezifische Kunden in genau definierten Märkten für einen ganz besonderen Bedarf und unterschiedliche Verwendungsanlässe zu erreichen. Händler werden ihre globale Stärke mit den Anforderungen lokaler Märkte und spezifischer Kenntnis über deren Shopper kombinieren müssen. „Retail is Detail" bedeutet auch, jedem einzelnen Outlet die notwendige Beachtung zu schenken. Vertriebstypengerechte Displays unserer Zeit sind lediglich der Anfang. Es geht darum, Lösungen für die unter-

Raphael Stix

The future of retail

Retail will have changed radically when we reach 2015: the environment will be completely different.

Everything will be smaller and simpler

Possibly, that will not be true for large distribution formats. All other formats, however, are facing a "decade of downsizing". Products, packaging, store chains, the average store size, all that will grow smaller. The trend towards sustainability will lead to a norm that ranks things according to their ecological and social "desirability". People and their behaviour are part of this trend: shoppers want things to be clear and simple.

Shoppers will look out for product ranges and stores that are smaller (and more refined) and answer more to their needs. In a world of unlimited choice, most evident in the Internet, which allows customers to compare offers while at the same time defining services themselves, many established (retail) products will disappear. There will be more and more small "niches". We will see two trends at the POS: standardised (display) solutions will increase efficiency and, quite the opposite, there will be more small, individualised displays.

Retail is detail

The next important step large retail companies will have to take is to offer differentiated product ranges that are tailored to "local" needs. Retail formats and concepts will differ increasingly and with these specialised concepts retailers will try to reach customers in clearly defined stores by offering a specialised product range for different uses. Retailers will have to combine their global strengths with the special requirements of stores in different regions and specific knowledge of the shoppers of these stores. "Retail is detail" also means giving each store the necessary attention. Displays that are tailored to the needs of different types of distribution today are only the beginning. What counts is to develop solutions for the different shopper missions at each store. Product diversity and the use of displays and secondary placement will be the consequence.

schiedlichen Shoppermissions eines jeden Outlets zu entwickeln. Varianz in Sortiment und Bestückung von Platzierungen und Zweitplatzierungen werden die Folge sein.

Die 80:20 Regel gilt nicht mehr

Die Zukunft des Handels liegt darin, weniger vom „Üblichen" zu verkaufen. Während heute 20% der Artikel für 80% der Verkäufe stehen, werden in 2015 die verbleibenden 80% der Artikel für einen zunehmenden Anteil des Verkaufs und vor allem des Gewinnes stehen. Grund: Da man heute alles fast überall bekommt, werden die Konsumenten weniger das kaufen, was alle haben, sondern das was, zu ihnen passt oder was sie differenziert. Trotz „Clean Store Policy" werden aktivierende und die Markenbotschaft transportierende Displays wieder gefragt sein. Entscheidend für den Erfolg ist es, diese Veränderung logistisch und organisatorisch zu bewerkstelligen.

Die „Entkettung" des Handels

Größe wird zunehmend kein Erfolgsfaktor mehr sein. Die Tage einer Ladenkette mit Hunderten von Outlets, die das gleiche Sortiment undabhängig von ihrem Standort überall verkaufen, ist vorbei.

Händler werden innovativer und daher aus neuen Konzepten zunehmend mehr Geschäft machen als aus etablierten. Für die Kreativen und die Hersteller von POP-Materialien ist dies einerseits eine große Chance, andererseits eine fast unlösbare Aufgabe: Wie „tailormade" kann man ein Vermarktungskonzept tatsächlich ausarbeiten und produzieren, um dem besonderen Anspruch auf Alleinstellung des Handels gerecht zu werden?

Zunehmende Handelskonzentration auf globaler Ebene

Bis 2015 gibt es eine weitere Konsolidierung im Handel auf internationaler Ebene. Diese (verbliebenen) Unternehmen werden versuchen, mit hoher Flexibilität und unterschiedlichen, Shopper Insightbasierten Vertriebstypen erfolgreich zu sein.

Hier ist Internationalität auch auf der „Zulieferer-Seite" gefragt. Welche Erfahrungen können international gebündelt werden? Welche Best Practise Cases gibt es? Wie sieht logistisch eine entsprechende Struktur aus?

Es werden wenige große Zulieferer in der POS-Industrie übrig bleiben, die über internationale Strukturen verfügen und das innovative und produktionstechnische Format haben, um für globale Hersteller und Händler zu arbeiten

The 80/20 rule no longer applies

In future retailers will focus on selling less of the usual. While 20% of all goods generate 80% of total sales today, the remaining 20% will account for an increasing percentage of sales, and even more so of profits, in 2015. The reason for that is simple: customers will tire of being able to buy everything everywhere. They will stop buying what everyone else has to buy more products they think suit them and distinguish them from other people. In spite of the "clean store policy", displays that stimulate customers and convey the brand message will be back in the spotlight. The critical factor for success will be to manage the logistical and organisational side of this change.

"Unchaining" retail

Size will be less and less important for success in the future. The days are over for chains with hundreds of stores that sell the same products in every single store everywhere. Retailers are increasingly innovative and will thus make more money with new concepts than with established ones in the future. On the one hand that creates a big opportunity for designers and manufacturers of POP materials. On the other hand it appears to pose an almost unsolvable problem: how "tailor made" can a marketing concept be and what must it look like to meet that special requirement of retailers of holding an unique position in the market?

Increasing retail consolidation on a global scale

By 2015, retail will have undergone further consolidation everywhere in the world. The (remaining) companies will try to score with great flexibility and strongly differing distribution concepts that are based on shopper insights. This calls for international cooperation on the "supply side". Which international activities can be combined? What kind of Best Practice Cases are there? What will the logistical structure have to look like?

In the future, the POS industry will be commanded by a small number of big suppliers with the necessary international networks and the innovative and technical format required to work for global manufacturers and retailers.

"Share of life" retailing

Retailers will focus on the services they can offer customers rather than on the products they sell. Again the task is to look at what the reason for consumption is and what the consumer's needs are. The shopping journey in the store must emotionally engage the shopper with extraordinary products, easy choice and new combinations of products and services. In this connection, retail will not be limited to the POS. It will include the pre-sales phase as well as after sales. Retailers are already the biggest media spenders and issuers of loyalty cards.

„Share of Life" Retailing

Der Handel wird sich mehr darum bemühen, mit welchem Dienstleistungsangebot er seine Kunde bedient, als darum welche Produkte er verkauft. Auch hier gilt es, auf Konsumanlässe und Konsumentenbedürfnisse abzuheben. Es geht darum, den Shop zu einem Erlebnis werden zu lassen, mit außergewöhnlichen Angeboten, einfacher Auswahl und neuen Kombinationen von Produkten und Dienstleistungen. Hierbei wird der Handel nicht nur der POS sein. Er wird auch die Vorkaufphase und den Bereich des After Sales für sich beanspruchen. Bereits heute sind Retailer die größten Mediaspender oder beispielsweise „Loyalty Card"-Herausgeber.

Handel findet nicht nur im Laden statt

Wir werden Handel nicht nur in Geschäften, Katalogen und online finden. Wir werden ihn größer und weiter wahrnehmen. Pop up Stores, Shop in Shops, Virtual Stores auf dem Smartphone, Partnerschaften mit anderen Dienstleistern (Reisen, Hotels, Tankstellen, Telekommunikationsanbieter, Paketdienste ...). Überall wird es darum gehen, sofortigen Service und Verkauf zu ermöglichen, die Händlermarke erlebbar zu machen und im „Relevant Set" des Shoppers zu etablieren. Man kann sagen: Der POP wird virtuell. Das Produkt und seine Inszenierung bleiben. Der „First Moment of Truth" ist plötzlich an der Haustüre, wenn der Kurier die bestellte Ware bringt. Hier wird die Umverpackung den ersten Markeneindruck vermitteln und dem Shopper das notwendige Maß an Rückversicherung geben müssen, dass dieser Kauf richtig war. Ein gutes Beispiel hierfür sind die Produkte von Apple.

Retail is not only the store

Retail is not limited to stores, catalogues and the Internet. Retail will expand to cover other formats like temporary stores, shop in shops, virtual smart phone stores and cooperation with service providers from the travel, hotel, service stations, telecommunications and parcel services businesses. In all cases, the important thing will be to offer immediate service and possibility to buy,

Der handschriftliche Hinweis schafft eine emotionale Verbindung.
The handwritten message creates an emotional connection with the customer.

involve customers with the retail brand and establish it as part of the shopper's "relevant set". It is safe to say that the POS will be virtual in the future. The product and its effective presentation at retail remain important. "The first moment of truth" suddenly occurs at the front door when the courier delivers the ordered goods. The packaging will be the first impression the brand makes on the customer and determines whether or not the customer

Beinahe jeder, der das iPhone gekauft hat, hat die dazugehörige Schachtel aufgehoben. Einfach, weil sie so mit dem Produkt „verbunden" ist, dass man es nicht „übers Herz bringt", sie in den Müll zu werfen. Emotionales Involvement pur!

Der Kunde als Mitgestalter

Die unüberwindbare Trennung zwischen Hersteller und Shopper/Consumer wird sich aufweichen. Der Point of Sale wird zunehmend zum „Point of Remixing", „Point of Customizing" oder „Point of Creation". Der POS wird ein wertvoller Platz, an dem „Forschung und Entwicklung" die notwendigen Informationen über Produkte und deren Verwendung bekommen oder an dem man seine eigene Kollektion zusammenstellen kann. Diesen Trend aus dem Internet wird es auch im „physischen" Handel geben. Der POS der Zukunft wird auch diesen Trend bedienen. Die M&M-Platzierung zeigt schon heute, wie es sein könnte.

Zunehmende Ausbreitung von Handelsmarken

Zur Differenzierung und eigenen Positionierung wird der Handel zunehmend Private Labels schaffen und aktiv vermarkten.

Power to the People

Shopper haben unbegrenzten Zugang zu allen Informationen über Produkte und Preise. Soziale Netzwerke werden mehr und mehr den Einkauf und die Haltung der Menschen zu Geschäften und Marken beeinflussen. Ganz davon abgesehen, dass moderne Technologie „Sammelbestellungen"

Entsprechend der Kundenpräferenzen können diese ihre eigene Mischung gestalten.
Customers can pick their own mix according to their preferences.

Der Handel nutzt alle Kommunikationskanäle.
Retailers use all communication channels.

feels good about the purchase. Apple products are a good example for this. Almost every shopper who bought the iPhone kept the box it comes in. Because customers believe the box "belongs" to the product and just "don't have the heart" to throw it away. That is true emotional involvement!

The customer as a co-architect

The deep divide between manufacturer and shopper or consumer will gradually disappear. The point of sale will convert to being a "point of remixing", "point of customizing" or "point of creation". The POS will be an important place for "research and development" to gather relevant information about a product and its use or a place for creating own collections. This trend that is already found online will feed through to "physical" retail. The POS of the future will serve this trend as well. The M&M display shows us today what the future may look like.

The growing presence of retail brands

To distinguish themselves from other brands and strengthen their position as retail brands, retailers will create and actively sell more private labels.

Power to the people

Shoppers will have unlimited access to any kind of product and price information. The influence of social networks on what people buy and what their attitude is towards stores and brands will increase. Apart from that, modern technology will make "collective ordering" possible,

Die Markenkommunikation für Coors verbindet erfolgreich die On- und Offline-Kanäle bis an den POS.
Coors brand communication successfully links online with offline channels, also at the POS.

ermöglicht und somit eine neue (alte) Art der Preisbildung entsteht. Trotzdem oder gerade deshalb wird der Point of Sale seine Stellung als Medium ausbauen. Denn hier wird die Marke und das Produkt tatsächlich physisch erlebbar. Gerade deshalb investieren viele Marken wieder mehr am POS.

Neue Technologien

Spätestens in 2011 wird die Haushaltspenetration von Smartphones die klassischer Mobiltelefone übertroffen haben. Dann beginnt mit WLAN, Store- und „Product-Findern", RFID, individuellen Shopper-Profilen, „Apps" für die besten Angebote in einem Geschäft oder einem Einkaufszentrum usw. die wirkliche Digitalisierung im Handel.

Aus dem „stummen Verkäufer" wird ein interaktiver Markenbotschafter. Das Zeitalter von DIGITAIL (Digital und Retail) hat begonnen.

thus leading to new (old) price formations. Despite this, or perhaps because of it, the importance of the POS as a medium will grow. At the POS, the customer can actually engage physically with the brand. That is why many brands have started to increasingly invest in the POS again.

New technologies

In 2011 at the latest, household penetration of smart phones will be higher than household penetration of regular mobile phones. That is when retail will really enter the digital age with wlan, store finders and "product finders", RFID, individual shopper profiles, "apps" for the best offers in stores or shopping centres and so forth. The digital age will reach the POS too. Terminals for product choice or "mobile coupons" will become standard at retail. Shelves and displays will communicate with shoppers.

The "silent salesperson" will turn into an interactive brand messenger. The DIGITAIL (digital and retail) age has dawned.

Raphael Stix

Tom Giessler

360°-Marketing: Displays als Erfolgsfaktor von Marken und Handel

Tom Giessler

360 degree marketing: the display as a success factor for brands and retailers

Wenn es darum geht, ein Schiff durch unbekannte Gewässer zu steuern, dann ist es wichtig, den Überblick zu behalten. Nicht umsonst hielt der Steuermann auf hoher See den direkten Kontakt zu seinem Matrosen im Mastkorb, der aus lichter Höhe einen „Rundumblick" hatte. Heute unterstützt ihn das Radar, das ebenfalls eine 360°-Perspektive ermöglicht.

Doch trotz moderner Technik geben auch heute noch Leuchttürme den Seeleuten in schwierigen Situationen eine wichtige Orientierung. Mit ihrem in alle Richtungen sichtbaren Signal vermitteln sie Sicherheit und sind „der Fels in der Brandung".

Marken – egal ob Handels- oder Hersteller-, Preiseinstieg- oder Premium-Marken – haben „Leuchtturmfunktion", geben den Verbrauchern auf ihrer Einkaufsreise (Customer Journey) Orientierung und wirken komplexitätsreduzierend in einer sich schnell verändernden Welt. Daher ist es wichtig, dass die Markenbotschaften in alle Richtungen kommuniziert werden und auf allen Kanälen identisch sind.

Der „Customer Journey" beschreibt den Weg des Kunden durch die verschiedensten Kontaktpunkte bis zum Kaufabschluss. Die Betrachtung dieser gesamten Wegstrecke ist entscheidend, um die Marketing-Budgets effizient zu planen. Den Kaufprozess aus Kundensicht darzustellen sowie die Exposition des potenziellen Käufers zu den unterschiedlichen Werbemitteln (TV, Print, Online, POS etc.) festzuhalten, hilft, die Marketing-Maßnahmen optimal auszusteuern.

Durch die direkte Verknüpfung von Angebot und Nachfrage übernimmt der POS auf der „Landkarte der Shopper" eine besondere Rolle. Dies bestätigt auch Deloitte in seiner Studie „Delivering the Promise of Shopper Marketing"[1] und betont eine zunehmende Bedeutung des Shopper-Marketings für eine erfolgreiche 360°-Kommunikation.

Vor diesem Hintergrund wurde in den letzten Jahren von den Werbetreibenden eine deutliche Verschiebung der Werbebudgets von klassischen zu nicht-klassischen Medien vorgenom-

When navigating a ship in unknown waters, it is important to keep a weather eye open. Not for nothing would the steersman of a ship on the high sea keep a close eye on the lookout in the crow's nest, who had an "all-round" view of things at his airy height. Today, the steersman can turn to radar for support, which also provides a 360 degree perspective.

But regardless of modern technology, it is still the lighthouses that guide sailors in choppy waters and give them the orientation they need. The signals of these beacons can be seen from all directions, creating a feeling of safety, as they "weather any storm".

Whether retail brand, manufacturer brand, entry-level brand or luxury brand – brands act as "beacons of orientation" for consumers during their shopping journey (customer journey) and reduce confusion in a rapidly changing world. This calls for brand messages that are delivered in all directions and are consistent in all channels.

The "customer journey" covers the customer's path along all the different points of contact before the actual purchase. The entire itinerary must be taken into consideration to ensure the effective planning of marketing budgets. Marketing measures can be best planned by seeing the buying process from the customer's point of view and recording how the potential buyer reacts to different forms of advertising (TV, print, online, POS etc.).

By directly linking supply to demand, the POS plays a special role on the "shopper's map". The Deloitte study "Delivering the Promise of Shopper Marketing"[1] confirms this and stresses the increasing importance of shopper marketing for successful 360 degree communication. Against this backdrop, advertisers have clearly shifted from above-the-line to below-the-line advertising in the past years. Today's meanwhile omnipresent online media and sales promotion activity alike benefit from this trend. Both have two key advantages over above-the-line advertising: an individual customer approach and direct ordering or buying function.

men. Hiervon profitieren die mittlerweile überall verfügbaren Online-Medien ebenso wie Verkaufsförderungsaktionen. Beide Medien haben gegenüber der klassischen Kommunikation zwei entscheidende Vorteile: die individuelle Ansprache und die direkte Bestell- bzw. Kauffunktion.

Erfolg auf dem letzten Meter – Die Bedeutung des POS steigt

Um in der Sprache des „Customer Journey" zu bleiben, bildet die POS-Kommunikation die werbliche Begleitung des potenziellen Kunden auf der Zielgeraden. Die Verkaufsförderung erreicht den Kunden, wenn er am aufnahmefähigsten für Informationen ist, die das auf ein Minimum reduzierte Handelspersonal nicht liefern kann.

Andreas Häderlein vom Zukunftsinstitut in Kelkheim spricht in der 2009 erschienenen Studie „Sales Design" von der Kraft der vernetzten Kommunikation: „Werbung ist effektiver, wenn der Kunde kurz vor der Kaufentscheidung steht."
Die emotionalisierte Ansprache über audiovisuelle Werbung am Verkaufsort ergänzt das Visual-Merchandising-Repertoire um eine unterhaltende Note. Werbung auf Flatscreens, Videoboards und Ähnlichem kommt so wirksam am Ende der Vertriebskette zum Tragen und stimuliert den Absatz. Yunchuan „Frank" Liu, Marketing-Professor an der Universität von Illinois, schloss 2009 die erste große Untersuchung zur Auswirkung von ladeninterner Werbung ab und konstatiert: „Künftig werden wir mehr Werbung in Stores erleben. Die Folge wird sein, dass mehr und mehr Marken und Produkthersteller ihre Werbeausgaben von den klassischen, ohnehin schwächelnden Kanälen TV und Print in den Bereich Instore-Media umverteilen."

Wertsteigerung am POS: Differenzierung erhöhen – Kosten reduzieren

Auch wenn die von Liu angesprochene Budgetverschiebung spürbar ist, stellt sich – wie bei allen Kommunikationsmaßnahmen – die Frage nach der Effektivität.

Diese kann am POS durch Kampagnen erreicht werden, die auf der einen Seite eine Differenzierung am Markt ermöglichen, d.h. durch Individualisierung wesentlich stärker Shopper-Typengruppen ins Visier nehmen und damit den Absatz beschleu-

Success at the final stage – the importance of the POS is increasing

In terms of the "customer journey", communication at the POS is the advertising escort that accompanies the potential customer on the home straight. Sales promotion kicks in with customers when they are most receptive to information that cannot be provided by a sales staff, which has been reduced to a minimum.

In the "Sales Design" study published in 2009, Andreas Häderlein from the Zukunftsinstitut in Kelkheim refers to the power of networked communication: "Advertising is more effective when the customer is just about to make the buying decision. An emotional approach by means of audiovisual advertising at the POS adds an entertaining tone to the repertoire of visual merchandising. In this way, advertising on flat screens, video boards and similar devices is effective at the end of the supply chain and stimulates sales. Yunchuan "Frank" Liu, marketing professor at the University of Illinois, was the first to carry out an extensive study on the effectiveness of in-store marketing and found: "In the future, we will see more advertising available in stores, and as a consequence, more and more brands and manufacturers of goods will shift advertising from traditional, already weakening media like TV and print, to in-store media."

Greater value at the POS: increasing differentiation – reducing costs

Even though the shift in budgeting mentioned by Liu can be observed, the question arises – as with all means of communication – whether this activity is effective.

Erfolgsmodell POS-Marketing				Successful POS marketing			
Differenzierung erhöhen Increasing differentiation				**Supply Chain-Kosten reduzieren** Reducing Supply Chain-costs			
1. Harmonisierung von Display und Verpackungsdesign	2. Integration multimedialer Effekte	3. Maßgeschneiderte Lösungen für unterschiedliche Shopper-Typen	4. Story Telling: Integrierte Kommunikation bis an den POS – und vice versa	5. Plattformentwicklung	6. Betrachtung der gesamten Supply Chain (TCO)	7. POS-Entwicklungskompetenz	8. Konfektionierung und Platzierung
1. Harmonisation of display and packaging	2. Integration of multimedia effects	3. Customised solutions for different shopper types	4. Story telling: integrated communication right up to the POS and vice versa	5. Development of platforms	6. Consideration of the entire supply chain (TCO)	7. Competence in POS development	8. Fulfilment

Quelle: STI-Group

Wertsteigerung durch erfolgreiches POS-Marketing
Increasing value through successful POS marketing

nigen und den Umsatz erhöhen. Auf der anderen Seite treten die Kosten der gesamten Supply Chain in den Fokus – von der Produktentwicklung über die Konfektionierung bis hin zur Platzierung im Handel.

Wo die Augen keinen Halt finden, gehen auch die Füße vorbei!

Die Verkaufsförderung macht sich die Wirkungsweise der AIDA-Formel (Attention, Interest, Desire, Action) zunutze, um den Abverkauf eines Produktes zu beschleunigen und Preisqualitäten zu steigern: die Aufmerksamkeit des Konsumenten auf sich ziehen, sein Interesse wecken, ein Bedürfnis bzw. einen Wunsch nach dem Produkt und letztendlich die Kaufhandlung auslösen. „Den Augen Halt zu geben", ist dabei die primäre Aufgabe einer POS-Kampagne.

Erst wenn die Neugier eines Konsumenten geweckt wurde, setzt sich dieser aktiv mit der Botschaft und damit auch mit dem Händlersortiment auseinander. Und das „Innehalten" ist Voraussetzung dafür, dass ein Kaufakt erfolgt.

1. Harmonisierung von Verpackungs- und Displaydesign

Die Verpackung ist das Verkaufsförderungsmedium Nr. 1 – mit keiner anderen Werbeform kommt der Kunde derart häufig in Kontakt. Verpackung ist „Werbung zum Anfassen". Aus diesem Grund greifen erfolgreiche Displaylösungen das Verpackungsdesign auf und inszenieren dieses – wie die Beispiele von Axe und Magic Fruits zeigen.

2. Integration multimedialer Elemente

Gleichzeitig ermöglicht zukünftig die POS-Kommunikation eine stärkere Vernetzung von On- und Offline-Inhalten – sei es durch die Integration von Flatscreens wie bei Russian Standard, den Einsatz von Printed Illuminated Paper (PIP) oder aber den

Das Verpackungsdesign stand Pate für das Displaydesign.
The design of the packaging was the inspiration for the display design.

Die taillierte Form kommuniziert das Produktversprechen: Genuss, der nicht dick macht.
The tapered form promises customers "pleasure without gaining weight".

Effectiveness can be increased by POS campaigns that, on the one hand, lead to market differentiation, i.e. an individualised approach leads to a stronger focus on groups of shopper types, thus promoting the sale of a product and increasing sales. On the other hand, the spotlight is now on the costs of the entire supply chain, from product design and packaging to the product's placement in the store.

If you can't fetch the eye, the feet will walk by

Sales promotion takes advantage of the effectiveness of the AIDA formula (attention, interest, desire, action) to boost the sale of a product and charge higher prices: attract the attention of the consumer, raise customer interest, convince customers that they want and desire the product, and, in the end, encourage the customer to buy. "Catching the customer's eye" is the main task of the POS campaign.

Only if customers' interest is raised will they actively engage in the product's message and the retailer's offer. Only if customers' "pause and reflect" about the product they may also buy it.

1. Harmonising packaging and display design

Packaging is the number one sales promotion tool, it is the form of advertising customers come in direct contact with the most. Packaging

Digital Signage kann auch in Displays integriert werden und rundet die POS-Platzierung ab.
Digital signage can be integrated into displays and rounds off the POS presentation.

Einbau von RFID-Chips oder Bluetooth in Dekorationselemente. Gerade in saturierten Märkten, in denen tendenziell eine hohe Reiz(über-)flut festzustellen ist, ist die wirksame Differenzierung ein entscheidender Vorteil.

PIP ist ein elektronisches Leuchtplakat, bei dem verschiedene Segmente via Steuerungseinheit beleuchtet und animiert werden können. Die Besonderheit liegt in der Materialdicke von nur etwa 3 mm. Untersuchungen in den USA weisen eine 89 %ige Abverkaufserhöhung durch PIP-Displays im Gegensatz zu + 39 % bei statischen Displays nach. Zudem positionieren Marktleiter 88 % aller Beleuchtungs- und Bewegungsdisplays in Haupt-Promotionenzonen, wohingegen 53 % der statischen Displays auch in weniger attraktiven Marktregionen platziert werden.

3. Maßgeschneiderte Lösungen für unterschiedliche Shopper-Typen

Es gilt: „Think global – act local", denn Individualisierung ermöglicht

Printed Illuminated Paper, d.h. elektronisches Papier, ermöglicht zukünftig interaktive Botschaften auf allen Flächen und Plätzen.
Printed Illuminated Paper, i.e. electronic paper, will make interactive messages possible in all stores and places in the future.

is "hands-on advertising". That is why successful display solutions, as demonstrated for example by Axe and Magic Fruits, use, and effectively present packaging design.

2. Integrating multimedia elements

At the same time, POS communication will allow for a greater cross-linking of online and offline content in the future, whether through the integration of flat screens as demonstrated by Russian Standard, the use of Printed Illuminated Paper (PIP), or the integration of RFID chips or Blue-tooth into display decoration. Effective differentiation proves to be an important advantage especially in saturated markets, where a high sensory (over) load is evident.

PIP is a programmable, dynamic electronic poster that lights up and creates the illusion of motion. The peculiarity of PIP is that it is only 3mm thick. Research in the US shows that PIP displays have increased sales by 89 %, while the sales increase reached by using static displays was 39 %. Further-more, store managers placed 88 % of digital signage displays in the main promotion areas, while 53 % of static displays were also placed in less attractive areas of the store.

Die digitale Fertigung ermöglicht die Umsetzung individueller Motive.
Digital printing leads to customised POS concepts in small lot sizes.

Wöchentlich wechselnde Angebote lassen sich in die Displaywand integrieren.
Weekly changing ranges can be integrated into the display backwall.

Ein individuell bedruckter Crowner stellt die Verbindung von Marke und Handelsunternehmen her.
An individually printed crowner establishes a link between brand and retailer.

Differenzierung. Das Display der Zukunft ist daher nicht nur hinsichtlich seiner Größe, sondern auch in Punkto Design an die Erfordernisse der verschiedenen Handelskanäle angepasst. So ermöglicht der großformatige Digitaldruck in Verbindung mit einer effizienten Workflowlösung die Umsetzung maßgeschneiderter POS-Kampagnen bis auf Marktebene. Davon profitieren Industrie und Handel gleichermaßen, denn der Handel kann sein Sortiment bzw. seine Werbebotschaft auf sein spezifisches Zielkundensegment zuschneiden. Das Beispiel „100 Jahre EDEKA" zeigt, wie mit einfachen Mitteln die POS-Platzierung zur Kommunikation wöchentlich wechselnder Aktionen eingesetzt werden kann. Selbst bei Langzeitdisplays ist – wie der Carlsen-Verlag in Kooperation mit dem Buchfachhandel beweist – eine derartige Individualisierung möglich.

4. Story-Telling und integrierte Kommunikation

Ein gutes Display ist in der Lage, die Geschichte zu Ende zu erzählen, die in der klassischen „Above-the-line"-Kommunikation begonnen wurde. So unterstreicht bei der POS-Kampagne für Grany ein Display aus offener Welle die natürliche Herkunft des Produktes. Geprägte Ähren betonen den Anspruch von LU als „Céréal Expert". Die Displays können zudem für unterschiedliche Sorten des Herstellers genutzt werden, so dass gleichzeitig die Differenzierung erhöht und die Kosten optimiert werden konnten.

Wie zukünftig Shopper-Insights in das Displaydesign integriert werden können, wurde mit der „World of Whisky (WoW)" be-

3. Customised solutions for different shopper types

We need to act according to the catchphrase: "Think global, act local", because differentiation is made possible by individualisation. Not only in terms of size, but also in terms of design will the display of the future have to cater for the needs of each distribution channel. Large digital prints paired with effective work flow solutions produce customised POS campaigns on all levels including the store. Manufacturers and retailers alike benefit from this kind of campaign because retailers are able to offer specific ranges or advertising messages for each target customer group. The "100 years of EDEKA" campaign shows nicely how POS displays can be used to run weekly changing promotions with little effort. In this way, even permanent displays can be turned into individual displays as demonstrated by publisher Carlsen-Verlag in cooperation with book retailers.

4. Story telling and integrated communication

A good display knows how to finish the story that traditional "above-the-line" communication started to tell. The POS campaign of Grany, for instance, uses a corrugated cardboard display to stress the product's natural origins. Embossed corn ears underpin LU's claim to being a "cereal expert". The display can be further used for the manufacturer's other varieties, thus increasing differentiation and lowering costs.

Die offene Welle steht für Authentizität und betont die natürliche Herkunft des Produktes.
The corrugated cardboard display stands for authenticity and stresses the product's natural origins.

Langzeitdisplays und Shop-in-Shop-Systeme unterstreichen nachhaltig und langfristig den Anspruch der Marktführer.
Permanent displays and shop-in-shop systems create a sustainable and lasting idea of market leaders' claims.

Großformatige Platzierungen dienen als Eye-catcher, Warendruck erzeugt „Kaufdruck" und stimuliert den Abverkauf.
Large displays act as eye-catchers, large amounts of product increase the "pressure to buy" and stimulate sales.

wiesen, bei der zehn Whiskysorten aus vier Ländern in einer Art Shop-in-Shop-Platzierung präsentiert wurden.

Die fließend harmonische Form des weißen Holzdesigns spricht die Zielgruppe der urbanen Männer und Frauen ab 25 Jahren an und fügt sich harmonisch in jedes Ladendesign ein. Die passend zum Display gestaltet Theke dient einem Sommelier als Beratungsplattform, um Kunden zu informieren und zum Ausprobieren neuer Geschmacksvarianten zu animieren. Damit steht erneut der Shopper im Mittelpunkt der Aktion.

Das Beispiel Sidroga zeigt, dass integrierte Kommunikation nicht zwangsläufig das Abspielen eines TV-Spots am POS bedeutet, sondern dass umgekehrt ein Display den Weg in einen TV-Spot schafft. So wurde im Fernsehen nicht nur die Sidroga Produktrange beworben, sondern auch das Display präsentiert, aus dem die Kundin in der Apotheke das Produkt entnimmt – eine sehr gelungene Verknüpfung von „Above-the-line-" und „Below-the-line-"Kommunikation.

Und noch zwei weitere wichtige Punkte wurden bei dieser POS-Kampagne berücksichtigt: Die Bestückung des Displays ist modular und auf die Wünsche der einzelnen Apotheken zugeschnitten. Außerdem erfolgt der Aufbau der Langzeitdisplays durch ein Merchandising-Team, so dass sich die Apotheker auf ihre eigentliche Aufgabe – die Beratung der Patienten und den Verkauf von Produkten – konzentrieren können. Die POS-

By presenting ten varieties of Whisky from four countries in a kind of shop-in-shop, the "World of Whisky (WoW)" has shown how shopper insights can be integrated into display design in the future.

The symmetric and harmonious shape of the white wooden display targets urban men and women aged 25 and older and fits nicely into any kind of store design. A counter in the same design as the display serves as a demonstration stand for the sommelier, who offers customers information and advice and encourages them to try new varieties of Whisky. This ensures that the shopper is again at the centre of the promotion.

A Sidroga campaign shows that integrated communication is not necessarily limited to showing a TV spot at the POS, but can achieve quite the opposite effect of featuring the display in the TV spot. Sidroga showed not only the product range, but also the display in its TV commercial. The spot, which shows a woman taking a product from the display in the chemist store, is an example of the very successful interaction between "above-the-line" and "below-the-line" communication.

Two further aspects that are important have been taken into account while designing this display: the arrangement of products on display is modular and customised to the needs of each chemist store. Furthermore, the permanent displays were assembled by a dedicated merchandising team allowing the chemist to concentrate on his furthermost task of giving customers advice and selling the product. This

Die Integration des Displays in den TV-Spot zeigt, dass integrierte Kommunikation auch in die andere Richtung funktioniert.
The integration of displays into TV commercials shows that integrated communication can also work the other way round.

Kampagnen der Zukunft berücksichtigen daher auch das Thema „Platzierung" und planen einen Teil des POS-Budgets für den Aufbau der Displays und Dekorationen ein.

Nachhaltigkeit und Verantwortung gewinnen in der Kommunikation an Bedeutung – dies spiegelt sich zukünftig auch verstärkt in der POS-Kommunikation wider, um die Sympathiewerte für und von Marken zu steigern.

Die vivesco-Apothekenkampagne zeigt, was am POS möglich ist: Interaktion mit dem Kunden und die Umsetzung einer Spendenkampagne, deren Erfolg direkt sichtbar wird. Um kleine Patienten in Krankenhäusern aufzuheitern, sammelten vivesco-Apotheken Geld für professionelle „Clown-Visiten". Ein lebensgroßes Clown-Display machte in den Apotheken auf die Spendenaktion aufmerksam.

5. Plattformentwicklung

Marken und nicht Länder definieren die Märkte; daher arbeiten Handel und Hersteller zunehmend an länderübergreifenden Konzepten, um den Markenauftritt globaler Marken in allen Ländern bzw. Regionen identisch zu gestalten.

Die Automobilindustrie sowie viele technische Produktionszweige zeigen, wohin die Entwicklung der Zukunft geht: Plattformkonzepte ermöglichen in der Produktentwicklung eine Reduzierung von Entwicklungszeiten (time-to-market) und Entwicklungskosten.

Hinzu kommen massive Potenziale zur Kostensenkung entlang der gesamten hochrationalisierten Supply Chain: So erhöhen länderübergreifende Kampagnen die Auflagen für POS-Materialien

means that the POS campaigns of the future include the question of where and how to position displays in the store. They will also allocate a part of the POS budget for the assembly and decoration of displays.

Sustainability and responsibility are gaining importance in communication. This will be increasingly reflected in POS communication, to boost the popularity of brands.

The vivesco campaign in chemist stores shows the great opportunities offered by POS campaigns: the vivesco promotion allowed direct interaction with the customer and the launch of a fundraising campaign, which showed immediate results. In the campaign, vivesco chemist stores collected money, so that professional clowns could be sent to children's hospitals to cheer up their small patients. A life-size clown display helped draw the customer's attention to the fundraising campaign.

5. Developing platforms

Markets are defined by brands, not countries. That is why retailers and manufacturers are increasing their efforts to develop concepts that work in various countries to ensure that the presentation of global brands is consistent in all countries and regions.

The automotive industry as well as many technical production branches are showing us what the future will look like: platform concepts contribute to reducing time-to-market and development costs during in the design process.

In addition, there is a massive potential to reduce costs along the entire, thoroughly streamlined supply chain: campaigns that can be used

Soziale Verantwortung steigert auch am POS die Sympathiewerte für Marken.
Social responsibility increases the popularity of brands also at the POS.

und senken damit die Kosten, die durch eine zentrale Beschaffung und die daraus resultierende Reduzierung der Komplexitätskosten nochmals minimiert werden können.

Doch die Umsetzung pan-regionaler Kampagnen ist nicht einfach, denn sowohl bei den Verbraucherpräferenzen als auch bei den Handelsanforderungen gibt es alleine in Europa große Unterschiede.

Die Lösung besteht in modularen Displaykonzepten, die es ermöglichen, globale Konzepte mit lokalen Bedürfnissen zu kombinieren. Die unter Berücksichtigung aller Anforderungen entstandenen Baukastensysteme lassen sich beliebig zusammenstellen. Auf diese Weise können mit einem Displaytyp Eurohakenpräsentationen genauso umgesetzt werden wie Regalböden und elektronische Preisauszeichnungen ebenso wie die bekannten Regalschienen.

Dies war auch einer der Beweggründe für Vileda, ein modulares Baukastensystem für POS-Platzierungen entwickeln zu lassen. Mit wenigen Standardelementen sollten unterschiedliche Displaytypen und Bestückungsvarianten umgesetzt werden können, so dass auch für neue Produkte innerhalb kürzester Zeit eine Zweitplatzierung realisiert werden kann.

Bei der Optimierung der gesamten Displaystruktur stehen nicht nur die Reduzierung der Herstellkosten, sondern in erster Linie auch die Reduzierung der Supply Chain-Kosten im Fokus.

Zwingende Voraussetzung für ein pan-regionales Plattformkonzept ist neben einem profunden technischen Wissen auch das Verständnis lokaler Kunden- und Handelspräferenzen.

in more than one country increase the amount of POS materials and reduce costs. These costs can be further cut by centralising procurement and the resulting reduction in variable costs.

Launching pan-regional campaigns, however, is not easy, considering that, alone in Europe, customer preferences and retail requirements differ largely.

The solution lies in modular display concepts that make it possible to combine global concepts with local requirements. The modular display systems were created considering any kind of requirement and can be designed in any possible way. In this way, the same display type can be used to present products on euro hooks, on shelves, with electronic price labelling, or on the well-known shelf rails.

VI.3 DISPLAYS ALS ERFOLGSFAKTOR VON MARKEN UND HANDEL | THE DISPLAY AS A SUCCESS FACTOR FOR BRANDS AND RETAILERS

Eine Standardisierung der eingesetzten Displaymaterialien reduziert Prozesskosten und die time-to-market und führt gleichzeitig zu einer Steigerung der Brand Visibility im Handel.
The standardisation of display materials used at the POS reduces costs and time-to-market while at the same time increasing brand visibility at retail.

In der Fachhandelskommunikation von Vileda stehen die Displays im Fokus. Eine Anpassung der Standarddisplays für Sub-Marken ist einfach umsetzbar.
Vileda's advertising in speciality stores focuses on the display. Standardised displays can be easily customised to meet the needs of sub-brands too.

6. Betrachtung der gesamten Supply Chain

Wie im gesamten kaufmännischen Prozess dürfen bei der Entwicklung und Bewertung von Displays und POS-Aktionen nicht nur die reinen Herstellkosten und Zusatzverkäufe analysiert werden. Vielmehr gilt im Sinne einer ganzheitlichen Optimierung der Prozesskette eine prozesskostenorientierte Betrachtung. Diese umfasst die Beschaffung und Lagerhaltung ebenso wie die Konfektionierung der Displays oder deren Platzierung am POS – um nur einige Elemente herauszugreifen. So führt beispielsweise ein integriertes Supply Chain Management zu einer Reduzierung von Durchlauf- und Wiederbeschaffungszeiten sowie einer Reduzierung der Lagerkosten.

Gleichzeitig können durch den Einsatz intelligenter Online-Tools, wie beispielsweise einen Displaykonfigurator sowie eine dezentrale Produktionslogistik, auch CO_2-Emissionen reduziert werden.

7. POS-Entwicklungskompetenz

Die ökologische Nachhaltigkeit von POS-Lösungen sowie eine weitere konsequente Reduzierung von Displaykosten werden in ihrer Bedeutung weiter steigen. Die hohe maschinelle Verfügbarkeit von Herstellern bzw. Produktionsmitteln für POS-Materialien führt mittelfristig zu einem Wettbewerb der Anbieter im Hinblick auf Kosten, Qualität, Schnelligkeit („time-to-market") sowie Umweltfreundlichkeit.

In der Produktentwicklung wird der Grundstein für eine nachhaltige, logistisch optimierte und damit in allen Bereichen effiziente Kampagne gelegt.

8. Konfektionierung und Platzierung

Wenn es darum geht, Prozesskosten entlang der gesamten Supply Chain zu optimieren, spielen auch die Konfektionierung und Platzierung von Displays eine wichtige Rolle. In vielen Warengruppen übernehmen Displays eine primär logistische Funktion, wenn es um die Platzierung großer Warenmengen zu Saisonzeiten im Handel geht.

Das Beispiel „Orion" aus Tschechien zeigt, wie Design und Logistik aufeinander abgestimmt werden können.

That was one of the reasons that motivated Vileda to design a modular display system for its POS presentations. The idea was to design different display types using only a small number of standard components to make secondary placements of new products possible in a very short time.

While optimising the entire display structure, the focus is not only on the reduction of production costs, but also on the reduction of supply chain costs.

Mit diesem in Australien für den WWF produzierten Displayplakat werden Pflanzen mit Nährstoffen versorgt.
This display was designed in Australia for the WWF. It supplies plants with nutrients.

Thorough technical knowledge as well as insights into the preferences of local customers and retailers are absolutely essential for creating pan-regional platform concepts.

6. Considering the entire supply chain

The importance of analysing manufacturing costs and additional sales applies not only to all commercial processes, but also to the development and evaluation of displays. To ensure optimization at all stages of the process chain, all process relevant costs must be taken into consideration. This includes sourcing and storage as well as the packing of displays and the placement of displays at the POS – to name only a few aspects. Integrated supply chain management, for example, will reduce cycle and replacement times as well as storage costs.

At the same time, the use of intelligent online tools like display configurators as well as a decentralised logistics system can also reduce CO2 emissions.

7. Competence in developing the POS

Ecologically sustainable POS solutions and the consequent further reduction of display costs will continue to gain importance. The high availability of machines and means of production of POS materials will lead

Die Logistik spielt bei der Displayplatzierung der Zukunft eine zentrale Rolle.
Logistics will play a central role in the future of secondary placements.

Um ein leichtes Befüllen der Displays mit verschiedenen Produkten sowie eine ansprechende Präsentation der Waren zu ermöglichen, wurden die Maße der Regalfächer an die der gängigen Regale angepasst. Somit können die Produkte samt der Shelf-Ready-Trays im Display platziert und damit auch große Warenmengen effizient im Handel platziert werden.

Dies muss bei der Bestückung der Displays berücksichtigt werden, denn eine einfache Konfektionierung der Displays und eine Nutzung vorhandener Verpackungsmaterialien reduzieren den Aufwand für alle Beteiligten.

Fazit

Der POS hat – auch im Internetzeitalter – eine zentrale Bedeutung. Die Verbraucher genießen es, Produkte mit allen Sinnen wahrzunehmen, sie zu sehen, riechen oder zu fühlen und ziehen diese Form der Präsentation sterilen virtuellen Marktplätzen vor. Grundvoraussetzung dafür ist, dass der (Super-)Markt auch wirklich als Marktplatz gestaltet ist, der den Verbraucher zum Verweilen einlädt und den Einkauf zum Erlebnis werden lässt.

Retainment – die Mischung aus Retail und Entertainment – lautet die Erfolgsformel für die Zukunft.

Im Mittelpunkt stehen der Shopper und seine Suche nach auf ihn zugeschnittenen Lösungen.

Integrierte Kampagnen, die klassische Werbung und POS-Marketing vernetzen, haben die höchste Erfolgsquote. Erfolgreiche Displaykampagnen verstehen es, die Differenzierung einer Marke zu erhöhen und gleichzeitig die Supply Chain-Kosten bei hinreichender Flexibilität zu optimieren und dabei die lokalen Bedürfnisse von Shoppern und Händlern zu berücksichtigen.

Tom Giessler

to fierce competition among suppliers when it comes to costs, quality, time-to-market and environmental friendliness.

In product development, the foundations are being laid for a sustainable and logistically optimised campaign that is effective in all areas.

8. Fulfilment

When aiming at reducing costs along the entire supply chain, design and placement of displays play an important role. For many product groups, the display's main function is a logistical one when large amounts of goods go into stores in seasonal times.

"Orion" from the Czech Republic shows how to synchronise design and logistics. The company adapted the shelf size of the displays to the average retail shelf size to allow easy filling with different kinds of products while at the same time offering an attractive presentation of goods. In this way, products can be placed in the display together with the shelf ready trays, thus making it possible to present large amounts of goods in an effective way.

This should be born in mind when filling displays because a simple design and the use of existing packaging materials reduces costs and efforts for all involved.

Conclusion

Even in the Internet era, the POS is of crucial importance. Consumers enjoy experiencing a product with all senses, they prefer presentations, which allow them to see, smell and feel the product to sterile virtual marketplaces. Naturally, this only works if the supermarket is designed as a marketplace that invites consumers to linger in the store and turns their shopping journey into a shopping experience.

"Retainment", the combination of retail and entertainment, will be the formula of success in the future.

Shoppers and their search for solutions that are tailored to their needs must be the centre of attention.

Integrated campaigns that link above-the-line advertising to POS marketing have the highest success rate. Successful display campaigns can increase a brand's differentiation while at the same time reducing supply chain costs, safeguarding flexibility and taking into account the local needs of shoppers and retailers alike.

Im Gespräch:
Dierk Frauen

Die Familie Frauen betreibt sechs EDEKA-Märkte an der Westküste Schleswig Holsteins. Dierk Frauen führt zusammen mit seinem Vater Peter und seinem Bruder Jan das 1926 gegründete Familienunternehmen und war darüber hinaus bis Anfang 2010 Präsident des Bundesverbandes des Deutschen Lebensmittelhandels e.V. in Berlin.

Talking to
Dierk Frauen

The Frauen family runs six EDEKA stores on the west coast of the German state of Schleswig-Holstein. Together with his father Peter and his brother Jan, Dierk Frauen leads the family-run company founded in 1926. He was also president of the German food retail association Bundesverband des Deutschen Lebensmittelhandels e.V. in Berlin until early 2010.

1. Ein Sprichwort sagt „das Auge isst mit", gleichermaßen gilt für Sie als Händler „das Auge kauft mit". Welchen Stellenwert hat für Sie die Art der Warenpräsentation?
Nur gut präsentierte Ware kann auch verkauft werden, und die Art der Warenpräsentation prägt auch das Image eines Handelsunternehmens. Sowohl im Regal wie auch als Sonderpräsentation muss die Optik stimmen. Aber: Die beste Präsentation hilft nichts, wenn Qualität und Preis nicht stimmen oder die Menschen im Markt keine Kompetenz und Sympathie ausstrahlen.

2. Die Entwicklung von Displays ist eng mit der Entwicklung der Handelsgeschichte verknüpft (siehe Beitrag von Prof. Hallier, Kapitel II). Seit Beginn der Selbstbedienung gehören Displays zum Alltag im Handel. Wie nutzen Sie Displays in Ihren Märkten?
Displays gehören auch heute noch zum Erscheinungsbild eines modernen Supermarktes. Aber die Bedeutung der Displays ist sicher im Vergleich zu früheren Zeiten zurückgegangen. Heute wollen die Händler vor allem sich selbst als Marke präsentieren und nicht zu viele Akzente mit Sonderaufbauten verschiedener Marken setzen. Darüber hinaus hat der Händler stets die Gesamtwirkung des Marktes im Blick. Zu viele Aktionspunkte können störend sein. Dem Händler geht es ja in erster Linie um die Treue zur Einkaufsstätte und nicht um die Verkaufsförderung für einzelne Produkte.

1. Just like food that looks appetizing tastes better, products at retail presented in an attractive way can sell better. How important is presentation for you?
Only products that are presented in the right way will sell, and the way the product is presented to the customer can be bad or good for the company's image. The visual effect, whether on the shelf or in a dedicated display, must be just right. However, even the best presentation will not do the job if the quality and the price of the product is not right, or fails to give the customer the impression of competence as well as a feeling of pleasure.

2. The development of the display is closely linked to the historical development of retail (see Prof. Hallier's article in chapter II). Ever since self-service was introduced into stores, the display has been part of daily retail life. How do you use displays in your stores?

3. Welche Faktoren kennzeichnen für Sie eine gute Promotion? Wie messen Sie den Erfolg einer Kampagne?
Eine gute Promotion wird ganzheitlich organisiert, in der Haushaltswerbung und im Markt. Sie muss für den Kunden attraktiv sein, sie muss Frequenz erzeugen und zusätzlichen Umsatz generieren, und das möglichst dauerhaft. Und an diesen Faktoren muss sicher der Erfolg einer Aktion auch messen lassen.

4. Gibt es eine POS-Kampagne aus den letzten zwei Jahren, die Ihnen besonders positiv in Erinnerung geblieben ist?
Vor allem bei Wein haben wir gute Erfolge mit Displays, besonders dann, wenn die Ware und nicht das Display im Vordergrund steht. Viel Produkt und wenig Pappe, das ist wohl das richtige Rezept. Allerdings bevorzugen wir ganzheitliche Aktionen, die mehr bieten als nur Sonderaufbauten. Ein Straßenfest zur Wiedereröffnung unserer Hauptgeschäftsstrasse war so zum Beispiel ein riesiger Erfolg, aber auch größere Aktionen gemeinsam mit dem Kinderschutzbund oder der Krebsgesellschaft.

5. Wie sieht aus Ihrer Sicht die „ideale POS-Kampagne" aus? Welche Wünsche haben Sie an die Markenartikelhersteller und die Displayentwickler? Wie nutzen Sie Displays für Ihre Eigenmarken?
Sicher sind nicht nur die Optik, sondern auch der einfache Auf- und Abbau sowie der bequeme Transport wichtige Kriterien bei der Gestaltung von Displays. Der Handel möchte seine ganze Kraft den Kunden zur Verfügung stellen und nicht seine wertvolle Zeit in das Handling von Displays investieren. Auf so manchen Schnickschnack könnten wir gut verzichten, einfache Lösungen sind oft mehr wert als raffinierte Konstruktionen, die kein Mensch versteht. Und natürlich müssen Displays heute auch unter Umweltaspekten gestaltet werden. Ein Aspekt, der immer wichtiger wird. Eigenmarken nehmen wir ins Regal bzw. in die Truhe, vor allem die Neuheiten präsentieren wir an möglichst prominenter Stelle. Dabei besteht aber kein grundsätzlicher Unterschied zwischen Herstellermar-

Displays are still an integral part of the modern supermarket. But compared to the past, its importance has declined. Today, retailers mainly want to present themselves as brands in their own right and tend to avoid confusion by focusing on displays of more than one brand. In addition, the retailer always focuses on the overall impression of the store. Too many promotions can be disturbing. The retailer's main interest is retaining the customer as a loyal shopper at the store rather than selling individual products.

3. What, in your opinion, makes a promotion a good promotion? How do you establish whether a campaign was successful or not?
A good promotion has been organised taking into account all aspects of the presentation, in household advertising and in the store. It must be attractive for the customer and, if possible, permanently increase traffic and generate additional sales. The success of a promotion will be measured by these factors.

4. Do you remember a POS campaign of the past two years that was particularly effective?
Our experience with wine displays has been very good, in particular when the wine and not the display is at the centre of attention. A lot of product and little cardboard seems to be the right recipe for success. But we expect more from the campaign than just the simple dedicated display. A street festival for example that was organised to celebrate the reopening of our high street was a huge success, but larger campaigns organised together with the German Child Protection Agency or the German Cancer Society were also very successful.

5. What do you believe does the "ideal POS campaign" look like? What would you want from manufacturers of branded goods and display designers? How do you put displays at use for your own brands?
Surely, a display must not only be visually attractive. Aspects that are important for the design of a display are also that it can be assembled, removed and transported easily. Retailers want to dedicate all their strength to the customer and not waste valuable time in handling displays. We can surely do without some of the frills. Often simple solutions are a lot better than sophisticated constructions nobody understands. And naturally, the

ken und Eigenmarken. Wir bieten dem Kunden beides, und er kann dann unbeeinflusst entscheiden.

6. Ein Blick über die Grenzen Deutschlands: Sind deutsche Verbraucher und auch deutsche Märkte aus Ihrer Erfahrung anders, was die Art der Warenpräsentation angeht? Gibt es ein Shop-Konzept, das Sie besonders begeistert?

Ich glaube, die Händler in Deutschland sind wegen des starken Wettbewerbs im Markt schon ausgesprochen gut. Dennoch können wir immer etwas von anderen Kaufleuten lernen. Gerade im Hinblick auf die Präsentation der Ware lohnt immer ein Blick in die USA, zum Beispiel zu Whole Foods. Dort werden die Produkte toll in Szene gesetzt und ausgesprochen verkaufsaktiv präsentiert. Allerdings sind die Lohnkosten in den USA auch deutlich niedriger und dadurch ergeben sich andere Möglichkeiten. Sicher kann man aber auch Beispiele in Italien oder in Frankreich nennen. Gerade bei Frischwaren schaffen es die Händler dort, eine Marktplatzatmosphäre zu schaffen.

7. POS 2020: Wie werden Ihre Märkte im Jahr 2020 aussehen? Gibt es dort Displays und wenn ja – welche Optik und Funktionalität werden diese bieten?

Die Tendenz wird zunehmen, eigene, wieder verwendbare Möbel zur Präsentation heranzuziehen, die das Marktkonzept passgenau unterstützen und für eine stimmige Atmosphäre sorgen. Schon heute nutzen wir Pappsockel mit unserem eigenen Firmenlogo. Eventuell gibt es in zehn Jahren Displays der Industrie, die auf die individuellen Formate abgestimmte Layouts vorweisen. Das ist natürlich aufwendig, aber auch sehr gut. Der Nutzen dieser Präsentationsform wird vermutlich neben der Optik die Chance nutzen, Produktinformation bereitzustellen, insbesondere bei Innovationen und erklärungsbedürftigen Waren.

design of displays must today take into account environmental issues. That is an aspect of growing importance. We put our own brands on the shelf or in the cabinets. New products in particular are presented in places in the store where they are noticed most, in doing so, we basically make no difference whether it is our own brand or a manufacturer's brand. We offer both without influencing customers, who can decide on their own which product to buy.

6. Let's take a look beyond German borders: is it your experience that German consumers and also German stores differ when it comes to product presentation? Can you think of a particularly compelling shop concept?

I believe that retailers in Germany have been forced by fierce competition to be very good retailers. But we can always learn from other retailers. When it comes to the presentation of goods, it is always good to keep an eye on what is happening in the US, for example at stores like Whole Foods. Product presentation at Whole Foods is truly inviting and enticing and has an incremental effect on sales. On the other hand, labour costs in the US are substantially lower, so retailers there have more possibilities. I could surely also mention companies in Italy or France. Especially when it comes to fresh foods, retailers in those countries know how to give customers the impression that they are buying their groceries in a market place and not in a store.

7. The POS in 2020: what will your stores look like in 2020? Will there still be displays in the store and, if yes, what will they look like, and what will their functions be?

The trend is that more and more retailers will use own, reusable display furniture that is tailored exactly to the store's concept and creates an overall harmonious atmosphere. We are already using cardboard pedestals that feature our logo. Possibly, display makers will offer layouts in ten years time that are tailored to the specific needs of the different retail formats. Naturally, that requires more work and increases costs, but it is also very good. This type of display is likely to focus not only on making the product's presentation attractive, but also on providing information, especially for products that are new and require explanation.

Dierk Frauen

VII. DER POS DER ZUKUNFT | THE POS OF THE FUTURE

DER POS DER ZUKUNFT –
DIE ZUKUNFT DES POS-MARKETINGS
THE POS OF THE FUTURE –
THE FUTURE OF POS MARKETING

Michael Schellenberger

Zurück in die Zukunft: „Greif zu und kauf mich!" – Die Umwerbung des hybriden Verbrauchers

Haben Promotions eine Zukunft? Wie ist es um den Absatz rund um den POS bestellt? Gibt es Mittel und Wege, um so etwas wie Selbstähnlichkeit in der Markenführung bei POS-Kampagnen zu gewährleisten? Diese Fragen standen und stehen auch zukünftig im Mittelpunkt des Handelsgeschehens.

Gezielte Sales-Promotion statt Kampagnenflut

Allzu oft brechen Promotion-Aktivitäten am POS geradezu sintflutartig über die Kunden herein. Auch moderne Informationstechnologien haben daran noch nicht viel geändert. Die Sorge um den Absatz und der zunehmende Warendruck führen zu einer wahren Kampagnenflut.

Bereits Anfang der 70er Jahre setzte sich im Handel die Erkenntnis durch, dass die Platzierungskapazitäten in der Regel überzogen werden. Damals wie heute drängt sich daher die Frage auf: Wie kann, wie muss eine Promotion-Aktion aufgezogen sein, um überhaupt zum Einsatz zu gelangen? Welche qualitativen Ansprüche muss eine gute Sales-Promotion erfüllen? Werden die Wünsche und Bedürfnisse des Handels auch hinreichend berücksichtigt? Wie wird der Erfolg einer Verkaufsförderung gemessen und welche Schlüsse zieht man anschließend daraus?

Shopper Convenience statt Shopper Confusion

Jeder gibt sein Bestes, um letztlich den Verbraucher, das hochsensible Wesen, als Käufer zu gewinnen. Doch was erwartet dieser eigentlich? Wie kann man ihn für sich gewinnen? Am einfachsten lässt sich sagen, was er nicht will:

Flackernde Leuchtstoffröhren, zertretene Obstreste auf dem Fußboden, blinde Vitrinenscheiben, zerschlissene Kittel, zugestellte Gänge, Anhäufung von Pappkameraden, große Regallücken, gereizte, übermüdete und gestresste Mitarbeiter am Regal, der Theke oder der Kasse usw. usw. – diese Reihe ließe sich weiter fortsetzen.

Michael Schellenberger

Back to the future: "Move people to buy more!" – How to reach the hybrid consumer

Is there a future for promotions? How well are products selling at the POS? Are there ways and means to make sure that the brand management of POS campaigns is consistent? These questions have been crucial for retail in the past and will continue to be in the future.

Systematic sales promotion instead of a flood of campaigns

All too often, customers are bombarded with promotional activity at the POS. Even the use of modern information technologies has not changed that much. Worries about sales figures and the increasing amount of goods retailers are forced to put on the sales floor have lead to a flood of campaigns.

As early as the 1970s, retailers realised that there were basically too many planned promotions for too little space. Then, as now, the inevitable question is: what must a promotion look like to be viable and actually make its way into stores? What quality requirements must a sales promotion meet to be a good sales promotion? Are the needs and wishes of retailers given sufficient consideration? How is a promotion's success measured and what conclusions are drawn?

Shopper convenience instead of shopper confusion

Everyone is doing their best to turn the consumer, and consumers are without doubt extremely sensitive, into a buyer. But what do customers really want? How can we win them over? It is easier to say what customers do not want than what they want:

The customer does not want flickering neon lights, squashed fruit on the floor, steamed up windows, badly dressed sales staff, crowded aisles, masses of cardboard dummies, empty shelf space, irritated, tired and stressed sales staff at the shelf, counter or check-out etc. etc., the list could go on forever.

The conclusion is: people are forced to make detours, queue, ask and search for things and ask questions all day, so they do not want to be

Fazit: Wer tagsüber immer wieder zu Umwegen gezwungen wird, anstehen, bitten, suchen und fragen muss, möchte nicht auch noch beim Einkaufen mit Reizen überflutet werden. Dann reagiert der Kunde mit „Reduktionsstrategien", kann die Flut der ihm angebotenen Informationen nicht mehr verarbeiten. Weniger Shopper Confusion, mehr Shopper Convenience lautet daher das Gebot der Stunde, so Prof. Hendrik Schröder vom Lehrstuhl für Marketing & Handel der Universität Duisburg-Essen. Die bloße Anhäufung von Warenmengen sind also nicht dazu angetan, die Gunst des Verbrauchers zu wecken, wohl aber Aktionen, die dem Kunden die Gelegenheit geben, selbst aktiv zu werden. Das passiert beispielsweise in einem Gespräch bei einer Verkostung. Wie sehr dies vom Verbraucher akzeptiert und nicht selten auch honoriert wird, zeigt das Echo der Verbraucherrunden, die die Lebensmittel Zeitung in den letzten Jahren durchgeführt und ausführlich protokolliert hat.

Gestatten Sie mir einige kurze Zitate. Sie lesen nun O-Ton: „Neulich gab es eine Aktionswoche von einem Schweizer Getränkehersteller. Die Aktion hat mir gefallen, weil sich nämlich herausgestellt hat, dass mir dieses Getränk nicht schmeckt. Und ich hätte mich ja geärgert, wenn ich mir einen ganzen Kasten gekauft hätte."

„Probieren finde ich gut. Ich will doch wissen, was ich kaufe. Aber ich will mich auf keinen Fall von jemandem zu etwas überreden lassen, was ich nicht will."

Ich könnte Ihnen noch beliebig viele Beispiele nennen, die die sehr persönliche Meinung der Verbraucher widerspiegeln. Aber ich glaube, wir können es damit bewenden lassen. Sie wissen schon, was ich meine. Die Qualität und das Konzept der POS-Aktion sind ausschlaggebend – das galt bisher und wird auch zukünftig gelten.

Handel als Category Leader

Generell ist festzuhalten, dass der Handel, vor allem der Lebensmittelhandel, sich längst emanzipiert hat. Er ist zunehmend der Category Leader und hat den Daumen auf dem Regal und den

overloaded with information when shopping. Customers will then react with "reduction strategies", they are no longer able to handle and filter the information offered in the store. As Prof. Hendrik Schröder, Professor for marketing and retail at the Duisburg-Essen University puts it, less shopper confusion and more shopper convenience is the order of the day. Retailers will not win customers by putting large amounts of products in the store, but by offering promotions that allow customers to play an active part in shopping. That happens, for instance, when the customer enters into a conversation during a tasting event. Consumer round tables like those that have been organised and recorded by the Lebensmittel Zeitung over the past years show that customers accept and often highly appreciate tasting promotions.

Please allow me to repeat some statements made by customers. Here are a few direct quotes: "The other day, there was a promotion of a Swiss drinks maker. I liked the promotion because I found out that I do not like the drink. I would have kicked myself if I had bought a whole case."

"I like trying products. Naturally, I want to know what I am buying. But, I definitely do not want to be talked into buying something I do not want to buy."

I could go on citing many similar examples that clearly reflect customers' personal opinions. But I believe we can leave it at that. I am sure you know what I am trying to say. The quality and the concept of POS promotions matter. It has always been like that and will continue to be so in the future.

Retailers as category leaders

Generally speaking, we can say that retailers, especially food retailers, have been emancipated for years. Retailers are category leaders, they are in control of shelves and promotions. It is their way of trying to stick in the minds of their customers. Retailers want customers to think of them as brands in order to stand out from competitors.

Traditionally, brand policy and brand awareness are the domain of manufacturers, and manufacturers still have a considerable advan-

Promotions. Er versucht auf diese Weise, Platz in den Köpfen der Verbraucher zu belegen. Die Händler möchten selbst als Marke erlebt werden, um sich deutlich vom Wettbewerb abzuheben.

Markenpolitik und Markenprofilierung sind naturgemäß eine Domäne der Markenhersteller, die nach wie vor in diesem Wettstreit über beträchtliche Vorteile, wie Technologie, Kommunikationsqualität sowie Konsumentenverständnis, verfügen. Aber: Der Handel hat ebenfalls wirkungsvolle Instrumente zur Hand:

- Er verfügt über die knappe Regalfläche.
- Er entscheidet über Art und Umfang der jeweiligen Platzierung.
- Er kann über Ladenmedien zum Zeitpunkt des Einkaufs auf Verbraucher einwirken.
- Er kontrolliert eine Reihe von variablen Größen im Marketing-Mix, wie Preis, Verkaufsförderung, Bemusterung usw.
- Über moderne Informationstechnologie hat er zudem Zugang zu detaillierten Informationen über Einkaufsverhalten und Markenpräferenzen.

Der gesamte stationäre Handel muss sich darüber hinaus in den nächsten Jahren der elektronischen Herausforderung in Gestalt des Internets stellen. Es ist die Versuchung des neuen Jahrtausends – eine echte Revolution. Viele werden sich daran wagen, aber nicht für alle wird es das Paradies werden. Das Internet belebt die Fantasien der Anleger und vor allem die der Akteure. Alles, was jung und kreativ ist oder sein möchte, stürzt sich darauf.

Entlastung statt Reizüberflutung

Und gegenüber dem Kunden gilt: Entlastung statt Reizüberflutung! Kreativität im Handelsmarketing lautet das Gebot der Stunde, und das gilt auch für die intelligente Gestaltung und den Einsatz von Displays, denn das Ziel von Handel und Hersteller ist identisch: Beide wollen mehr verkaufen.

tage over competitors when it comes to technologies, the quality of communication and consumer insights. Still, retailers also have effective tools they can use:

- *The retailer controls the limited shelf space.*
- *The retailer decides on the kind and extent of a presentation in the store.*
- *The retailer can use store media to influence consumers during their shopping journey.*
- *The retailer controls various marketing mix variables like price, sales promotion, sampling etc.*
- *The retailer has detailed information about buying behaviour and brand preferences, provided by modern information technology.*

What is more, all retailers operating stores are facing the challenges the Internet will pose in the coming years. The Internet is the temptation of the new millennium, and a real revolution. Many will try to live up to the challenge, but it will not be the promised land for everyone. The Internet tickles the fancies of investors and even more of manufacturers and retailers using the Internet as a new distribution channel. Everybody, who is, or wants to be young and creative, jumps at the chances the Internet seems to offer.

Assistance instead of information overload

When dealing with the customer, it should be remembered that what counts is to assist and not overload customers with information! Retail marketing needs to be creative. That means that displays must also be cleverly designed and used, because retailers and manufacturers have the same objective: they both want to sell more.

Michael Schellenberger

Michael Gerling, Marlene Lohmann

The future of POS marketing

Once again, the economic crisis makes evident that when sales falter, price pressure rises and investments in marketing and brand are slashed as a knee-jerk reaction. That is how the automotive and finance industries in particular are currently driving the advertising industry into stagnation. Crisis-tested retailers are taking a different attitude by investing in advertising in spite of the economic downturn. More than ever, retailers need to defend their market share and strengthen their presence as a brand. They spend a lot of money on that. According to figures from EHI Retail Institute[1] retailers spend 8bn euros on advertising, making the retail trade the biggest advertiser in Germany. In marketing the POS is a crucial lever because it is still the most important point of contact with the customer. At the POS, the retailer is close to the customer, it is where the retailer can thrill the customer and make a lasting impression. And thrill is good for business.

1. Knowing why the customer buys

The customer, the unknown creature. Today, he shops at the discounter, tomorrow at the health food store and then he treats himself to a luxury item from an Italian designer. How does the customer think? What are the possibilities to turn a customer into a loyal long-term shopper? What are the factors that motivate the buying decision?

Customers hardly ever plan their shopping. That makes it even more important for retailers to find out how customers think. Successful retailers like ECR award-winning Douglas Group already make their decisions according to the premise: what is the benefit for the customer? This approach marks a paradigm shift. Knowledge of the product and all the processes that regard the product is already at a high standard. Knowing and understanding the customer is an increasing priority and is becoming the key factor for success.

A tried and at the same time current method to know how customers tick is the customer council. A panel of customers helps retailers with advice. By being actively involved in decisions of assortment and products, the council qualifies as a good ambassador for retailers and their decisions. The positive experience with this kind of market re-

Kaufentscheidungen fallen emotional.
Buying decisions are emotional.

Botschafter des Handels und seiner Entscheidungen. Die positiven Erfahrungen dieser Art der Marktforschung, die der EDEKA-Vorzeige-Händler Hieber mit dem Kundenbeirat seit Jahren macht, werden von vielen Händlern geteilt. Auch für den Discounter Penny ist der Kundenbeirat ein optimales Instrument, sein Geschäft noch kundenorientierter auszurichten.[2]

Weitergehende Einsichten in die Wahrnehmungs- und Entscheidungsprozesse des Kunden liefern heute in hohem Maße die Psychologie und das Neuromarketing: Der Handel hat die

search Edeka's model retailer Hieber has had with the customer council over several years is shared by many retailers. Discounter Penny also values the customer council as a perfect means to make business even more customer oriented.[2]

Today, psychology and neuromarketing give further insights into the customer's perceptual and decision-making processes. Retailers have discovered the methods of brain research and use the new knowledge to react to the customer's buying needs. This becomes clearly evident in the placing of products, the choice of display as well as in-store marketing.

Methoden der Hirnforschung für sich entdeckt und nutzt die gewonnenen Erkenntnisse, den Kunden beim Einkauf bedarf- und bedürfnisgerecht zu unterstützen, was sich u. a. in der Platzierung von Produkten, in der Art der Warenpräsentation und im Instore-Marketing deutlich zeigt.

Diese und weitere Methoden werden von erfolgreichen Händlern genutzt, um den Kunden mit seinen Anforderungen und Wünschen zu verstehen und daraus Strategien und Maßnahmen für mehr Erfolg am POS abzuleiten.

2. Kaufentscheidungen fallen emotional

„Heute besteht die größte Kunst darin, den Kunden zu verführen, ihn zu inspirieren, Wünsche zu wecken. Um das zu schaffen, muss der Kunde aber erstmal möglichst lange bei uns verweilen", so Georg Rothacher, ehemaliger Geschäftsführer der toom Baumarkt GmbH.[3]

Ein Kunde, der emotional stimuliert wird, verweilt einer empirischen Forschung der Universität Köln zufolge im Mittelwert doppelt so lange, nimmt mehr Informationen der Ladenwelt wahr, ist dabei vergnügter, erlebnisorientierter, fühlt sich optimal beansprucht, merkt nicht, wie die Zeit vergeht und gibt letztlich wesentlich mehr Geld für ungeplante Käufe aus.[4]

Der Trend zur „Emotionalisierung am POS" findet auf unterschiedlichen Ebenen statt: Neben der Ladeninszenierung, die zum unverwechselbaren Store-Brand beiträgt (Beispiel: IKEA) und in Erlebniswelten einlädt (Beispiel: Globetrotter), dem Personal, das mit Herz und Kompetenz berät (Beispiel: EDEKA) ist es das POS-Marketing, das den kleinen Unterschied macht. Dies zeigen Beispiele des Duft-Marketings, der digitalen Klang- und Bilderwelten und des Event-Shoppings.

Wo es (gut) riecht, hält man sich gern auf

Abercrombie & Fitch macht sich mit seinem Corporate-Duft unverwechselbar und auch in Deutschland setzen innovative Händler

Successful retailers use these and other methods to understand customers and their requirements and desires and to derive strategies and measures to amplify success at the POS.

2. Buying decisions are emotional

„Today, the art lies foremost in seducing the customer, inspiring him, generating desire. To succeed in that the customer has to stay in the store as long as possible," Georg Rothacher, the former managing director of Toom Baumarkt GmbH, says.[3]

According to empirical research from the University of Cologne, an emotionally stimulated customer in average remains in the store twice as long, takes in more information about the store, is happier and more experience-oriented doing so, feels totally engrossed, does not notice how time goes by and in the end spends considerably more money on unplanned purchases.[4]

„Emotionalising the POS" is a trend and takes place on different levels. Apart from the store design that makes a store brand unique (example: IKEA) and offers interactive experience (example: Globetrotter) and staff that gives friendly and competent advice (example: EDEKA) it is POS marketing that makes the difference. Examples of scent marketing, digital soundscapes and imagery and event shopping show that.

In a (nicely) scented place people like to linger

With its corporate scent, Abercrombie & Fitch has become truly distinctive. In Germany, retailers are relying increasingly on the emotional effect of scent marketing. The sense of smell has a subconscious influence on feelings, wellbeing and moods. Sensory perception finds its direct and unfiltered way from the nose to the brain and generates feelings within seconds. The scent Rewe retailer Nüsken uses includes pepper and lemon. It makes customers feel good and conclude "it is so nice here"[5]. This concept brings the desired success and therefore will be multiplied in further stores.

auf die emotionale Wirkung des Duft-Marketings. Der Geruchssinn beeinflusst unterbewusst Gefühle, Wohlbefinden und Stimmung. Die direkt von der Nase ungefiltert ins Hirn geleiteten Sinneswahrnehmungen erzeugen dort blitzschnell ein Gefühl. Der Duft, den Rewe-Händler Nüsken einsetzt, enthält zum Beispiel Komponenten wie Pfeffer und Zitrone und führt dazu, dass die von Marktforschern befragten Kunden sich wohlfühlen und sagen, dass es „hier so schön ist".[5] Ein Konzept, das zum gewünschten Erfolg führt und deshalb in weiteren Filialen zum Einsatz kommt.

Bewegtbild bewegt

Der POS bietet ein Umfeld, in dem der Konsument mit Werbebotschaften geradezu bombardiert wird. Mit neuen Varianten der digitalen Klang- und Bilderwelten sorgt der Handel dafür, dass sich Werbung und Information in diesem Umfeld durchsetzen können. Der Einsatz von Digital Signage, also bewegten Medieninhalten auf Flachbildschirmen, fängt bei der Kundenführung an („Was finde ich wo?"), präsentiert Werbespots der Händler bzw. von deren Lieferanten, kündigt Veranstaltungen an, informiert aktuell über Wetter und Börse und geht hin bis zur Vorstellung neuer Produkte. Die Zeit auf der Rolltreppe, im Fahrstuhl oder auf dem Weg zur gewünschten Abteilung wird mit Videos verkürzt – kombiniert mit effektiver Werbung.

Der Handel verbindet EHI-Marketing-Studien zufolge[6] mit dem Einsatz von elektronischen Medien am POS vor allem die Möglichkeit der Verlängerung der Kampagnenidee bis zum POS, die Erhöhung der Kundenbindung und eine stärkere Emotionalisierung der Kommunikation. Weiterhin nutzt der Handel Synergien mit anderen Werbeformen, wie TV aus – mit positiven Effekten auf den effizienten Einsatz von Budgets.

Event-Shopping

Interaktion mit dem Kunden und Community-Building sind zwei Kerntrends im Handelsmarketing. Im Online-Marketing bereits geschickt umgesetzt, finden Aktionen, die dem Kunden ein Wir-Gefühl vermitteln und eine Beziehung zum Handel aufbauen, gerade am POS eine perfekte Bühne. Outdoor-Aktionen à la Globetrotter, Modeschauen à la Peek&Cloppenburg, S. Oliver-Partys in angesagten Clubs oder Event-Cooking in Möbelhäusern sind nur einige Beispiele, die eigene Marke emotional aufzuladen, dem Handel ein unverwechselbares Gesicht zu geben und auf Qualität statt auf Geiz und Gier zu setzen.

Düfte stimulieren nicht nur Emotionen, sondern auch die ungeplanten Einkäufe.
Scents not only stimulate emotions, but unplanned purchases too.

Moving images move

The POS offers a surrounding that pelts consumers with advertising messages. New forms of digital soundscapes and imagery help retailers to successfully advertise and provide information in that surrounding. Digital Signage, moving media content on flat screens, starts with customer orientation (where is what?), presents advertising spots of retailers and their suppliers, highlights events, gives weather forecasts and share prices and presents new products. On escalators, in lifts, or on their way to the targeted department cus-tomers are entertained with videos that are combined with effective advertising.

EHI marketing studies show[6] that retailers use electronic media at the POS mainly to extend the idea of the campaign to the POS, increase customer loyalty and make communication more emotional. Retailers also create synergy with other advertising forms like TV, which has a positive effect on the efficient use of budgets.

Event shopping

Interaction with the customer and community building are two key trends in retail marketing. Already cleverly used in online marketing, campaigns that give customers a feeling of belonging and build a relationship with the retailer make for a perfect stage at the POS. The outdoor events typical of Globetrotter, the fashion shows Peek & Cloppenburg is known for, the parties S. Oliver throws in hip clubs or the cooking events staged by furniture stores are only a few examples of how to emotionally charge a brand, give retail a distinctive touch and focus on quality rather than penny-pinching and greed.

3. Der Handel investiert in Medien, die Kundenorientierung fördern

Wie wichtig es dem Handel ist, den Kunden mit seinen Anforderungen und Wünschen in den Mittelpunkt seines Tuns zu stellen, verdeutlicht einerseits der Anteil der Mediainvestitionen in die kundenorientierte Kommunikation und andererseits eine nachhaltige Umschichtung in eben diese Medien, wie die jährliche Erhebung des „EHI Marketingmonitor Handel"[7] zeigt.

Dem Handel stehen mannigfaltige Medien und Mittel bereit, um die Verbraucher zu mobilisieren. Dabei setzt er nach wie vor primär auf die bewährten klassischen Handelsmedien. Die Schwerpunkte verschieben sich jedoch:

EHI-Forschungsergebnissen zufolge[8] bleibt die klassische Printwerbung (Flyer, Kataloge, Magazine und Anzeigen) mit einem mittelfristig erwarteten Budgetanteil von 63% nach wie vor die tragende Säule der Handelswerbung. Aufgrund des zunehmenden Medienangebots und des veränderten Mediennutzungsverhaltens wird der Mediamix im Handel jedoch bunter, die Fragmentierung der Kommunikationskanäle nimmt zu. Der Mediamix verändert sich in kleinen Schritten weg von der Gießkannenwerbung, hin zu Medien, wie Direktmarketing, Online-Marketing und Instore-Marketing, die dem Aufbau und der Pflege des Retail-Brands dienen und eine gezielte Kundenansprache ermöglichen.

Direktmarketing

Um den Kunden emotional eng mit dem Unternehmen zu verbinden und zu begeistern, reicht es nicht, Leistungen anzubieten, die der Kunde erwartet, sondern solche Leistungen, die den Kunden überraschen. Diese Erkenntnisse der Kundenbegeisterung hat der Handel entdeckt und nutzt die Chancen durch nachhaltige Investitionen in den Dialog. Nach EHI-Hochrechnungen nahm der Handel in 2008 für Direktmarketingmaßnahmen 576 Millionen Euro in die Hand. Das entspricht einem Budgetanteil von gut 7% und einer Steigerung gegenüber dem Vorjahr von 1,7 Prozentpunkten.

3. Retailers invest in media that improve customer orientation

Media investments in customer-oriented communication and the shift towards a lasting focus on media show how important it is for retailers to put the spotlight on customers and their requirements and desires, according to the annual survey EHI Marketing Handel.[7]

Retailers have innumerable media and means they can use to mobilise consumers. They focus mainly on the tried and tested above-the-line retail media. But the focus is shifting:

Research from EHI shows[8] that above-the-line print advertising like flyers, catalogues, magazines and advertisements remain the very backbone of retail advertising with an expected budget share of 63% in the medium term. But the increased media offer and the changing media usage patterns make for a more varied media mix at retail and the fragmentation of communication channels is increasing. Gradually, the media mix is abandoning untargeted advertising in favour of media that help build and maintain retail brands and offer direct customer dialogue. Media like direct marketing, online marketing and in-store marketing.

Direct marketing

It is not sufficient to offer customers services they expect to thrill them and make them emotionally loyal to a company. The task is to surprise the customer. Retailers have discovered the ways of thrilling customers and are taking advantage of opportunities by making sustained investments in customer dialogue. Extrapolations from EHI indicate that retailers invested 576m euros in direct marketing in 2008. That amounts to 7% of the entire budget and represents an increase of 1,7%.

New media

With blogs and online forums retailers can win new target groups and perfectly respond to the customer's desire to exert influence and exchange information in communities with like-minded people.

Digital Signage: Bewegtbild bewegt
Digital Signage: Moving images move

Neue Medien

Mit Blogs und Foren können Händler neue Zielgruppen an ihre Märkte binden und die Wünsche der Kunden, nämlich Einfluss zu nehmen und sich in gleichgesinnten Communities auszutauschen, perfekt erfüllen.

Die Bildung von echten Communities wird zurzeit im deutschen Handel insbesondere von Freßnapf betrieben. Und auch Globetrotter setzt anstelle des Preises auf Events und Aktionen, wie z. B. Impfstationen oder Modeschauen, um damit tatkräftig die Bildung von Communities zu unterstützen.

Wenn Produktpreis und -qualität gleichauf liegen, geht die Orientierung des Kunden auf den Nutzen und das Servicedesign. Insofern bietet das Internet mit seiner Kundenorientierung große Potenziale, die der Handel mit einem verstärkten Invest in dieses Medium zu nutzen sucht. Die Budgetanteile für Neue Medien lagen in 2007 bei 2,8 %, kletterten im darauf folgenden Jahr auf 3,7 % und werden mittelfristig nach Einschätzungen des Handels steigen und bei knapp 7 % liegen.

Instore-Marketing

Über 70 % der Verbraucher treffen ihre Kaufentscheidung am POS. Neben der Verkaufsförderung und dem Einsatz von Displays tragen Mehrwertkonzepte, wie Emotionalisierung und Services oder sortimentsnahe Dienstleistungen, wesentlich dazu bei, diese Entscheidung zu beeinflussen und zu erleichtern. Denn sie bieten in besonderem Maße die Möglichkeit, mit dem Kunden direkt in Kontakt zu treten und dabei nicht ausschließlich den Preis in den Vordergrund zu stellen. Aus diesem Grund investierte der Handel

Freßnapf is one of the companies strongly driving the building of real communities. Globetrotter also focuses on events and actions rather than on price by setting up vaccination points in its stores or by organising fashion shows, both steps that lead to the building of communities.

When the quality and the price of a product are on the same level customers pay attention to the benefit they get from the product and its service design. That is why the Internet and its focus on customer orientation offers big opportunities retailers are increasingly taking advantage of by investing more money. The budget share of new media was 2.8 % in 2007, rose to 3,7 % in 2008 and is expected by retailers to increase to roughly 7 % in the medium term.

In-store marketing

More than 70 % of consumers make their buying decision at the POS. Apart from sales promotion and the use of displays, concepts that create additional value like emotionalisation, services, or product-related service contribute considerably to influencing and encouraging the buying decision. These concepts represent a great opportunity to come into direct contact with the customer without focusing entirely on the price question. That is why retailers invested around 5.5 % of their budgets in in-store marketing in 2007 and 7,9 % a year later. In 2008, gross advertising investment at retail amounted to 8 bn euros. Total investments stood at 520 m euros in 2007 and at 632 m euros in 2008.[9]

VII.2 DIE ZUKUNFT DES POS-MARKETINGS | THE FUTURE OF POS MARKETING

Aktionen sind wichtig – die leichte Handhabung ebenfalls.
Promotions are important – and so is easy handling.

2007 etwa 5,5 % seines Budgets in Instore-Marketing, 2008 stieg der Anteil auf 7,9 %. Bezogen auf die Brutto-Werbeinvestition des Handels von insgesamt 8 Milliarden Euro, beliefen sich die absoluten Investitionen auf eine Höhe von 520 Millionen Euro in 2007 bzw. auf 632 Millionen Euro in 2008.[9]

4. Der Handel investiert in die eigene Marke

Von großer Bedeutung für ein zukünftiges Marketing am POS ist die Tatsache, dass der Handel immer mehr und konzentrierter in die Stärkung seiner Marke investiert. Dies ist nicht zwangsläufig eine Investition in Eigenmarken, in vielen Fällen hängt aber der Ausbau der Eigenmarken mit der Stärkung der eigenen Marke eng zusammen.

Bereits seit vielen Jahren können wir verfolgen, dass der Markenauftritt der Markenartikelindustrie in den Geschäften des Einzelhandels immer engeren Restriktionen unterworfen wird. Längst darf die Markenartikelindustrie auf der Fläche des Handels nicht mehr uneingeschränkt agieren, sondern sie muss sich an den Wünschen und Vorstellungen der Händler orientieren.

Dies betrifft insbesondere das Geschäft mit Aktionen und Sonderplatzierungen. Hier wurde die Zahl der Sonderaktionen auf der Fläche in den letzten Jahren deutlich reduziert, und alle Maßnahmen, die heute in der Verkaufsstätte stattfinden, werden eng zwischen Handel und Markenartikelindustrie abgestimmt.

Dabei gilt bei den Aktionen mehr denn je, dass vor allem die Ware im Vordergrund stehen sollte und der Markt nicht in erster Linie als Werbeplattform für die Marke dient. Daraus leiten sich für Sonderaktionen eine Reihe von funktionellen und gestalterischen Folgen ab. Die Einbindung der Aktionen in das Gesamtdesign des Ladens liegt dem Einzelhandel ebenso am Herzen wie eine leichte Handhabung von Sonderplatzierungen und -aufbauten. In diesem Zusammenhang steht sicherlich auch, dass die Handelsunternehmen längst von der Markenartikelindustrie Aktionen erwarten, die auf die speziellen Erfordernisse ihrer Gruppe bzw. ihres Marktes zugeschnitten sind.

4. Retailers invest in own brands

Retailers are increasingly investing in strengthening their presence as a brand, which is of great importance for future marketing at the POS. That does not necessarily imply investments into own brands, even though building own brands often helps strengthen the presence of the retailer as a brand.

For many years, suppliers of branded articles have been facing increasing restrictions in the presentation of their brands. The branded goods industry is no longer free to decide on its presentation at retail, but is obliged to adapt more and more to the requirements and ideas of retailers.

That is valid in particular for regular promotions and special promotions. In the past years, the number of special promotions in stores has fallen sharply and all promotional activity in stores today is organised in close cooperation with the branded goods industry.

More than ever, the product and not the brand must be in the focus of all POS promotions. That has various functional and creative implications for special promotions. For retailers, harmonising actions with the design of the store is just as important as the easy handling of special promotions and displays. Surely, today retailers expect promotions from suppliers of branded goods that are tailored to the individual needs of their groups or stores.

In Verbindung mit einer stärkeren Markenbildung im Handel wird auch darauf geachtet, dass das Marktbild nicht über Gebühr durch Aktionen und Sonderplatzierungen gestört wird. Kundenorientierung und ein klares, übersichtliches Leitsystem sind dem Handel heute wichtiger als viele zusätzliche Kaufimpulse. Selbst an der Kasse gehen heute die besonders innovativen Einzelhandelsunternehmer dazu über, vollkommen auf Warenplatzierungen zu verzichten. Sonderaufbauten und Zweitplatzierungen in jedem Gang und an jedem Gondelkopf – diese Zeiten sind vorbei.

Unbesehen davon erfüllt das Display auch weiterhin seine Funktion als Logistikelement, wenn keine entsprechende Regalfläche zur Verfügung steht. Bei Aktionsware ist es häufig sinnvoll, diese komplett auf Palette im Handel zu platzieren. Das so genannte Logistikdisplay übernimmt hierbei gleich zwei Aufgaben: die der Verpackung und die des Displays.

5. Technische Infrastruktur

Auch die technische Infrastruktur der Märkte wird sich in den kommenden Jahren weiter verändern und damit auch die Zukunft des POS-Marketings deutlich prägen. Die Kunden von heute verlangen deutlich mehr Informationen über ihre Einkaufsstätte, über die dort angebotenen Waren und auch darüber, unter welchen Bedingungen diese Waren produziert und distribuiert worden sind. Es geht also nicht nur darum, welche Produkte mit welchen Inhaltsstoffen verkauft werden, sondern auch um die Frage, ob diese Produkte im Einklang mit der Natur und der Gesellschaft erzeugt worden sind.

Immer mehr Kunden wollen eben nicht nur ein gutes Produkt in guter Qualität, sondern sie wollen auch über die Auswirkungen ihres Kaufverhaltens informiert werden. Welche Düngemittel und Pestizide werden auf den Gemüseplantagen eingesetzt? Wie sehen die Arbeitsbedingungen der Beschäftigten dort aus? Stammt der Fisch aus einem Bestand, der nachhaltig bewirtschaftet wird? Wie viel Kalorien enthält ein Produkt? Wie hoch ist der Anteil an Fett, Salz und Kohlehydraten? Oder: Sind gegebenenfalls Stoffe in einem Produkt enthalten, die beim Verzehr Allergien verursachen können?

Viele, viele Fragen, die immer wieder von den Kunden gestellt werden und die künftig auch kompetent vom Handel beantwortet

In order to increase brand building at retail, it is important to avoid that regular and special promotions interfere too much with the store concept. Today, customer orientation and a clear signage are more important to retailers than many additional buying impulses. Today, highly innovative retailers are stopping to display products even at prominent places as the checkout. Special structures and secondary placements in every aisle and end-of-aisle display are a thing of the past.

Still, where shelf space is missing, displays continue to be a logistical element. It may be useful to display campaign goods always on pallets in the store. The so-called logistical display has both a packaging and displaying function.

5. Technical infrastructure

The technical infrastructure of markets will continue to change in the coming years, thus shaping the future of POS marketing. Today's customers demand substantially more information about the places they shop, about the products on offer and the conditions they are produced and distributed under. So the question is not only what product with what content is being sold, but also the question if the product is produced in harmony with nature and society.

More and more customers want a good product of good quality, but also want to know what effect their buying behaviour has. What kind

Schnelle Bereitstellung von Informationen durch neueste Technologie.

The latest technology allows quick provision of information.

VII.2 DIE ZUKUNFT DES POS-MARKETINGS | THE FUTURE OF POS MARKETING

Inspirierte Kunden verwenden mehr Geld auf ungeplante Käufe.

Inspired customers spend more on unplanned purchases.

werden müssen. Die Verpackung der Produkte allein reicht bei weitem nicht aus, um all diese Informationen bekanntzumachen. Auch eine Beschilderung stößt an ihre Grenzen. Es bleibt also kaum etwas anderes übrig, als die Produktinformation über neue technische Mittel verfügbar zu machen.

Der Schlüssel dazu wird nach heutigem Stand der Erkenntnisse zunächst der Barcode sein, der bereits auf allen Produkten angebracht ist, später wird es vielleicht einmal die Radiofrequenz-Identifikationstechnik sein, die eines Tages mit hoher Wahrscheinlichkeit den Barcode ersetzen wird.

Über den Barcode werden di Kunden zukünftig auf vielerlei Produktinformationen zugreifen können. Bereits heute gibt es hier mit SA 2 Worldsync einen weltweiten Datenpool, der sämtliche Informationen zur Beschreibung verschiedener Artikel zentral speichert. Während aktuell in erster Linie warenwirtschaftliche Daten in dieser Produktdatenbank abgelegt sind, werden zukünftig mehr und mehr verbraucherbezogene Informationen gespeichert werden. Über den Barcode wird dann der Verbraucher auf diese Datenbank zugreifen und Informationen zu all den genannten Fragen erhalten.

Ob dies nun im Markt an einem Scanner passiert, an einer Waage über die Eingabe von PLU-Nummern oder vielleicht über das Mobiltelefon, technisch gibt es hier eine ganze Reihe von Möglichkeiten, die von Fall zu Fall unterschiedlich geeignet sein dürften. Von großer Bedeutung wird sicherlich auch die Tatsache sein, dass die Geschäfte in der Regel schon heute eine permanente breitbandige Internetverbindung besitzen. Gleichzeitig gibt es

of pesticides and fertilizers are used in vegetable gardening? What are workers' conditions? Is that fish from a sustainable source? How many calories does the product contain? How much fat, salt and carbohydrates does it contain? Or does the product contain substances that can cause an allergic reaction?

These are just a few of the many questions customers continue to ask and that demand competent answers from retailers. Packaging alone does not suffice to give all the information needed. Labelling has its limits too. So the only answer is to use new technical means to transport information.

As things stand today, the barcode, already present on all products, is a key player. In the future, it may be radio frequency identification, which in all probability is likely to replace the barcode one day.

The barcode will make vast product information accessible to customers in the future. Today, there is already SA 2 Worldsync that

einen massiven Preisverfall bei den Monitoren, der dazu führen wird, dass immer mehr Bildschirme in die Geschäfte Einzug halten werden. Ob an der Kasse, an der Waage oder im Markt selbst – überall werden wir zukünftig die Möglichkeit haben, digitale Informationen ausgesprochen flexibel und gleichzeitig kostengünstig zu vermitteln. Ob Preisauszeichnung oder Plakatwerbung, in vielen Bereichen wurde bereits eine neue Ära eingeläutet und Etiketten und Plakate dürften strategisch gesehen nur noch eine begrenzte Lebensdauer haben.

6. Kundenorientierung auch in Krisenzeiten?

Ist die Orientierung an Kundenwünschen und die Investition in „kundennahe" Medien ein Luxus für wirtschaftlich gute Zeiten oder markiert sie eine nachhaltige Entwicklung?

Alle Indikatoren weisen darauf hin, dass der Handel es ernst meint mit der Hinwendung zum Kunden – gerade in herausfordernden Zeiten. Der Handel ist es gewohnt, sich in einem schwierigen Umfeld zu bewegen, denn von der positiven gesamtwirtschaftlichen Entwicklung der letzten Jahre hat er kaum profitiert. Der Umsatz im deutschen Einzelhandel stagniert seit Beginn der 90er Jahre. Gleichzeitig sinkt der Anteil des Handels am privaten Konsum kontinuierlich, während sich das Verkaufsflächenwachstum fortsetzt.[10]

Unter diesen ökonomischen Rahmenbedingungen stieg die Summe der Budgetanteile für „kundennahe" Medien – Direktmarketing, Neue Medien, POS-Marketing – von 14,8 % in 2007 auf stolze 18,8 % in 2008. Tendenz steigend. Das EHI geht davon aus, dass dieser Trend mittlerweile auch jenseits der Konjunkturdelle unumkehrbar scheint.[11]

offers a global central data pool containing all information about products. The focus of this data base is still on product data, but in future will include more and more consumer-oriented information. The consumer will then be able to use the barcode to get information about all the questions mentioned above.

Whether this will happen at a scanner in the store, by introducing a PLU code at the scales in the supermarket or possibly by using a mobile phone will depend on the individual situation. There is a whole range of technical options. The fact that most stores already have a broadband Internet connection will be of great importance. At the same time, falling screen prices mean that there will be more and more screens in stores. Whether at the checkout, the scales, or in the middle of the store, retailers will be able to transport digital information in an extremely flexible and cost-efficient way. Times have already changed for pricing and poster advertising so that under strategic aspects, labels and posters are likely to disappear before long.

6. Customer orientation in a crisis?

Is the focus on customer desires and investments in customer-oriented media possible only in healthy economic times or is it a lasting development?

All indicators point to the fact that retailers are serious about customer orientation, especially in hard times. Retailers are used to tough conditions considering that retail has hardly benefited from the over-all positive development over the past years. Retail sales have been stalling since the early 1990s. At the same time, the share of retail in private consumption is falling steadily, while selling space growth is continuing.[10]

Under these economic conditions, total budget share of customer-oriented media like direct marketing, new media, POS marketing has grown from 14,8 % in 2007 to 18,8 % in 2008. And the trend is rising. EHI reckons that the trend is irreversible regardless of the recession.[11]

Michael Gerling   Marlene Lohmann

Claudia Endl

Werbeformen für die Märkte von morgen

1. Entwicklung der Handelslandschaft

1.1 Das Umfeld von POS-Marketing – Ein Rückblick

Selbstständig geführte Einzelhandelsgeschäfte, die ihre Kunden lokal mit Waren versorgten, waren früher sozialer Treffpunkt, Beschaffung und Warenverteilung in einem. Auch heute noch dient der nostalgische Begriff des „Tante-Emma-Ladens" als Synonym für die intakte Beziehung zwischen dem lokalen Einzelhändler und seinen Kunden. Absatzförderung als Dialog mit Kunden ist der Schlüssel zur Absatzsteigerung - heute wie damals. Supermarktketten, die sich seit den 60er Jahren entwickelt haben, konnten mit größerer Ladenfläche, mit mehr Vielfalt und der damit verbundenen Produktauswahl aufwarten.
Spezialisierte Fach- und Verbrauchermärkte hielten Einzug in die Handelslandschaft, der Weg von der Bedienung in die Selbstbedienung war vorgezeichnet. Mit der Eröffnung des ersten Lebensmitteldiscounters zog mit Aldi 1962 ein neues Format und eine neue Produktwelt, die Handelsmarke, in die Welt des Handels ein. Charakteristisch für Aldi waren und sind die Konzentration auf ein relativ begrenztes Warensortiment von wenigen umsatzstarken bis schnell drehenden Produkten (zunächst knapp 400, heute 1.200 Artikel bei Aldi Nord), eine einfache Warenpräsentation und sparsamer Service.[1]

Beginnend mit den 90er Jahren zeichnete sich im Einzelhandel bundesweit eine beachtliche Dynamik ab. Die Wiedervereinigung, der Aufbau des Handelsnetzes in Ostdeutschland, neue Wettbewerber wie Tankstellen, E-Commerce, die Vertikalisierung und der Systemhandel führten zu einem Wandel in der Einzelhandelswelt. Neue Betriebs- und Vertriebsformen konkurrierten um das Budget der Kunden.[2] Fachmärkte, Einkaufszentren, Factory-Outlet-Center und Urban-Entertainment-Center veränderten mit ihren neuen Strukturen das Einkaufs- und das Absatzförderungsverhalten. Bedarfsdeckung durch preiswerte Anbieter und Erlebniswelten auf der anderen Seite förderten neben volumenorientierten Sonderangeboten saisonale und themenorientierte Vermarktung.

Claudia Endl

Advertising for the stores of the future

1. The development of the retail environment

1.1 A review of the POS marketing environment

The store of the independent retailer who locally supplied customers with products used to be a social meeting place, procurement and distribution of goods all in one. A nostalgic look back reveals the traditional "corner shop" to be synonymous with a good relationship between retailer and customer. Promoting sales by entering into dialogue with the customer was the key to increasing sales and still is today.
The supermarket chains that started to develop in the 1960s had stores with more floor space and a more diverse product range that offered customers a greater choice.
New formats like specialist stores and hypermarkets began to change the retail environment and paved the way for the shift from service to self-service. In 1962, Aldi established a new format and a new "product world", the retail brand, in the world of retail with the opening of the first discount food store. Aldi's business model was and still is characterised by a relatively reduced range of strong selling products with a high turnover ratio (initially 400 products, today 1,200 products at Aldi North), a simple product presentation and hardly any service.[1]

From the 1990s onwards, retail across the whole of Germany experienced dynamic changes. The reunification, the emergence of retail networks in eastern Germany, new competitors like petrol stations, e-commerce, vertical integration and retail partnerships changed the world of retail.[2] Companies started to compete for customer budgets with new business forms and retail concepts. With their new structures, specialist stores, shopping centres, factory outlets and urban entertainment centres changed customers' shopping behaviour and retailers' approach to sales promotion. On the other hand, customer demand was now also covered by discounters and specially designed interactive areas in stores not only drove the sale of volume oriented bargain offers, but also the sale of seasonal products and products of campaigns run under a particular theme.

The introduction of the euro in 2002 sparked a debate about the so-called "teuro",[3] from teuer meaning expensive in German. With

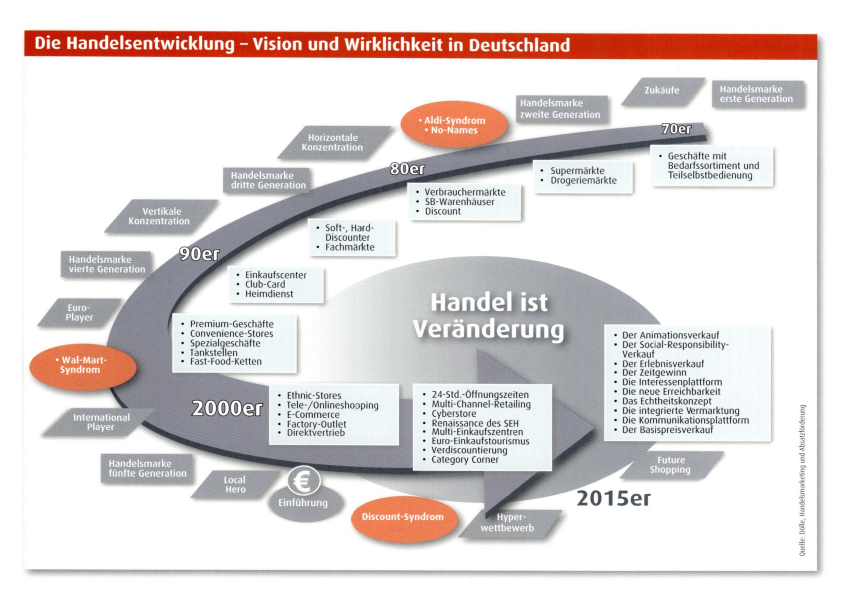

Die Einführung der Euro-Währung im Januar 2002 führte zu einer „Teuro"-Diskussion.[3] Dabei forcierten die Discounter über Preissenkungsrunden handelsgetriebene Konditionsforderungen an die Hersteller. Mit einer neuen Innovationskraft entstehen heute themenbezogene Produktangebote und Markenpartnerschaften. Umweltschutz, Verantwortung für Dritte rufen Labels wie „FAIRTRADE" auf den Plan. Ein Wertewandel, sowohl in der Angebots- als auch in der Nachfrage, wird sichtbar. „Die Verbraucher vergegenwärtigen sich aktuell, was hinter der eigentlichen Ware steckt." Veränderte Konsumentenwerte stellen neue Anforderungen an die Warenpräsentation und die Umfeldinformation.[4]

1.1.1 Entwicklung auf der Unternehmensebene

Eng verbunden mit den Entwicklungstrends auf der betrieblichen Ebene ist auf Unternehmensebene seit Jahren ein Konzentrationsprozess zu beobachten, der durch einen europaweiten Verdrängungswettbewerb und Unternehmensfusionen forciert wird. In 2010 liegt in Deutschland der Marktanteil der fünf größten Lebensmittelhändler bei fast 70 %.[5]

their price-cutting campaigns discounters put downward pressure on manufacturers, allowing them to work out favourable conditions. Innovation at retail has led to the creation of tie-in merchandise lines that take particular themes, as well as brand partnerships. Concern for the environment and responsibility for others has brought forth labels like "FAIRTRADE". We are seeing a change in values on both the supply and the demand side. "Consumers are starting to be aware of what is actually behind the product". Due to changing customer values, retailers face the challenge of finding new ways to present products and information about the products at the POS.[4]

1.1.1 Developments at the corporate level

Similarly to the trends on the operational level we have been witnessing consolidation on the corporate level over the past years that is mainly due to predatory competition and company mergers. In 2010, Germany's five biggest food retailers have a combined market share of almost 70 %.[5]

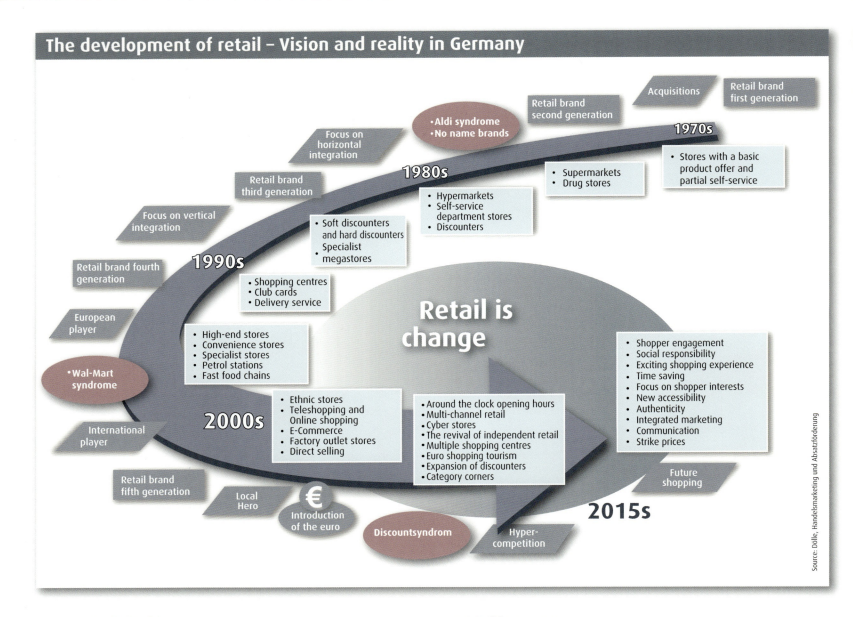

1.1.2 Die Discounter

Der Siegeszug der Discounter war zunächst ein deutsches Phänomen. Das Discountprinzip schwappte schnell auf andere Branchen über und konnte sich mittlerweile europaweit etablieren.

Der große Erfolg der Lebensmitteldiscounter der vergangenen Jahre beruht auch auf der Ausdehnung des Warenangebots auf nicht erklärungsbedürftige Grundbedarfs- und Basisprodukte des Non-Food-Bereiches. Gezielt wurde Aktionsware, die nur an wenigen Tagen im Jahr verkauft wurde, genutzt, um Frequenz zu schaffen.

1.1.3 Der Handel heute

Auf der Handelsseite werden mit zunehmendem Retailwettbewerb die eigenen Markenprofile verstärkt vorangetrieben. Der Handel will selbst mehr zur Marke werden.[6] Denn mit dem Preis allein lässt sich kein für den Konsumenten interessanter Unterschied zum Wettbewerb erreichen.[7]

1.1.2 Discounters

At first, the success of discounters was mainly a German phenomenon. The discount concept soon spilled over to other industries and is meanwhile accepted everywhere in Europe. The big success food discounters have experienced over the past years is also due to their policy to extend their ranges to include basic non-food products that require no explanation. To increase in-store traffic, retailers made strategic use of bargain offer goods that could be sold only on certain days of the year.

1.1.3 Retail today

At the retail level, increasing competition is strengthening the profile of retailers' brands. More and more retailers want to become brands in their own right. The price alone is not enough to keep the customer from switching to rival retailers.[6] This means that the manufacturer will be required to increasingly work together with retailers on activity that is in the interest of both the manufacturer and the retailer.

Dies bedeutet für die Hersteller, dass verstärkt Co-Maßnahmen - also Aktivitäten, bei denen Handel und Hersteller mit gleichen Interessen Ziele verfolgen - gewünscht werden. Auf der Herstellerseite erhält das POS-Marketing eine neue Wertschätzung. Diese wird ausgelöst durch die steigende Nutzung des Internets und die damit verbundenen medialen Plattformen, die Promotions zu jeder Zeit und in jeder Ausprägung ermöglichen. Über die letzten 50 Jahre hat sich Verkaufsförderung zu einer perfekten, strukturierten Vermarktung entwickelt, bei der nichts mehr dem Zufall überlassen wird.

1.1.4 Die Zukunft der Handelslandschaft

Neue Ladenkonzepte und Veränderungen im Sortimentsangebot sowie Spezialformate entstehen. Damit reagiert der Handel auf die sich ständig verändernden wirtschaftlichen, demografischen

Manufacturers will come to appreciate the POS because the POS allows promotions of all kinds at any time. This is made possible by the increased use of the Internet and connected media platforms. In the past 50 years, sales promotion has become a perfect and structured form of marketing that leaves nothing to chance.

1.1.4 Retail in the future

Retailers will roll out new store concepts, new product ranges and specialist concepts as a reaction to the constantly changing economic, demographic and structural conditions.[8] The future does not lie in maintaining a status quo. It should be a motivation for change for retailers to understand and adapt to the new situations in the life of consumer groups that are becoming more and more difficult to retain. Price and procurement leadership as well as perfectly organised logistics will be basic fundamental elements that are prerequisites for

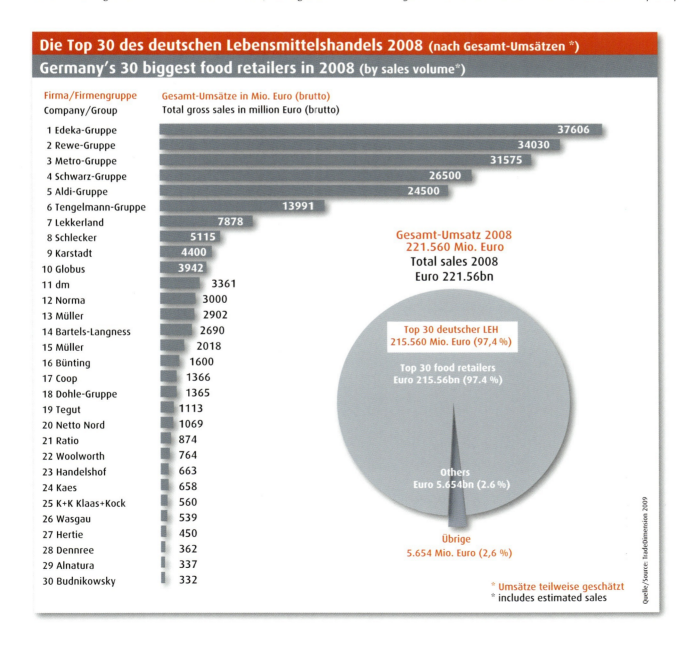

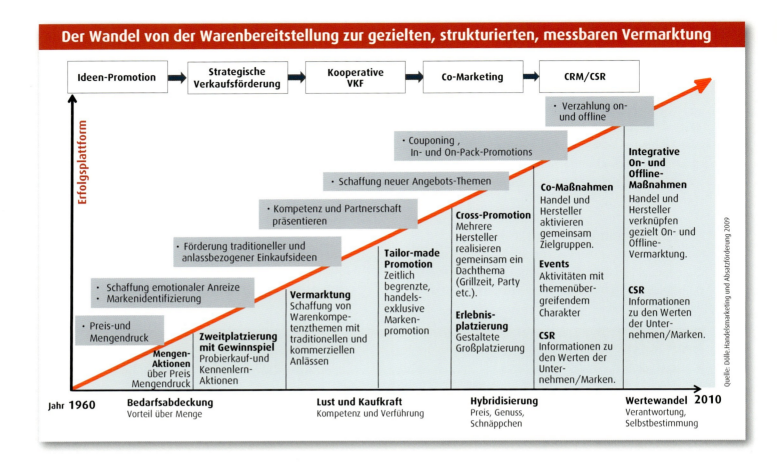

und strukturellen Rahmenbedingungen.⁸ Nicht die Fortschreibung vom Bestehenden ist die Zukunft, sondern die Adaption und die Einstellung zu den neuen Lebenswirklichkeiten der immer stärker entgleitenden Verbrauchergruppen ist Ansporn zum Wandel. Preis- und Beschaffungsführerschaft sowie logistische Perfektion werden zu Basiselementen als Grundleistungen für erfolgreiche Verkaufskonzepte. Das eröffnet Spielraum für kreative Konzepte in der Absatzförderung. Die Handelslandschaft von morgen muss ihre Konsumenten in der jeweiligen Bedürfnisstruktur abholen und mit ihren Plattformen im Sinne einer ganzheitlichen Absatzförderung für Nachfrage sorgen. Ziel ist es, aus Shoppern Konsumenten zu machen und dabei sowohl die Kunst der Verführung, als auch die Anziehungskraft niedriger Preise zu nutzen.

Orientierungsgröße sind die Verbraucher, die nicht müde sind, sich über Verkaufsförderung sowohl emotional als auch rational abholen zu lassen. Allerdings sind sie anspruchsvoller geworden, was die Qualität und die Botschaft der jeweiligen Aktion angeht.

2. Werbeformen für die Märkte von morgen

2.1 Die neuen Klassiker

Klassische Werbeträger im Outlet werden sich hinsichtlich Art und Inhalt verändern. Dabei übernehmen die Unternehmen einen success. That creates leeway for creative sales promotion concepts. In the retail environment of the future it will be fundamental to know what each customer needs and, in the spirit of a holistic sales promotion, stimulate his demand. The objective is to turn shoppers into consumers by tempting them with attractive products and prices. Retailers will have to centre their attention on the consumer who will not tire to respond emotionally and rationally to sales promotion. Customers, however, are more demanding today and expect a high standard of quality and content when it comes to promotions.

2. Advertising in tomorrow's stores

2.1 The new classics

The type and content of conventional displays and advertising media in the store will change. Companies will have to focus on information and communication that benefits their brand and its positioning in the market. The vast number of displays available offer solutions based on competence and product know-how that are tailored to the individual needs of retailers. Combined with ideas and imagination these solutions will pay off.⁹ At the same time, content of the messages delivered to customers is becoming increasingly important: for many shoppers sustainability and corporate responsibility are good reasons to buy a product. The key element of sales promotion will still

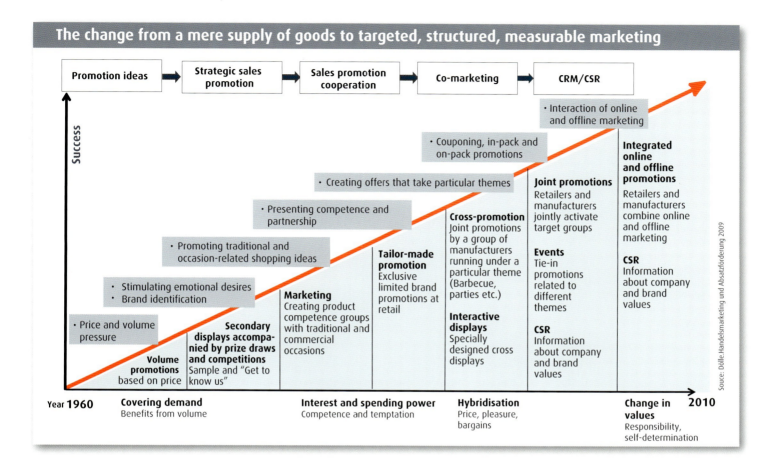

kommunikativen und informativen Auftrag, der in ihre Marke und deren Positionierung investiert. Dafür bietet die Welt der Displays maßgeschneiderte Lösungen mit Waren- und Kompetenzthemen, untermauert mit Ideen und Phantasie, die sich auszahlen.⁹ Gleichzeitig nimmt die Bedeutung der Botschaften zu: Nachhaltigkeit und unternehmerische Verantwortung sind für viele Shopper heute entscheidende Kaufargumente. Wesentliches Element der Verkaufsförderung wird das Produkt in seiner Verpackung bleiben, die den neuen Anforderungen an Information, Lesbarkeit und Convenience sowie Form und Farbe gerecht werden muss. Auch der Handzettel wird für den Handel ein strategisches Verkaufsförderungstool bleiben. Der Handzettel muss sich jedoch neu erfinden, die aktuelle Positionierung darstellen, den Kunden in seiner Themenwelt abholen und zur Einkaufsstätte einladen.

2.2 Digitale Medien

Digitale Medien sind auf dem Vormarsch, sie erlauben eine zielgruppen- und anlassgerichtete Ansprache über den Tag, wodurch die Bewerbung unterschiedlicher Produkte zu den entsprechenden Tageszeiten möglich ist.¹⁰ Der Kunde kauft nur das, was er sieht.¹¹ In den Outlets werden vermehrt Multimediaterminals eingesetzt, die dem Kunden die Möglichkeit bieten, sich jederzeit aktuell zu Produkten und Themen zu informieren. Digital Signage, z.B. als elektronisches Plakat oder Schild zur Vermittlung von statischen

be the product and its packaging, the packaging now challenged with meeting the new demands on information, readability, convenience, form and colour. Flyers will also continue to be a strategic sales promotion tool. But the flyer will have to re-invent itself, show the store's current market position, know exactly what customers want and make them want to come to the store.

2.2 Digital media

Digital media are gaining ground, they cater for specific target groups and specific occasions at different times of the day. In this way, it is possible to promote different products at a specific time of day.¹⁰ Customers only buy what they see.¹¹
There will be more and more multimedia terminals in stores where customers can get the latest information about individual products or campaigns at any time. It is impossible to imagine tomorrow's advertising world without digital signage like electronic posters or signs that convey static and dynamic advertising and information content.¹² With information and entertainment, digital media turns the customer's shopping journey into a special experience.

2.3 Mobile marketing

Technologies like Bluetooth and RFID deliver individual messages and information about products right when they are needed. Retailers can take advantage of the permanent presence of the mobile device that

und dynamischen Werbe- und Informationsinhalten, ist aus der Werbewelt von morgen nicht mehr wegzudenken.[12] Digitale Medien schaffen für ihre Kunden durch Informationen und Unterhaltung ein besonderes Kauferlebnis.

2.3 Mobile Marketing
Technologien wie Bluetooth und RFID sorgen dafür, dass individuell und zeitnah Werbebotschaften oder Informationen über Produkte übermittelt werden können. Das mobile Endgerät trägt durch seine ständige Präsenz - der fast ununterbrochenen Mitführung am Körper - zur Individualisierung und Personalisierung der Botschaft an den Kunden bei. Zusätzlich können Streuverluste und Kosten minimiert werden.[13]

2.4 Partnerschaften
Partnerschaften als Form der Bündelung von mindestens zwei selbstständigen Marken respektive Produkten unterstützen gegenseitig das jeweilige Image, sorgen für Bekanntheitssteigerung und erweitern Leistungen und Zusatznutzen. Zur gleichen Zeit erschließen sie neue Kunden, neue Kompetenzfelder und zusätzliche Absatzkanäle. Bekanntestes Co-Promotion-Beispiel ist McDonald's mit Monopoly. Die geschickte Verknüpfung von Spiel und Abverkauf fördert Frequenz, Image und Ertrag. Auch Cross-Partnerschaften wie beispielsweise die Verbindung von Mumm-Sekt und WMF fördern Absatz und Image.

2.5 Couponing
Kunden finden und binden: Diese Ziele lassen sich mit Hilfe von Bonuspunkten und Gutscheinen erreichen.[14] Coupons, Punkte und Kundenkarten werden von Kunden als Service bzw. als Zusatznutzen gegenüber Wettbewerbsprodukten gewertet und bilden eine Art „Sparwährung". Bis zu 70 % des durch Coupons eingesparten Geldes werden beim gleichen Einkauf für andere Dinge ausgegeben. Damit erhöhen sich der Wert des Durchschnittsbons

customers almost always carry carries around with them to deliver individual messages. These technologies also help minimize spreading losses and costs.[13]

2.4 Partnerships
Partnerships between at least two independent brands and their products mutually support and promote the partners' image, increase brand awareness and provide additional services and benefits. Partnerships help acquire new customers and new fields of competence and open new sales channels. The best-known co-promotion alliance is that between McDonald's and Monopoly. The clever combination of playing and sales process boosts traffic, image and profits. Cross partnerships like the one between Mumm sparkling wine and WMF also improve the companies' sales and image.

und der Umsatz als solcher. Kundenkarten funktionieren durch direkte Rabatte und Bonuserstattungen als eine Art des automatischen Sparens und unterstützen den Abverkauf von Produkt, Dienstleistung und ergänzenden Serviceleistungen.

3. Verzahnung von On- und Offline-Kommunikation am POS

Der Point of Sale bietet einen entscheidenden Vorteil gegenüber anderen Kommunikationsmitteln: Er ermöglicht die zeitnahe Interaktion zwischen dem Handel und dem Kunden. Über interaktive Maßnahmen lässt sich sowohl Nutzen für den Kunden schaffen, der sich vor Ort über Produkte informieren kann, als auch die Erinnerung an vorher geschaltete Werbemaßnahmen gezielt fördern.[15]

2.5 Coupons

To find and bind customers: bonus points and vouchers can help achieve that goal.[14] Customers regard coupons, bonus points and loyalty cards as additional benefits not offered by competitors. These coupons and bonus points can be considered a kind of "piggy bank" currency. Customers spend up to 70 % of the money they save by using their coupons on other products they buy during the same shopping journey. This increases the average spending per purchase and total sales. Loyalty cards with their direct discounts and bonus points rewards represent a sort of automatic saving system and support the sale of products and services.

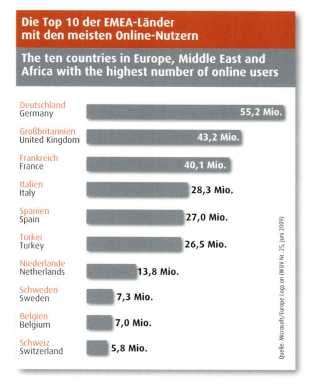

Die Top 10 der EMEA-Länder mit den meisten Online-Nutzern
The ten countries in Europe, Middle East and Africa with the highest number of online users

Deutschland / Germany	55,2 Mio.
Großbritannien / United Kingdom	43,2 Mio.
Frankreich / France	40,1 Mio.
Italien / Italy	28,3 Mio.
Spanien / Spain	27,0 Mio.
Türkei / Turkey	26,5 Mio.
Niederlande / Netherlands	13,8 Mio.
Schweden / Sweden	7,3 Mio.
Belgien / Belgium	7,0 Mio.
Schweiz / Switzerland	5,8 Mio.

Quelle: Microsoft/Europe Logs on (W&V Nr. 25, Juni 2009)

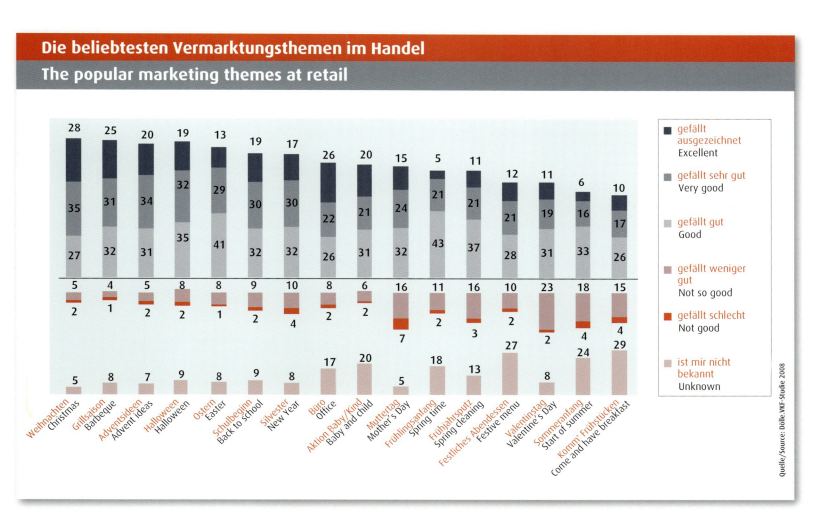

Die beliebtesten Vermarktungsthemen im Handel
The popular marketing themes at retail

Quelle/Source: Dölle-VKF-Studie 2008

Der Wirkungsverlust klassischer Medien kann durch Online-Kommunikation ersetzt werden und den vernetzten Dialog zwischen Hersteller, Handel, POS und themenbasierten Aktionen fördern. Coupons on Demand, die sich der Verbraucher im Internet herunterladen kann, fördern die Beschäftigung mit dem Produkt oder der Dienstleistung und damit die Interaktion zwischen Kunde und Marke. Direkt mobil abrufbare Vorteile - zum Beispiel die Integration von Bonus Codes in Fanta-Flaschendeckeln - zeigen die forcierte Verknüpfung von mobiler Kommunikation und POS-Marketing. Die Resonanz ist positiv.[16]

3.1 Medienkonvergenz

Die Grundzüge des werblichen Handels werden sich zunehmend verändern. POS Marketing als ein strategisches Instrument des 360°-Marketings wird interaktiv und integrativ zwischen Hersteller und Handel an Bedeutung gewinnen, integrativer Bestandteil eines strategischen Kommunikationsmanagements werden und eine andere Planungsqualität erhalten müssen.

Die Annäherung und das Zusammenspiel einzelner Medien erfordern eine zielgerichtete formale und inhaltliche Abstimmung aller Maßnahmen. Die integrierte 360°-Kommunikation sorgt für die Durchgängigkeit von Botschaften und Inhalten über alle Medien hinweg.

4. Die Bedeutung der Präsentation für die Marken von morgen

4.1 Der Kunde im Mittelpunkt

POS-Marketing muss sich auf Kunden einstellen, die heute kritischer, souveräner, informationshungriger und spielbereiter denn je sind. Sie leben in einer für sie jederzeit transparenten und interaktiven Welt. Der Kunde ist Dreh- und Angelpunkt und belohnt mit seinem Kauf den Marketingeinsatz des Herstellers: Verkaufsförderung ist die Optimierung der Beziehungsqualität. Der Wunsch der Kunden nach optisch ansprechender Ware hat sich noch verstärkt.[17] Die Verkaufs-

3. The interaction of online and offline communication at the POS

The POS has a distinct advantage over other means of communication: the POS is a platform for immediate interaction between the retailer and the customer. Interaction at the POS creates value for the customer who can get information about products right at the POS, and systematically increases recall of previous advertising efforts.[15]

The loss of effectiveness of above-the-line media can be compensated with online communication and encourages networked communication between manufacturers, retailers, the POS and product-specific promotions. Coupons on demand that can be downloaded from the Internet increase customers' engagement with the product or service and their interaction with the brand. Direct mobile services like those allowing the customer to save bonus codes collected from Fanta bottle caps over the phone are examples of interaction of mobile communication and POS marketing. The response is positive.[16]

3.1 Media convergence

The main features of retail marketing will see increasing change in the future. The importance of POS marketing as a strategic tool of 360 degree marketing for both manufacturers and retailers in terms of interaction and integration will increase, it will become an integral part of strategic communication management and will require a new planning policy.

Einflüsse der Verpackung auf die Kaufentscheidung
Influence of the packaging on the buying decision

Kaufgründe der Deutschen
Why shoppers in Germany buy a product

Geschmack / Taste	17,1 %
Empfehlung / Recommendation	14,6 %
Produktnutzen / Product value	11,8 %
Preis / Price	7,5 %
Qualität / Quality	5,5 %
Sonderaktion / Special promotion	4,6 %
Verpackung / Packaging	4,1 %
Marke / Brand	3,6 %
Geruch / Smell	3,0 %
Inhaltsstoffe / Ingredients	2,7 %

Trends | Trends

Veredelung	Refinement
Nachhaltigkeit	Sustainability
Zielgruppenspezifische Gestaltung	Customised design for each target group

Verpackung als Qualitätsindikator
Packaging as an indicator of quality

Verbraucherempfinden in ausgewählten Warengruppen
Customer opinion regarding select product groups

Süßwaren / Confectionary	45,5 %
Kosmetik / Cosmetics	35,9 %
Waschmittel / Washing powder	29,7 %
Reis / Rice	29,2 %

Preisbereitschaft der Verbraucher für besondere Verpackungen (Mehrpreis je Einheit)
Price customers were willing to pay for special packaging (extra cost per unit)

Kosmetikprodukt / Cosmetics	0,74 Euro
Waschmittel / Washing powder	0,49 Euro
Cerealien/Müsli / Cereals/Muesli	0,42 Euro
Süßwarenartikel / Confectionary	0,38 Euro
Reis / Rice	0,37 Euro

Quelle/Source: Nielsen; Pro Caron 2009

---

förderung wird morgen auf viel mehr Wissen um den Kunden, den Konsumenten, sein Kaufverhalten, seine Kaufmotive, seine Lebenswerte und seinen Informationsbedarf aufbauen müssen, um erfolgreich zu sein. Dieser Erfolg wird sich dafür zukünftig verstärkt methodengestützt messen lassen.

Marken sind dabei Fixpunkte: Sie vermitteln Authentizität und bieten ein Heimatgefühl in der globalen Welt. Sie stehen für Vertrauen, Zuverlässigkeit, Innovation, Qualität und Prestige. Marken leisten mit ihren Kernwerten ein Leistungsversprechen, auf das der Konsument besteht. Die Marke wird selbst zum Werttreiber und transportiert innerhalb von Sekunden Emotionswelten und Identifikationsmerkmale. Entscheidend dabei bleibt, dass die Produkte auf eine für den Kunden relevante Art und Weise erlebbar werden.[18]

Themenbezogene Vermarktungsaktionen, die emotional ansprechen und den Kunden in seinem Interessenfeld treffen (Freizeit,

The convergence and interaction of various media requires the targeted coordination of all advertising efforts in terms of form and content. Integrated 360 degree marketing provides consistent messages and content across all forms of media.

4. The importance of presentation for future brands

4.1 The customer at centre stage

POS marketing will have to adjust to customers who have never been as critical, confident, information hungry and playful as they are today. They live in a world that becomes transparent and interactive whenever they want it to. Customers are the pivot around which the marketing world revolves and their purchase is the reward for the manufacturer's marketing efforts: sales promotion takes the quality of the relationship between customer and manufacturer to the highest possible level. Today's customers have become even more demanding when it comes to the visual attractiveness of products.[17] In order to

Verbraucher nutzen Infos am POS
Consumers use information at the POS

Bewertung der POS-Maßnahmen aus Sicht der Marktleiter   How store managers rate POS activity

	Gesamtnote* Total*	Praktische Umsetzbarkeit Practicability	Abverkaufs-steigerung Sales increase	Steigerung der Attraktivität des Marktes Increase in the store's attractiveness
Handzettel/Werbezettel Flyers/leaflets	1,3	1,3	1,3	1,4
Dekorierte Warenaufbauten/Displays Decorated fixtures/displays	1,7	1,6	1,8	1,6
Werbedamen Female promotional models	1,7	1,7	1,7	1,6
Themeninseln/Saisonaktionen Walk-around displays/seasonal promotions	1,7	1,6	1,9	1,6
Gondelkopf (Regalstirnseite) End-of the aisle display	1,7	1,7	1,6	1,9
Vorteilspack Value packs	1,8	1,7	1,7	1,9

*Notensystem von 1–5 mit 1 = „stimme voll zu" und 5 = „stimme überhaupt nicht zu"
*Five point rating scale 1 = "strongly agree", 5 = "strongly disagree"

Quelle/Source: GfK (Lebensmittel Zeitung Nr. 14, April 2009)

Urlaub, Sport, Familie) fördern die Zielsetzungen der Marken und eine nachhaltige Entscheidung beim Produktwechsel.

4.2 Die Warenpräsentation
Die alternde Gesellschaft, der Anstieg von Ein- und Zweipersonenhaushalten, die Veränderungen im Lebens- und Ernährungsstil haben Einfluss auf die Warenpräsentation und die Sortimentsführung. Der Kunde kauft nur das, was er sieht, was in seine täglichen Rituale passt oder ihn verführt. Dabei kreiert Visual Merchandising Emotionen und Lebenswelten der Marken und wird zu einem wichtigen Erfolgsbaustein der Verkaufsförderung.
Kooperationen mit Medien, gemeinsame Verkaufsförderungsaktionen von Handel und Herstellern werden zunehmen. Sie dienen als Auslöser einer Faszination beim Kunden, als Impulsgeber für neue Absatzideen, motivieren die eigenen Mitarbeiter und erschließen neue Verwendergruppen für bestimmte Sortimente. Das Display hilft, Marken-Erlebniswelten zu inszenieren und ist für viele Produkte als flankierende Maßnahme sinnvoll.

Neben einer wachsenden Anzahl von Aktionen am POS wächst die Förderung des Warenverkaufs aus dem Regal. Die wachsende Breite und Tiefe der Warengruppe und Sortimente machen neue Visibilitäts-, Warenpräsentations- und Absatzförderungskonzepte erforderlich.

4.3 Der Handel
Gute Verkaufsförderungsmaßnahmen zahlen sich für Handel und Industrie aus. Auf der Fläche entscheiden Sekunden. In die

be successful, sales promotion in the future will have to be based on much more knowledge about customers, consumers, their buying behaviour and buying motivation, values and information demand. In return, it will be easier to measure this success with the appropriate methods.

Brands are constants in this context: they evoke authenticity in the customer's mind and create a sense of home in the global world. Brands stand for trust, reliability, innovation, quality and prestige. Brands and their intrinsic values make a promise to perform according to the customer's wishes and the customer will insist that this promise is kept. The brand itself becomes a value driver that conveys emotional worlds and identification with the product within seconds. What's crucial here is that the product "comes to life" providing the customer with a relevant experience.[18]

Promotions that take a particular theme emotionally engage customers and address their interests (free time, holidays, sports, family), work towards the brand's objectives and encourage the customer to make a permanent change to a new product.

4.2 Product presentation
Our ageing society, the increasing number of one-adult and two-adult households and the changes in people's ways of living and eating have an influence on product presentation and management. Customers buy only what they see, what fits into their daily rituals or represents a temptation. Visual Merchandising helps to create emotions and build entire worlds

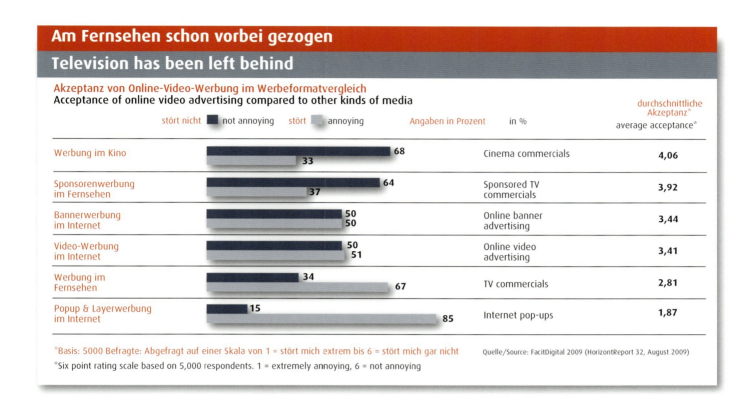

Marketingwelt der Hersteller müssen neben den logistischen und administrativen Anforderungen des Handels modulare Konzepte zu Platzierung, zur Ansprache des Verbrauchers am POS, Platzierungsentwürfe und Preisempfehlungen für die themenbezogene Vermarktung einbezogen werden.[19]

Zu integrieren ist das Internet. Inhaltlich und methodisch werden damit völlig neue temporäre und langfristige Verkaufsförderungskonzepte initiiert werden können. Nur die Vernetzung zwischen Marken- und Handelswelt kann zu einer dauerhaften Kundenbindung für beide Partner führen.

around brands. That makes it a central element for the success of sales promotion. Cooperation with different kinds of media and joint sales promotion efforts of retailers and manufacturers will increase. This will trigger customer fascination and new sales promotion ideas, motivate employees and create new customer groups for specific product ranges. Displays are helpful in creating a brand experience and useful as an additional promotion tool for many products.

While promotion activity at the POS is growing, on-shelf sales promotion is also increasing. New visibility, presentation and sales promotion concepts are needed for product groups and ranges that are expanding in terms of choice and number of products.

4.3. Retail

Both manufacturers and retailers benefit from good sales promotion efforts. Seconds matter at the POS. Next to the logistic and administrative needs of retailers, the manufacturer's marketing world must also take into consideration modular display concepts, customer activation concepts at the POS, display concepts and retail price recommendations for customised marketing efforts.[19]

Good sales promotion must also include the Internet. The Internet will help initiate completely new concepts for both temporary and permanent sales promotion. Only the interaction and cooperation between brands and retailers can create lasting customer loyalty on both sides.

Claudia Endl

VIII. INTEGRIERTE KOMMUNIKATION: VOM SOLISTEN ZUM ORCHESTER | INTEGRATED COMMUNICATION: FROM SOLOIST TO ORCHESTRA

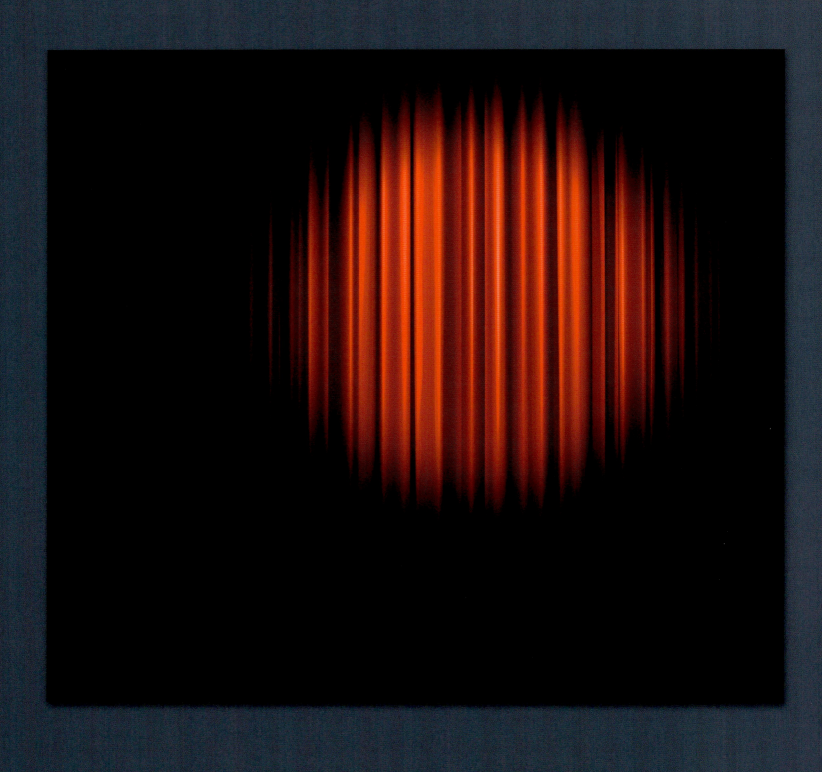

INTEGRIERTE KOMMUNIKATION:
VOM SOLISTEN ZUM ORCHESTER

INTEGRATED COMMUNICATION:
FROM SOLOIST TO ORCHESTRA

Frank-Michael Schmidt,
Henk Knaupe

Integrierte Kommunikation: Vom Solisten zum Orchester

Marken kämpfen um Kunden und die finale Schlacht tobt am Point of Sale. Bei bis zu 150.000 Verkaufspunkten alleine in Deutschland wird von den Unternehmen ein wahrer Kraftakt zur Abdeckung des Universums verlangt. Das Resultat: Armeen von Außendienstmitarbeitern durchkämmen systematisch Supermärkte, Fachhändler, Tankstellen, Shops und kleine Kioske. Sie sind ausgestattet mit Pappen, Displays, Aufstellern und Mobiles und sie eint ein Ziel: eine nachhaltig sichtbare Präsenz am POS.

Trotz dieses Feldzugs bleiben die Erfolge häufig aus und das Ziel unerreicht. Dieser Eindruck verstärkt sich durch konkrete Erfahrungen bei Spontanbesuchen beliebiger Supermärkte oder Shops auf der ganzen Welt: Nur selten sieht eine Warenpräsentation in der Realität so aus, wie es in der Theorie vorher abgesprochen war und wie es sich Unternehmen und Agenturen gleichermaßen vorgestellt hatten.

1. Die Wahrnehmung am POS ist oft ernüchternd. Und warum aus Soldaten Künstler werden müssen.

Der POS bietet unvergleichbare Voraussetzungen für eine wirksame Kommunikation: Bis zu 70 % der Kaufentscheidungen werden final am POS getroffen.[1] Doch dieses Potenzial bleibt derzeit weitgehend ungenutzt. Ein Selbstversuch zeigt: Oft genug steht man als Kunde im Supermarkt allein und verlassen vor einem Regal mit breiter Auswahl. Wo ist meine Lieblingsmarke? Oder: Für welches Produkt soll ich mich entscheiden? Man sieht den Wald vor lauter Bäumen nicht und Verkaufspersonal ist meist nicht in Sicht.

Genau der Zeitpunkt, den eine Marke für sich beanspruchen könnte! Doch nutzen die Marken in dieser Situation ihre Chance, mit dem Konsumenten zu sprechen? Preisen sie sich an, umwerben und präsentieren sie ihre Vorteile? Wenn wir ehrlich sind – meistens nicht! Sie sind da, aber sie sind kaum sichtbar.

Der Blick durch die professionelle Brille ist dann oft ernüchternd: Es mangelt nicht an Werbebotschaften, doch sind diese versteckt,

Frank-Michael Schmidt,
Henk Knaupe

Integrated communication: From soloist to orchestra

Brands fight over customers and the final battlefield is the point of sale. With up to 150,000 POS in Germany alone companies are forced to produce a huge effort to cover the entire market. The result is that armies of field staff systematically comb the supermarkets, specialist retailers, petrol stations, shops and kiosks. They are armed with cartons, displays, stands and mobiles and all have the same aim, to create a lasting and visible presence at the point of sale.

These campaigns are often without success and the goal is not reached. The experience made during spontaneous visits to supermarkets or shops of any kind around the world confirms that impression. Rarely what you find is what had been agreed in theory and what companies and agencies alike had imagined.

1. POS visibility is often sobering. And why soldiers must become artists.

The POS offers unique conditions for effective communication. In the end, up to 70 % of all buying decisions are made at the point of sale.[1] But this potential remains untapped. Everybody knows how it feels to stand in front of a shelf full of goods, alone and abandoned in search of the favourite brand. Or undecided which product to buy. It's hard to see the wood for the trees and there is no salesperson in sight.

That is the moment a brand could take advantage of. But do brands seize the opportunity to communicate with the customer? Do they praise their strengths and court the customer? To be honest they hardly ever do. The brands are there, but they are invisible.

From the professional point of view the result is often sobering. The advertising messages are there, but they are hidden, complicated, complex and delivered in the wrong places. Recent research shows that only 14 % of customers remember the advertising messages of brands on posters, signs and ceiling danglers at the POS.[2]

For some time now all those involved in the process have had the feeling that the battle at the POS cannot be won in the traditional

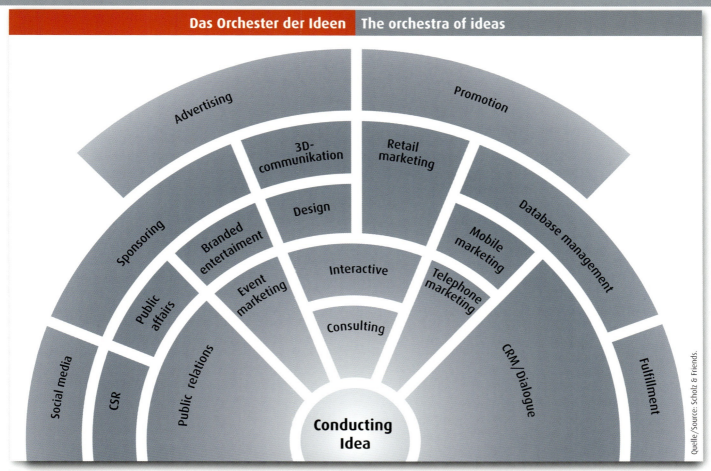

Abbildung/Figure 1

kompliziert, uneinheitlich und an den falschen Stellen platziert. Aktuelle Studien untermauern diesen Eindruck: Nur 14 % der Kunden erinnern sich am POS an markenspezifische Botschaften über Schilder, Plakate und Deckenhänger.[2]

Bereits seit einiger Zeit schwant es den Beteiligten: Die Schlacht am POS kann auf herkömmliche Art und Weise nicht gewonnen werden. Und somit ist es an der Zeit, sich von der Metapher des Krieges zu lösen und den POS aus der Perspektive der Kunden zu betrachten: der Konsumenten und des Handels. Eine wirksame Bearbeitung des POS braucht keine Offiziere und Soldaten, sondern Verständnis und Gefühl. Wir sollten Kommunikation am POS als Kunst betrachten.

2. Orchestrierte Kommunikation bedeutet: Alle Instrumente spielen dieselbe Melodie.

Die Notwendigkeit einer inhaltlichen Vernetzung der Kommunikation über alle Instrumente hinweg ist unumstritten. Doch viele Erklärungsansätze greifen zu kurz. Tatsächlich beschreibt der Begriff der Orchestrierung am treffendsten den richtigen Weg einer abgestimmten ganzheitlichen Kommunikation: Die Kommunikation muss sich wie ein Orchester verschiedener Instrumente

way. The time has come to drop the war metaphor and try to see the POS through the customer's eyes: the eyes of consumers and retailers. The effective handling of the POS needs no soldiers and officers, but understanding and sensitivity. We should view communication at the POS as a high art.

2. Orchestrated communication means all instruments play the same melody.

It is undisputed that all instruments of communication need to interact in terms of content. But many methods of explanation do not go far enough. In fact, the term orchestration best describes the right way to synchronised overall communication. Like an orchestra, communication relies on different instruments (see figure 1). The true listening pleasure is created by the perfect interplay between all instruments.

To be honest, the communications industry is still miles away from such an interplay. There is no director in sight and the instruments are playing their parts without bothering about the others. Often they are not even coordinated which means that sometimes they are not even playing the same piece. Often a brand that yesterday had a high-end appearance on TV, accompanied by the music of Mozart,

bedienen (siehe Abbildung 1). Der wahrhaftige Hörgenuss entsteht dann bei einem perfekten Zusammenspiel dieser Instrumente.

Seien wir ehrlich: Von diesem Zusammenspiel ist die Kommunikationsbranche noch weit entfernt. Vom Dirigenten fehlt jede Spur, und die Instrumente spielen ihren Part, ohne gegenseitig auf sich zu hören. Oft stimmen sie sich noch nicht einmal ab. So passiert es auch, dass nicht einmal das gleiche Stück gespielt wird. Häufig wird eine Marke, die noch gestern im TV filigran und hochwertig im zarten Streicherklang von Mozart auftrat, am POS im Stile einer bayrischen Blaskapelle präsentiert. Eine fatale Folge: Versteht der Kunde die Kommunikation nicht, blendet er sie aus und nimmt sie nicht mehr wahr. Für die Marke ist das verschwendetes Geld.

Wirksame Kommunikation am POS muss sich in die Gesamtkommunikation einfügen und Wertigkeit, Inhalte und Tonalität der Marke transportieren, die der Dirigent vorgibt. Es geht darum, das Kommunikationsguthaben der Marke zu nutzen und mit der POS-Kommunikation ein stimmiges Gesamtbild abzugeben.

3. Preispromotions sind wie die Sirenen des Odysseus – einmal genossen, kann man sich ihnen nicht mehr entziehen.

Das gefährlichste Gift am POS sind (isoliert eingesetzte) Preispromotions. Sie haben die Verlockung einer hohen Wahrnehmung und einer direkten Wirksamkeit im Abverkauf. Der Handel liebt sie, der Vertrieb häufig auch.

Für die Marke aber kann dies ihren schleichenden Tod bedeuten. Preispromotions können als taktisches Mittel sinnvoll und wirksam sein. Aber sie sind zu häufig „Geister", die man nicht mehr los wird. Nicht nur der Handel, sondern vor allem die Konsumenten gewöhnen sich zu schnell an die reduzierten Preise. So wird der Promotionpreis ganz schnell als Normalpreis wahrgenommen. Abgesehen von den desaströsen Auswirkungen auf Margen und Profitabilität untergraben Preispromotions den Wertanspruch der Marke. Warum wird viel Geld für eine Premiumpositionierung ausgegeben, wenn das Produkt am POS mit 20 % Nachlass und

today presents itself at the POS playing Bavarian wind music. When customers fail to understand communication, it fades out and is no longer noticed. For a brand that is money wasted.

3. Price promotions are like the Odyssey sirens – once you have heard their singing you cannot resist their effect.

The most potent of poisons at the POS are (isolated) price promotions. They promise high visibility and a direct effect on sales. Retailers and distributors alike love them. But brands using them may just be facing slow death.

Price promotions can be useful and effective when used as a tactic means. But mostly they are like ghosts you cannot get rid of. Retailers, but mainly customers, get used to reduced prices. Quickly the reduced price starts to feel like the regular price. Apart from the disastrous effect on margins and profitability, price promotions undermine the brand's value. Why invest lots of money in positioning a product at the high end of the market when it is later sold at the POS at a discount of 20% promoted by a "special bargain "sign in bright red letters? That makes no sense. For many brands it is a painful experience to see that it is difficult, if not entirely impossible, to later compensate the reductions.

In contrast, raising prices at retail requires courage and strength. In most cases they cause considerable declines in sales volume. Retailers also threaten to stop selling a product and like to set an example as a warning. Unfortunately, many companies lose their staying power in spite of the substantial effects on profitability, even absolute profitability, experienced also by retailers.

4. Orchestrated communication means making perfect use of every instrument and its individual strengths. Or: why blatant advertising can strike the right chord.

One of the fallacies of integrated communication is believing that every kind of communication, including POS communication, must sing

leuchtend rotem Sonderangebot-Schild verkauft wird? Das passt nicht zusammen. Viele Marken machen die bittere Erfahrung, dass es schwer bis nahezu unmöglich ist, Preisnachlässe im Nachhinein wieder einzufangen.

Dagegen erfordert die Durchsetzung von Preiserhöhungen im Handel Mut und Kraft, sie sind nahezu immer mit deutlichen Absatzeinbrüchen im Volumen verbunden. Zudem droht der Handel oft genug mit Auslistung und statuiert immer wieder gern ein Exempel. Leider fehlt den Unternehmen in der heutigen Zeit zu oft der lange Atem, das durchzustehen, obwohl Effekte auf die (auch absolute) Profitabilität - im Übrigen auch für den Handel - erheblich sind.

4. Orchestrierte Kommunikation heißt, jedes Instrument seinen eigenen Stärken entsprechend einzusetzen. Oder warum Schweinebäuche richtig Musik machen können.

Ein weiterer Trugschluss der integrierten Kommunikation liegt in dem Glauben, dass jede Art von Kommunikation – auch die POS-Kommunikation – im Einheitssingsang versinken muss. Das Ergebnis sind Kampagnen am POS, die die Besonderheiten der Handelskommunikation nicht berücksichtigen.

Besonders beliebt sind ellenlange Copytexte, die möglicherweise im Printbereich die Geschichte der Marke erzählen und ihre kommunikative Wirkung entfachen, am POS jedoch völlig fehl am Platze sind. Niemand liest sich derartige Texte, möglichst noch in 12-Punkt-Schriftgröße, am POS durch. Am POS wirken Drei-Wort-Sätze. Es muss schnell, kurz, laut und umfeldrelevant kommuniziert werden. Der Mehrwert muss sich sofort erschließen. Die Konsumenten möchten direkte Informationen zum Produkt, im Idealfall verbunden mit einem Angebot, das mitnichten immer ein Preisangebot sein muss.

Das ist kein Widerspruch zur orchestrierten Kommunikation, sondern vielmehr deren wirksame Umsetzung. Es gilt, die besonderen Vorzüge des Instruments im Orchester geltend zu machen. Genauso wie beispielsweise die Bläser im Orchester gemeinhin für die lauteren Töne verantwortlich sind, so muss das Instrument POS-Kommunikation die Markenmelodie ausdrucksstark und weithin wahrnehmbar präsentieren.

So ist es keine Überraschung, dass Handzettel und Zweitplatzierungen am POS besonders wirksam sind. Dabei gilt der Handzettel zu Unrecht in der Kommunikationsbranche als Schmuddelkind. Er

the same chant. The result is that campaigns appear at the POS that do not take into account the individuality of retail communication.

Endless copy texts are particularly popular. In magazines they may have a communicative effect by telling the brand's story. At the POS, however, they are completely misplaced. Nobody reads texts like that, possibly even in type size 12. Advertising at the POS needs three-word sentences. The message has to be short, quick and loud and be delivered in accordance with its context. Customers must immediately understand the benefit the product offers. They want direct information about the product, ideally linked to an offer that not necessarily has to be a price offer.

That does not contradict the idea of orchestrated communication, it is its effective realisation. The task is to highlight the strengths of the individual instruments playing in the orchestra. As the wind players in the orchestra usually play the loudest, the instrument POS communication must loudly and clearly play the brand's melody.

It will thus not come as a surprise that flyers and secondary placements have a great effect at the POS. Flyers are wrongly considered the pariah of the communications industry. Their quality has risen considerably and they are undoubtedly an information media for the customer: More than 60 % of customers definitely pay attention to flyers.[3]

In combination with secondary placements, flyers are of particular importance for impulse products. Both attract the necessary attention and represent a platform to effectively present the brand. Here, the brand can be presented in an adequate way and give direct impulses for the selling process.

5. Retailers love orchestration.

Retailers want to sell. They love everything that aids the selling process. That is why retailers are open to clearly structured orchestrated campaigns. They know that by means of these campaigns the advertising spend of above-the-line communication feeds directly through to the POS and supports the sale of a product.

The resistance of more and more retailers against traditional cartons, shelve signs and wobblers consequently mirrors the whole picture. These forms of advertising not only fail to produce the hoped-for effect, they also destroy the harmonious overall impression the sales floors make, an aspect that is of increasing importance to retailers. In the end, personalised customer communication targets both customers and retailers. POS communication must be sold to retailers (sell-in) and take their needs into account as well.

VIII. INTEGRIERTE KOMMUNIKATION: VOM SOLISTEN ZUM ORCHESTER | INTEGRATED COMMUNICATION: FROM SOLOIST TO ORCHESTRA

Abbildung 2: Die Grafik zeigt den prozentualen Anteil, den qualitative Aktionen in den einzelnen Warengruppen ausmachen. Zu qualitativen Promotions zählen Displays und kommunikative Maßnahmen, wie beispielsweise Handzettelwerbung.

hat in letzter Zeit deutlich an Qualität gewonnen und ist einer der Informationsmedien für die Konsumenten: Über 60 % der Kunden schenken ihm konkrete Beachtung.[3]

In Kombination mit Zweitplatzierungen sind Handzettel vor allem bei Impulsprodukten von immanenter Bedeutung. Gemeinsam bringen beide die notwendige Aufmerksamkeit und bieten den Raum, die Marke am POS tatsächlich zu inszenieren. Hier kann sich die Marke adäquat präsentieren und direkte Verkaufsimpulse geben.

5. Der Handel liebt die Orchestrierung.

Der Handel will verkaufen. Er liebt alles, was den Verkauf unterstützt. Deshalb ist der Handel besonders für klar durchdeklinierte orchestrierte Kampagnen offen. Er weiß, dass in diesem Fall die Werbeausgaben der klassischen Kommunikation direkt am POS ihre nachhaltige Wirkung entfalten und den Abverkauf unterstützen.

Es ist nur eine konsequente Abrundung des Gesamtbildes, wenn immer mehr Händler sich gegen die althergebrachten Pappen, Regalschilder und Wobbler wehren. Sie verfehlen nicht nur die erhoffte Wirkung, sondern sie zerstören auch das für den Handel inzwischen immer wichtigere stimmige Gesamtbild seiner Verkaufsflächen. Letztlich bezieht sich die kundenspezifische

Retailers often decide right on the spot whether or not and how to use POS marketing (see figure 3). Decision makers attach particular importance to good ideas, creativity and materials that are both high-end and practical. A glance at the warehouses and waste containers shows that low-quality and ill-conceived POS marketing campaigns often do not reach the sales floors. It is better not to think about how much money and value has been destroyed in that way.

6. A good orchestra needs a big stage.

POS marketing has become more sophisticated over the past years. That applies not only to the content of communication but also to the quality and creativity in developing and producing POS materials.

Today, only communication is used that has been coordinated in the companies' retail departments and complies with retail's idea of "clean store policy". That means that clearly defined sales spaces for brand communication have been made available at retail. The days are over when field workers placed the materials at the POS as they wished after having a cup of coffee with the store manager.

It is exactly this development that highlights the opportunities POS marketing offers for retailers. Supermarkets with a select product offer are increasingly seeking partners from the branded goods industry to stand out against discounters. In their strive to offer customers a unique shopping experience, retailers more than welcome

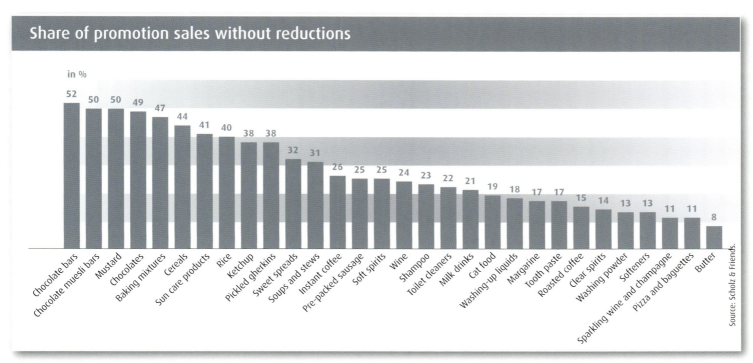

Figure. 2: The graph shows the share of quality promotional activity in the individual product groups. Quality promotions include displays and communication means such as flyer advertising.

Ansprache nicht nur auf die Konsumenten, sondern ebenfalls auf den Handel. Die POS-Kommunikation muss auch in den Handel hineinverkauft werden (Sell-in) und seine Ansprüche berücksichtigen.

Der Handel entscheidet in hohem Maße und oft erst vor Ort, ob und wie die POS-Kommunikation tatsächlich platziert wird (siehe Abbildung 3). Dabei legen die Entscheidungsträger Wert auf gute Ideen, auf eine hohe Kreativität und auf hochwertige und praktikabel einsetzbare Materialien. Ein Blick in die Tiefen der Lager und Sperrmüllcontainer zeigt, dass minderwertige und nicht durchdachte POS-Kommunikationsansätze zu häufig den Gang auf die Handelsfläche gar nicht schaffen. Man mag gar nicht daran denken, welche Werte über diesen Weg schon vernichtet wurden.

6. Ein gutes Orchester braucht eine große Bühne.

POS-Kommunikation ist in den letzten Jahren anspruchsvoller geworden. Das betrifft nicht nur den Inhalt der Kommunikation, sondern auch die Qualität und Kreativität bei der Entwicklung und Produktion der POS-Materialien.

Heute wird nur noch die Kommunikation platziert, die vorher zentral in den Handelszentralen abgesprochen wurde und die sich in das Bild der „Clean-Store-Policy" des Handels einfügt. Das bedeutet, dass klar definierte Flächen im Handel für Markenkommunika-

sophisticated ideas and concepts for the presentation of brands and products. Brands have to seize these opportunities. It presents them with nothing less than the desired possibility to present their brands at the POS in the best possible way.

The brand must not only be presented in an adequate way, the presentation must also be realised in a way that can and must meet the highest standards in design, size and content and, most importantly, in the materials and displays used at the POS. Without doubt these ways of presentation are more expensive than traditional presentations. The benefit is a more adequate presentation for the brand and an increased visibility. It also offers the possibility of a permanent presentation and permanent presence that can be tailored to the special needs of retailers and their customers.

The future challenge will be to create an adequate stage for the sophisticated brand orchestra at the POS. Speed is also an issue. Every stage is unique and retailers will allocate space used for presentation to a product category only once. All other product categories run the risk of becoming travelling buskers at the POS.

7. Orchestrated communication can unfold only in an orchestra.

It is a long way from production to the shelve and many POS campaigns stand little chance of making it to the sales area. Consequently, communication at the POS must be targeted and largely visible.

Abbildung/Figure 3

tion zur Verfügung stehen und die Zeiten vorbei sind, in denen der Außendienst die Materialien nach einem gemeinsamen Kaffee mit dem Marktleiter nach Gutdünken im Markt platzieren konnte.

Doch gerade in dieser Entwicklung liegt für die Marken die entscheidende Chance der POS-Kommunikation. Gut sortierte Supermärkte suchen inzwischen in der notwendigen Abgrenzung von den Discountern nach Partnern aus der Markenartikelindustrie. Im Bestreben des Handels, Einkaufserlebnisse zu ermöglichen, sind hochwertige Ideen und Konzepte zur Marken- und Produktpräsentation mehr als willkommen. Die Marken müssen diese Chance nutzen. Nichts ist wichtiger, als die lang ersehnte Möglichkeit einer Markeninszenierung am POS zu forcieren.

Dazu gehört neben der zur Marke passenden Präsentationsidee auch eine Umsetzung, die in der Gestaltung, in Größe und Umfang und vor allem in der Qualität der verwendeten POS-Materialien und Displays höchsten Ansprüchen genügen kann und muss. Ohne Frage sind diese Präsentationsformen teurer als herkömmliche Produktionen. Sie zahlen sich jedoch nicht nur über eine höhere Wahrnehmung und eine markengerechte Präsentation aus, sondern auch über die damit verbundene Möglichkeit einer Dauerplatzierung und Dauerpräsenz, die darüber hinaus noch für den jeweiligen Handel kundenindividuell gestaltet werden kann.

Die zukünftigen Herausforderungen liegen darin, dem hochwertigen Markenorchester eine adäquate Bühne am POS zu bauen.

Using a limited number of identical advertising means in all stores in a country often proves ineffective. It makes more sense to reach a higher visibility at the stores of select retail partners. The objective is to make all instruments available to the brand at every POS and communicate with customers on their way to POS.

The customer's journey starts outside the POS, continues in the entrance area and right up to the shelve or secondary placement. This means that POS communication in the store also needs its own orchestration and, in the ideal case, the brand will send a chamber orchestra to the POS. Orchestration at the POS ensures that both brand and product are actually noticed. Experience has shown that at least three touch points are needed at the POS (see figure 4) to really get customers' attention and encourage them to buy.

8. The grand finale of communication takes place at the POS.

No crystal ball is needed to anticipate that POS communication will become increasingly important. The potential of effective retail communication has not been fully explored. Especially in times when the effectiveness of communication for the sale process is questioned, POS communication will become a growing focus of interest.

It would be a false conclusion, however, to believe that retail communication can replace other forms of communication. Every

Dabei geht es auch um Schnelligkeit. Denn genauso wie es jede Bühne nur einmal gibt, wird der Handel diese Präsentationsflächen je Produktkategorie nur einmal vergeben. Wer zuletzt kommt, steht vor dem Risiko, zumindest am POS als „Straßenmusikant" zu enden.

7. Orchestrierte Kommunikation entfaltet ihre Kraft nur im Orchester.

Der Weg vom Hersteller ins Regal ist weit, viele POS-Kampagnen bekommen nicht einmal die Chance, in das Sichtfeld der Konsumenten zu kommen. Deshalb gilt gerade am POS: Kommunikation muss konzentriert und breit aufgestellt sein. Eine landesweite Bearbeitung aller denkbaren Märkte mit wenigen Werbemitteln verfehlt häufig ihre Wirkung. Es macht deutlich mehr Sinn, bei ausgewählten Handelspartnern eine breite Sichtbarkeit zu erreichen. Es gilt, die verschiedenen verfügbaren Instrumente an jedem POS für die Marke nutzbar zu machen und den Weg der Konsumenten am POS kommunikativ zu begleiten.

Dieser Weg beginnt im Umfeld des POS, setzt sich über den Eingangsbereich fort und führt den Konsumenten direkt an das Regal oder zur vereinbarten Zweitplatzierung. Das heißt, auch POS-Kommunikation vor Ort braucht eine eigene Orchestrierung, und im Idealfall schickt die Marke ein kleines, aber exzellentes Kammerorchester an den POS. Dieser orchestrierte Auftritt garantiert, dass Marke und Produkt tatsächlich wahrgenommen werden. Erfahrungen zeigen, dass mindestens drei Touchpoints (siehe Abbildung 4) notwendig sind, um eine signifikante und zielführende Wahrnehmung zu erreichen.

8. Das kommunikative Finale findet am POS statt.

Es ist keine Hellseherei zu behaupten, dass POS-Kommunikation an Bedeutung gewinnen wird. Das Potenzial einer wirksamen Handelskommunikation ist noch längst nicht ausgeschöpft. Gerade in Zeiten, die auch von der Kommunikation einen direkten Wirksamkeitsnachweis in Bezug auf den Verkauf verlangen, wird die POS-Kommunikation stärker in den Fokus rücken.

Es ist jedoch ein Trugschluss zu glauben, dass Handelskommunikation andere Kommunikationsformen ersetzen kann. Jedes Instrument hat seine individuellen Stärken, und die Herausforderung besteht vielmehr in der Entwicklung orchestrierter Kommunikationskonzepte, die den Gesamtklang der Marke über alle Bereiche und in allen Kanälen wirksam erlebbar und präsent machen.

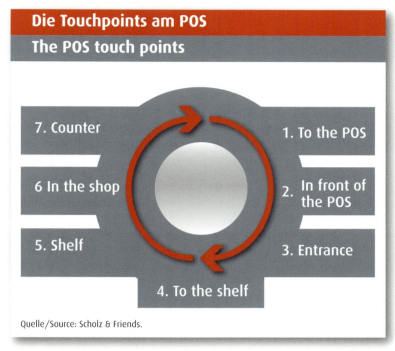

Quelle/Source: Scholz & Friends.

Abbildung/Figure 4

instrument has its individual strengths, so the challenge is rather to create orchestrated communication concepts that make the brand's overall sound an effective experience and presence across all areas and channels.

Frank-Michael Schmidt   Henk Knaupe

IX. | DIE ZUKUNFT DES DISPLAYS | THE FUTURE OF THE DISPLAY

DIE ZUKUNFT DES DISPLAYS
THE FUTURE OF THE DISPLAY

Christoph Häberle
Die Zukunft des Displays

Keine Branche ist dem Verbraucher und seinen Wünschen näher als der Einzelhandel. Resultierend aus ökonomischen und soziokulturellen Veränderungen der Gesellschaft entwickeln Verbraucher permanent neue Formen des Kaufverhaltens. Im Folgenden soll daher eine grobe Beschreibung elementarer gesellschaftlicher Strömungen helfen, potenzielle Auswirkungen auf zukünftige Funktionen des Displays erschließen zu können. Zwei eng miteinander verbundene Entwicklungen sind hier entscheidend:

1. Strukturelle und wirtschaftliche Entwicklungen im Einzelhandel
2. Allgemeine soziokulturelle Entwicklungen in der Gesellschaft

Hybrides Kaufverhalten statt Power-Shopping

Wie sehr Einkaufen als Freizeitbeschäftigung in unserem Bewusstsein verankert ist, veranschaulicht die bekannte, witzig-ironische Begriffsschöpfung „Power-Shopping". Die ernsthaften Folgen übersteigerten Konsumverhaltens in Form privater Überschuldung, Privatinsolvenzen oder krankhafter Kaufsucht füllen immer häufiger öffentliche Schlagzeilen. Die wachsende private wie öffentliche Verschuldung limitieren zunehmend die Konsummöglichkeiten von Privathaushalten und Staat und damit das systembedingende Wirtschaftswachstum. Besonders in den letzten zehn Jahren sind heftige und immer rascher aufeinanderfolgende Phasenwechsel zwischen wirtschaftlicher Rezession (wie z. B. 2001–2003, 2005 und 2008–2009) und kurzen, weniger intensiven Konjunkturschüben zu beobachten. Vor diesem volkswirtschaftlichen Hintergrund erklärt sich der seit mehreren Jahren langsam vollziehende Wandel zum „hybriden Kaufverhalten". Die Verknappung der verfügbaren Mittel der Privathaushalte erzwingt zunehmend einen ökonomischeren Umgang in Form einer effizienten Kombination aus niedrigstpreisigen und hochpreisigen Produkten.

Oberste Handlungsmaxime: Effizienz

Für Kunden, Hersteller und Handel gilt mehr denn je Effizienz als oberste Handlungsmaxime. Für den Einzelhandel bedeu-

Christoph Häberle
The future of the display

No industry is closer to consumers and their desires than the retail industry. Consumers are constantly changing their buying behaviour as a reaction to economic and socio-cultural changes in society. The following rough description of fundamental societal trends aims at helping retailers to identify factors that could possibly influence the display's functions in the future. Two closely linked developments are decisive in this context:

1. Structural and economic developments at retail
2. General socio-cultural developments in society

Hybrid buying behaviour instead of power shopping

The well-known, humorous and ironic coinage "power shopping" shows how deeply shopping is rooted in the minds of people as a pastime. More and more frequently, we read about the serious implications of excessive consumption in the headlines, leading to increasing personal indebtedness, personal insolvencies or compulsive buying. The rise in the personal and public accumulation of debt is increasingly impeding consumption of both private households and the state, thus limiting economic growth. In the past ten years, in particular, the periods of economic downturns have become longer and intervals between recessions shorter (i.e. 2001 – 2003, 2005 and 2008 – 2009), while economic upturns have been less frequent and intensive. Against this economic backdrop, gradually, the phenomenon of "hybrid buying behaviour" has developed in recent years. In view of the declining disposable income of private households, consumers are forced to manage their budgets more tightly by efficiently combining discounter purchases with purchases of high priced products.

Key guiding principle: Efficiency

Efficiency is the key guiding principle for customers, manufacturers and retailers alike. For the selling strategies of retailers this means achieving the highest possible efficiency in their

tet dies verkaufsstrategisch höchste Effizienz in Sortiments-, Ein- und Verkaufs- sowie Distributionspolitik. Der europäische Einzelhandel befindet sich während der letzten zehn Jahre in einem fundamentalen strukturellen Wandel. Speziell in Deutschland tobt aktuell ein unerbittlicher Preiskrieg und ein massiver Verdrängungswettbewerb. Durch Fusionen, Übernahmen und Aufkäufe entsteht zunehmend eine vertikale Konzentration im Einzelhandel in Form filialisierender Unternehmensgruppen, die wiederum Bestandteil von Konzernen sind, die auch im Großhandel tätig sind. Große Abnahmemengen vergünstigen die Einkaufskonditionen, welche wiederum als Preisreduktion an den Verbraucher weitergegeben werden können. Das Preisniveau im deutschen Lebensmitteleinzelhandel ist innerhalb eines Jahrzehnts auf das niedrigste in Europa gesunken. Die Effizienz des Selbstbedienungsprinzips verbunden mit massiven Einsparungen von Personalkosten scheint hierfür unumstößliche Bedingung zu sein. Die kundenrelevante Entwicklung der Sortimentsstruktur (Auswahl an Produkten) bestimmt mehr und mehr die Effizienz eines Unternehmens und wird zum ausschlaggebenden Argument für dessen Wirtschaftlichkeit. Allein aus Effizienzgründen befinden sich Handelsmarken bzw. „Private Labels" ungebrochen auf dem Vormarsch. Schwache Herstellermarken werden am Markt substituiert, lediglich starken, häufig historisch gewachsenen, nicht imitierbaren Herstellermarken und wenigen neuen Herstellermarken wenngleich nur unter enormen Marketinganstrengungen gelingt der dauerhafte Verbleib im Markt.

Vergrößerung der Verkaufsfläche versus Urbanisierung

Ungebrochen ist dabei die Tendenz zur Vergrößerung der Verkaufsfläche und zu steigendem Umsatz bei gleichzeitiger Verringerung der Anzahl der Einzelhandelsbetriebe. Während die zehn größten Handelshäuser 1990 einen Marktanteil von 45 % auf sich vereinten, erreichten sie bereits 2004 84 %. Die Analyse der Umsatzentwicklung verschiedener Einzelhandelsformate lässt momentan eine deutliche Tendenz zu Discount- und Verbrauchermärkten mit eingeschränktem Warensortiment erkennen. Der Vergrößerung der Verkaufsfläche steht jedoch eine Entwicklung entgegen: die Urbanisierung. Mit zunehmendem „Entwicklungsstand" (Human Development Index) eines Landes ist eine deutliche Tendenz zur Verstädterung zu beobachten. Während 1920 in Europa etwa 34,7 % der Bevölkerung in Städten lebte, waren dies 1960 44,2 % und 2000 bereits 75 %. Gerade in großen Ballungszentren limitieren jedoch die begrenzten und teuren Innenstadtlagen inklusive benötigter Parkmöglichkeiten die Flächenausdehnung großer Einzelhandelsformate. Hier ist momentan eine Tendenz zu kleineren Verbrauchermärkten zu beobachten. Speziell älteren Menschen in Städten kommt diese Versorgungsform auch aufgrund kurzer Wege, sozialer Anbin-

product range, buying and selling and distribution policies. Retail in Europe has been experiencing fundamental structural change in the past ten years. Germany, in particular, is witnessing fierce price wars and massive cutthroat competition. Mergers, acquisitions and takeovers are leading to increasing consolidation at retail, creating more and more vertical retail chains. These chains, in turn, are usually part of large groups that, apart from retail, operate in the wholesale business as well. The buying of large amounts of merchandise improves buying conditions and allows retailers to pass price reductions on to the consumer. Price levels at food retail in Europe have fallen to a ten-year low. The efficiency of self-service combined with massive payroll cost cuts appears to be an absolute prerequisite for lowest price levels. The efficiency of a company is increasingly dependent on how customer-oriented its offer (choice of products) is and will decide on how profitable the company is. For reasons of efficiency alone, retail brands, or "private labels", are continuing to gain ground at retail. Weak manufacturer's brands will be replaced, only strong manufacturer's brands, often with a rich heritage and impossible to imitate, as well as a limited number of new manufacturer's brands will manage to survive in the market in the long run, and they will survive only by making enormous marketing efforts.

Expansion of retail space versus increasing urbanisation

There is an ongoing trend towards larger stores and higher sales volumes while, at the same time, the number of retail companies is declining. In 1990, the ten leading retailers together accounted for a market share of 45 %. In 2004, that figure reached 84 %. When analysing the sales development of different retail formats it becomes clear that the trend is towards discounters and hypermarkets with a limited product offer. Expansion of retail space, however, is hampered by increasing urbanisation. Countries with a high "human development" (Human Development Index) show high rates of urbanisation. In 1920, 34,7 % of Europe's population lived in cities. That figure increased to 44,2 % in 1960 and to 75 % in 2000. In areas of high population density, however, limited sites and high rents in prime locations as well as necessary parking space make it difficult for large retailers to add space. This is leading to an obvious trend towards smaller stores. Elderly people in cities, in particular, are benefiting from this trend, because they do not have to walk too far to the store, are better involved in social life and are offered more assistance in-store. Rising energy prices further this development because shorter distances mean more time and less costs. In times of declining disposable income they reduce expenses and increase efficiency.

dung und etwas höherer Kundenberatung entgegen. Unterstützt wird diese Entwicklung auch durch steigende Energiepreise, kurze Wege sind zeit- und kostensparend und tragen angesichts der Verknappung verfügbarer Mittel zur Reduzierung von Ausgaben und höherer Effizienz bei.

Dem Bestreben des Einzelhandels zur möglichst effizienten Standardisierung des Sortiments stehen wie beschrieben die Anforderungen des Verbrauchers entgegen. Obwohl dem Handel eine immer zentralere und mächtigere Position zukommt, entscheidet letztlich immer die Kompatibiliät zu Kundenvorstellungen über den Erfolg eines Einzelhandelsunternehmens. Der Verbraucher ist dabei in seinem Verhalten grundlegend beeinflusst von den gesellschaftlichen Bedingungen seines Lebensumfeldes. Hierzu zählen die aktuellen, hinlänglich bekannten Entwicklungen, wie soziodemografische Überalterung der Gesellschaft, wachsende Anzahl von Singlehaushalten, Fragmentierung der Familienstrukturen, wachsender Zeitdruck mit Stresssymptomen, ungesündere Ernährung in Verbindung mit körperlichem Übergewicht, zunehmende globale Vernetzung, wachsender Wohlstand in Verbindung mit wachsender Verschuldung, rasch wechselnde Wirtschaftsschwankungen – Phasen heftiger Rezession mit drohender Arbeitslosigkeit in immer rascherem Wechsel mit kurzen Konjunkturphasen, steigende Gefahr des Verlustes sozialer Sicherheit, zunehmender Zwang zu wirtschaftlicher Effizienz etc.

Wandel des Verbraucherverhaltens

Vor diesem Hintergrund wandelt sich das Verbraucherverhalten massiv. Während sich in der breiten Masse bis 2003 noch mit dem Slogan „Geiz ist Geil" die „Ich will alles und sofort"-Mentalität aktivieren ließ, entsteht sowohl durch Einsicht aus negativer Erfahrung mit Billigschnäppchen und deren Haltbarkeit als auch unter dem wachsenden Zwang zu effizientem Wirtschaften eine neue Qualitätsvorstellung, die langfristigere Effizienz verspricht. Die Marke erlebt dabei als Sicherheit gebendes Garantiesiegel für Qualität eine neue Bedeutung in Bezug auf Effizienz, vorausgesetzt das Budget des Kunden gestattet dies. Die Preis-Leistungsbeurteilung des Verbrauchers wird zunehmend differenzierter

As described earlier, consumer requirements are hindering retailers in their ambition to standardise their product offer as they attempt to be as efficient as possible. Even though the influence and power of retailers is rising continuously, success will always depend on their capability of responding adequately to their customers' needs. And consumer behaviour is fundamentally influenced by the social conditions people live in. These include recent, well-known, socio-demographic developments like ageing populations, the increase in single households, the breakdown of traditional family structures, increasing time pressure accompanied by stress symptoms, unhealthy eating accompanied by overweight, globalisation, increasing wealth paired with increasing accumulation of debt, the rapid succession of intense recession with the threat of unemployment and short economic upturns, the growing risk of falling out of the social security system, increasing pressure to be economically efficient etc.

Changing of consumer behavior

Consumer behaviour is changing radically against this backdrop. In 2003, slogans like Saturn's "Cheap is cool" ("Geiz ist geil") still managed to create an "I want everything now" ("Ich will alles und sofort") mentality. Today, the bad experiences customers have had with discount products and their poor durability paired with constraints on income and spending are prompting them to embrace a knew concept of quality that promises longer-lasting efficiency. As confidence-inspiring warranties of quality, brands are taking on new significance in terms of efficiency, provided the customer can afford to buy the brand. Consumers will grow increasingly sensitive and discerning when it comes to the question of value for money. Surely, these reflections about efficiency appear to somewhat contradict the prediction that the mid-market will break down while the discount and small luxury industries will flourish.

The change in the customer's attitude is accompanied by a public debate over the "sustainability" of people's actions in connection with long-term efficiency considerations. As the

und kritischer ausfallen. Diese Effizienzüberlegungen arbeiten sicherlich etwas gegen das propagierte Verschwinden des mittleren Marktsegmentes zugunsten eines großen Billig- und kleinen Luxussektors.

Begleitet wird dieser Haltungswandel des Verbrauchers durch die wachsende öffentliche Diskussion um „Nachhaltigkeit" unseres Handelns in Verbindung mit langfristigeren Effizienzbetrachtungen. Mit zunehmender Labilität des Wirtschaftssystems formt sich nach und nach die Einsicht, dass die Vorstellung von grenzenlosem Wachstum und Wohlstand für alle womöglich Utopie ist. Vor dieser Erfahrung werden auch die Folgen unseres Handelns wie z. B. die technische Umweltverschmutzung, deren Folgen zunehmend Kosten verursacht, ebenso wie die psychosozialen Folgen und Folgekosten im gesellschaftlichen Umgang mit anderer Gewichtung bewertet. Nachdem zehn Jahre lang die Verführung zu „Luxus" und „Status" als sozial differenzierendes und wirtschaftlich lukratives Wertschöpfungspotenzial ausgereizt wurde, wandelt sich nun der „Luxusbegriff" unter dem Einwirken beschriebener Entwicklungen massiv. Gegenüber der egoistischen „Ich will alles und sofort"-Haltung setzt sich – wenn auch sehr langsam – eine neue, womöglich aus der Not geborene „Wir"-Haltung durch (vgl. den Wahlslogan von Barack Obama: „Yes we can" oder ähnlichen aus der aktuellen deutschen Bundestagswahl). Zunehmend werden wir uns der Folgen unseres Handelns bewusst und versuchen langfristigere Ziele zu formulieren. Dabei werden vermehrt wirtschaftliche, moralische und ethische Bewertungskriterien eingeführt und ein neues Bewusstsein für effizientes und verantwortliches Handeln auch für unsere nachfolgenden Generationen beginnt zu entstehen.

Fazit – Das Display der Zukunft

Vorauszusehen, welche neuartigen Anforderungen dem Display in Zukunft zukommen werden, ist sicherlich nur schwer möglich. Während in der Vergangenheit das Display verstärkt mit der Generierung von bedingungslosem Mehrkonsum betraut wurde, werden dem Display im Zuge „nachhaltiger" Strategien wieder verstärkt sachorientierte Funktionen der Effizienzsteigerung zukommen:

- Berücksichtigung „nachhaltiger" Strategien, z. B. Ökobilanz eingesetzter Materialien, kurze Produktionswege, moralisch-ethische Anforderungen wie Sicherung lokaler Arbeitsplätze, sozial verträgliche Arbeitsbedingungen etc.
- Verstärkte Kommunikation des Preis-Leistungsverhältnisses, qualitative Repräsentation der Marke
- Generierung von Einsparpotenzial im Bereich der In-Store-Logistik: Präsentation vorkonfektionierter Ware, Bewahrung eines Ordnungsprinzips trotz Selbstbedienung, Vermeidung von Pflegeaufwand der Warenpräsentation und damit Perso-

economic system grows increasingly unstable, people are gradually starting to realise that unlimited growth and wealth for everyone may be Utopia. Under the influence of this insight, people now judge and weigh the consequences of their actions differently in society. The consequences of their actions include technical pollution, which is increasingly creating costs, as well as psycho-social implications and consequential costs. After ten years of tempting consumers towards "luxury" and "status" to create social differentiation and potential profitable value, the concept of luxury and its perception in society is undergoing dramatic change as a result of the described developments and influences. Albeit very slowly, a new "we" attitude (consider Barack Obama's electoral slogan "Yes we can", or similar recent electoral slogans in other countries), born possibly from necessity, is starting to prevail over the self-centred "I want everything now" attitude. People are increasingly aware of the implications of their actions and attempt to set longer-term objectives for themselves. In doing so, they are increasingly adopting economic, moral and ethical evaluation criteria. This is creating a growing awareness for efficient and responsible actions that is passed on also to the following generations.

Conclusion – the display of the future

Surely, it is rather difficult to predict what new requirements the display will be facing in the future. In the past, it was the display's implicit function to make customers buy more, but, as retailers increasingly pursue "sustainable" strategies, they will use the display as a means of increasing efficiency, in a more targeted way, again:

- *"Sustainable" strategies, i.e. the ecological footprint of the used materials, shorter production cycles, moral and ethical requirements like safeguarding local jobs, decent working conditions etc., are taken into consideration*
- *Value-for-money is better communicated to the customer, the focus of the brand's presentation is on quality*
- *Potential is created to cut logistical costs in-store: presentation of pre-packed goods, a certain level of order and organisation is maintained despite self-service, product presentation requires no maintenance, there are no potential personnel costs that must be passed on to the product's price*
- *The flexibility of the individual retail formats is safeguarded: the display can be easily used for changing product ranges, i.e. for special offers that are not limited to permanent shelves*
- *Space is saved, which improves orientation in a product assortment that tends to be increasingly diversified*

These observations show clearly that the display's function always reflects the societal and economic conditions of a certain period.

IX. DIE ZUKUNFT DES DISPLAYS | THE FUTURE OF THE DISPLAY

nalkosten, welche auf den Produktpreis umzulegen sind
- Gewährleistung der Flexibilität der Einzelhandelsformate: flexible Anpassung an wechselndes Produktsortiment z. B. im Bereich von Aktionswaren ohne Bindung an fixe Regalsysteme
- Raumbildende Funktion zur Verbesserung der Orientierung in zunehmend zur Diversifizierung neigendem Warensortiment

Die Ausführungen zeigen deutlich, dass die Funktionen des Displays immer eine Reflexion gesellschaftlicher und ökonomischer Bedingungen einer bestimmten Zeit sind. Immer steht das Display dabei an vorderster Front der Verkaufsförderung, es ist der Katalysator in der Kunde-Produkt-Beziehung:

- Es konfrontiert den Kunden mit der Ware und bietet diese produktadäquat an.
- Es verringert die Distanz zwischen Kunde und Ware.
- Es fokussiert die Aufmerksamkeit auf die Ware.
- Es schafft formale Differenzierung gegenüber Wettbewerberprodukten.
- Es verbessert die Orientierung in einem unübersichtlichen Warensortiment.
- Es kommuniziert dem Betrachter inhaltlich die Qualitäten eines Produktes, dessen Marke und evoziert Wertvorstellungen in unserem Bewusstsein.
- Es fordert vom Betrachter mentale Auseinandersetzung und verankert sich bleibend in der Erinnerung.

In this context, the display is the key means of sales promotion, it acts as a catalyst in the relationship between the customer and the product:

- *It confronts the customer with the product and presents the product in an adequate way.*
- *It reduces the distance between the customer and the product.*
- *It focuses the customer's attention on the product.*
- *It formally distinguishes the product from competitor products.*
- *It improves orientation in a confusing product assortment.*
- *It communicates the product's qualities to customers and evokes value propositions in their minds.*
- *It forces the customer to mentally engage with the product, it makes a lasting impression and will not be forgotten by the customer.*

Christoph Häberle

ABBILDUNGS-, QUELLEN- UND LITERATURNACHWEISE | REFERENCE

ABBILDUNGS-, QUELLEN- UND LITERATURNACHWEISE
REFERENCE

X. ABBILDUNGS-, QUELLEN- UND LITERATURNACHWEISE | REFERENCE

I. Die Ursprünge des Displays – Von der Antike bis zur Selbstbedienung

Sophie Wittl, Christoph Häberle

Abbildungen

Abbildung Kapitelseite
Wandbild aus Grab 1 der Pyramide von Sakkara
(angelehnt an) Hardach, G.; Schilling, J. (1980): Das Buch vom Markt – Eine Wirtschafts und Kulturgeschichte, Luzern/Frankfurt am Main

Abbildung 1
Geflügelverkauf, dargestellt auf einem Sarkophag aus Ostia
Weeber, K.-W. (2000): Alltag im Alten Rom, Düsseldorf/Zürich

Abbildung 2
Straßenszene in Pompeji
Sédillot, R. (1966): Vom Tauschhandel zum Supermarkt – Die Story der Händler und Märkte, Stuttgart

Abbildung 3
Laden für Lebensmittel und Haushaltswaren, um 1390
Österreichische Nationalbibliothek, Wien, C 30091-C (=Cod. S.N. 2644, fol. 46r)

Abbildung 4
Fliegender Händler mit Bauchladen, um 1480
Proverbes en rimes, Walters Art Museum, Baltimore

Abbildung 5
Tante-Emma-Laden
Wikipedia
http://de.wikipedia.org/w/index.php?title=Datei:Lebensmittel-einzelhandel_in_den_1950er.jpg&filetimestamp=20070421105509

Abbildung 6
Versandschachteln, die gleichzeitig als Thekendisplay dienten, links 1905, rechts 1933
Dr. August Oetker Firmenarchiv

Abbildung 7
Verkaufsschränke „Dr. Oetker" für 300 bzw. 500 Päckchen, 1914 Dr. August Oetker Firmenarchiv

Abbildung 8
Haus, aus Persilpackungen gebaut
Konzernarchiv der Henkel AG & Co. KGaA

Abbildung 9
Display „Persil" mit Roll-Palette, 1966/67
Konzernarchiv der Henkel AG & Co. KGaA

Abbildung 10
Bodendisplay „Pretty Hair", 1969
Konzernarchiv der Henkel AG & Co. KGaA

Abbildung 11
Bodendisplay „Perla", 1960er Jahre
Konzernarchiv der Henkel AG & Co. KGaA

Abbildung 12
Augsburg, erster Selbstbedienungsladen
Bundesarchiv, Bild 183-2005-0807-506

I. The Origins of the Display – From Antiquity to Self-Service

Sophie Wittl, Christoph Häberle

Illustrations

Chapter opening page illustrations
Mural from tomb 1 of the Saqqara pyramid
(based on) Hardach, G.; Schilling, J. (1980): Das Buch vom Markt – Eine Wirtschafts und Kulturgeschichte, Luzern/Frankfurt am Main

Figure 1
The sale of poultry as shown on a sarcophagus from Ostia
Weeber, K.-W. (2000): Alltag im Alten Rom, Düsseldorf/Zürich

Figure 2
Street scene in Pompei
Sédillot, R. (1966): Vom Tauschhandel zum Supermarkt – Die Story der Händler und Märkte, Stuttgart

Figure 3
Food and houseware store, around 1390
Österreichische Nationalbibliothek, Wien, C 30091-C (=Cod. S.N. 2644, fol. 46r)

Figure 4
Hawker with vending tray, around 1480
Proverbes en rimes, Walters Art Museum, Baltimore

Figure 5
Corner Shop
Wikipedia
http://de.wikipedia.org/w/index.php?title=Datei:Lebensmitteleinzelhandel_in_den_1950er.jpg&filetimestamp=20070421105509

Figure 6
Shipping boxes that could also be used as counter displays, left 1905, right 1933
Dr. August Oetker Firmenarchiv

Figure 7
"Dr Oetker" display cabinets for 300 or 500 packs, 1914
Dr. August Oetker Firmenarchiv

Figure 8
House built of Persil packs
Konzernarchiv der Henkel AG & Co. KGaA

Figure 9
"Persil" roll pallet display, 1966/1967
Konzernarchiv der Henkel AG & Co. KGaA

Figure 10
"Pretty Hair" floor stand display, 1969
Konzernarchiv der Henkel AG & Co. KGaA

Figure 11
"Perla" floor stand display, 1960s
Konzernarchiv der Henkel AG & Co. KGaA

Figure 12
The first self-service store in Augsburg
Bundesarchiv, Bild 183-2005-0807-506

Abbildung 13
Bodendisplay „Plantschi", 1960er Jahre
Firmenarchiv STI Group, Lauterbach

Figure 13
"Plantschi" floor stand display, 1960s
STI Group

Literatur- und Quellenangaben

[1] Reitz, M. (1999): Alltag im alten Ägypten, Augsburg
[2] Gutgesell, M. (2004): Wirtschaft und Handel, in: R. Schulz und M. Seidel (Hrsg.): Ägypten – Die Welt der Pharaonen, Königswinter
[3] Strauß-Seeber, C. (2004): Geschenke des Nils – Agrarwirtschaft einer Flußoase, in: R. Schulz und M. Seidel (Hrsg.): Ägypten – Die Welt der Pharaonen, Königswinter
[4] Barceló, P. (2005): Kleine römische Geschichte, Darmstadt
[5] Weeber, K.-W. (2000): Alltag im Alten Rom, Düsseldorf/Zürich
[6] Spufford, P. (2004): Handel, Macht und Reichtum, Stuttgart
[7] Bohner, T. (1955): Der offene Laden – Aus der Chronik des Einzelhandels, Frankfurt am Main
[8] Metzger, W. (2002): Handel und Handwerk des Mittelalters im Spiegel der Buchmalerei, Graz
[9] Buchli, H. (1962): 6000 Jahre Werbung, Bd. 1, Berlin
[10] Spiekermann, U. (1999): Basis der Konsumgesellschaft: Entstehung und Entwicklung des modernen Kleinhandels in Deutschland, München
[11] Berekoven, L. (1986): Geschichte des deutschen Einzelhandels, Frankfurt am Main
[12] Andersen, A. (1997): Der Traum vom guten Leben. Alltags- und Konsumgeschichte vom Wirtschaftswunder bis heute, Frankfurt am Main

Bibliography

[1] *Reitz, M. (1999): Alltag im alten Ägypten, Augsburg*
[2] *Gutgesell, M. (2004): Wirtschaft und Handel, in: R. Schulz und M. Seidel (ed.): Ägypten – Die Welt der Pharaonen, Königswinter*
[3] *Strauß-Seeber, C. (2004): Geschenke des Nils – Agrarwirtschaft einer Flußoase, in: R. Schulz und M. Seidel (ed.): Ägypten – Die Welt der Pharaonen, Königswinter*
[4] *Barceló, P. (2005): Kleine römische Geschichte, Darmstadt*
[5] *Weeber, K.-W. (2000): Alltag im Alten Rom, Düsseldorf/Zürich*
[6] *Spufford, P. (2004): Handel, Macht und Reichtum, Stuttgart*
[7] *Bohner, T. (1955): Der offene Laden – Aus der Chronik des Einzelhandels, Frankfurt am Main*
[8] *Metzger, W. (2002): Handel und Handwerk des Mittelalters im Spiegel der Buchmalerei, Graz*
[9] *Buchli, H. (1962): 6000 Jahre Werbung, Vol. 1, Berlin*
[10] *Spiekermann, U. (1999): Basis der Konsumgesellschaft: Entstehung und Entwicklung des modernen Kleinhandels in Deutschland, München*
[11] *Berekoven, L. (1986): Geschichte des deutschen Einzelhandels, Frankfurt am Main*
[12] *Andersen, A. (1997): Der Traum vom guten Leben. Alltags- und Konsumgeschichte vom Wirtschaftswunder bis heute, Frankfurt am Main*

II. Die Entwicklung des POS-Marketings

Bernd Hallier

Abbildungen

Abbildung 6, Seite 33
Modernes Einkaufszentrum: Europa Passage in Hamburg
Allianz Center Management GmbH

Abbildung 7, Seite 34
Moderne Zahlprozesse funktionieren wahlweise via Mobiltelefon oder Fingerabdruck.
Metro Future Store

II. The Development of POS Marketing

Bernd Hallier

Illustrations

Figure 6, page 33
A modern Shopping center: The Europa Passage in Hamburg
Allianz Center Management GmbH

Figure 7, page 34
Modern payment processes include payment by mobile phone or fingerprint.
Metro Future Store

III. „Draußen zuhause": Markenführung – Am Point of Sale
Acht POS-Biografien besonders prominenter Marken

Hans-Georg Böcher

Abbildungen

GILLETTE

Abbildung, Seite 41
Früh krümmt sich... Echte Männer können mit dem Rasieren gar nicht jung genug anfangen. Anzeige aus der Frühzeit der Marke.
Procter & Gamble, Company Archive

Abbildungen, Seite 42/43
Der „Safety Razor" diente von Beginn der Etablierung eines Systems,

III. "At home outdoors": Brand Management – At the Point of Sale
Eight exemplary POS biographies of well-known brands

Hans-Georg Böcher

Illustrations

GILLETTE

Figure, page 41
Practice makes perfect. For real men, it is never too early to start shaving. Advertisement in the brand's early years.
Procter & Gamble, Company Archive

Figures, page 42/43
Right from the beginning, the „safety razor" aimed to establish a system

X. ABBILDUNGS-, QUELLEN- UND LITERATURNACHWEISE | REFERENCE

das auf den Vertrieb der Klingen zielte. Diese trugen das Bildnis des Unternehmers um die Welt.
Procter & Gamble, Company Archive

In Deutschland nahm das Produkt in einem solchen Etui seinen Anfang. Eine beigefügte Bedienungsanleitung illustrierte mit Grafiken umständlich, wie die Selbstrasur stattzufinden habe (um 1908).
Copyright: The Boecher Brand & Package Design Collection, Wiesbaden

King Camp Gillette war nicht nur ein Erfinder, sondern auch ein Pionier des Marketing. Er wusste sich selbst als sein eigener „Testimonial" exzellent in Szene zu setzen.
Procter & Gamble, Company Archive

Gillette, der auch als Autor sozialutopischer Bücher auf sich aufmerksam machte, war durch das Konterfei auf jeder Klinge eines der bekanntesten Gesichter der Welt. Er starb (als Folge des Börsencrashs) als armer Mann.
Procter & Gamble, Company Archive

Abbildungen, Seite 44/45
Zur Einführung seines „Safety Razor" setzte Gillette Packungen ein, die den Charakter von Geldnoten imitierten. Sich selbst gab er auf der fiktiven „Banknote" als „treasurer" ein amtlich-seriöses Auftreten (Karton, um 1908).
Copyright: The Boecher Brand & Package Design Collection, Wiesbaden

Die „Blue Blade"-Klinge, eingeführt um 1930, war über Jahrzehnte hinweg der „Klassiker" des Hauses. Werbung in China, um 1985.
Procter & Gamble, Company Archive

Aus der „Blue Blade" wurde „Fusion": Mit dieser Retro-Grafik gratulierte sich die Marke selbst zum 100. Geburtstag, Deutschland 2001.
Procter & Gamble, Company Archive

Das Sortiment wurde spätestens ab 1970 recht unübersichtlich. Eine klare Leitfarbe gab es nicht. Sortimentsübersicht um 1980.
Procter & Gamble, Company Archive

In Deutschland folgte auf die „Blaue Klinge" die „Blaue Klinge Extra". Frühe Blisterpackung, Deutschland um 1960. Die Farbe Blau gab der Marke Halt.
Copyright: The Boecher Brand & Package Design Collection

Abbildungen, Seite 46/47
Patriotismus war gut für den Abverkauf. Gillette Service Week Campaign, USA 1917.
Procter & Gamble, Company Archive

Zweiteiliger Bodenaufsteller, Deutschland 1977
Firmenarchiv STI Group, Lauterbach

Regaldisplay in Form eines Formel-1-Rennwagens, Deutschland 1996
Firmenarchiv STI Group, Lauterbach

for the distribution of the blades. The blades carried the image of the businessman all over the world.
Procter & Gamble, Company Archive

In Germany, the product started in a case like the one shown above. The enclosed instructions awkwardly explained in pictures how to shave (around 1908).
Copyright: The Boecher Brand & Package Design Collection, Wiesbaden

King Camp Gillette was not only an inventor, but also a pioneer in marketing. He knewhow to effectively promote himself as his own "brand ambassador".
Procter & Gamble, Company Archive

The face of Gillette, who also gained attention as an author ofsocial-utopian books, was on every single blade. His face was one of the best-known faces around the world. He died poor (owing to the stock market crash).
Procter & Gamble, Company Archive

Figures, page 44/45
For the launch of the "safety razor" onto the market, Gillette used packs that resembled banknotes. The notes featured the image of Gillette as "Treasurer", lending him an official and respectable appearance (Cardboard, around 1908).
Copyright: The Boecher Brand & Package Design Collection, Wiesbaden

The "Blue Blade" was introduced around 1930 and was the brand's "classic"for decades. Advertisement in China, around 1985.
Procter & Gamble, Company Archive

"Blue Blade" was later renamed "Fusion". In this retro-style advertisement, the brand congratulated itself for its 100 birthday, Germany 2001.
Procter & Gamble, Company Archive

In 1970, the product range started to be rather confusing. There was no dominating colour that could be identified with the brand. An overview of Gillette products, around 1980.
Procter & Gamble, Company Archive

In Germany, the successor to the "Blue Blade" was the "Blue Blade Extra". Early blister pack, Germany around 1960. The colour blue supported the brand in building an identity.
Copyright: The Boecher Brand & Package Design Collection

Figures, page 46/47
Patriotism helped boost sales. Gillette Service Week Campaign, US 1917.
Procter & Gamble, Company Archive

Two-piece floor stand display, Germany 1977
Firmenarchiv STI Group, Lauterbach

Formula One racing car shelf display, Germany 1996
Firmenarchiv STI Group, Lauterbach

„Arctic Ice", schwarzes Regaldisplay, 2000
Firmenarchiv STI Group, Lauterbach

Gillette Blue II Plus, Bodendisplay als Schütte auf Chep-Palette, Deutschland 2002
Firmenarchiv STI Group, Lauterbach

Abbildungen, Seite 48/49
Kombiniertes Display für Herren- und Damen-Shaver, Deutschland 2002
Firmenarchiv STI Group, Lauterbach

Gillette Sensor, blaues Bodendisplay mit großem 3D-Dummy des Rasierers, 2003
Firmenarchiv STI Group, Lauterbach

Gillette Venus Divine, Thekendisplay, 2004
Procter & Gamble, Company Archive

M3 Power, schwarzes Regaldisplay, 2005
Firmenarchiv STI Group, Lauterbach

Gillette Satin, Regal-Doppeldisplay, 2005
Firmenarchiv STI Group, Lauterbach

Abbildungen, Seite 51
Gillette Fusion, Thekendisplay, 2007
Procter & Gamble, Company Archive

Gillette Fusion, Bodendisplay, 2007
Procter & Gamble, Company Archive

Gillette Fusion, Displayeinsatz mit integriertem Vorschubsystem, 2007
Procter & Gamble, Company Archive

Gillette Fusion, Regaldisplay, 2007
Procter & Gamble, Company Archive

Doppeldisplay (Kombination für Herren- und Damen-Shaver), Skandinavien 2008
Firmenarchiv STI Group, Lauterbach

Abbildungen, Seite 53
Gillette Fusion, attraktives Shape-Display (mit Sylvie van der Vaart), Deutschland 2010
Procter & Gamble, Company Archive

Gillette Fusion, Regaldisplay 2010
Procter & Gamble, Company Archive

Gillette Fusion, Bodendisplay, 2010
Procter & Gamble, Company Archive

Gillette Venus Embrace, Bodendisplay, 2010
Procter & Gamble, Company Archive

Gillete Venus Embrace Regalhänger, 2010
Procter & Gamble, Company Archive

Gillette Venus Embrace Regaldisplay mit vier Präsentations-ebenen und Schaupräsentation eines Rasierers, Deutschland 2010
Procter & Gamble, Company Archive

MILKA

Abbildung, Seite 55
Dass Kühe ein lila Fell haben können, ist allgemein bekannt. Und zwar seit der legendären Werbekampagne von Young & Rubicam von 1972.
Kraft Foods Deutschland, Company Archive

Black "Arctic Ice" shelf display, 2000
Firmenarchiv STI Group, Lauterbach

Gillette Blue II Plus floor stand display consisting of a bin on a Chep pallet, Germany 2002
Firmenarchiv STI Group, Lauterbach

Figures, page 48/49
Display for both men's and women's razors, Germany 2002
Firmenarchiv STI Group, Lauterbach

Blue Gillette Sensor floor stand display with large three-dimensional razor dummy, 2003
Firmenarchiv STI Group, Lauterbach

Gillette Venus Divine counter display, 2004
Procter & Gamble, Company Archive

Black M3 Power shelf display, 2005
Firmenarchiv STI Group, Lauterbach

Twin Gillette Satin shelf display, 2005
Firmenarchiv STI Group, Lauterbach

Figures, page 51
Gillette Fusion counter display 2007
Procter & Gamble, Company Archive

Gillette Fusion floor stand display, 2007
Procter & Gamble, Company Archive

Gillette Fusion display tray with integrated feed system, 2007
Procter & Gamble, Company Archive

Gillette Fusion shelf display, 2007
Procter & Gamble, Company Archive

Twin display for both men's and women's razors, Scandinavia 2008
Firmenarchiv STI Group, Lauterbach

Figures, page 53
Attractively shaped Gillette Fusion display (with Sylvie van der Vaart), Germany 2010
Procter & Gamble, Company Archive

Gillette Fusion shelf display, 2010
Procter & Gamble, Company Archive

Gillette Venus Embrace floor stand display, 2010
Procter & Gamble, Company Archive

Gillette Fusion, Floor stand display, 2010
Procter & Gamble, Company Archive

Gillette Venus Embrace clip strip for shelves, 2010
Procter & Gamble, Company Archive

Gillette Venus Embrace shelf display with four levels and product demonstration of the Gillette razor, Germany 2010
Procter & Gamble, Company Archive

MILKA

Figure, page 55
Purple cows exist. Everybody knows that since the famous Young & Rubicam campaign in 1972.
Kraft Foods Deutschland, Company Archive

ABBILDUNGS-, QUELLEN- UND LITERATURNACHWEISE | REFERENCE

Abbildungen, Seite 56/56
Der Unternehmensgründer Philippe Suchard (1797–1884), ein echter Schweizer, war von der stärkenden Kraft der Schokolade fasziniert.
Kraft Foods Deutschland, Company Archive

Der Schwiegersohn des Firmengründers war ein Deutscher: Carl Russ (1838–1925). Er war der Erfinder der „Milka".
Kraft Foods Deutschland, Company Archive

Milka war ein Werbepionier. Plakat um 1905.
Kraft Foods Deutschland, Company Archive

Der „Milka-Bernhardiner" ist längst Reklamegeschichte. Er interpretiert einen Mythos und „apportiert" der Marke die „Herkunftsenergie" der Schweiz. Plakat um 1910.
Kraft Foods Deutschland, Company Archive

Auf der Schokolade (hier Packungen von 1901, 1909, 1922, 1960 und 1988) wandelte sich nicht nur die Darstellungsweise der Kuh. Genial war der zart schmelzende Schriftzug des Markennamens, eingeführt 1909.
Kraft Foods Deutschland, Company Archive

Abbildungen, Seite 58/59
Genuss, wie ihn nur die „lila Kuh" verkörpert: Anzeige von 1981
Kraft Foods Deutschland, Company Archive

Palettendisplay (1970er Jahre) zu einer markentypischen Promotion-Aktion, wie sie später Geschichte schreiben sollte. Denn 1995, als bei einem ähnlichen Malwettbewerb allein 40.000 Bauernhof-Motive zum Ausmalen an Kindergärten versendet wurden, malte jedes dritte Kind die Kuh mit einem lila Fell! Dies löste erregte Debatten über den Wirklichkeitsverlust und die Macht der Werbung aus.
Firmenarchiv STI Group, Lauterbach

Abbildungen, Seite 60/61
Alpenhütte als „Knusperhäuschen" mit „Milka-Bernhardiner" und lila Kuh: eine erlebnisstarke Platzierung – und ein traumhafter Spielort für Kinder. Bodendisplay 1996.
Firmenarchiv STI Group, Lauterbach

Sekundendisplay zum 25-jährigen Geburtstag der Milka-Kuh, 1999
Firmenarchiv STI Group, Lauterbach

Heiße Hits auf „kuhlen" Scheiben bewarben den 25. Geburtstag der lila Kuh, Bodendisplay 1999
Firmenarchiv STI Group, Lauterbach

Sechseckige Schütte, Bodendisplay 2002
Firmenarchiv STI Group, Lauterbach

Abbildungen, Seite 62/63
Palettendekoration mit Hase als Paraglider, Ostern 2003
Firmenarchiv STI Group, Lauterbach

Figures, page 56/55
Founder Philippe Suchard (1797–1884), a true Swiss, was fascinated by the strengthening effect chocolate has on the body.
Kraft Foods Deutschland, Company Archive

The company founder's son-in-law was German: Carl Russ (1838–1925). He invented Milka.
Kraft Foods Deutschland, Company Archive

Milka was a pioneer in advertising. Poster, around 1905.
Kraft Foods Deutschland, Company Archive

Milka's St Bernhard has already gone down in advertising history. The dog represents a myth and "fetches" the "original energy" of Switzerland for the brand. Poster, around 1910.
Kraft Foods Deutschland, Company Archive

Not only the image of the cow changed on the chocolate over time (bars from 1901, 1909, 1922, 1960 and 1988). The new smooth logo that appeared on Milka bars in 1909, with letters that seemed to be melting, was a work of genius.
Kraft Foods Deutschland, Company Archive

Figures, page 58/59
No figure better embodies relish than the "purple cow": advertisement from 1981
Kraft Foods Deutschland, Company Archive

Pallet display (1970s) for a typical Milka promotion that would later make history. In 1995, when 40,000 farmhouse colouring book images were sent out to children as part of a painting competition, one in three children painted a purple cow. An intense debate was sparked over the loss of reality and the power of advertising.
Firmenarchiv STI Group, Lauterbach

Figures, page 60/61
"Gingerbread" mountain hut with the "Milka St Bernhard" and the purple cow: an exciting display – and a wonderful playground for children. Floor stand display 1996.
Firmenarchiv STI Group, Lauterbach

Quick assembly display introduced for the Milka cow's 25th anniversary, 1999
Firmenarchiv STI Group, Lauterbach

A display offered cds with latest hits for the purple cow's 25th anniversary, floor stand display 1999
Firmenarchiv STI Group, Lauterbach

Hexagonal dump-bin 2002
Firmenarchiv STI Group, Lauterbach

Figures, page 62/63
Paragliding bunny for pallet displays, Easter 2003
Firmenarchiv STI Group, Lauterbach

Palettendekoration „Halloween", Herbst 2003
Firmenarchiv STI Group, Lauterbach

„Choco & Rice", Regaldisplay 2003
Firmenarchiv STI Group, Lauterbach

„Von Herzen", Chep-Palettendisplay „Von Herzen", 2006
Firmenarchiv STI Group, Lauterbach

Bodendisplay, Tschechien 2007
Floor stand display, Czech Republic 2007
Firmenarchiv STI Group, Lauterbach

Schachtdisplay mit Innendruck auf Palettenbreite, 2004
Firmenarchiv STI Group, Lauterbach

Palettendekoration mit Milka-Kuh als Plüschtier, Muttertag 2009
Firmenarchiv STI Group, Lauterbach

Abbildungen, Seite 64/65
Mega-Platzierung mit Alpenhüttendekoration, 2008
Firmenarchiv STI Group, Lauterbach

Umfassende Regaldekoration für den Auftritt in Osteuropa, 2006. Auf drei Metern Regalbreite entfesselt die Marke hier auch in der Erstplatzierung ein Feuerwerk an Werbe-Ideen.
Firmenarchiv STI Group, Lauterbach

NESCAFÉ

Abbildung, Seite 67
Der „Aufstieg" der Marke nahm mit der „Patentdose" und der – für damalige Verhältnisse sehr convenience-orientierten – Portionspackung für eine Tasse ihren Anfang. Plakat, Schweiz 1949.
Archives Historiques Nestlé, Vevey. Copyright: Nestlé S.A./SPN (Société des Produits Nestlé)

Abbildungen, Seite 68/69
Der filterlose, lösliche Kaffee war neu. Seine Zubereitung musste damals noch umständlich erklärt werden. Bedienungsanleitung, um 1950.
Archives Historiques Nestlé, Vevey. Copyright: Nestlé S.A./SPN (Société des Produits Nestlé)

Markenauftritt in der „Patentdose", um 1945
Brand presence in the "patented tin", around 1945
Archives Historiques Nestlé, Vevey. Copyright: Nestlé S.A./SPN (Société des Produits Nestlé)

Abbildungen, Seite 70/71
Schaufensterdisplays (mit „Störer" von 1961 und Weihnachten 1960)
Archives Historiques Nestlé, Vevey. Copyright: Nestlé S.A./SPN (Société des Produits Nestlé)

Thekendisplay für Aktivumsatz mit den Portions-Tuben, Deutschland 1952
Archives Historiques Nestlé, Vevey. Copyright: Nestlé S.A./SPN (Société des Produits Nestlé)

Bodendisplay mit Drahtkonstruktion, um 1960
Firmenarchiv STI Group, Lauterbach

Bodendisplay mit Drahtkonstruktion, frühe 1960er Jahre
Firmenarchiv STI Group, Lauterbach

Wellpappe-Verkaufsaufsteller der 1960er Jahre zur Aufnahme eines Versandkartons (beidseitig begehbar)
Firmenarchiv STI Group, Lauterbach

"Halloween" spooky castle for pallet displays, autumn 2003
Firmenarchiv STI Group, Lauterbach

"Choco & Rice", shelf display 2003
Firmenarchiv STI Group, Lauterbach

"From the heart", Chep pallet display, 2006
Firmenarchiv STI Group, Lauterbach

Floor stand display, Czech Republic 2007
Firmenarchiv STI Group, Lauterbach

Pallet-size tier display with inside printing, 2004
Firmenarchiv STI Group, Lauterbach

Milka cow plush toy for pallet displays, Mother's Day 2009
Firmenarchiv STI Group, Lauterbach

Figures, page 64/65
Huge display construction with mountain hut, 2008
Firmenarchiv STI Group, Lauterbach

Large display construction designed for Eastern Europe, 2006. On a three-metre shelf, the brand produces a firework of advertising ideas, also at its traditional in-store department.
Firmenarchiv STI Group, Lauterbach

NESCAFÉ

Figure, page 67
The brand's "rise" started with the "patented tin" and the – for the time very convenience oriented – one cup sachet. Poster, Switzerland 1949.
Archives Historiques Nestlé, Vevey. Copyright: Nestlé S.A./SPN (Société des Produits Nestlé)

Figures page 68/69
The filterless instant coffee was a novelty. Explaining its preparation was still rather awkward at the time. Instructions, around 1950.
Archives Historiques Nestlé, Vevey. Copyright: Nestlé S.A./SPN (Société des Produits Nestlé)

Brand presence in the "patented tin", around 1945
Archives Historiques Nestlé, Vevey. Copyright: Nestlé S.A./SPN (Société des Produits Nestlé)

Figures, page 70/71
Shop window displays (with "eye-catcher" in 1961 and at Christmas in 1960)
Archives Historiques Nestlé, Vevey. Copyright: Nestlé S.A./SPN (Société des Produits Nestlé)

Counter display to boost sales of the one-portion Nescafé "tubes", Germany 1952
Archives Historiques Nestlé, Vevey. Copyright: Nestlé S.A./SPN (Société des Produits Nestlé)

Wire based floor stand display, around 1960
Firmenarchiv STI Group, Lauterbach

Wire based floor stand display, early 1960s
Firmenarchiv STI Group, Lauterbach

Corrugated cardboard floor stand holding double-sided shipping boxes, 1960s
Firmenarchiv STI Group, Lauterbach

ABBILDUNGS-, QUELLEN- UND LITERATURNACHWEISE | REFERENCE

„Der neue Nescafé", Bodendisplay aus Wellpappe, 1968
"The new Nescafé", corrugated cardboard floor stand display, 1968
Firmenarchiv STI Group, Lauterbach

Abbildungen, Seite 72/73
Vorsteck-Regaldisplay als Zweitplatzierung, Wellkiste in Metalldraht-Konstruktion, Deutschland 1973
Archives Historiques Nestlé, Vevey. Copyright: Nestlé S.A./SPN (Société des Produits Nestlé)

Necafé Gold, Anzeige mit Bodendisplay, Deutschland 1979
Archives Historiques Nestlé, Vevey. Copyright: Nestlé S.A./SPN (Société des Produits Nestlé)

Regaldisplay, 2000
Firmenarchiv STI Group, Lauterbach

Regaldisplay aus der „italienischen"
Phase, 2001
Firmenarchiv STI Group, Lauterbach

„Nescafé Eiskaffee", Bodendisplay als Palettenmantel, 2002
Firmenarchiv STI Group, Lauterbach

Kombiniertes Bodendisplay für die Marken „Nescafé" (Regal) und „Orion" (Schütte), 2003
Firmenarchiv STI Group, Lauterbach

Abbildung, Seite 74
Modularisierte Zweitplatzierung für diverse Nestlé-Getränke, Frankreich, 2008
Firmenarchiv STI Group, Lauterbach

Abbildung, Seite 75
Aktuelle Dekoration für eine Standplatzierung
Firmenarchiv STI Group, Lauterbach

NESQUIK

Abbildung, Seite 77
Eine der sympathischsten Werbefiguren ist der Hase „Quiky". Er fungiert seit 1972-73 als Begleiter der Marke Nesquik
(Tray, Deutschland 2008-2009).
Copyright: The Boecher Brand & Package Design Collection, Wiesbaden.

Abbildungen, Seite 78/79
Am Anfang stand die vornehme Marke „Nescao". Dieser Kakao konnte gleichwohl nur in warmer Milch gelöst werden (Packung um 1930).
Archives Historiques Nestlé, Vevey. Copyright: Nestlé S.A./SPN (Société des Produits Nestlé)

"The new Nescafé", corrugated cardboard floor stand display, 1968
Firmenarchiv STI Group, Lauterbach

Figures, page 72/73
Display tray used as secondary placement. The corrugated cardboard box could be attached to shelves by its metal hooks, Germany 1973
Archives Historiques Nestlé, Vevey. Copyright: Nestlé S.A./SPN (Société des Produits Nestlé)

Nescafé Gold, advertisement featuring floor stand display, Germany 1979
Archives Historiques Nestlé, Vevey. Copyright: Nestlé S.A./SPN (Société des Produits Nestlé)

Shelf display, 2000
Firmenarchiv STI Group, Lauterbach

"Italian phase" shelf display, 2001
Firmenarchiv STI Group, Lauterbach

"Nescafé Eiskaffee" iced coffee, open wrap-around display for pallets, 2002
Firmenarchiv STI Group, Lauterbach

"Floor stand display for the brands "Nescafé" (shelf) and "Orion" (bin), 2003
Firmenarchiv STI Group, Lauterbach

Figure, page 74
Modular displays for the secondary placement of various Nestlé drinks, France 2008
Firmenarchiv STI Group, Lauterbach

Figure, page 75
Recent decoration for a floor stand display
Firmenarchiv STI Group, Lauterbach

NESQUIK

Figure, page 77
One of the most likeable advertising characters was the „Quiky" bunny. He has accompanied the Nesquik brand since 1972/73 (tray, Germany 2008-2009).
Copyright: The Boecher Brand & Package Design Collection, Wiesbaden.

Figures, page 78/79
At the beginning, there was the refined brand "Nescao". The cocoa could be prepared only with warm milk (packaging around 1930).
Archives Historiques Nestlé, Vevey. Copyright: Nestlé S.A./SPN (Société des Produits Nestlé)

Mit „Nestlés Quik" nahm die Marke in den USA ihren Anfang. Hier erscheint bereits ein Schokoladehase zur Auslobung, den Bruce Kellet 1972/73 entwickelt hatte (dieser ist gleichwohl noch kein Bestandteil des Labels). Anzeige, USA 1975.
Archives Historiques Nestlé, Vevey. Copyright: Nestlé S.A./SPN (Société des Produits Nestlé)

Nestlés Quik, Packungsdesign (noch ohne den Hasen), USA um 1965
Archives Historiques Nestlé, Vevey. Copyright: Nestlé S.A./SPN (Société des Produits Nestlé)

Nestlés Quik, Packungsdesign mit dem „Erdbeerhasen", dem Vorläufer der späteren „Quiky"-Figur (Sorte Erdbeergeschmack), Wickler, USA 1966/67
Archives Historiques Nestlé, Vevey. Copyright: Nestlé S.A./SPN (Société des Produits Nestlé)

Abbildungen, Seite 80/81
Thekendisplay mit integriertem Strohhalmspender, Deutschland 1960
Archives Historiques Nestlé, Vevey. Copyright: Nestlé S.A./SPN (Société des Produits Nestlé)

Thekendisplay mit trinkendem Jungen, Deutschland um 1959/60
Archives Historiques Nestlé, Vevey. Copyright: Nestlé S.A./SPN (Société des Produits Nestlé)

Bodendisplay aus Wellpappe mit ausladender Schütte und Aufsteckschild, Deutschland 1960er Jahre
Firmenarchiv STI Group, Lauterbach

Display in Kakaofarbe, Wellpappe, Schütte mit Regalaufbau, Deutschland 1960er Jahre
Firmenarchiv STI Group, Lauterbach

Bodendisplay aus Wellpappe, Gewinnspielaktion, Deutschland um 1967/68
Firmenarchiv STI Group, Lauterbach

Abbildungen, Seite 82/83
Nesquik, Packungsdesign mit „Quiky" für den englischsprachigen Markt, von (oder nach) 1991
Copyright: The Boecher Brand & Package Design Collection, Wiesbaden.

Sockelgestaltung mit „Quiky" für ein stabiles Bodendisplay (Schütte), Deutschland 2002
Firmenarchiv STI Group, Lauterbach

Nesquik Bodendisplay mit Stapelschütten, Frankreich 2005
Firmenarchiv STI Group, Lauterbach
Palettendekoration als „Standee" für eine Sommer-Promotion, Deutschland 2005
Firmenarchiv STI Group, Lauterbach

Ricoré, Nescafé, Nesquik etc., modulares (ökologisch nachhaltiges) Displaykonzept mit veränderbaren Modul-Standards, Frankreich 2008
Firmenarchiv STI Group, Lauterbach

NIVEA

Abbildung, Seite 85
Markenwerbung am Point of Sale. Vorschlag zur Schaufenster-Dekoration, 1928
Beiersdorf AG, Firmenarchiv

The brand started in the US as "Nestlés Quik". The packaging already features the chocolate bunny created by Brunce Kellet between 1972 and 1973 (the bunny is not yet part of the label). Advertisement, US 1975.
Archives Historiques Nestlé, Vevey. Copyright: Nestlé S.A./SPN (Société des Produits Nestlé)

Packaging design for Nestlés Quik (still without the bunny), US around 1965
Archives Historiques Nestlé, Vevey. Copyright: Nestlé S.A./SPN (Société des Produits Nestlé)

Packaging design for Nestlés Quik featuring the "strawberry bunny", the predecessor to the "Quiky" (for the strawberry flavour), Wickler, US 1966-67
Archives Historiques Nestlé, Vevey. Copyright: Nestlé S.A./SPN (Société des Produits Nestlé)

Figures, page 80/81
Counter display with integrated drinking straw dispenser, Germany 1960
Archives Historiques Nestlé, Vevey. Copyright: Nestlé S.A./SPN (Société des Produits Nestlé)

Counter display featuring a boy drinking Nesquik, Germany around 1959-60
Archives Historiques Nestlé, Vevey. Copyright: Nestlé S.A./SPN (Société des Produits Nestlé)

Corrugated cardboard display with protruding bin and header card, Germany in the 1960s
Firmenarchiv STI Group, Lauterbach

Cocoa-coloured corrugated cardboard display with shelf structure, Germany in the 1960s
Firmenarchiv STI Group, Lauterbach

Corrugated cardboard display with integrated prize draw, Germany around 1967-68
Firmenarchiv STI Group, Lauterbach

Figures, page 82/83
Nesquik packaging design for English-speaking markets featuring "Quiky", in (or later than) 1991
Copyright: The Boecher Brand & Package Design Collection, Wiesbaden.

"Quiky" pedestal decoration for a solid floor stand display (dumpbin), Germany 2002
Firmenarchiv STI Group, Lauterbach

Nesquik floor stand display with stackable bins, France 2005
Firmenarchiv STI Group, Lauterbach

"Quiky" standee for pallet displays in a summer promotion, Germany 2005
Firmenarchiv STI Group, Lauterbach

Ricoré, Nescafé, Nesquik etc., modular (ecologically sustainable) display concept with exchangeable standardised modules, France 2008
Firmenarchiv STI Group, Lauterbach

NIVEA

Figure, page 85
Brand advertising at the point of Beiersdorf AG, Firmenarchiv

X. ABBILDUNGS-, QUELLEN- UND LITERATURNACHWEISE | REFERENCE

Abbildungen, Seite 86/87
NIVEA war immer „schneeweiß", aber die Packung war anfangs noch nicht blau. Werbeplakat 1912, Entwurf Hans Rudi Erdt.
Beiersdorf AG, Firmenarchiv

NIVEA Creme, Anzeige von 1912
Beiersdorf AG, Firmenarchiv

NIVEA Creme, Puder, Seife. Grafisch anspruchsvolle Anzeige, 1922
Beiersdorf AG, Firmenarchiv

Das Jahr 1925 war die Geburtsstunde der weiß-blauen Dose.
Copyright: The Boecher Brand & Package Design Collection, Wiesbaden

Abbildungen, Seite 88/89
Verkaufshilfe für den Point of Sale: NIVEA-Verkaufsschränkchen, 1925
Beiersdorf AG, Firmenarchiv

NIVEA, Verkaufsschränkchen, 1927
Beiersdorf AG, Firmenarchiv

NIVEA, drehbares Verkaufsschränkchen, gemischte Sortierung, 1932
Beiersdorf AG, Firmenarchiv

NIVEA, Theken-Holzdisplay (auch hängbar), 1954
Beiersdorf AG, Firmenarchiv

NIVEA, Theken-Holzdisplay, 1960
Beiersdorf AG, Firmenarchiv

Abbildungen, Seite 90/91
„NIVEA: FÜR LICHT-LUFT-U. SONNEN-FREUNDE", Vorschlag zur Schaufensterdekoration, 1928
Beiersdorf AG, Firmenarchiv

„Ihr bester NIVEA-Verkäufer", Werbung für den „Verkaufsschrank", 1929
Beiersdorf AG, Firmenarchiv

„NIVEA nicht vergessen!", Sommer-Schaufenster, Dekorationsvorschlag, 1955
Beiersdorf AG, Firmenarchiv

„8 x 4" und NIVEA, Sommer-Schaufenster, Dekorationsvorschlag, 1955
Beiersdorf AG, Firmenarchiv

Abbildungen, Seite 92/93
NIVEA-Ball, Hinweise zum Werbemittel-Einsatz, 1965
Beiersdorf AG, Firmenarchiv

Bodendisplay mit doppelter Schütte, Wellpappe, um 1965
Firmenarchiv STI Group, Lauterbach

Bodendisplay, Drahtkonstruktion mit schwebendem NIVEA-Ball, 1964
Beiersdorf AG, Firmenarchiv

Figures, page 86/87
NIVEA has always been "snow-white", but its packaging was not always blue. Advertising poster designed by Hans Rudi Erdt in 1912.
Beiersdorf AG, Firmenarchiv

NIVEA creme, advertisement from 1912
Beiersdorf AG, Firmenarchiv

NIVEA creme, powder and soap. Graphically sophisticated advertisement, 1922
Beiersdorf AG, Firmenarchiv

1925 marked the birth of the blue and white jar.
Copyright: The Boecher Brand & Package Design Collection, Wiesbaden

Figures, page 88/89
Sales promotion at the point of sale: NIVEA display cabinet, 1925
Beiersdorf AG, Firmenarchiv

NIVEA display cabinet, 1927
Beiersdorf AG, Firmenarchiv

Rotating display cabinet for various NIVEA products, 1932
Beiersdorf AG, Firmenarchiv

Wooden NIVEA counter display (that could also be hung on the wall), 1954
Beiersdorf AG, Firmenarchiv

Wooden NIVEA counter display, 1960
Beiersdorf AG, Firmenarchiv

Figures, page 90/91
"NIVEA: for lovers of light, air and sun", suggestion for window shop decorations, 1928
Beiersdorf AG, Firmenarchiv

"Your best NIVEA seller", advertisement for the "NIVEA display cabinet", 1929
Beiersdorf AG, Firmenarchiv

"Don't forget your NIVEA!", suggestion for a summer shop window decoration, 1955
Beiersdorf AG, Firmenarchiv

"8 x 4" and NIVEA, suggestion for a summer shop window decoration, 1955
Beiersdorf AG, Firmenarchiv

Figures, page 92/93
NIVEA ball, help for the use of advertising material, 1965
Beiersdorf AG, Firmenarchiv

Two-tier corrugated cardboard floor stand display, around 1965
Firmenarchiv STI Group, Lauterbach

Ein Kajak als Schütte: Displays und Werbemittel (T-Shirts etc.) für den POS, 1978
Beiersdorf AG, Firmenarchiv

Palettendekoration mit NIVEA-Bällen, 1977
Beiersdorf AG, Firmenarchiv

NIVEA-Marktstand als „Pflegecenter", Zweitplatzierung 1978
Beiersdorf AG, Firmenarchiv

Beispiel für Aktionsplatzierung, 1985
Beiersdorf AG, Firmenarchiv

Verkaufsförderung mit der Strandkorb-Palette, 1987
Beiersdorf AG, Firmenarchiv

Abbildungen, Seite 94/95
NIVEA Visage, rollbares Regaldisplay, 1994
Firmenarchiv STI Group, Lauterbach

NIVEA (und Atrix), Universaldisplay mit auswechselbaren Aufsteckschildern, 2000
Firmenarchiv STI Group, Lauterbach

NIVEA Beauté, zierliches Bodendisplay mit Aufsatz, der auch als Thekendisplay verwandt werden kann, 1999
Firmenarchiv STI Group, Lauterbach

Regaldisplay (Weiterentwicklung) mit ausklappbarem Fach (Nachbestückung), oben: vorgeblocktes Motiv mit integriertem Licht-Effekt (Fenster leuchtet), 2002
Firmenarchiv STI Group, Lauterbach

NIVEA Beauté, Verkaufshilfe für das gesamte Sortiment, Langzeitplatzierung, schwenkbar, Schweiz 2002
Firmenarchiv STI Group, Lauterbach

Abbildungen, Seite 97
NIVEA Beauté, Langzeit-Display-Platzierung, seitlich herausziehbare Böden, Schweiz 2005
Firmenarchiv STI Group, Lauterbach

NIVEA Beauté, Co-Branding mit „Chantal Thomass", Theken- und Bodendisplay im Boudoir-Stil, 2009
Firmenarchiv STI Group, Lauterbach

NIVEA Visage, Pop-Up-Store, 2009
Beiersdorf AG, Firmenarchiv

PHILIPS

Abbildung, Seite 99
Der unter seinem Künstlernamen A. M. Cassandre berühmt gewordene Grafiker (1901–1968) war einer der ersten
„Designer-Stars" der Werbung. Plakat von 1951.
Philips Company Archives, Eindhoven

Abbildungen, Seite 100/101
Plakatgestaltung von Mathieu Clement, unter der künstlerischen Leitung von Louis Kalff, Holland 1928
Philips Company Archives, Eindhoven

Werbeplakat, 1958
Advertising poster, 1958
Philips Company Archives, Eindhoven

„Miniwatt", Design für Plakat und Produktverpackung (Radioröhren), A.

Wire based floor stand display with levitating NIVEA ball, 1964
Beiersdorf AG, Firmenarchiv

Display with a canoe instead of a bin. Display and POS advertising material such as T-shirts, 1978
Beiersdorf AG, Firmenarchiv

NIVEA balls for pallet displays, 1977
Beiersdorf AG, Firmenarchiv

NIVEA "care centre" market stall, secondary placement 1978
Beiersdorf AG, Firmenarchiv

A NIVEA promotional campaign display, 1985
Beiersdorf AG, Firmenarchiv

Sales promotion with beach chair pallet displays, 1987
Beiersdorf AG, Firmenarchiv

Figures, page 94/95
NIVEA Visage shelf display on wheels, 1994
Firmenarchiv STI Group, Lauterbach

Universal display with exchangeable header cards for NIVEA and Atrix, 2000
Firmenarchiv STI Group, Lauterbach

Petite NIVEA Beauté floor display with attachment that could also be used as counter display, 1999
Firmenarchiv STI Group, Lauterbach

Advanced shelf display variant with fold-out case for refill. Above: posters with illuminated dimensional
structures (light shining through the window), 2002
Firmenarchiv STI Group, Lauterbach

Display for the entire NIVEA Beauté product range, swivelling permanent display, Switzerland 2002
Firmenarchiv STI Group, Lauterbach

Figures, page 97
Permanent NIVEA Beauté display, its trays pulled out sideways, Switzerland 2005
Firmenarchiv STI Group, Lauterbach

NIVEA Beauté, co-branding with Chantal Thomass, boudoir style counter and floor stand displays, 2009
Firmenarchiv STI Group, Lauterbach

NIVEA Visage pop-up store, 2009
Beiersdorf AG, Firmenarchiv

PHILIPS

Figure, page 99
The graphic designer A. M. Cassandre (1901–1968), also known as Adolphe Jean Marie Mouron, was one of the first "designer stars" in advertising. Poster from 1951.
Philips Company Archives, Eindhoven

Figures, page 100/101
Commercial poster created by Mathieu Clement under the creative direction of Louis Kalff, Holland 1928
Philips Company Archives, Eindhoven

Advertising poster, 1958
Philips Company Archives, Eindhoven

"Miniwatt", design for posters and product packs (radio valves), A. M. Cas-

X. ABBILDUNGS-, QUELLEN- UND LITERATURNACHWEISE | REFERENCE

M. Cassandre 1931
Philips Company Archives, Eindhoven

Anzeige für Fernsehgeräte, Apparatus Design Gruppe, 1950er Jahre
Philips Company Archives, Eindhoven

Abbildungen, Seite 102/103
Live-Marketing am Point of Sale: Philips setzte bereits 1937 beleuchtbare Holzdisplays ein.
Philips Company Archives, Eindhoven

Display für eine der ersten Mikrowellen, späte 1970er Jahre.
Firmenarchiv STI Group, Lauterbach

Abbildungen, Seite 104/105
Bodendisplay, 1980er Jahre
Firmenarchiv STI Group, Lauterbach

Home Cinema, Manteldisplay für ein (interaktives) Originalgerät, 1998
Firmenarchiv STI Group, Lauterbach

Spielserie „amBX", Multimediadisplay zur multisensorischen Konsumentenansprache (inklusive Windmaschine und Full-around-Sound), 2008
Firmenarchiv STI Group, Lauterbach

Abbildung, Seite 107
„Television", Marken-Präsentation u. a. auf der „Crossroads" Wien, 1994/95
Philips Company Archives, Eindhoven

Abbildungen, Seite 108/109
„Podium" (= Leuchtenserie von Philips, Frankreich), elektrifiziertes Langzeitdisplay, 2009
Firmenarchiv STI Group, Lauterbach

Philips Experience Showroom (Singapur), konzeptioneller Flagship-Store für ein totales Marken-Erlebnis, Design von Low Cheaw Hwei, errichtet ab 2004.
Philips Company Archives, Eindhoven

REXONA

Abbildung, Seite 111
Rexona war als erste desodorierende Seife im Markt eine absolute Innovation. Mit vollen Segeln ging die Marke von Beginn an auch am Point of Sale ins Rennen. Bodendisplay, um 1960.
Firmenarchiv STI Group, Lauterbach

Abbildungen, Seite 112/113
Rexona, Entwicklung des Packungsdesigns von 1953 bis um 1980.
Abbildungen 1–4
Copyright: The Boecher Brand & Package Design Collection, Wiesbaden

sandre 1931
Philips Company Archives, Eindhoven

Advertisement for televisions, Apparatus Design Gruppe, 1950s
Philips Company Archives, Eindhoven

Figures, page 102/103
Live marketing at the point of sale: Philips used illuminated wooden displays as early as 1937.
Philips Company Archives, Eindhoven

Display for one of the first-ever microwaves, late 1970s.
Firmenarchiv STI Group, Lauterbach

Figures, page 104/105
Floor stand display, 1980s
Firmenarchiv STI Group, Lauterbach

Home Cinema, display for a real (interactive)Philips Home Cinema device, 1998
Firmenarchiv STI Group, Lauterbach

The "amBX" games series, multimedia display offering a multi-sensory customer approach (including wind machine and all-around sound), 2008
Firmenarchiv STI Group, Lauterbach

Figure, page 107
"Television", brand presentation as staged at the "Crossroads" in Vienna, 1994/1995
Philips Company Archives, Eindhoven

Figures, page 108/109
"Podium" (Philips lamp series, France), electrically powered permanent display, 2009
Firmenarchiv STI Group, Lauterbach

Philips Experience Showroom in Singapore, a concept flagship s Low Cheaw Hwei tore for a complete brand experience, designed by Low Cheaw Hwei and opened in 2004.
Philips Company Archives, Eindhoven

REXONA

Figure, page 111
Rexona was the first deodorising soap and a complete novelty. Right from the beginning the brand sailed through the retail race, also at the point of sale. Floor stand display, around 1960.
Firmenarchiv STI Group, Lauterbach

Figures, page 112/113
How the Rexona soap's packaging changed between 1953 and 1980
Figures 1–4
Copyright: The Boecher Brand & Package Design Collection, Wiesbaden

Abbildung 5
Unilever Deutschland
Abbildung 6
Copyright: The Boecher Brand & Package Design Collection, Wiesbaden

Zwei Anzeigen mit ermahnenddirekter Konsumenten-Ansprache, beide um 1955
Abbildung 1
Copyright: The Boecher Brand & Package Design Collection, Wiesbaden
Abbildung 2
Unilever Deutschland

Abbildungen, Seite 114/115
„Deo-Lotion", Anzeige 1971
Copyright: The Boecher Brand & Package Design Collection

Der „Tick" ist weltweit identisch, der Markenname variiert.
Unilever Deutschland

Abbildungen, Seite 116/117
ABBA lässt grüßen: Rexona Girl ließ 2008 disco-begeisterte „Tanz-Königinnen" nach dem „perfekten Typ" und einem „Sexy Duft" suchen...
Unilever Deutschland

„Fan Pack" zur Weihnachtszeit (mit Beach Bag), abgestimmt auf die Tanz-Promotion der Sub-Marke „Rexona Girl"
Unilever Deutschland

Für die Sub-Marke „Rexona Girl" wurden 2007 unter der Ägide des Tanz-Trainers Detlef D! Soost junge Mädchen für einen Werbe-Tanzspot gecastet. Und „Hello Kitty" drückte „ganz fest die Daumen".
Unilever Deutschland

Abbildungen, Seite 118/119
Bodendisplay als Segelschiff, am Mast gab eine echte Blinkleuchte Signal, 1960er Jahre
Firmenarchiv STI Group, Lauterbach

Bodendisplay als einfache Schütte, 1960er Jahre
Firmenarchiv STI Group, Lauterbach

Bodendisplay mit aufblasbarem Paddelboot auf Wellpappe-Sockel, 1960er Jahre
Firmenarchiv STI Group, Lauterbach

„New Rexona", Live-Marketing auf dem schwarzen Kontinent, Bodendisplay, 1970er Jahre
Copyright: The Boecher Brand & Package Design Collection, Wiesbaden

Abbildungen, Seite 121
Rexona Girl, Bodendisplay 2006
Firmenarchiv STI Group, Lauterbach

Rexona Girl, „Dance Energy", Bodendisplay 2008
Unilever Deutschland

Rexona, ovales Shape-Regaldisplay in Form der Packung mit rotierendem Deo im Plakat, 2008
Unilever Deutschland

Shape-Regaldisplay in Form der Packung, 2009
Unilever Deutschland

Shape-Regaldisplay in Form der Packung, 2009
Unilever Deutschland

Rexona Woman, Bodendisplay mit Konturfigur einer nostalgischen Anzieh-Puppe, passend zur Promotion 2009
Unilever Deutschland

Figure 5
Unilever Deutschland
Figure 6
Copyright: The Boecher Brand & Package Design Collection, Wiesbaden

Two advertisements taking a menacingly direct consumer approach, both around 1955
Figure 1
Copyright: The Boecher Brand & Package Design Collection, Wiesbaden
Figure 2
Unilever Deutschland

Figures, page 114/115
"Deo-Lotion", advertisement 1971
Copyright: The Boecher Brand & Package Design Collection

The "tick" is largely identical, the brand name changes.
Unilever Deutschland

Figures, page 116/117
Almost like ABBA: in 2008, Rexona Girl sent disco-loving "dancing queens" out to find the "perfect guy" as well as a "sexy scent"...
Unilever Deutschland

The "Fan Pack" (with beach bag) launched for Christmas that accompanied the "Rexona Girl" sub-brand's dance promotion campaign
Unilever Deutschland

For the sub-brand "Rexona Girl", dancing trainer Detlef D! Soost casted young girls for a dance commercial in 2007. And "Hello Kitty" "kept fingers rossed" for the contestants.
Unilever Deutschland

Figures, page 118/119
Sailing boat floor stand display, a real flashing light on its mast sending out signals, 1960s
Firmenarchiv STI Group, Lauterbach

Simply dump-bin, 1960s
Firmenarchiv STI Group, Lauterbach

Floor stand display with an inflatable canoe on a corrugated cardboard pedestal, 1960s
Firmenarchiv STI Group, Lauterbach

Live marketing for "New Rexona" on the black continent, floor stand display, 1970s
Copyright: The Boecher Brand & Package Design Collection, Wiesbaden

Figures, page 121
Rexona Girl, floor stand display 2006
Firmenarchiv STI Group, Lauterbach

Rexona Girl, "Dance Energy", floor stand display 2008
Unilever Deutschland

Rexona, oval shelf display repeating the product pack's oval shape, with a rotating roll-on on the back card
Unilever Deutschland

Shelf display repeating the product pack's shape, 2009
Unilever Deutschland

Shelf display repeating the product pack's shape, 2009
Unilever Deutschland

Rexona Woman, floor stand display featuring the cut-out figure of an old-fashioned dress up paper doll, 2009
Unilever Deutschland

RICOLA

Abbildung, Seite 123
Für kleine Kunden „ganz groß": Von Beginn an hatte Ricola unter kleinen Kindern große Freunde.
Ricola AG, Laufen

Abbildungen, Seite 124/125
Am Ursprung der Marken-Kommunikation stand die klassische Bonbon-Tüte. Hier Ausführungen aus der Anfangszeit um 1940 sowie Designs aus der Zeit um 1954, um 1960, um 1970, 1980 bis Mitte 1990er Jahre, ab der Mitte 1990er Jahre, ab 2005.
Ricola AG, Laufen

Schon 1981 wurde die neue „Böxli-Packung" beworben (Anzeige, Schweiz 1981).
Ricola AG, Laufen

Zur „Entfaltung" der Marke trägt der klassische Wickler des Bonbons bei (Anzeige, Schweiz 1981).
Ricola AG, Laufen

„Wer hat's erfunden?" – TV-Spot mit Kult-Faktor. Das Konzept begann 1998 mit der Finnen-Sauna – und wurde im Laufe der Jahre auf viele andere Länder übertragen. So behaupten immer mehr Nationen, die Erfinder der originalen Schweizer Ricola-Bonbons zu sein: Ende 1999 postulierten dies die Australier, im Jahr 2000 die Engländer, dann 2001 die Mexikaner, 2004 wurde der Spot in Rio gedreht, bis 2005 auch die Chinesen und Ende 2009 gar die Eskimos ihre Ansprüche anmeldeten.
Ricola AG, Laufen

Abbildungen, Seite 126/127
Thekendisplay für Ricola (Beutel), um 1975
Firmenarchiv STI Group, Lauterbach

Achteckiges Thekendisplay für Kräutertee, 1978
Firmenarchiv STI Group, Lauterbach

Bodenaufsteller, Ende 1970er Jahre
Firmenarchiv STI Group, Lauterbach

Sortimentsdisplay (Kräutertee und Kräuterzucker), 1978
Firmenarchiv STI Group, Lauterbach

Stapelschütten auf Chep-Palette vor Matterhorn-Motiv (Konturstanzung, dreidimensionales Dach), 1997
Firmenarchiv STI Group, Lauterbach

Palettendisplay, Almhütte vor konturgestanztem Matterhorn, 2000
Firmenarchiv STI Group, Lauterbach

RICOLA

Figure, page 123
Ricola went over big with small customers. Right from the beginning the brand was highly popular with small children.
Ricola AG, Laufen

Figures, page 124/125
Ricola's brand communication started with the traditional sweets bag. See variants from the brand's early days around 1940 as well as designs from around 1954, 1960, 1970, 1980 to the mid-1990s, from 1990 and 2005.
Ricola AG, Laufen

The new „Böxli pack" was promoted as early as 1981 (Advertisement, Switzerland 1981).
Ricola AG, Laufen

The sweet's classic wrapper contributes to the brand's "unfolding" (Advertisement, Switzerland 1981).
Ricola AG, Laufen

„Who invented it?" – A TV commercial that achieved cult status. The concept started with the Finnish sauna in 1998 and was later applied to many other countries. More and more nations came to claim to have invented the original Ricola lozenge: in late 1999 it was the Australians, in 2000 the English and the Mexicans in 2001. The spot was then filmed in Rio in 2004, and in the end even the Chinese claimed to have invented Ricola in 2005 and the Eskimos in 2009.
Ricola AG, Laufen

Figures, page 126/127
Ricola counter display (bag), around 1975
Firmenarchiv STI Group, Lauterbach

Octagonal herbal tea counter display, 1978
Firmenarchiv STI Group, Lauterbach

Floor stand display, late 1970s
Firmenarchiv STI Group, Lauterbach

Display for herbal tea and Kräuterzucker lozenges, 1978
Firmenarchiv STI Group, Lauterbach

Stacking bins on a Chep pallet, its back card featuring a die-cut image of the Matterhorn (three-dimensional roof)
Firmenarchiv STI Group, Lauterbach

Pallet display, mountain hut in front of a cut-die image of the Matterhorn, 2000
Firmenarchiv STI Group, Lauterbach

Abbildungen, Seite 128/129
Sechseckiges Bodendisplay, 1998
Firmenarchiv STI Group, Lauterbach

Thekendisplay für „Böxli"- und Probepackungen, 2007
Ricola AG, Laufen

Thekendisplay für „Böxli"-Packungen, um 2007
Ricola AG, Laufen

Sekundendisplay mit konkav-konvexem Sockel, 2007
Ricola AG, Laufen

Bodendisplay mit Hartschalen-Trolley, 2009
Firmenarchiv STI Group, Lauterbach

Rollbares Langzeitdisplay, 2009
Ricola AG, Laufen

Abbildungen, Seite 131
Bodendisplay mit Alpenpanorama, 2007
Firmenarchiv STI Group, Lauterbach

Dreieckiges Display für Regalseiten, 2009
Firmenarchiv STI Group, Lauterbach

Thekendisplay als echter Flechtkorb (mit Konturschild), 2009
Ricola AG, Laufen

Bodendisplay, 2009
Ricola AG, Laufen

Verkaufsförderungsaktion mit Paletten- und Sortimentsplatzierung, 2009
Ricola AG, Laufen

Display-Säule für „Böxli"-Packungen, um 2007
Ricola AG, Laufen

Literatur- und Quellenangaben

Anders, S.; Franz, S. (2001): Milka. Das Jahrhundertbuch der Schokolade, München

Böcher, H.-G. (2009): TOP BRANDS. Marken, die die Märkte prägten, 21 Porträts kulturell bedeutender Marken, Arbeitskreis Prägefoliendruck e. V. (Hrsg.), Berlin

Böcher, H.-G. (2004): Kunst und Markenartikel, in: Bruhn, M. (Hrsg.): Handbuch Markenführung. Kompendium zum erfolgreichen Markenmanagement, Strategien – Instrumente – Erfahrungen, Bd. 2, Wiesbaden, S. 1293–1345

Böcher, H.-G. (2000): Design in Hülle & Fülle. Gefaltete Schachteln – entfaltete Marken. Die schönsten Faltschachteln aus über 100 Jahren Design- und Kulturgeschichte der künstlerischen Warenverpackung, Ulm (Klassiker des modernen Verpackungsdesigns, Bd. 2)

Böcher, H.-G.(1999): Kulturgut Verpackung. Ein Beitrag zur Kulturgeschichte eines künstlerischen Mediums, Kaiserslautern

Böcher, H.-G.(1998): Erlebniswelten im Verpackungsdesign – Markenbild, Wunschbild, Weltbild, in: Stabernack, W. (Hrsg.): Verpackung – Medium im Trend der Wünsche, Marketinginstrument Verpackung, München, S. 154–177

Böcher, H.-G. (1998): Von der Packmittelnot zum Luxus. Verpackung

bringt den Warenumschlag auf Tempo, in: Stickel, A.; Tröscher, M. (Hrsg.): 48,98 Tante Emma Megastore. 50 Jahre Lebensmittelhandel in Deutschland, zum fünfzigjährigen Bestehen der Lebensmittel Zeitung, Ingelheim, S. 88-94

Hansen, C. (2001): NIVEA – Entwicklung einer Weltmarke, Hamburg

Pfiffner, A. (2002): „A real winner one day": Die Entwicklung des „Nescafés" in den 1930er Jahren, in: Rossfeld, Roman (Hrsg.): Genuss und Nüchternheit. Geschichte des Kaffees in der Schweiz vom 18. Jahrhundert bis zur Gegenwart, Baden

Wachtel, J. (1965): Vom Ballenbinder zur Selbstbedienung, Verpackung – anno dazumal und heute, zum 150jährigen Bestehen hrsg. von Wolff & Co., Walsrode/Gütersloh 1965

IV. Shopper Insights: Was Kunden bewegt

Abbildung Kapitelseite
Firmenarchiv STI Group, Lauterbach

1 „Point of Purchase-Marketing im Einzelhandel – Weniger Shopper Confusion, mehr Shopper Convenience

Hendrik Schröder

Abbildungen

Abbildung 4
Shopper Confusion: Zu viele Stimuli und zu viele Menschen machen für den Kunden das Einkaufen anstrengend.
Lebensmittel Zeitung; Fotograf: Hans-Rudolf Schulz

Abbildung 5
Im Raiffeisen-Markt in Borken zieht ein Traktor oder ein lebensgroßer Gartenzwerg die Aufmerksamkeit der Kunden auf sich. Terres Marketing und Consulting GmbH, Münster

Abbildung 6
Die Zweitplatzierung in diesem Beispiel kann zu Missverständnissen beim Kunden führen.
Lebensmittel Zeitung; Fotograf: Thomas Fedra

Abbildung 7
Das Frischecenter EDEKA-Zurheide kombiniert geschickt eine ansprechend gestaltete Ruhezone mit der Möglichkeit, Produkte auszuprobieren.
Lebensmittel Zeitung; Fotograf: Reinhard Rosendahl

---

den Warenumschlag auf Tempo, in: Stickel, A.; Tröscher, M. (ed.): 48,98 Tante Emma Megastore. 50 Jahre Lebensmittelhandel in Deutschland, zum fünfzigjährigen Bestehen der Lebensmittel Zeitung, Ingelheim, p. 88-94

Hansen, C. (2001): NIVEA – Entwicklung einer Weltmarke, Hamburg

Pfiffner, A. (2002): „A real winner one day": Die Entwicklung des „Nescafés" in den 1930er Jahren, in: Rossfeld, Roman (ed.): Genuss und Nüchternheit. Geschichte des Kaffees in der Schweiz vom 18. Jahrhundert bis zur Gegenwart, Baden

Wachtel, J. (1965): Vom Ballenbinder zur Selbstbedienung, Verpackung – anno dazumal und heute, zum 150jährigen Bestehen herausgegeben Wolff & Co., Walsrode/Gütersloh 1965

IV. Shopper Insights: How Customers tick

Chapter opening page illustrations
Firmenarchiv STI Group, Lauterbach

1 Point of purchase marketing at retail – Less shopper confusion, more shopper convenience

Hendrik Schröder

Illustrations

Figure 4
Shopper confusion: information overload and a crowded store turn shopping into an exhausting experience.
Lebensmittel Zeitung; Photographer: Hans-Rudolf Schulz

Figure 5
A tractor or life-size garden gnome attracts the customer's attention in the Raffeisen store in Borken.
Terres Marketing und Consulting GmbH, Münster

Figure 6
The secondary placement in this example could be misleading and might confuse the customer.
Lebensmittel Zeitung; Photographer: Thomas Fedra

Figure 7
EDEKA cleverly uses the attractively designed rest area in its store in Zurheide as a demonstration area where customers can test-taste its products
Lebensmittel Zeitung; Photographer: Reinhard Rosendahl

Bibliography

Baun, D. (2003): Impulsives Kaufverhalten am Point of Sale, Wiesbaden

Hauschildt, J. (1977): Entscheidungsziele, Tübingen

Heinen, E. (1976): Grundlagen betriebswirtschaftlicher Entscheidungen. Das Zielsystem der Unternehmung, 3rd edition, Wiesbaden
Hurth, J. (2006): Angewandte Handelspsychologie, Stuttgart

Kreutz, A. (2000): Der französische Zehnkämpfer, in: Textilwirtschaft, Nr. 2 v. 13.1., p 178–182

Kroeber-Riel, W.; Weinberg, P.; Gröppel-Klein, A. (2009): Konsumentenverhalten, 9th edition., München

Liebmann, H.-P. (2006): Handelsmanagement im Umbruch: Neue Ideen und Impulse, 10 Jahre HL Display in Österreich, Vortrag am 22.6.2006

Reith, C. (2007): Convenience im Handel, Frankfurt am Main

Schröder, H. (2003): Category Management – eine Standortbestimmung, in: Schröder, H. (ed.): Category Management – Aus der Praxis für die Praxis. Konzepte – Kooperationen – Erfahrungen, Frankfurt am Main, p 11–38

Schröder, H. (2004): Wie sicher ist die Position eines Herstellers als Category Captain? – Kooperation zwischen Handel und Industrie aus der Perspektive von Prinzipal und Agent, in: Bauer, H. H.; Huber, F. (ed.): Strategien und Trends im Handelsmanagement, München 2004, p 231–249

Schröder, H.; Berghaus, N. (2005): Blickaufzeichnung der Wahrnehmung am Regal – Methodendemonstration am Beispiel Süßgebäck, in: Trommsdorff, V. (ed.): Handelsforschung 2005, Stuttgart, p. 315–335

Schröder, H.; Berghaus, N.; Zimmermann, G. (2005): Das Blickverhalten der Kunden als Grundlage für die Warenplatzierung im Lebensmitteleinzelhandel, in: Der Markt, issue 1, p. 31–43

Schröder, H.; Möller, N.; Zimmermann, G. (2007): Die Messung der Wahrnehmung von Warenplatzierungen mit Hilfe der Videobeobachtung und der Blickaufzeichnung – dargestellt am Beispiel der Warengruppe Wasch-, Putz- und Reinigungsmittel, in: Schuckel, W.; Toporowski, W. (ed.): Theoretische Fundierung und praktische Relevanz der Handelsforschung, Wiesbaden, p. 257–282

Schweizer, M. (2005): Consumer Confusion im Handel, Wiesbaden

Swoboda, B.; Janz, M. (2002): Einordnung des Pay on Scan-Konzeptes in die modernen Ansätze zur unternehmensübergreifenden Wertkettenoptimierung in der Konsumgüterwirtschaft, in: Trommsdorff, V. (ed.): Handelsforschung 2001/2002, Wiesbaden, p. 203-222

3 Solving for shoppers

Jon Kramer

Bibliography

[1] *Presentation by Bob Michelson, CEO, Goliath Solutions, Shoppability 2.0 Conference: Collaborating Through Technology, Indiana University, Kelley School of Business, 2007*

[2] *Shopper Marketing (2007): Capture a Shopper's Mind, Heart and Wallet, study by Deloitte Consulting and the Grocery Manufacturers Association (GMA)*

X. ABBILDUNGS-, QUELLEN- UND LITERATURNACHWEISE | REFERENCE

V. Was Verkaufsförderung bewegt: Die Effizienz von POS-Maßnahmen

Abbildung Kapitelseite
fotolia

1. Was Verkaufsförderung bewegt: Die Effizienz von POS-Maßnahmen
Von Shopper Insights zu betriebswirtschaftlichen Erfolgskennziffern

Susanne Czech-Winkelmann

Literatur- und Quellenangaben

Birkigt, K. (1983): Angewandte Verkaufsförderung, Hamburg

ECR Europe Board (1997): in: Lebensmittel Zeitung – Journal Nr. 17, 25.04.1997, S. 52

Fuchs, W.; Unger, F. (2003): Verkaufsförderung. Konzepte und Instrument im Marketing-Mix, 2. Aufl., Wiesbaden

Gedenk, K. (2005): Efficient Promotion. Vortrag anläßlich der Jahrestagung der Akademischen Partnerschaft ECR Deutschland, Köln

Gedenk, K. (2002): Verkaufsförderung, München

GfK (2006): Werbeklima-Studie I/2006 http://www.gfk.com/imperia/md/content/presse/studien_und_publikationen/gfk-wiwo-werbeklimastudie_2006.pdf

GfK (2006): POS-Maßnahmen im Verbrauchermarkt http://www.gfk.com/group/press_information/press_releases/001010/index.de.html

Koinecke, F.-J./ Großklaus, R. (1985): Die besten Promotion-Aktionen. Ziele, Konzept, Budget, Erfolg, Bd. 1, Landsberg a. Lech

Lauermann, D. (2009): Effizienz von POS- und Verkaufsförderungsmaßnahmen in der Gebrauchsgüterindustrie – eine empirische Untersuchung ausgewählter Zulieferer von Bau- und Gartenmärkten, Bachelor-Thesis, Wiesbaden Business School

Schmidt, D. (2009): Effizienz von POS-und Verkaufsförderungsmaßnahmen in der Konsumgüterindustrie – eine empirische Stärken/Schwächen Untersuchung bei den Marktleitern in LEH- und Getränkemärkten, Bachelor-Thesis, Wiesbaden Business School

V. Driving sales promotion: the effectiveness of POS activity

Chapter opening page illustrations
fotolia

1. Driving sales promotion: the effectiveness of POS activity
From shopper insights to economic success indicators

Susanne Czech-Winkelmann

Bibliography

Birkigt, K. (1983): Angewandte Verkaufsförderung, Hamburg

ECR Europe Board (1997): in: Lebensmittel Zeitung – Journal Nr. 17, 25.04.1997, p. 52

Fuchs, W.; Unger, F. (2003): Verkaufsförderung. Konzepte und Instrument im Marketing-Mix, 2nd edition, Wiesbaden

Gedenk, K. (2005): Efficient Promotion. Vortrag anläßlich der Jahrestagung der Akademischen Partnerschaft ECR Deutschland, Köln

Gedenk, K. (2002): Verkaufsförderung, München

GfK (2006): Werbeklima-Studie I/2006 http://www.gfk.com/imperia/md/content/presse/studien_und_publikationen/gfk-wiwo-werbeklimastudie_2006.pdf

GfK (2006): POS-Maßnahmen im Verbrauchermarkt http://www.gfk.com/group/press_information/press_releases/001010/index.de.html

Koinecke, F.-J./ Großklaus, R. (1985): Die besten Promotion-Aktionen. Ziele, Konzept, Budget, Erfolg, Vol. 1, Landsberg a. Lech

Lauermann, D. (2009): Effizienz von POS- und Verkaufsförderungsmaßnahmen in der Gebrauchsgüterindustrie – eine empirische Untersuchung ausgewählter Zulieferer von Bau- und Gartenmärkten, Bachelor-Thesis, Wiesbaden Business School

Schmidt, D. (2009): Effizienz von POS-und Verkaufsförderungsmaßnahmen in der Konsumgüterindustrie – eine empirische Stärken/Schwächen Untersuchung bei den Marktleitern in LEH- und Getränkemärkten, Bachelor-Thesis, Wiesbaden Business School

Wellhöfer, A./ Weng, J. (2008): Von den Besten lernen: Kunden profitabel managen, in akzente, S. 53-59 http://www.mckinsey.de/downloads/publikation/akzente/2008/akzente_0803_52_kundenmanagement.pdf

VI. Das Display der Zukunft: POS 2.0 – Display 2.0

Abbildung Kapitelseite
Firmenarchiv STI Group, Lauterbach

1. Die Rolle des Displays im Supermarkt der Zukunft

Günter Bauer

Literatur- und Quellenangaben

[1] Maslow, A. H.: A Theory of Human Motivation, in: Psychological Review 50 (4) (1943):370–396

2. The Future of Retail

Raphael Stix

Abbildungen

Abbildung, Seite 200
Der handschriftliche Hinweis schafft eine emotionale Verbindung. Foto privat, USA

Abbildungen, Seite 201
Entsprechend der Kundenpräferenzen können diese ihre eigene Mischung gestalten. (Customers can pick their own mix according to their preferences.)
Foto privat, USA

Der Handel nutzt alle Kommunikationskanäle. (Retailers use all communication channels.)
www.Stroeer.de

Abbildung, Seite 202
Die Markenkommunikation für Coors verbindet erfolgreich die On- und Offline-Kanäle bis an den POS.
The Integer Group, Denver, Colorado

3 360°-Marketing: Displays als Erfolgsfaktor von Marken und Handel

Tom Giessler

Abbildungen

Abbildung, Seite 207
Digital Signage kann auch in Displays integriert werden und rundet die POS-Platzierung ab.
Campari Deutschland und Global Shopper GmbH

Wellhöfer, A./ Weng, J. (2008): Von den Besten lernen: Kunden profitabel managen, in akzente, p. 53-59 http://www.mckinsey.de/downloads/publikation/akzente/2008/akzente_0803_52_kundenmanagement.pdf

VI. The Display of the Future: POS 2.0 – Display 2.0

Chapter opening page illustrations
Firmenarchiv STI Group, Lauterbach

1. The display in the supermarket of the future

Günter Bauer

Bibliography

[1] *Maslow, A. H.: A Theory of Human Motivation, in: Psychological Review 50 (4) (1943):370–396*

2. The future of retail

Raphael Stix

Illustrations

Figure, page 200
The handwritten message creates an emotional connection with the customer.
Private photo, USA

Figure, page 201
Entsprechend der Kundenpräferenzen können diese ihre eigene Mischung gestalten. (Customers can pick their own mix according to their preferences. Private photo, USA

Der Handel nutzt alle Kommunikationskanäle. (Retailers use all communication channels.)
www.Stroeer.de

Figure, page 202
Coors brand communication successfully links online with offline channels, also at the POS.
The Integer Group, Denver, Colorado

3 360 degree marketing: the display as a success factor for brands and retailers

Tom Giessler

Illustrations

Figure, page 207
Digital signage can be integrated into displays and rounds off the POS presentation.
Campari Deutschland und Global Shopper GmbH

Abbildungen, Seite 212
Eine Standardisierung der eingesetzten Displaymaterialien reduziert Prozesskosten und die time-to-market und führt gleichzeitig zu einer Steigerung der Brand Visibility im Handel.
Vileda GmbH

In der Fachhandelskommunikation von Vileda stehen die Displays im Fokus. Eine Anpassung der Standarddisplays für Sub-Marken ist einfach umsetzbar.
Vileda GmbH

Literatur- und Quellenangaben

[1] Delivering the Promise of Shopper Marketing: Mastering Execution for Competitive Advantage, 2008 GMA/Deloitte Shopper Marketing Studie

VII. Der POS der Zukunft – Die Zukunft des POS-Marketings

Abbildung Kapitelseite
Andreas Habicht, Firmenarchiv STI Goup, Lauterbach

2 Die Zukunft des POS-Marketings

Michael Gerling, Marlene Lohmann

Abbildungen

Abbildung, Seite 225
Kaufentscheidungen fallen emotional.
Sensarama, Graz

Abbildung, Seite 227
Düfte stimulieren nicht nur Emotionen, sondern auch die ungeplanten Einkäufe.
Scentcommunication

Abbildung, Seite 229
Aktionen sind wichtig – die leichte Handhabung ebenfalls.
Container Centralen

Abbildung, Seite 230
Schnelle Bereitstellung von Informationen durch neueste Technologie.
EHI

Abbildung, Seite 231
Inspirierte Kunden verwenden mehr Geld auf ungeplante Käufe.
Laslo Regos Photography/All the Hoopla, Michigan, USA

Figures, page 212
The standardisation of display materials used at the POS reduces costs and time-to-market while at the same time increasing brand visibility at retail.
Vileda GmbH

Vileda's advertising in speciality stores focuses on the display. Standardised displays can be easily customised to meet the needs of sub-brands too.
Vileda GmbH

Bibliography

[1] *Delivering the Promise of Shopper Marketing: Mastering Execution for Competitive Advantage, 2008 GMA/Deloitte Shopper Marketing Studie*

VII. The POS of the future – the future of POS marketing

Chapter opening page illustrations
Andreas Habicht, Firmenarchiv STI Group, Lauterbach

2 The future of POS marketing

Michael Gerling, Marlene Lohmann

Illustrations

Figure, page 225
Buying decisions are emotional.
Sensarama, Graz

Figure, page 227
Scents not only stimulate emotions, but unplanned purchases too.
Scentcommunication

Figure, page 229
Promotions are important – and so is easy handling.
Container Centralen

Figure, page 230
The latest technology allows quick provision of information.
EHI

Figure, page 231
Inspired customers spend more on unplanned purchases.
Laslo Regos Photography/All the Hoopla, Michigan, USA

Literatur- und Quellenangaben

[1] EHI-Marketingmonitor Handel 2008-2012
[2] Horizont, 36, 2009
[3] Tim Inteeworn (2007): Bestimmungsfaktoren der Verweildauer im Einzelhandel, unveröffentlichte Diplomarbeit, Universität Köln
[4] Tim Inteeworn (2007): Bestimmungsfaktoren der Verweildauer im Einzelhandel, unveröffentlichte Diplomarbeit, Universität Köln
[5] Stores +Shops, 03, 2008
[6] EHI-Marketingmonitor Handel 2007-2011
[7] EHI-Marketingmonitor Handel 2008-2012
[8] Marketing Monitor Handel 2008-2012
[9] EHI-Marketingmonitor Handel 2007-2011/EHI-Marketingmonitor Handel 2008-2012
[10] HDE, Destatis
[11] HDE, Destatis

3 Werbeformen für die Märkte von morgen

Claudia Endl

Abbildungen

Abbildung, Seite 240
Tesco.com

Abbildung, Seite 242
Coca-Cola GmbH, Deutschland, Aktion: Fanta trinken und Freiminuten gewinnen, Juli 2009

Literatur- und Quellenangaben

[1] Zur Geschichte von Aldi vgl. insbesondere Brandes (1998) und GfK
[2] Münsteraner Führungsgespräche, 06. Februar 2004 Köln, Auswirkungen der Discountwelle auf die Handelslandschaft, Holger Wenzel, Hauptgeschäftsführer, HDE
[3] Lebensmittel Zeitung, 04.09.2002
[4] Göpel Fairtrade leistet Pionierarbeit, in: Der Handel 09/2009
[5] TradeDimension 2009
[6] Lebensmittel Zeitung, Rewe Big bang , 09.08.2009
[7] GfK, POS Maßnahmen-/Medienstudie 2009
[8] KPMG, Trends im Handel 2010
[9] Display 3/2009 Welfhard Kraiker, Die Gedanken sind frei
[10] EHI Retail Institute: rt spezial, Supplement to retail technology, Content Management für digitale POS Medien, 2007, S.8
[11] Vkf-Trends: Vom Stiefkind zum Shootingstar, Agenda 2010, Lebensmittel Zeitung,15.06.2007
[12] Vgl. Nagel, M.: Neue Werbung für den Handel – Erscheinungsformen, Effizienzmessung, Einsatzmöglichkeiten, Cross-Media, 2007
[13] Mobile Couponing, Couponing Vorteile der über 60 der deutschen Handynutzer akzeptiert, Artikel 15.03.2007
[14] Robert L. Desatnick, Managing to keep the customer
[15] FHTW Berlin, Prof. Dr. Andrea Rumler 2009
[16] Der Markt wächst langsam, in: Absatzwirtschaft 9/2009
[17] H.-G. Lemke, Mehr Umsatz mit besserer optimaler Warenpräsentation im Einzel- und Fachhandel
[18] Dr. Markus Pfeiffer, Vivaldi GmbH, Studie zu Marken und Innovation
[19] Capgemini, The future value chain, Herausforderung Marketing, Diskussion um die Effektivität des Marketing, Harald Münzberg 2006

Bibliography

[1] EHI-Marketingmonitor Handel 2008-2012
[2] Horizont, 36, 2009
[3] Tim Inteeworn (2007): Bestimmungsfaktoren der Verweildauer im Einzelhandel, unveröffentlichte Diplomarbeit, Universität Köln
[4] Tim Inteeworn (2007): Bestimmungsfaktoren der Verweildauer im Einzelhandel, unveröffentlichte Diplomarbeit, Universität Köln
[5] Stores +Shops, 03, 2008
[6] EHI-Marketingmonitor Handel 2007-2011
[7] EHI-Marketingmonitor Handel 2008-2012
[8] Marketing Monitor Handel 2008-2012
[9] EHI-Marketingmonitor Handel 2007-2011/EHI-Marketingmonitor Handel 2008-2012
[10] HDE, Destatis
[11] HDE, Destatis

3 Advertising for the stores of the future

Claudia Endl

Illustrations

Figure, page 240
Tesco.com

Figure, page 242
Coca-Cola GmbH, Deutschland, Aktion: Fanta trinken und Freiminuten gewinnen, Juli 2009

Bibliography

[1] For the history of Aldi cf. in particular Brandes (1998) und GfK
[2] Münsteraner Führungsgespräche, 06. Februar 2004 Köln, Auswirkungen der Discountwelle auf die Handelslandschaft, Holger Wenzel, Hauptgeschäftsführer, HDE
[3] Lebensmittel Zeitung, 04.09.2002
[4] Göpel Fairtrade leistet Pionierarbeit, in: Der Handel 09/2009
[5] TradeDimension 2009
[6] Lebensmittel Zeitung, Rewe Big bang , 09.08.2009
[7] GfK, POS Maßnahmen-/Medienstudie 2009
[8] KPMG, Trends im Handel 2010
[9] Display 3/2009 Welfhard Kraiker, Die Gedanken sind frei
[10] EHI Retail Institute: rt spezial, Supplement to retail technology, Content Management für digitale POS Medien, 2007, p.8
[11] Vkf-Trends: Vom Stiefkind zum Shootingstar, Agenda 2010, Lebensmittel Zeitung,15.06.2007
[12] Cf. Nagel, M.: Neue Werbung für den Handel – Erscheinungsformen, Effizienzmessung, Einsatzmöglichkeiten, Cross-Media, 2007
[13] Mobile Couponing, Couponing Vorteile der über 60 der deutschen Handynutzer akzeptiert, Artikel 15.03.2007
[14] Robert L. Desatnick, Managing to keep the customer
[15] FHTW Berlin, Prof. Dr. Andrea Rumler 2009
[16] Der Markt wächst langsam, in: Absatzwirtschaft 9/2009
[17] H.-G. Lemke, Mehr Umsatz mit besserer optimaler Warenpräsentation im Einzel- und Fachhandel
[18] Dr. Markus Pfeiffer, Vivaldi GmbH, Studie zu Marken und Innovation
[19] Capgemini, The future value chain, Herausforderung Marketing, Diskussion um die Effektivität des Marketing, Harald Münzberg 2006

VIII. Integrierte Kommunikation: Vom Solisten zum Orchester

Frank-Michael Schmidt, Henk Knaupe

Abbildungen

Abbildung Kapitelseite
fotolia

Abbildung 2
Die Grafik zeigt den prozentualen Anteil, den qualitative Aktionen in den einzelnen Warengruppen ausmachen. Zu qualitativen Promotions zählen Displays und kommunikative Maßnahmen, wie beispielsweise Handzettelwerbung.
Rundschau für den deutschen LEH, Beilage, „Warum es auch ohne Rotstift geht", März 2008

Abbildung 3
Einflussnahme von Handelszentral- und Marktmanagern
Lebensmittel Zeitung „Trend zu vernetztem Marketing", 12.12.2008.

Literatur- und Quellenangaben

[1] Vgl. GfK, „Store Effects", 27.03.2009.
[2] Vgl. Konzept & Markt, „Einkaufsverhalten am POS", Januar 2009
[3] Vgl. ebd.

IX. Die Zukunft des Displays

Christoph Häberle

Abbildung Kapitelseite
pixelio, Zarkow

Literatur- und Quellenangaben

Andersen, A. (1997): Der Traum vom guten Leben. Alltags- und Konsumgeschichte vom Wirtschaftswunder bis heute; Frankfurt am Main

Barceló, P. (2005): Kleine römische Geschichte, Darmstadt

Berekoven, L. (1986): Geschichte des deutschen Einzelhandels, Frankfurt am Main

Bohner, T. (1955): Der offene Laden – Aus der Chronik des Einzelhandels, Frankfurt am Main

Buchli, H. (1962): 6000 Jahre Werbung, Bd. 1, Berlin

VIII. Integrated communication: From soloist to orchestra

Frank-Michael Schmidt, Henk Knaupe

Illustrations

Chapter opening page illustrations
fotolia

Figure 2
The graph shows the share of quality promotional activity in the individual product groups. Quality promotions include displays and communication means such as flyer advertising.
Rundschau für den deutschen LEH, Beilage, „Warum es auch ohne Rotstift geht", März 2008

Figure 3
The influence of retail and store managers
Lebensmittel Zeitung „Trend zu vernetztem Marketing", 12.12.2008.

Bibliography

[1] Cf. GfK, „Store Effects", 27.03.2009.
[2] Cf. Konzept & Markt, „Einkaufsverhalten am POS", Januar 2009
[3] Cf. ibid

IX. The future of the display

Christoph Häberle

Chapter opening page illustrations
pixelio, Zarkow

Bibliography

Andersen, A. (1997): Der Traum vom guten Leben. Alltags- und Konsumgeschichte vom Wirtschaftswunder bis heute; Frankfurt am Main

Barceló, P. (2005): Kleine römische Geschichte, Darmstadt

Berekoven, L. (1986): Geschichte des deutschen Einzelhandels, Frankfurt am Main

Bohner, T. (1955): Der offene Laden – Aus der Chronik des Einzelhandels, Frankfurt am Main

Buchli, H. (1962): 6000 Jahre Werbung, Vol. 1, Berlin

Gutgesell, M. (2004): Wirtschaft und Handel, in: R. Schulz und M. Seidel (Hrsg.): Ägypten – Die Welt der Pharaonen., Königswinter

Heinritz, G.; Klein, K.; Popp, M. (2003): Geographische Handelsforschung, Berlin/Stuttgart

Hofmeister, B. (1999): Stadtgeographie, Braunschweig

Metzger, W. (2002): Handel und Handwerk des Mittelalters im Spiegel der Buchmalerei, Graz

Reitz, M. (1999): Alltag im alten Ägypten, Augsburg

Spiekermann, U. (1999): Basis der Konsumgesellschaft: Entstehung und Entwicklung des modernen Kleinhandels in Deutschland, München

Spufford, P. (2004): Handel, Macht und Reichtum, Stuttgart

Strauß-Seeber, C. (2004): Geschenke des Nils – Agrarwirtschaft einer Flußoase, in: R. Schulz und M. Seidel (Hrsg.): Ägypten – Die Welt der Pharaonen, Königswinter

Sturm, N. (2004): Aldi, Lidl und mehr, in: Süddeutsche Zeitung vom 29.03.2004

Weeber, K.-W. (2000): Alltag im Alten Rom, Düsseldorf/Zürich

Wortmann, M. (2003): Strukturwandel und Globalisierung des deutschen Einzelhandels, WZB Discussion Paper SP III 2003-202a, Berlin

XI. DIE AUTOREN | THE AUTHORS

DIE AUTOREN
THE AUTHORS

Günter P. Bauer

Günter P. Bauer ist seit 2006 Creative Director bei Jos de Vries The Retail Company in Maarssen (Niederlande). Nach seinem Studium zum Master Industrial Design Engineering an der Delft University of Technology war er von 1999 bis 2001 als Industrial Design Engineer bei Albert Heijn in Zaandam beschäftigt. Anschließend arbeitete er fünf Jahre als freier Retail Designer in Alkmaar. Nebenberuflich lehrt er als Dozent an der Faculty Industrial Design Engineering der Delft University.

Günter P. Bauer has been Creative Director of Jos de Vries The Retail Company in Maarssen in the Netherlands since 2006. He is also a part-time lecturer at the Faculty of Industrial Design Engineering of the Delft University. Before joining Jos de Vries, Mr Bauer worked as a freelance retail designer in Alkmaar. Between 1999 and 2001, he was industrial design engineer at Albert Heijn in Zaandam. He holds a Master of Industrial Design Engineering from Delft University of Technology.

Hans-Georg Böcher

Hans-Georg Böcher ist Direktor des Deutschen Verpackungs-Museums in Heidelberg, einer Einrichtung, die von 230 Unternehmen unterstützt wird (BASF, Beiersdorf, Coca-Cola, Nestlé, Unilever). Daneben baute er über viele Jahre ein privates historisches Archiv mit einer umfassenden Sammlung zum künstlerischen Verpackungsdesign auf. Der studierte Kunsthistoriker verfügt somit über eine mehrere tausend Originalobjekte umfassende einzigartige Privatsammlung, mit der er regelmäßig Ausstellungen sowie Film- und Dreharbeiten (z. B. auch die Hollywood-Produktion „The good German" von Steven Sonderbergh mit Kate Blanchett und George Clooney, 2006) unterstützt. Er ist Autor zahlreicher Fachbücher und Bildbände zum Thema Verpackung und Marken-Design sowie Mitglied mehrerer Design- und Kreativ-Wettbewerbe.

Hans-Georg Böcher is the director of the German packaging museum Deutsches Verpackungs-Museum in Heidelberg, which is supported by 230 companies, including BASF, Beiersdorf, Coca-Cola, Nestlé and Unilever. Over many years, he has succeeded in building a private historical archive and a comprehensive artistic packaging collection. The art historian's private collection consists of thousands of originals that are regularly shown in exhibitions and used in film shootings such as the Hollywood production "The good German" by Steven Sonderbergh, starring Kate Blanchet and George Clooney in 2006. Mr Böcher is an author of various trade books and illustrated books on packaging and brand design and is also member of several design and creative competition organisations.

Susanne Czech-Winkelmann, Prof. Dr.

Seit 1997 ist Susanne Czech-Winkelmann Professorin für Vertriebsmanagement/International Sales Management an der Wiesbaden Business School der Hochschule RheinMain – University of Applied Sciences. Zuvor war sie im Marketing- und Vertriebsmanagement u. a. als Geschäftsführerin Marketing/Vertrieb tätig und sammelte berufspraktische Erfahrungen in den Branchen OTC-Arzneimittel, Kosmetik und Lebensmittel (Wick Pharma/Procter & Gamble, Milupa u. a.). Neben ihrer Lehrtätigkeit arbeitet sie als Beraterin und Gutachterin.

Susanne Czech-Winkelmann has been a professor of International Sales Management at the Wiesbaden Business School of the Hochschule RheinMain – University of Applied Sciences since 1997. Before her time as professor, she held various marketing and sales management positions, including general manager marketing and sales. She gained practical experience at companies in the OTC drug, cosmetics and food industries, including Wick Pharma/Procter & Gamble and Milupa. Ms Czech-Winkelmann also works as a consultant and reviewer.

Claudia Endl, Dipl.-Kffr.

Claudia Endl ist Geschäftsführerin der Dölle Managementberatung Handelsmarketing und Absatzförderung mit dem Schwerpunkt Strategieberatung zur Erschließung neuer Märkte und zur Einführung neuer Produktkonzepte. Sie studierte Betriebswirtschaft an der Universität Giessen und der University of Texas in El Paso (USA) und war anschließend langjährig als Beraterin (Marketing und Vertrieb) im Bereich Handel und Dienstleistung tätig. Außerdem baute sie ihr eigenes Unternehmen für LEH-Mediendienstleistungen auf, das sie heute leitet.

Claudia Endl is general manager of consultancy Dölle Managementberatung Handelsmarketing und Absatzförderung. She is a strategic consultant specialised in the opening of new markets and the launch of new product concepts. Ms Endl graduated in business management at the University of Giessen in Germany und the University of Texas in El Paso in the US and later worked as a marketing and sales consultant for retail and services for many years. She founded and today heads a food retail media services company. Ms Endl holds a business administration degree.

Dierk Frauen, Dipl.-Kfm.

Mit seinem Eintritt in den elterlichen Betrieb 1997 übernahm Dierk Frauen die Geschäftsführung der Peter Frauen & Co. oHG in Brunsbüttel und wurde Gesellschafter der neu gegründeten Frauen Lebensmittel KG. In diesen Positionen ist er weiterhin tätig. Vor seinem Studium der Betriebswirtschaftslehre an der Universität Hamburg absolvierte er eine Ausbildung zum Fachgehilfen in steuer- und wirtschaftsberatenden Berufen. Frauen war darüber hinaus bis Anfang 2010 Präsident des Bundesverbandes des Deutschen Lebensmittelhandels e.V. und Mitglied des Vorstandes des HDE e.V.

Dierk Frauen is general manager and owner of food company Frauen Lebensmittel KG. He joined his family's business as general manager in 1997, when it was still called Peter Frauen & Co. oHG. He then became the owner of the newly founded company Frauen Lebensmittel KG. Before graduating in business management at the University of Hamburg in Germany, Mr Frauen was trained as a tax and economic consultant. He was chairman of German food association Bundesverband des Deutschen Lebensmittelhandels e.V. and member of the board of German retail body HDE e.V. until early 2010. Mr Frauen holds a business administration degree.

DIE AUTOREN | THE AUTHORS

Michael Gerling, Dipl.-Kfm.

Als Geschäftsführer des EHI Retail Institute ist Michael Gerling für Forschungsarbeiten und Arbeitskreise sowie für die weiteren Geschäftsfelder verantwortlich. Nach dem Studium an der Universität Münster begann er seine berufliche Karriere 1983 als Trainee bei der Edeka Handelsgesellschaft Münsterland. Von 1990 bis 1993 war er u. a. im Ausland in verschiedenen Positionen tätig. Anschließend wechselte er als Senior Consultant zum EHI-EuroHandelsinstitut. Er übt darüber hinaus mehrere ehrenamtliche Tätigkeiten aus, so als Hauptgeschäftsführer des Bundesverbands des Deutschen Lebensmittelhandels e. V.

As a general manager of EHI Retail Institute, Michael Gerling is in charge of research and working groups as well as the other business areas. After graduating from the University of Münster in Germany, he started his career as a trainee at Edeka Handelsgesellschaft Münsterland in 1983. Between 1990 and 1993, Mr Gerling worked for various companies abroad and later joined EHI-EuroHandelsinstitut as senior consultant. Among his various honorary positions, he is managing director of German food association Bundesverband des Deutschen Lebensmittelhandels e. V. Mr Gerling holds a business administration degree.

Tom Giessler, Dr.

Tom Giessler ist Geschäftsführer der STI Group. Sein Parallelstudium der Betriebswirtschaftslehre und des Maschinenbaus an der RWTH Aachen schloss er mit einer Promotion ab. Anschließend trat er in die interne Beratung eines internationalen Industriekonzerns ein – die Schwerpunkte seiner Tätigkeit waren die Entwicklung und Implementierung von Strategien für Geschäftsbereiche und Technologien. Nach verschiedenen Tätigkeiten im international geprägten Corporate Finance sowie bei einer strategischen Unternehmensberatung wechselte Giessler 2007 zur STI Group. Seitdem zeichnet er als CFO für die kaufmännischen Bereiche und die internationalen Standorte des Unternehmens verantwortlich.

Tom Giessler is a general manager of STI Group. He graduated in business management and engineering at the RWTH Aachen university and completed his studies with a doctorate. He later worked as a consultant for an international group with a focus on the development and implementation of business and technology strategies. Mr Giessler held various international corporate finance positions and worked for a strategic consulting company before joining STI Group in 2007. As Chief Financial Officer, he has been in charge of commercial operations and the company's international branches since.

Christoph Häberle, Prof. Dr.

Seit 2005 ist Christoph Häberle Studiendekan für den Masterstudiengang Packaging, Design & Marketing an der Hochschule der Medien in Stuttgart. Nach seinem Studium der Produktions- und Automatisierungstechnik an der FHT Esslingen arbeitete er von 1989 bis 1992 u. a. im Bereich Zertifizierung und Entwicklung. Anschließend folgte ein Studium zum Industriedesigner an der Staatlichen Akademie der Bildenden Künste in Stuttgart und 1996 eine Promotion in Philosophie/Design an der Universität und Gesamthochschule Wuppertal. 2000 erhielt er eine Professur im Studiengang Verpackungstechnik, Bereich Verpackungsdesign der Fachhochschule Stuttgart, Hochschule für Druck und Medien. Sein Forschungsschwerpunkt ist der Bereich Farbforschung

Christoph Häberle has been Dean of Students for the master degree Packaging, Design and Marketing at the Hochschule der Medien university in Stuttgart since 2005. After graduating in production and automation technology at the FHT Esslingen, he held various certification and development positions between 1989 and 1992. He then graduated in industry design at the Staatliche Akademie der Bildenden Künste university in Stuttgart and gained a doctorate in philosophy and design at the University of Wuppertal. In 2000, he became professor of packaging technology at the packaging design department of the Hochschule für Druck und Medien university in Stuttgart. His main area of research is colour research.

Bernd Otto Hallier, Prof. Dr.

Bernd Otto Hallier ist seit 1985 Geschäftsführer des EHI Retail Institute, einer Forschungs-, Bildungs- und Beratungsinstitut für den Handel und seine Partner. Das internationale EHI-Netzwerk umfasst 500 Mitgliedsunternehmen aus Handel, Konsum- und Investitionsgüterindustrie. Des Weiteren ist er Gründer der Orgainvent (Rückverfolgbarkeit von Tieren), Mitinitiator EUREPGAP (heute GlobalGAP), Vorsitzender des EuroShop-Beirats, Gründer der European Retail Academy HYPERLINK „http://www.european-retail-academy.org" und des European Competence Center for Vocational Training (EuCVoT). Als Referent zahlreicher Handelsthemen hat er alle Kontinente bereist und ist Autor von Fachbüchern und über 200 Artikeln.

Bernd Otto Hallier has been general manager of EHI Retail Institut since 1985. The research, training and consulting institute for retailers and their partners has 500 member companies from the retail, consumer and capital goods industries. Mr Hallier is also the founder of German meat labelling organisation Orgainvent, co-founder of EUREPGAP (today known as GlobalGAP), chairman of the EuroShop advisory council and founder of the European Retail Academy and European Competence Center for Vocational Training (EuCVoT). He has travelled the world to give lectures on retail and is an author of trade books and more than 200 articles.

Henk Knaupe

Henk Knaupe ist Partner der Commarco und Geschäftsführer von Scholz & Friends Sales Affairs. Nach seinem Studium (Moderne Nahostwissenschaften in Leipzig und Volkswirtschaftslehre in Berlin) war er in den 1990er Jahren sowohl in der Forschung als auch in verschiedenen Marketingpositionen tätig. 2001 und 2008 gründete er zwei weitere Unternehmen mit Schwerpunkt Handelskommunikation (Scholz & Friends Brand Affairs GmbH sowie Scholz & Friends Sales Affairs der Scholz & Friends Gruppe). Mit der RessourcenReich GmbH folgte 2009 eine weitere Firmengründung, diesmal mit den Schwerpunkten „ganzheitliche Vertriebskonzepte" und „nachhaltige Distribution".

Henk Knaupe is a partner at Commarco and general manager of Scholz & Friends Sales Affairs. After graduating in Near East Studies in Leipzig and Applied Economics in Berlin, he conducted research and held various marketing positions in the 1990s. In 2001 and 2008, Mr Knaupe founded two retail communications companies (Scholz & Friends Brand Affairs GmbH and Scholz & Friends Sales Affairs within the Scholz & Friends Group). The foundation of RessourcenReich GmbH followed in 2009. RessourcenReich GmbH is specialised in "holistic retail concepts" and "sustainable distribution".

Jon Kramer

Jon Kramer ist Chief Marketing Officer bei Rock-Tenn Merchandising Displays in Cincinnati. Er ist spezialisiert auf die Entwicklung von Handelsmarketingstrategien für internationale Markenartikelhersteller wie Kraft Foods, PepsiCo oder Campell's. Kramers Vision ist die Konvergenz von Verkaufsförderung, Werbung und neuen Medien am POS, um den First Moment of Truth des Shoppers zu gewinnen.

Jon Kramer is the Chief Marketing Officer of Rock-Tenn Merchandising Displays in Cincinnati. He has specialised in developing retail marketing strategies for international suppliers of branded goods such as Kraft Foods, PepsiCo and Campell's. Kramer believes in the convergence of sales promotion, advertising and new media at the POS to win the First Moment of Truth.

Marlene Lohmann, Dipl.-Kffr.

Marlene Lohmann ist seit 2005 Leiterin des Forschungsbereichs Marketing & Projektleiterin EHI Wissenschaftspreis Handel am EHI Retail Institute e. V. Nach einer Ausbildung zur Bankkauffrau und dem Studium der Wirtschaftswissenschaft (Schwerpunkt Marketing) an der Universität Paderborn leitete sie in verschiedenen Unternehmen den Bereich Werbung und Marketing (Konsumgenossenschaft Dortmund-Kassel, Stinnes Baumarkt/Esslingen, Paderborner Brauerei Haus Cramer u. a.). Darüber hinaus ist sie ehrenamtliches Mitglied in mehreren Jurys (EHI Wissenschaftspreis Handel, STI Design Award u. a.)

Marlene Lohmann has been head of marketing research and project manager of EHI Wissenschaftspreis Handel at the EHI Retail Institute e. V. since 2005. After training to be a bank clerk and graduating in economics, with a focus on marketing, at the University of Paderborn in Germany, she led the marketing of various advertising and marketing companies, including Konsumgenossenschaft Dortmund-Kassel, Stinnes Baumarkt in Esslingen and the Paderborner Brauerei Cramer brewery. She is also an honorary jury member of various organisations, including EHI Wissenschaftspreis Handel and STI Design Award. Ms Lohmann holds a business administration degree.

Bram Nauta

Bram Nauta studierte Marketing Management an der Universität Rotterdam. Er begann seine Marketing-Management-Karriere bei Van Nelle Confectionary und Johma Salads. Ab 1986 war er für verschiedene Werbeagenturen tätig und betreute für die Agentur AYER als International Client Services Director Kunden wie Beiersdorf, SEAT und Dentsu. 1992 gründete er sein eigenes Beratungsunternehmen für Retail Marketing. 1998 kam er so in Berührung mit POPAI Benelux. Aufgrund seiner Erfahrungen in den Bereichen Brand Marketing, Werbung und Einzelhandel wurde er 1998 in das Management Board von POPAI Benelux aufgenommen und 2000 zum Geschäftsführer ernannt. Bram Nauta ist unter anderem zuständig für die Entwicklung und Ausführung von POPAI Marktforschung auf dem Gebiet Konsumentenverhalten sowie für Effizienz- und Ausgaben-Studien. Er referiert häufig über diese Themen.

Bram Nauta graduated from the University of Rotterdam in Marketing Management and started his career in marketing management with Van Nelle Confectionery and Johma Salads. From 1986 he worked with different advertising agencies and was international client services director in the AYER agency on Beiersdorf, SEAT and Dentsu. In 1992 he started his own consultancy agency in retail marketing. In this capacity he got into contact with POPAI Benelux in 1998. Having experience in brandmarketing, advertising and retailing he joined the Benelux Board and was appointed general manager in 2000. Nauta is among other things responsible for developing methodology and executing POPAI marketresearch on consumer behaviour, effectiveness and expenditures studies and is frequently giving lectures on these issues.

Michael Schellenberger

Michael Schellenberger ist seit Mai 2000 Geschäftsführer im Deutschen Fachverlag, zuständig für die LZ-Medien, das Wirtschaftsmagazin „Der Handel" sowie die Agrartitel „AZ" und „Feed Magazine". Zuvor war er 17 Jahre als Chefredakteur der Lebensmittel Zeitung tätig, die wöchentlich über aktuelles Geschehen aus Handel und Industrie berichtet. Der gelernte Einzelhandelskaufmann trat nach Verkäufer- und Substitutenjahren in einem führenden Warenhauskonzern sowie einem dreijährigen Studium an der damaligen Höheren Wirtschaftsfachschule in Siegen im Alter von 25 Jahren in die Redaktion der Lebensmittel Zeitung ein. Er begann als Assistent der Chefredaktion, wurde nach zwei Jahren Leiter des Handelsressorts und im Alter von 31 Jahren zum stellvertretenden Chefredakteur bestellt. Fünf Jahre später übertrug man ihm gemeinsam mit Jürgen Wolfskeil die Chefredaktion der Lebensmittel Zeitung, für die heute immerhin 42 Redakteure und weit über 200 Autoren tätig sind.

Michael Schellenberger has been a general manager at Deutscher Fachverlag with responsibilities for LZ-Medien, business trade journal "Der Handel" as well as the agricultural publications "AZ" and "Feed Magazine" since 2000. Before, the 62-year old was chief editor of the Lebensmittelzeitung, a weekly magazine for food manufacturers and retailers. After training as a retail salesman, Mr Schellenberger worked as a salesman and substitute for several years. He also studied at the business school Höhere Wirtschaftsfachschule in Siegen for three years. At the age of 25, he joined the Lebensmittelzeitung. He started his career as an assistant to the chief editor, was named head of retail after two years and promoted to deputy chief editor at the age of 31. Five years later, Mr Schellenberger was appointed co-chief editor next to Jürgen Wolfskeil. Today, 42 editors and more than 200 authors work for the Lebensmittelzeitung.

XI. DIE AUTOREN | THE AUTHORS

Frank-Michael Schmidt

Seit April 2008 ist Frank-Michael Schmidt CEO der Scholz & Friends Group und CEO der Holding Commarco. Nach seinem Studium der Publizistik, Philosophie und Politikwissenschaft an der Freien Universität Berlin (Abschluss Magister Artium) begann er 1989 als Assistent der Geschäftsführung bei Wilkens Ayer in Hamburg. Seit 1991 war er in verschiedenen Positionen im Bereich Brand Consulting und Strategische Planung tätig, bis er im Jahr 2000 die Funktion des Chief Strategic Officers für die deutsche J. Walter Thompson Group übernahm. Im Jahr 2003 wechselte er als Deutschlandchef zu Scholz & Friends, wo er die Gesamtverantwortung für die deutschen Agenturen der Scholz & Friends Group übernahm.

Frank-Michael Schmidt has been CEO of Scholz & Friends Group and CEO of the Commarco holding since April 2008. After graduating from the Freie Universität of Berlin university, he joined Wilkens Ayer in Hamburg as a management assistant in 1989. Mr Schmidt held various brand consulting and strategic planning positions between 1991 and 2000, when he was appointed as Chief Strategic Officer at the German branch of J. Walter Thompson Group. In 2003, he joined Scholz & Friends as general manager Germany with responsibility for the group's German agencies. Mr Schmidt holds a Master of Arts.

Hendrik Schröder, Univ.-Prof. Dr.

Hendrik Schröder ist seit 1996 Inhaber des Lehrstuhls für Betriebswirtschaftslehre, insbesondere Marketing & Handel, an der Universität Duisburg-Essen (www.marketing.wiwi.uni-due.de) und Leiter des Forschungszentrums für Category Management in Essen (www.cm-net.wiwi.uni-due.de). Seine Forschungsschwerpunkte sind Shopper Research, Handelsmanagement und Handelscontrolling, Customer Relationship Management und Multi-Channel-Retailing.

Hendrik Schröder has been holding the Chair of Business Management at the University of Duisburg-Essen (www.marketing.wiwi.uni-due.de) since 1996. His focus is marketing and retail. Also since 1996, he has been head of the research centre for Category Management in Essen (www.cm-net.wiwi.uni-due.de). His main areas of research are shopper research, retail management and retail controlling, customer relationship management and multi-channel retailing.

Louise Spillard

Louise Spillard ist seit 2008 Forschungsdirektorin bei IGD, London. Sie betreut dort seit 1999 nationale und internationale Forschungsprojekte im Bereich Retail und Kundenforschung. Sie studierte Hotel & Catering Management an der University Surrey und arbeitete vor ihrer Forschungstätigkeit als Einkäuferin bei Waitrose.

Louise Spillard has been research director at IGD in London since 2008. Since 1999, she has been in charge of the company's retail and customer research divisions. Ms Spillard graduated in Hotel and Catering Management at the University of Surrey and worked as a buyer at Waitrose before taking up research.

Raphael Stix

Raphael Stix ist Geschäftsführer der Globalshopper GmbH in Hamburg. Zuvor war er über 17 Jahre in der FMCG Industrie (Bestfoods und Unilever) in unterschiedlichen Sales-, Key Account- und Marketingfunktionen tätig. Seit 2005 beraten er und sein Unternehmen bedeutende internationale Markenartikelunternehmen auf dem Gebiet des Shoppermarketings.

Raphael Stix is general manager of Globalshopper GmbH in Hamburg. Before joining Globalshopper, he held various sales, key account and marketing positions with fast moving consumer goods companies like Bestfoods and Unilever for 17 years. Since 2005, Mr Stix has been a shopper marketing consultant to leading international branded goods companies.

Sophie Wittl, Dipl.-Ing. Verpackungstechnik (FH)

Als Produktentwicklerin der STI Group betreut Sophie Wittl internationale Key-Accounts. Sie studierte Verpackungstechnik an der Hochschule der Medien (HdM) in Stuttgart sowie an der Ecole Supérieure d'Ingénieurs en Emballage et Conditionnement (ESIEC) in Reims. In ihrer Diplomarbeit beschäftigte sie sich mit den Ursprüngen und der Geschichte des POS-Displays.

Sophie Wittl is product developer at STI Group with responsibility for international key accounts. She graduated in packaging technology at the Hochschule der Medien (HdM) University in Stuttgart in Germany. She also graduated from the Ecole Supérieure d'Ingénieurs en Emballage et Conditionnement (ESIEC) university in Reims. Ms Wittl holds an engineering degree in packaging technology. She wrote her thesis on the origins and history of POS displays.